SOCIAL RESEARCH in Developing Countries

SURVEYS AND CENSUSES IN THE THIRD WORLD

Edited by
Martin Bulmer
University of Southampton
Donald P. Warwick
Harvard Institute for International Development

UCL

PRESS

First published in paperback in 1993 by UCL Press.
Originally published in hardback in 1983 by John Wiley & Sons Ltd.

UCL Press Limited
University College London
Gower Street
London WC1E 6BT
England

The name of University College London (UCL) is a registered
trade mark used by UCL Press with the consent of the owner.

ISBN: 1-85728-137-3

A CIP catalogue record for this book
is available from the British Library.

Typeset by Inforum Ltd, Portsmouth.
Printed and bound by Athenæum Press Limited, Newcastle upon Tyne.

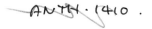
ANTH · 1410 .

CONTENTS

v

PREFACE

This book has its origins in an interest which we both share, from different backgrounds, in the conduct of empirical social research in developing countries. The conditions under which social science research is carried out in the Third World differ in significant respects from conditions in the industrial world in North America, western Europe and Australia. The guidance available from standard texts — particularly those on survey methods — for the most part assumes as background the conditions that exist in the developed world. When such texts are transposed to the context of the developing countries, although they provide guidance on how to proceed, they do not pay attention to the particular local conditions and problems which are likely to arise. One aim of this book is to provide a collection of material which specifically addresses the problems of conducting social surveys in developing countries.

Sceptics about the indiscriminate use of social surveys in those countries have often suggested that other research methods — particularly extended fieldwork and participant observation — may be more appropriate. Without wishing to take sides in a fruitless polemic between left arm and right arm, between the survey *or* participant observation, we recognize the seriousness of such criticisms. This collection therefore also considers briefly the alternatives to the social survey, and includes a section on methodological marriages specifically addressed to the most fruitful ways of using multiple methods in empirical research in the Third World.

A subsidiary aim of the book is to throw light on the conduct of surveys in the *developed* world. Examining the problems encountered in poorer countries can indirectly expose the general assumptions on which survey practice rests, and lead to a better understanding of the effective conduct of surveys wherever they are carried out. The aim of this book is constructive, to promote more effective research. It is not meant to tear down, to show that certain types of research are not possible or, if possible, so vitiated by non-sampling error that these are not worthwhile. Improving the tools of social research, however, involves facing up to their weaknesses as well as their strengths.

ix

This book is written primarily for use by local social scientists working in the developing countries. We hope it will be of interest also to social scientists in industrial countries who have occasion to work in or on the Third World. Unlike much of the literature of the 1960s, however, this book is not aimed at the 'safari' social scientist on an (often brief) field trip from developed to developing world, who then disappears again to his home base once the data has been collected. The day of that kind of scientist has passed and will not return.

This book is the result of collaboration between us over a period of 2 years (1980–82). One of us (Bulmer) has taken the lead in selecting material and preparing drafts of some of the linking chapters. The other (Warwick) has concentrated particularly on the last two sections of the book, but also provided advice and comments on the earlier sections. The book is a joint effort, though authorship of different chapters indicates where we have concentrated our efforts.

One of us (Bulmer) came to the subject from a background in the teaching of social research methodology, of which he has had 15 years' experience. Research in the Third World throws up more sharply many critical issues present in research in the developed world, and he has welcomed an opportunity to explore this further. The specific opportunity to do so came through an invitation from Professor Ruth Glass and Dr Richard Jones to teach from 1978 to 1980 on a 3-month summer course on Social Research for Development held at the Centre for Urban Studies at University College, London. Since 1980 he has taught a more extended seminar to students on the MSc course in Social Planning in Developing Countries at the London School of Economics, and is grateful to his colleagues Mrs Margaret Hardiman and Dr James Midgley for the opportunity to do so. The invaluable contact on these courses with a variety of administrative and research workers from the developing world, almost all of them mature students attending an advanced· course in mid-career, has been a most rewarding teaching experience.

The other of us (Warwick) has had extensive first-hand research experience in the developing countries. While in graduate school at the University of Michigan he learned the basics of survey research by taking part in two separate studies at the Survey Research Center. From 1964 to 1966 he worked with that Center in helping the Peruvian government to establish a survey unit within its Ministry of Labour. That experience made him aware of both the uses and the limitations of standard survey research methodology in the developing countries. Then, while Director of the Comparative International Studies Program in the Department of Social Relations at Harvard University (1967–71) he pursued many of the intellectual questions raised in this book in an annual graduate seminar on the methodology of comparative research. In 1973 he became project manager of a study on the formulation and implementation of population policies in eight developing countries. Through this project, which lasted until 1981, he had the opportunity to work closely with colleagues from several countries and to live for a year in Mexico.

In 1977 and 1978, he was part of a project investigating the organization and impact of educational planning in both El Salvador and Paraguay. Since 1978 he has been conducting research in Indonesia, working most recently with Indonesian and American colleagues on a large-scale field study of the implementation of development programmes. These research experiences and allied teaching have brought home to him the acute need for high-quality social research in the developing countries, the practical difficulties in conducting such research, and the benefits of methodological integration.

The idea of the book occurred to Martin Bulmer on 25 August 1979, while he was staying at the home of Henry and Phoebe Roper in Halifax, Nova Scotia. For advice and assistance of various kinds during the preparation of the book he is indebted to Professor Ronald Dore (then of the Institute of Development Studies, University of Sussex, now at The Technical Change Centre, London); to Professor Asher Tropp of the University of Surrey and Patricia O. Fuellhart of the Statistical Research Division of the US Bureau of the Census for bibliographical assistance; to Mrs Catherine Marsh of the University of Cambridge, to Professor Robert E. Mitchell of the Agency for International Development, Washington, DC, and to Professor William H. Form of the University of Illinois at Urbana. Dr M.N. Murthy of the UN Statistical Institute for Asia and the Pacific in Tokyo provided assistance well beyond the call of duty in preparing Chapter 9 for publication.

Donald Warwick would like to thank especially his colleagues from the developing countries who have educated him about the realities of their countries and inspired him to seek research approaches with greater cross-cultural applicability than those in which he was trained. He is particularly grateful to Francisco Codina and Abel Centurion of Peru, his first mentors in this area; to Saad Gadalla of Egypt, Luis Leñero of Mexico, Maria Elena Lopez of the Philippines; and Kivuto Ndeti of Kenya, all collaborators on the Project on Cultural Values and Population Policies; and to his Indonesian colleagues on the Development Programme Implementation Study. In different ways and at different times he has also learned a great deal about cross-cultural research from Alex Inkeles, David McClelland, Noel McGinn, Donald Snodgrass, and Marguerite Robinson.

Parts of the manuscript were typed by Valerie Campling and Gay Grant in London and by Mary Lavallee and Irene McCall in Cambridge, Massachusetts. Michael Coombs at Wiley has been a considerate editor whom we thank for encouraging our collaboration on this book.

Martin Bulmer
*Department of Social Science
and Administration
London School of Economics*

Donald P. Warwick
*Harvard Institute for
International Development
Harvard University*

August, 1982

NOTES ABOUT THE CONTRIBUTORS

MARTIN BULMER (editor) teaches the methodology of social research and the applications of social research in policy making in the Department of Social Science and Administration at the London School of Economics and Political Science. Previously he was a statistician in the Office of Population Censuses and Surveys, London, and lecturer in sociology at the University of Durham. His main research interests are currently in the areas of the use of social science in policy-making, the sociology of privacy, and the history of the social sciences in the 1920s. His recent publications include *The Uses of Social Research: Social Investigation in Public Policy-making* (Allen and Unwin, 1982) and several edited anthologies including *Social Research Ethics* (Macmillan and Holmes and Meier, 1982), and *Censuses, Surveys and Privacy* (Macmillan and Holmes and Meier, 1979). He jointly edited a special issue, (**Vol 15, no 4**, 1981) of *Sociology* on The Teaching of Research Methodology. He is currently a member of the Research Resources and Methods Committee of the (British) Social Science Research Council.

DONALD P. WARWICK (editor) is an Institute Fellow at the Harvard Institute for International Development and Lecturer in both the Graduate School of Education and the Sociology Department at Harvard University. He received his PhD in Social Psychology from the University of Michigan in 1963, where he also worked with the Survey Research Center of the Institute for Social Research. He has held teaching positions at Harvard University, York University, the University of Michigan, the National University of San Marcos in Lima, Peru, and Oberlin College. From 1964 to 1966 he was adviser to the government of Peru in establishing a survey research center. From 1973 to 1981 he served as Project Manager of the UN-sponsored Project on Cultural Values and Population Policies, an eight-nation comparative study. As part of that project he lived in Mexico for 1 year. Most recently he has been working in Indonesia where he is consultant to a large-scale field study of the implementation of development programmes. He is author of *Bitter Pills: Population*

Policies and their Implementation in Eight Developing Countries (Cambridge University Press, 1982); *A Theory of Public Bureaucracy* (Harvard University Press, 1975); and *The Teaching of Ethics in the Social Sciences* (The Hastings Center, 1980); co-author of *The Sample Survey: Theory and Practice* (McGraw-Hill, 1975); and co-editor of *Comparative Research Methods* (Prentice-Hall, 1973).

BENJAMIN GIL (Chapter 3) is currently Senior Technical Adviser and Project Manager of a UNFPA-sponsored Civil Registration Demonstration Project covering about one-tenth of the Kenyan population. Previously he has worked as a statistician for the United Nations, the International Labour Office and the UN Economic Commission for Africa. He has published widely on population topics in Africa.

E.N. OMABOE (Chapter 3) is Managing Director of E.N. Omaboe Associates Ltd., business, investment and economic consultants, in Accra, Ghana. From 1960 to 1969 he was a statistician with the Ghanaian government. He is the joint editor (with W. Birmingham and I. Neustadt) of *The Survey of Contemporary Ghana* (1966).

J. MAYONE STYCOS (Chapter 4) is Professor of Sociology and Director of the International Population Program at Cornell University, Ithaca, New York. He has been a consultant to the Population Council, International Planned Parenthood Federation, the Population Reference Bureau, the World Health Organization, and the United Nations Fund for Population Activities. Currently working on the evaluation of family planning programmes in Egypt, he has had research or consulting experience in most of Latin America and the Caribbean. He is the author of *Human Fertility in Latin America* (1968); *Ideology, Faith, and Family Planning in Latin America* (1971); and *The Clinic and Information Flow* (1975).

PHILIP M. HAUSER (Chapter 5) is Senior Fellow at the East–West Population Institute, East-West Center, Hawaii. He is also Lucy Flower Professor Emeritus of Urban Sociology at the University of Chicago, where he spent his academic career. From 1938 to 1947 he worked for the US Bureau of the Census, ending as Deputy Director, and in 1949–50 returned as Acting Director. His main publications include *World Population and Development* (editor, 1979), *The Population Dilemma* (editor, 1963), and *The Study of Population* (editor with O.D. Duncan, 1959). He has carried out research and consultancy work in many parts of the Third World, particularly in most of the countries in South and South-East Asia.

MARGARET PEIL (Chapter 6) is Reader in Sociology in the Centre of West African Studies, University of Birmingham. From 1963 to 1968 she taught sociology at the University of Ghana and has also held visiting teaching posts in

Nigeria and Sierra Leone. Her main teaching and research interests are urban, industrial and educational sociology with a focus upon West Africa. Her publications include *Social Science Research Methods: An African Handbook* (with P. Mitchell and D. Rimmer, 1982); *The Ghanaian Factory Worker*; *Nigerian Politics*; and *Cities and Suburbs: Urban Life in West Africa*. Her main Third World research experience has been in The Gambia, Ghana, Nigeria and Sierra Leone.

SLOBODAN S. ZARKOVICH (Chapter 8) was from 1975 to 1979 Director of the Institute of Statistics, Belgrade, Yugoslavia. Previously, from 1955 to 1975, he worked for the Food and Agriculture Organization (FAO) in Rome developing agricultural statistics. His numerous publications include *Quality of Statistical Data* (1966); *Statistical Development* (1975); and *Utilization of Statistical Data* (1976). While with the FAO, he travelled extensively and visited most of the less developed countries to assist in building up statistical development programmes, organize training and advise on survey and census-taking.

M.N. MURTHY (Chapter 9) has been a member of the staff of the United Nations Statistical Institute for Asia and the Pacific, Tokyo since 1970. Previously he was Chief of the Division of Sampling Design, Research and Training, in the National Sample Survey Department, Indian Statistical Institute, Calcutta. He is the author of *Sampling Theory and Methods* (Statistical Publishing Society, Calcutta, 1967) and of several technical publications, as well as editor of several major symposia.

A.S. ROY (Chapter 9) is Deputy Director of the Division of Survey Design and Research of the National Sample Survey Organisation, Department of Statistics, in the Indian Ministry of Planning, Calcutta. Since 1957 he has worked as a survey statistician on the Indian National Sample Survey. He is the author of several papers on sampling theory and survey methods, and (jointly) of the *Manual of Food Consumption Surveys* (FAO).

MICHAEL WARD (Chapter 10) is a Fellow of the Institute of Development Studies at Sussex University. He is director of the Institute's statistics programme. Previously he was in the Department of Applied Economics at Cambridge University. He has undertaken numerous technical assistance assignments in statistics in developing countries under the auspices of the British government and international agencies. From 1972 to 1975 he was the UNESCO programme director for statistical training in southern Africa. He is the author of several books and a large number of articles on development problems.

GABRIELE WUELKER (Chapter 12) is Professor Emeritus of the Sociology of Development at the University of Bochum, Ruhr, Federal Republic of

Germany. From 1960 to 1965 she was Director of the Institute for Research in Developing Countries in Bonn. Her work in the sociology of development has included public opinion research in India, Nepal, Thailand, Taiwan and Korea, and also studies in Nigeria, Togo and Ghana. Her main publications include *Togo: Tradition und Entwicklung* (Stuttgart, 1966) and *In Asien und Afrika; Sociale und Soziologische Wandlungen* (Stuttgart, 1962).

BRIAN R. FLAY (Chapter 13) is Assistant Director of the Health Behavior Research Institute at the University of Southern California, Los Angeles. Previously he taught at the University of Waterloo, Ontario, Canada. He is a New Zealander by birth. His research interests include the prevention of cigarette smoking and the use of mass media for health promotion. He has published extensively in professional journals on health-related subjects and evaluation research.

PATRICK E. BULL (Chapter 13) is Senior Lecturer in Business at Massey University, New Zealand.

JOHN TAMAHORI (Chapter 13) is an industrial manager in New Zealand. He is a member of the National Polynesian Advisory Committee of the Vocational Training Council of New Zealand.

SHANTO IYENGAR (Chapter 14) is Visiting Research Scholar and Associate Professor, Department of Political Science, Yale University. His main areas of research are political psychology, mass communications, voting and attitudes. He has published widely in professional journals such as *The American Political Science Review*, *Public Opinion Quarterly*, *The Journal of Developing Areas* and *Comparative Political Studies*. His main Third World research experience has been of longitudinal survey research in India.

J. OSCAR ALERS (Chapter 15) is Coordinator of the Puerto Rican Migration Research Consortium, New York City. He has also taught sociology and development studies at the City College of New York, Cornell University and Boston College. He has had research experience in the Third World in Peru, Thailand, Venezuela, Honduras and the Caribbean. He has more than 30 publications, centering on Peruvian community development, Thai family planning and Puerto Rican migration.

J.C.G. BLACKER (Chapter 16) is Senior Research Fellow in the Centre for Population Studies at the London School of Hygiene and Tropical Medicine. He has also been a demographic adviser to the UN Economic Commission for Africa and a demographer for the East African and Kenyan governments. He has published widely in professional journals such as *Population Studies*, and is the author (with C. Scott) of *Manual on Demographic Sample Surveys in Africa* (UNECA, 1974).

WILLIAM BRASS (Chapter 16) is Professor of Medical Demography in the University of London and Director of the Centre for Population Studies at the London School of Hygiene and Tropical Medicine. His publications include *Biosocial Aspects of Demography* (editor), and *The Demography of Tropical Africa* (with others). He is currently President of the International Union for the Scientific Study of Population.

ROBERT EDWARD MITCHELL (Chapter 18) is currently with the Cairo Mission of the United States Agency for International Development (USAID). He has also taught at Florida State University, been Director of the Social Survey Research Centre of the Chinese University of Hong Kong, and Deputy Director of the Survey Research Center, University of California, Berkeley. His principal Third World research experience has been in Egypt, Jordan, Nigeria, Hong Kong, Taiwan, Singapore, Malaysia and Thailand.

ALLAN F. HERSHFIELD (Chapter 19) is a political scientist at the University of California. He has had research experience in Ethiopia, Nigeria and Somalia.

NIELS G. ROHLING (Chapter 19) teaches at the Agricultural University of Wageningen, Netherlands. He has had research experience in Kenya and Nigeria.

GRAHAM B. KERR (Chapter 19) has been a senior demographer in the Central Statistical Office of Afghanistan, and has also worked in Nigeria.

GERALD HURSH-CESAR (Chapter 19) is Acting Director of the Office of Research, US International Communication Agency. Previously he was Regional Consultant for Research to UNICEF in India, Nepal and Afghanistan, and Data Systems Director for the Ford Foundation in India. He is the co-author of *Third World Surveys* (Macmillan of India, 1976) and of *Survey Research* (Wiley, 1981).

EMILY L. JONES (Chapter 20) has been on the staff of the Coordination Centre for South East Asian Studies, Bangkok, Thailand.

HARVEY M. CHOLDIN (Chapter 21) is Professor of Sociology at the University of Illinois at Urbana-Champaign. Previously he taught at Michigan State University and was on the staff of the Population Council. His main Third World research experience was in Bangladesh (when it was East Pakistan).

A. MAJEED KHAN and H. HOSNE ARA (Chapter 21) teach at Rajshahi University, Bangladesh.

WILLIAM F. WHYTE (Chapter 23) is Professor Emeritus of Sociology at the New York State School of Industrial and Labor Relations, Cornell University, Ithaca, New York. His best known work is *Street Corner Society* (1943), but his main research and teaching interests have been in industrial relations in the United States and in agricultural development in Latin America. His publications on the latter include *Toward an Integrated Theory of Development* (1968) and *Organizing for Agricultural Development* (1975). He has recently collaborated on a five-nation study of agricultural research and development in Central America to be published as *High Yielding Human Systems: Participatory Approaches to Agricultural Research and Development*. Professor Whyte has been President of the American Sociological Association and of the Society for Applied Anthropology.

GIORGIO ALBERTI (Chapter 23) is Professor of Political Science at the University of Bologna, Italy, where he is Director of the Gino Germani Centre for the Comparative Study of Modernization and Development. His main areas of research are the politics of development and peasant movements. Most of his field research has been done in Peru.

RICARDO B. ZUNIGA (Chapter 25) is Associate Professor in the School of Social Work, University of Montreal, Canada, and Assistant Dean in the Faculty of Adult Education. Formerly he was Professor of Sociology at the Catholic University, Santiago, Chile. His main teaching and research interests are in the fields of action and participatory research, professional education, and research methodology. He has several publications on action research. His main Third World research experience has been in Chile.

CHARLES D. KLEYMEYER (Chapter 27) is a social science analyst for the Inter-American Foundation working primarily in Ecuador. He has also worked in Colombia, Peru and Guatemala. His main research interests are in power-dependency relations across ethnic boundaries, humanization of health care, and the conduct of applied research. He has published articles in *Ethics in Social Science and Medicine* and *The American Behavioral Scientist*, and has a book forthcoming on Peru.

WILLIAM E. BERTRAND (Chapter 27) is Associate Professor of Biostatistics and Epidemiology, School of Public Health and Tropical Medicine, Tulane University, New Orleans, where he is also Adjunct Associate Professor of Sociology. His main areas of research are social epidemiology, cross-cultural methodologies and the evaluation of social action and health programmes. He has published extensively on epidemiology and evaluation research. In the Third World, he has carried out social research in Colombia, Zaire, Bolivia, Guatemala and Niger.

SECTION I

INTRODUCTION

Social Research in Developing Countries
Edited by M. Bulmer and D.P. Warwick
© 1983, John Wiley & Sons, Ltd.

CHAPTER 1

GENERAL INTRODUCTION

MARTIN BULMER

The conduct of social research in developing countries is an important issue. For Third World countries rely increasingly upon social science methods to gather data which is used by government both for development planning and in day-to-day administration. The results of social inquiry are not just fed back to fellow academics, but are used to influence the life chances of millions upon millions of people. The means by which social data are collected, and the quality of the data which result, are therefore issues of major importance which this book seeks to examine.

'Developing countries' are defined as all countries in Latin America, Africa and Asia with the exception of Japan, Australia, New Zealand and South Africa. They tend to have economies in which agriculture is the dominant activity, and to have low *per capita* income, nutritional standards, literacy and productivity. Health, water and social service provisions and transport and communication facilities tend to be poor by comparison with the industrial countries of the 'developed' world. Developing countries also tend to have rather high birth and death rates, short life expectancy, and a marked incidence of ill-health, malnutrition and disease. A simple dichotomy between the 'developed' and 'developing' world conceals the very wide variation within each group, particularly among developing countries, where some are much more industrialized than others. Singapore, for example, is very different from neighbouring Indonesia, which is generally much poorer.

Another dimension of difference is geographical scale. In conducting survey research, a city-state like Singapore or small countries like Jamaica or the Netherlands pose fewer problems for sampling and organizing a field force than large, farflung countries such as Indonesia, India or the United States. Moreover, much of what is said in this book also applies equally well to research in the poorer and more marginal areas of the more affluent countries in the world. Nevertheless, it is useful to treat the subject of research methods as applying to *all* developing countries, for by comparison with the industrial countries of the western and eastern *blocs*, Third World countries do have

3

many social and economic characteristics in common which directly influence the conduct of social research.

A major issue in the use of social science methods to provide social data for Third World government is: how can such methods produce data which those who use the data can trust? Do the procedures and techniques used give an adequate picture of the state of the society (or one aspect of it) at the time of the study? Is the evidence provided consistent and meaningful? Does it represent the true state of affairs at the local level, and do its measurements really measure what they claim to measure? Is the evidence provided as objective and free from bias as possible? How well does the evidence stand up if the exercise is repeated, and the results of a second enquiry under the same conditions are compared with the first? Is it possible to conduct high-quality research that avoids political controversy and avoids ethical difficulties? These questions require a critical examination of the means by which social data is collected and the social conditions of its production.

The limitations of administrative data

Discussion of these issues is vitally necessary because it is widely recognized that the social data available to governments in the Third World is often highly unsatisfactory (Rimmer, 1982).

If a serious study of the availability of reliable data is undertaken, the situation in many developing countries is likely to be found to be quite alarming. It is not only a question of lack of data; in many situations, the position is more a case of poor quality data than of no data. Further, there are situations where data are available, but minimal or no use is made of the same owing to lack of proper infrastructure or suitable opportunity (Murthy, 1978, p. 232).

Development officials often lack adequate data on basic population parameters and indicators of development such as agricultural production or infant mortality. A study of methods of estimation for yields of wheat and maize crops in 120 countries, for example, showed that in 80 countries eye estimates were used to provide such data. In 74 countries such methods were used to estimate the total number of cattle (Zarkovich, 1975, p. 15).

Particularly serious defects are likely in official statistics collected as a byproduct of administration. Government statistical offices have developed slowly, and on a limited scale, according to what Third World governments could afford to spend on information gathering. More basic economic needs have to be met first. The nature of social problems — with masses of people living in appalling and unquantified social conditions — is more intractable than in the developed world and creates major difficulties for social inquiry.

Developing countries have limited adminstrative capacity and a restricted supply of trained manpower. Trained statisticians are particularly likely to be scarce at the middle and senior levels.

The official statistical collection system and infrastructure in many developing countries is much more fragile than in developed ones, and in social statistics, which have relied primarily on administrative sources, the collection system is particularly weak. The central statistical offices in many developing countries have not yet established a field organisation with a network of provincial offices and still rely heavily on the use of local administrators or *ad hoc* staff (Goldstone, 1977, p. 758).

There are, however, variations in the availability of trained manpower. In a few developing countries, for example India and Korea, such skills are more plentiful than in, say, Indonesia, Mali or Brazil. India in particular has an impressive record in statistics and quantitative social research (as is evident in Chapter 9), but this is the exception rather than the rule in the developing world.

Reliance for data upon administrative sources can be dangerously misleading. Casley and Lury (1981, p. 10) cite examples of crop surveys where officials preferred (inaccurate) administrative estimates of acreage to (more accurate) estimates derived from sample surveys, basing their preference fallaciously upon the basis of personal experience. This sort of experience is not uncommon. In many developing countries, despite nominal affirmations of interest, traditional adminstrators do not really believe in the value of social science data in formulating and implementing public policy. The demand for quality data may thus be low.

Even where there is a real demand, many administrators do not know what to do with quality data. Most have not been trained in social science methodology, most do not have the intellectual background to make real sense of the usual tables, and most do not have the time available for serious study of the results. Hence research reports are often either ignored or are boiled down to such an extent that nuances of substance and methodology are lost.

Moreover, in the developing even more than in the developed world it is by no means the case that information, and particularly objective information produced by social science research, is the prime ingredient either in making or in assessing government policies (Lindblom and Cohen, 1979). Politics is more often the order of the day than statistics.

Even so, purpose designed inquiries, particularly sample surveys, have in principle a great deal to contribute to the process of data collection and analysis in developing countries. Population censuses clearly play a major role, and more intensive methods of field research based on the case study may also be of value. They are superior to data from administrative sources because their sole purpose is research and investigation; they are not byproducts of some administrative process.

The rationale for this book

This book has been produced because there is a need to examine critically the research methods which are available for use in the Third World. Apart from the large literature, mainly American, on comparative research methods (among which the most outstanding is Warwick and Osherson, 1973), there is a growing literature on methods of research in the Third World (see, for example, Casley and Lury, 1981; Hursh-César and Roy, 1976; O'Barr et al., 1973; Peil et al., 1982. For bibliographies see Frey et al., 1969; and Dixon and Leach, 1981). This book has been planned to complement these existing texts and raise critical questions about the research process in the developing world. At each stage in the research process, problems may be encountered which are not found to the same extent in the developed world, and difficulties are often added or compounded by foreign sponsorship and/or funding (for one example of this, see Chapter 27). For example, in most developing countries, languages spoken are much more diverse than in a single industrial country, with resultant complications for the conduct of survey research, both in ensuring linguistic equivalence of research instruments and in training and sending interviewers out into the field.

The book is mainly concerned with the conduct of social surveys, and to a lesser extent population censuses in Third World countries. The extracts included consider different stages of the research process, with a particular emphasis upon sampling, data collection and the organization of fieldwork. It is in these areas that the most critical problems of conducting surveys arise. Basic conditions taken for granted in standard western textbooks on research methods (Babbie, 1973; Backstrom and Hursh-César, 1981; Moser and Kalton, 1971) are lacking:

To begin with, the available statistical description of the economic and physical and human setting of the research is often defective. Census figures are usually out of date and frequently unreliable, if indeed they are available at all. Aggregate estimates give little guidance as to the questions it is important to ask in particular local settings. No list of potential interviewees is available from which to draw a sample. The research worker may speak a different language than his respondents . . . often the respondents (and the communities in which they live) have never encountered the idea of social science field data; surveys arouse both curiosity and suspicion. At the same time, rural studies usually involve scattered and remote settings; provision of transport and food and lodging for interviewers may require some inventiveness. The choice of enumerators will be both crucial and limited. . . . Supervision of field staff and checks on the reliability of their work offer special problems. . . . (Kearl, 1976, p. xx).

The following sections explore in detail the source and nature of the problems encountered, and ways of dealing with them. The articles selected for inclusion are all written by social scientists with first-hand experience of research in developing societies. Some are themselves from those countries, some from western Europe or North America or Australasia. The main criterion for selecting articles has been their relevance to the topic being considered, and the extent to which they highlight the methodological difficulties arising at that particular stage of the research process. Slight preference has been given to articles dealing with Asian or Latin American experience. The extracts have been selected after an exhaustive search of the available literature, as those which in the judgement of the editors highlight the problems of conducting survey research most sharply.

Although the main emphasis is upon social survey research this is not exclusively so. Some comparison is made between extensive and intensive research methods, and the complementarity of large-scale survey and small-scale case studies is emphasized in Section VI on methodological marriages. One way in which the defects arising from errors in large-scale inquiries may be countered is by also using ethnographic methods, though these too have their limitations.

It would be a mistake to draw too sharp a distinction between methods of research used in the developed and in the developing world. It is true that most general textbooks on research methodology assume that the reader lives in western Europe or North America or perhaps Australasia, and that social conditions in those societies provide the backcloth for the carrying out of the procedures described in the texts. Indeed, one purpose of the present book is to provide a collection which, read alongside a standard text, may give a more realistic picture of social research in the developing world. Nevertheless, the procedures described are not qualitatively different. They differ in degree, perhaps, but not in kind.

There are no fundamental differences in principle or in logic between cross-cultural survey research and within-cultural survey research. . . . Important 'subcultural' variations between classes, educational groups, regional populations, and other social echelons plague the domestic survey researcher in a manner quite analogous to the more pronounced full-cultural variations that loom before the cross-cultural survey researcher. This is true in the areas of sampling, interviewer recruitment and training, instrument preparation, interviewer–respondent interaction, coding and analysis. The differences are in degree and not really in kind. These differences in degree — in the relative severity of problems, if not in their intrinsic character — do, however, have weighty implications for cross-cultural survey research. Not only are the problems more severe, but their existence is more conspicuous. One can ignore a mouse-like problem, but when it assumes elephantine proportions, one ignores it only at the peril of being overwhelmed (Frey, 1970, p. 184).

One secondary purpose of the present book is to give a fresh perspective upon social survey research in the *developed* world. Survey research practitioners do themselves no harm by re-examining the assumptions upon which their procedures rest. Looking at the practice of survey research in developing countries is one way of doing this, for as Frey indicates many of the problems encountered in the Third World are merely problems writ large which exist in all survey research. For example, intercultural and intracultural problems of linguistic equivalence (Deutscher, 1973; 1977) differ only in degree rather than in kind.

Methods of social research distinguished

The different methods of research discussed in this collection will now be defined rather more clearly. *Aggregate data* derived from official statistics, already referred to, are normally the byproduct of administrative processes whose primary function is not the collection of data. Acute conceptual and measurement problems can therefore arise in trying to adapt such official data for research purposes where there is not a match between administrative and social science research categories. For example, official data on inmigration and outmigration from a country is likely to be based on administrative or legal categories, while social researchers would tend to use the demographic definition approved by the United Nations (a person entering a country intending to stay at least 1 year, or leaving the country for at least 1 year). In developed societies such official data poses considerable problems (see, for example, Halsey, 1972; Morgenstern, 1963). For the reasons discussed earlier, its quality in many developing countries is quite suspect. First-hand social investigation is therefore in many cases preferable.

The population census

The population census is a complete enumeration of the population of a country carried out simultaneously by the government usually every 10 years. A decennial census is an extremely costly operation requiring massive resources and manpower since large numbers of enumerators must be recruited and given some training, and must then cover the whole country at one and the same time. Usually census gathering has the force of law behind it; compliance is compulsory. Even so, considerable problems of data quality may arise, due to problems of enumerating a partly illiterate and uncomprehending population, and to the use as enumerators of relatively untrained and even unsuitable personnel. Supervision of field staff in a large national census is also a very difficult matter to regulate properly. Because of its scale and cost, censuses take place infrequently, and the data they provide rather rapidly becomes out of date for policy-making purposes.

The social survey

The social survey, however, provides a feasible and relatively economical alternative means of collecting social data. Probability sampling is at the heart of survey procedures, for they enable inferences to be made from a small sample (from whom data are collected) to a very much larger population (whose characteristics are unknown or inadequately known). The development of sampling is one of the major intellectual achievements in the twentieth century in social science, and it gives to the social researcher a very powerful tool. The unit of response (the respondent) in a survey is usually a person. A number of respondents large enough to permit generalization are selected as the sample, and are then asked questions, the answers to which form the data to be analysed at the end of the research process. Usually in surveys in the Third World these questions are asked by means of a personal intrview, in which a trained interviewer asks the respondent questions face to face and records the verbal answers given in writing on an interview schedule. (Mail questionnaires are rarely suitable for use in developing countries, except for a few inquiries with the educated minority or individual firms.) Most large-scale surveys use a structured interview schedule, in which responses are standardized to a limited range of alternatives permitting rapid numerical analysis of the results. The duration of the interview is usually relatively brief. A primary aim of the survey is to collect standardized information from a relatively large number of individuals in order to generalize from the sample to the population from which it is drawn.

All data collection in social science is liable to error and no method is free from error. In the case of sample surveys, this error is divisible into sampling error and non-sampling error. Social surveys in developing countries are particularly prone to non-sampling error (discussed extensively later in the book), and this has led some social scientists to argue the superiority of more intensive methods of research over social surveys.

The case-study method

The case-study method, the use of intensive methods, participant observation or ethnographic research lacks a commonly agreed name but shares a number of characteristics. It usually involves the indepth study of a particular milieu (village, association, organization, institution) rather than of a random sample of individuals drawn more widely. The researcher, rather than briefly interviewing a large number of respondents using a standardized instrument, relies on a repertoire of methods to gather data including informal interviewing, the use of knowledgeable informants in the locale being studied (to interpret that locale to the social investigator) and participation in and observation of events in the setting as and when they occur. In terms of coverage, such methods are much more limited than the social survey, but their proponents argue that they gain in greater richness of data and depth and penetration of analysis. As noted in Chapters 22 and 23, intensive methods can fruitfully be combined with extensive methods, including a local census and one or more sample surveys.

Criteria for choosing the appropriate method(s)

The position taken in this book is that different research methods are not alternatives to be chosen between on *a priori* grounds, but methods which are more or less appropriate to particular problems. In total, different methods are *complementary* to each other rather than in competition, a point emphasized in the later section on methodological marriages. Nevertheless, criteria may be suggested in terms of which the relative appropriateness of different methods may be evaluated.

Appropriateness to the research objectives

One important criterion is appropriateness to the objectives of the research. Will the method produce the kinds of data needed to answer the questions posed in the study? Is the purpose of the research to develop hypotheses, to test hypotheses, to evaluate an action programme, to provide an interpretative account or what? Are historical data required? What level of analysis is aimed at? Not all methods are equally appropriate for all problems. In particular, what survey methods can accomplish and what they cannot accomplish needs to be appreciated.

Reliability

A second major criterion is the reliability of the method used. Would that method, if repeated by a different person at the same time, or the same person at a later point in time, yield the same results on a second occasion? Are the results achieved reproducible under other circumstances? A frequent criticism of case-study research, for example, is that its reliability is low since so much depends on the capacity and personality of the observer. There is, however, ample evidence of problems of reliability in the conduct of censuses and sample surveys in the Third World. The use of a standardized interview schedule administered by interviewers or enumerators is not in itself a guarantee that the results will be reliable, if, for example, respondents do not understand the question, fail to respond in terms of the alternatives provided, or believe that the interviewer is a government agent whom they must placate and give socially acceptable (rather than true) answers.

Validity

A third criterion, over which there is much contention, is the validity of the method of data collection. Does the researcher obtain measurements of what he is really trying to measure? Does an attitude scale, for example, really measure the underlying attitudes which it purports to measure? Validity is a difficult and complex issue which has a number of aspects (Campbell and Stanley, 1963), but it has to be considered in assessing the value of particular methods.

Representativeness or generalizability

A further criterion, of particular importance to policy-makers, is the representativeness of the sample, or the generalizability of the data in a particular case. To what extent can one go beyond the data about the sample in case to a wider population? The census would appear to score most strongly at this point, and does except in so far as it is an unwieldy method of data collection which only covers a limited number of topics. Generalizability is in fact the strongest card of the sample survey. Using probability sampling methods, the sample survey is an elegant and powerful method of gathering data on a small number of cases to make statements about (or estimates for) a much larger universe. Case study methods tend to be notably weak in relation to this criterion; the representativeness of the particular cases studied is uncertain or unknown.

Explanatory power

Methods may be evaluated, too, in terms of their explanatory power. Social scientists are often seeking the answer to 'why?' type questions in the investigations that they conduct. Both social surveys and case studies are superior in this respect to reliance upon census data or aggregate statistics, which are frequently deficient either in terms of topic coverage (the census) or fineness with which the data can be broken down (aggregate data analysis is also liable to the ecological fallacy (Robinson, 1950)).

Administrative convenience

A final consideration is administrative convenience, involving considerations of cost, speed and organizational complexity. Low cost, rapid speed and a minimum of organizational difficulties are usually desired, but are difficult to realize. Censuses are extremely expensive and slow to produce data. Social surveys involve complex adminstrative arrangements for fieldwork and data analysis. Participant observation is less expensive but slow. These practical considerations, including the question of who is paying for the research, cannot be ignored.

Problems of the equivalence of data

A major intellectual problem of the survey researcher in the Third World is the problem of equivalence of data. Not only are there major differences *between* developing countries, there are also major variations *within* developing countries. There are major differences between urban and rural areas, as well as within them. Population mobility is high. Geographical, cultural and regional diffrences may be extreme; for example, different types of agriculture may be found in the same society, ranging from nomadic pastoralism through small-scale subsistence farming to modern commercial production. Ethnic and racial differences are not uncommon. Language differences are widespread, and most developing countries use more than one language.

Such heterogeneity poses formidable problems, particularly for the survey researcher. For the social survey, as it has developed in the industrial west, tends to assume a *degree* of homogeneity in the population being studied. Thus, if British or American respondents are asked about their attitudes towards major political parties or political leaders, it is assumed that this is a meaningful question for them and a dimension in terms of which they can answer. The much greater variation within developing countries poses a sharp challenge for the survey researcher, which it is difficult to meet.

This is clearest in relation to language and problems of ensuring linguistic equivalence in the development and administration of a survey instrument. The issue is most acute in translating a question from one language to another. The meaning of words is seldom identical across cultures. 'Friend' in English, *'amie'* in French and *'amigo'* in Spanish, for example, all have different meanings. Words, as language terms, depend on the context in which they are used, usually a particular culture. The thought-patterns of people in different cultures are expressed in terms of language, and are often profoundly different one from another.

Securing equivalence in designing research is by no means merely an operational or technical problem of exact translation. Literal translation may overlook the different meaning which words have in different cultures. In general, the primary aim in designing research instruments is to secure *conceptual* equivalence, to ensure so far as possible that one is getting at the same concept in the different languages being used. Operational equivalence is secondary, and in some circumstances one may measure the concepts differently in order to achieve conceptual equivalence. These issues are discussed in more detail in Section IV.

Can third world surveys yield reliable and valid data?

The value of the social survey as an instrument of social research has not been uncontested. A number of general critiques have been mounted, alleging that, for example, surveys entail 'measurement by fiat' (Cicourel, 1964). Becker and Geer (1957) suggested that participant observation was to be preferred to interviewing because of its sensitivity to language, its ability to probe difficult topics and the researcher's participation in events that he is studying. Cicourel has recently returned to the attack (1982) urging greater attention to the linguistic and cognitive processes which frame exchanges between interviewer and respondent in a survey. A strong defence of the survey has however been mounted; Marsh (1982) is a distinguished recent example. Becker and Geer's critique was met head on by Martin Trow (1957), who argued that one method was not inherently superior over another. It was not a question of whether one method was better than another, but what the problem was to which a particular method — or combination of methods — was appropriate. Proponents of survey research are the first to admit the problems of bias and error which can occur (see Schuman, 1982), but see these difficulties as drawbacks to be overcome rather than insuperable objections to that research method.

The use of survey methods in developing countries is a particular case of the appropriateness of the use of the method. There has been considerable dispute about the appropriateness of survey methods, much of the argument turning on issues of the reliability and validity of survey data. The sharpest critics have been anthropologists, who have questioned whether extensive methods using standardized questionnaires really yield meaningful results.

Sir Edmund Leach, the British anthropologist, for example, has argued that the survey methods yield results inferior to the indepth ethnographic methods of the social anthropologist.

(T)here is a wide range of sociological phenomena which are intrinsically inaccesible to statistical investigation of any kind. . . . The anthropologist is constantly made aware of the difficulty of fitting items of human behaviour and experience into numerical categories. It is not that the numbers are necessarily false but that they draw the inquirer's attention away from what is of crucial significance (Leach, 1967, pp. 77, 82).

This argument is documented by means of a detailed comparison of a survey-based and an ethnographic study of Ceylonese villages. Leach argues that the results of the social survey gloss over important features of social structure. For example, the survey data appear to show that one can quantify the predominance of male over female inheritance. Leach doubts this. Apart from the fact that the subject is the very last topic on which one could expect a respondent to offer candid and straightforward information, there is in the area a very strong cultural prejudice that working the land of one's father is respectable while a husband working the land of his wife or sister is less respectable. This would influence responses given to survey questions: 'It is in the very nature of questionnaire investigation that the "results" tend to err in the direction of ideal stereotypes. Hence any attempt to investigate, by questionnaire research, the degree of fit between an ideal stereotype and actual practice is a waste of time' (Leach, 1967, p. 85).

Indian anthropologists have also criticized the social survey as the favoured digging tool of social inquiry. Data collected may not be all it appears to be. One government official in India told a visiting anthropologist: 'We have all categories [of data]. We have some ready for survey research people who come here periodically; we have a similar one for students who come for dissertation research and bother us. But we have what I call the green-room data, one concealed behind the screen' (Srinivas, Shah, and Ramaswamy, 1979, p. 13). Their general critique is of the failings of data collection in survey research in practice.

Survey research based on schedules and questionnaires is the most popular form of research in the social sciences. Research is generally organised in such a way — particularly the huge and expensive projects — that there is a sharp division of labour between high level analysts, who decide such matters as the problem to be investigated, and the methodology to be employed and who write the final draft, and low level investigators who canvass the questionnaires and punch, code and tabulate the replies. The former are the upstairs people while the latter live below. The investigators who collect the information are generally not highly motivated; as a result, the data gathered in the big surveys do not have a high degree of reliability. However, this is not peculiar to India — it is a universal phenomenon. No amount of statistical sophistication can set right the distortions and falsifications introduced by wrong data (Srinivas, Shah, and Ramaswamy, 1979, p. vii).

No more specific indications of the limitation of survey data are given, though the advantages (and difficulties) of fieldwork are discussed at length.

Other evidence illustrates the problems that can arise in village surveys in India (though the problems arising can be generalized to the Third World in general). Neale, for example, has criticized the quality of data in Indian agricultural surveys:

Questions are asked of the cultivator to which he does not know the answer; sometimes because the questions are not asked in the cultivator's terminology, sometimes because the cultivator has no means of knowing the answers, sometimes because the questions are not ones to which the cultivator normally gives consideration. Thus 'acres' and 'guntas' are English revenue measures, not indigenous measures, while the cultivator cannot be expected to know yields by weight if there are no scales in the village (Neale, 1958, pp. 394–395).

His respondents were invariably pleasant and courteous, but did not give the impression of trying hard to make sure the answers were correct. Deference and social hierarchy, particularly marked in a caste society, encourage the respondent to give an acceptable answer. Surveys in India, Neale concludes, do not and cannot be expected to provide accurate data.

Another Indian study by political scientists concluded that Western survey techniques could not be applied *pari passu* in the Indian context: 'One experience indicates that *some* of the questions which the opinion survey can answer in the West can be better answered, at least for the present, by the anthropologist using methods of clinical observation' (Rudolph and Rudolph, 1958, p.

242). For example, these investigators found that the egalitarian premises of opinion research were often challenged. Consulting a random sample of individuals whose opinions were held to have equal weight and importance was frequently challenged, both by those in authority (such as village headmen) or by respondents of inferior social status ('Why ask me? I am only an ignorant woman! Ask my husband'). The researcher's status is also at best uncertain. The interviewer may be taken for a government official, policeman or tax inspector. The role of social research interviewer is an unfamiliar one as are the appropriate behaviours for a social survey respondent.

Another strain of criticism of survey research in developing countries has concerned so-called KAP (Knowledge–Attitude–Practice) Surveys in the family planning field, developed by demographers to study reproductive behaviour and the use of contraception. Population issues are among the most important facing developing countries, and KAP surveys had a particular vogue in the 1950s and 1960s. Considerable doubts have been expressed about the inferences made using such survey data about the likely success of family planning programmes. Some of these reservations are discussed further by Philip Hauser in Chapter 5, but they serve as an example of the general criticisms levelled at the uncritical policy use of survey data (Bulmer, 1982, Chapter 1) with too ready a tendency to jump from attitudes expressed in verbal responses (which may be influenced, for example, by what the respondent thinks the interviewer wants to hear) to the behaviour of the respondent and (in the case of KAP surveys) changes in the behaviour of the respondent.

Such criticisms of the reliability and validity of survey data collected in developing countries are, however, strongly contested. Many survey practitioners maintain that survey data can be collected quite satisfactorily in the Third World, and while admitting that care is needed in the conduct of research, point to the successful outcome of large-scale inquiries such as the Indian National Sample Survey (NSS) whose design is discussed in Chapter 9. Some would go further to point out that the sample design for this survey, which began in 1950, was developed by the great Indian statistician P.C. Mahalanobis, a close friend of R.A. Fisher, and one of the earliest pioneers in the world of the use of survey sampling. Far from applying western methods uncritically, in the sample design of the NSS India was leading the developed world at the time rather than following it.

Even among anthropologists, the blanket criticisms of Leach would not be very widely accepted. As noted in Chapter 22, anthropologists have often combined observational research with surveys and other quantitative approaches (for methodological discussions see Burgess, 1982, pp. 163–188; Henry, 1967; Mitchell, 1967; Speckmann, 1967). Even if one grants Leach's point about surveys and ideal stereotypes, there are many other areas where sample survey methods can be applied to effect in village studies.

Hard evidence of the feasibility and accuracy of surveys in non-western countries is available. The first two examples are again drawn from India, but the results may be generalized. Ralis, Suchman and Goldsen examined the reliability and validity of data derived from a survey of 984 respondents in Uttar Pradesh, to evaluate Shramdan (voluntary contribution to public work). An internal reliability check between two similar questionnaire items showed a high degree of similarity and consistency. Two validity checks examined the internal consistency of relationships among independent variables measured in the survey. High internal correlations were obtained, offering presumptive evidence that the data were valid and meaningful. Some interviewer bias was detected when comparisons were made between responses obtained by interviewers who were government employees compared with responses obtained by interviewers who were private citizens (Ralis, Suchman, and Goldsen, 1958, pp. 245–50).

Joseph Elder (1973), in the course of survey research in Lucknow and Madurai in India into attitude change, made a systematic examination of six methodological problems in terms of which he compared intrasocietal and cross-cultural research: unit comparability, sampling, instrument construction, instrument translation, interviewer selection and training, and field response. He concluded that for five of the six problems there were no qualitative differences, only differences of degree. He did conclude, however, that the problem of instrument translation was qualitatively different; there was a major difference between supplying an occasional word-substitute for sub-cultural groups in the same language pool, and supplying an entire research instrument in a different language.

Other evidence of the feasibility of survey research in developing countries is provided by studies by social scientists in several societies. William Form, for example, successfully carried out a comparative survey of automobile workers in four countries, Italy, the United States, Argentina and India. In the Indian stage of the research, the interview schedule had to be translated into the mother-tongues of the workers: Marathi, Hindi, Urdu, Gujarati and Punjabi. The principal researcher was fluent in three of these languages and interviewers speaking the other languages were trained to carry out those inter-other three countries, mainly spent trying to make sure the questions were understood: 'On the whole, satisfactory interviews were obtained, with a refusal rate of only three percent' (Form, 1976, p. 275).

A political science study carried out in India sought to carry out the first national sample survey of Indian electoral behaviour. Its authors concluded that the use of survey methods was feasible in the Indian context:

Despite the difficulties posed by this electoral setting, as well as the problems attending the transference of a research technology from one culture to another, our national surveys were satisfactorily concluded, both in the sense of utilising scientific procedures from design to analysis, and in the sense of producing reliable and valid data (Eldersveld and Ahmed, 1978, p. 13)

Some observers had questioned whether this could be done in a country like India, citing the ignorance and disinterest of the citizens, lack of comprehension of questions, impossibility of eliminating bias in the interviewer–respondent relationship (because of the caste system), courtesy bias and translation problems.

Our position . . . based on our extensive experience in two national surveys and in smaller studies, is that in principle the problems of survey research are no different in India than elsewhere. Obstacles of a special character do indeed exist in India, but by careful planning, training, and supervision those which might seriously bias the results can be dealt with. Error does occur and must be allowed for in all studies everywhere — sampling error, interviewing error, coding error — but India is basically no different from other countries in this respect (Eldersveld and Ahmed, 1978, p. 13).

Turning to demographic research, the World Fertility Survey (WFS) provides a counter-example to the criticism directed at KAP surveys. This major international survey, begun in 1972, is designed to enable developing countries in particular to carry out nationally representative, internationally comparable and scientifically conducted surveys of fertility behaviour. The WFS is administered by the International Statistical Institute with funds from United Nations agencies (World Fertility Survey, 1980).

Under the guidance of a central research staff located in London, national surveys have been conducted during the late 1970s in a considerable number of developing countries. This is not the place for a full review of the scope of the WFS but it may be noted that although various problems have been encountered, the quality of data collected has been generally high. An assessment by Chidambaram *et al.* (1980) suggests that coverage of vital events in the survey data on individuals has been good, and particularly good on infant and child mortality (though poor on fetal losses). Detailed birth histories provided by individual women were judged of reasonable quality in about half the countries, but errors in the dating of births rendered the data for other countries less satisfactory. The experience of this major project goes some way to quieten the criticisms of fertility research using survey methods arising from the earlier KAP surveys.

This long discussion of the pros and cons of using survey research in developing countries highlights a major purpose of this book — to examine the problems of conducting surveys in developing countries, to show the difficulties which there undoubtedly are, to evaluate their seriousness, and to consider possible solutions.

Survey research is not alone in suffering from methodological limitations. Some discussions make it appear as if, because the sample survey has the problems noted, other approaches, particularly ethnographic research, are relatively trouble-free. Such is far from the case. Most basically the typical village study suffers from limitations of coverage and thus difficulties in generalizing its findings beyond the case or cases chosen. In projects aiming at policy relevance that is no small limitation. Moreover, many of the problems of sample surveys, including lack of comprehension by local respondents, suspicions about the purposes of the research, and distortions in responses, repeat themselves in different form in the observational study. Many of these problems have been ably set forth in the now-classic essay by Gerald Berreman (1972, pp. xvii–lvii) on his field experiences in the Himalayas.

The issue is not an either/or choice for or against the use of survey methods. As emphasized at length in Section VI on methodological marriages, there is much to be gained by complementing the use of a single method with another method or methods: 'Every extension of survey methods to a new cultural milieu requires a cautious examination not only of how techniques may be best adapted to the new setting but also a thoughtful reconsideration of basic principles' (Bonilla, 1964, p. 140).

Survey methods, for example, may be more appropriate where quantitative data are required, where the information sought is reasonably specific and familiar to the respondents, and where the researcher has prior knowledge of the range of responses likely to be obtained. These conditions are met in areas of research which are the traditional strongholds of the survey — public opinion, voting, attitudes and beliefs and economic behaviour.

Participant observation, on the other hand, may be more appropriate when the study requires an examination of complex social relationships or intricate patterns of interaction, such as kinship relations; or where observational data on social processes, such as leadership or small group dynamics, are required; or where the aim is to build up an indepth picture of a particular social context or milieu. Participant observation may be superior to the survey in this regard because it does not require detailed prior knowledge; it does not depend on a short, structured interview with a relative stranger; it enables ongoing processes to be studied; and it permits attention to the intricacy and complexity of the data.

On the other hand, the survey is a much more effective and efficient means of obtaining quantitative data, and offers greater possibilities for replication. Its results can be generalized, and the survey provides a representative picture in a way that the participant observer cannot do.

In short, there is no magic to either of these methods, or to any other. Each is useful for some purposes and useless for others. The strength of the sample survey lies in its potential for quantification, replication, and generalisability to a broader population. Participant observation normally has the edge on qualitative depth and flexibility for the observer. In many studies the ideal solution is to develop a methodological mixture which will capitalise on the strengths of each approach. A design which combines participant observation or other qualitative methods with a sample survey provides opportunities for cross-checking and for a much more complete picture of the situation being studied (Warwick and Lininger, 1975, p. 12).

The research process

The organization of the book follows the research process through its several stages. Section II, on research strategy, discusses the use of censuses and sample surveys for research purposes in the developing world, and the problems which arise in using sample survey methods developed and codified in industrial countries under different Third World conditions. Section III, on sampling, considers the problems that arise in adapting standard procedures to the special conditions in the Third World, and also examines the relative merits of extensive and intensive types of inquiry.

The core of the book lies in Section IV on data collection and analysis and Section V on interviewing and field organization. It is in the area of the collection of data that the most intractable problems arise in conducting survey research in the developing world. Topics covered include the design of questionnaires, the construction of reliable cross-cultural research instruments, problems of translation in the preparation of research instruments, and problems in the reliability and validity of data collected by survey methods. The discussion of fieldwork and interviewing focuses upon relations between research teams, interviewers and respondents, the actual conditions under which surveys are carried out and the kinds of methodological problems which can arise, particularly in rural areas in the Third World, when using standard techniques. The material provides the opportunity for a critical assessment of the uses and limitations of survey research methods in the developing world.

The following section, on methodological marriages, considers the extent to which survey methods may be combined with other research methods such as participant observation, the use of archival records and official statistics. The value of combining different methods is emphasized, taking the discussion beyond the simple either/or, for/against, discussion of the uses of the social survey. The final section of the book examines the political and ethical context of social inquiry in the Third World, an increasingly important issue. Social research is a form of intervention touching sensitive personal and political nerves. As well as technical competence and professional standards, its use entails ethical and political considerations. Deception, manipulation and abuses of trust need to be avoided both as morally harmful but also because they can provoke a public backlash against social science. The position of western social scientists as 'outsiders' in developing countries needs to be carefully considered, to avoid the taunt of exploitation or abuse of both indigenous social scientists and of respondents. Increasingly, collaborative research between 'outsiders' and 'insiders' is favoured (the World Fertility Survey provides a notable example) as is the development of indigenous social science in the countries of the developing world. The influence of the political context is emphasised in Chapter 25 on Chile by Zuñiga.

No book on methods of social research is ever complete, and this one is no exception. There are several aspects of the research process which are not treated or treated only lightly. One is the important issue of conceptualization in social science research. Though this is discussed at several points, detailed attention is not paid to the origin of social science concepts, the way that concepts are specified in particular pieces of empirical research, and how concepts are operationalized in the course of research. This is discussed elsewhere in texts on research methods, to which reference should be made (for example, Bulmer, 1977, pp. 78–91; Warwick and Lininger, 1975, p. 20–45; see also Bulmer, 1979).

Data analysis does not feature significantly in this book, because the subject is well treated in standard textbooks on methods of social research. It is in the area of data analysis that the differences between research practice in the developed and developing world are least important. There are, to be sure, some technological differences. Computers are now universally used in the industrial world to handle quantitative social data, while their use in the developing world is less general, the counter-sorter still being a great standby. (For an excellent review of the practical and technological aspects of data processing, see Hursh-César and Roy, 1976, pp. 347–98.) The logic of data analysis and the statistical procedures associated with it are, however, the same wherever a survey is conducted, and differences of degree are less in different types of society because social conditions do not impinge directly upon how data is analysed in the many ways that they do upon how data is collected. Hence the reader may much more safely rely upon the accounts of data analysis in standard texts for a guide to practice in the Third World than upon comparable sections dealing with the design of research, sampling or the collection of data. In these latter areas differences of degree, if not of kind, are very marked.

Political and ethical difficulties of research in developing countries

The early history of social science research in the Third World is the history of colonial social science. In anthropology, for example, the vast majority of scholars were of western origin, usually coming to spend a relatively brief period of fieldwork in an African, Asian or Latin American country before returning home. Sometimes they taught at local universities (staffed, in the social sciences, predominantly by Europeans or Americans). Some worked in an applied capacity for colonial governments (see Asad, 1973). There was also some movement in the other direction. A few promising young people in colonial societies were given opportunities to study social science in the metropolitan centres, becoming academic social scientists in some cases and in others entering the professions or following a political career.

So far as research methods, particularly survey research methods, were concerned, the great expansion occurred after the Second World War, particularly in the United States. In the 1950s and early 1960s there was a major growth of survey research in the Third World, mainly conducted (with the exception of certain countries such as India) by western social scientists applying methods developed in their own societies in new and unfamiliar conditions. A spate of publications reflected this experience, and sought to systematize knowledge about problems of cross-cultural survey research (see, for example Armer and Grimshaw, 1973; Berting *et al.*, 1979; Brislin *et al.*, 1973; Delamater, 1968; Hauser, 1964; Holt and Turner, 1970; Merritt and Rokkan, 1966; Moore, 1961; Przeworski and Teune, 1970; Rokkan, 1968; Szalai and Petrella, 1977; Triandis and Berry, 1980; Ward, 1964; Warwick and Osherson, 1973). Typically the authors were North Americans or western Europeans.

The typical research project in a developing nation in the 1950–1960 period consisted of 'data-mining' by the sojourning social scientist. He came to the host country, gathered his data, and went home to complete his analysis. This 'safari' research expedition left no lasting imprint on the host country's research capability. If anything, the visitor left disappointed hosts who expected useful research results, correction of social problems, or even joint publications (Hursh-César and Roy, 1976, p. 8).

This era of the 'safari' scholar is now at an end. There remain, nevertheless, problems in the relation between 'outsiders' (that is, foreign scholars) and 'insiders' (that is, indigenous scholars), problems of sponsorship and provision of resources, recruitment of personnel, and their institutional affiliation (Roy and Fliegel, 1970). To replace 'outsiders' by indigenous research workers is no panacea. It depends on whom the insiders are. For example, in rural surveys

because they are well-educated, can be hired inexpensively, often express an interest in social science research, and can be found quite easily from a variety of ethnic backgrounds, college students in particular are frequently used in studies of developing nations — often disastrously. Like it or not, most students are 'elitist', already or becoming members of the privileged urban classes. Their employment can cause serious communication problems. They may have great difficulty stepping out of their high-status roles and adopting the behaviour and demeanour required to establish rapport with illiterate subsistence-level farmers (Hursh-César and Roy, 1976, p. 308).

Experience of field research in India, for example, shows that sensitivity to the local context and awareness of the fieldworker's role is all important (Berreman, 1972, pp. xvii–lvii; Beteille and Madan, 1975; Beteille, 1976; Srinivas, Shah and Ramaswamy, 1979).

Research relations involving 'outsiders' and 'insiders' in the contemporary developing world are too complex for easy summary (see Fahim, 1982). A common thread in the research experience in the Third World, however, is the salience of ethical and political problems. Many of the most acute have arisen as a result of actions by 'outsiders', the most notorious of which is probably Project Camelot in Chile (Horowitz, 1967). The last section of this book therefore considers some of the political and ethical difficulties of research. The story is brought forward to more recent times by Ricardo Zuniga, who discusses the position of social science during the Popular Unity government of Salvador Allende in Chile (Chapter 25). Two other examples from the study of population are discussed by Donald Warwick (Chapter 26) and by Charles Kleymeyer and William Bertrand (Chapter 27). The materials in this section emphasize that the problems of adapting survey methods for successful use in the Third World are not merely technical ones of methodology, but involve the broader political, social and ethical context and purposes of social scientific inquiry.

References

Armer, M. and Grimshaw, A.D. (Eds) (1973). *Comparative Social Research: Methodological Problems and Strategies*, Wiley, New York.

Asad, T. (ed) (1973). *Anthropology and the Colonial Encounter*, Ithaca Press, London.

Babbie, E.R. (1973). *Survey Research Methods*, Wadsworth, Belmont, Cal.

Backstrom, C.H. and Hursh-César, G. (1981). *Survey Research, 2nd Edition*, Wiley, New York.

Becker, H.S. and Geer, B. (1957). Participant observation and interviewing. *Human Organisation*, **16**, 28–32.

Berreman, G.D. (1972). *Hindus of the Himalayas: Ethnography and Change, 2nd Edition* University of California Press, Berkeley.

Berting, J. *et al.* (eds) (1979). *Problems of International Comparative Research in the Social Sciences*, Pergamon, Oxford.

Beteille, A. (1976). The limitations of research methodology. *International Social Science Journal*, **28**, 195–197.

Beteille, A. and Madan, J.N. (Eds) (1975). *Encounter and Experience*, Vikas, New Delhi.

Bonilla, F. (1964). Survey techniques. In R.E. Ward (Ed.), *Studying Politics Abroad*, pp. 134–152, Little Brown, Boston.

Brislin, R.W. *et al.* (1973). *Cross-cultural Research Methods*, Wiley, New York.

Bulmer, M. (Ed) (1977). *Sociological Research Methods*, Macmillan, London.

Bulmer, M. (1979). Concepts in the analysis of qualitative data. *Sociological Review*, **27**, 651–677.

Bulmer, M. (1982). *The Uses of Social Research*, Allen and Unwin, London.

Burgess, R. (ed) (1982). *Field Research: A Sourcebook and Field Manual*, Allen and Unwin, London.

Campbell, D.T. and Stanley, J.C. (1963). *Experimental and Quasi-Experimental Designs for Research*, Chicago, Rand McNally.

Casley, D.J. and Lury, D.A. (1981). *Data Collection in Developing Countries*, Clarendon Press, Oxford.

Chidambaram, V.C. *et al.* (1980). *Some Aspects of World Fertility Survey Data Quality*, International Statistical Institute, *World Fertility Survey Comparative Studies* **No. 16, May**, Voorburg, Netherlands.

Cicourel, A.V. (1964). *Method and Measurement in Sociology*, Free Press, New York.

Cicourel, A.V. (1982). Interviews, surveys and the problem of ecological validity. *American Sociologist*, **17**, 11–20.

Delamater, J., Hefner, R. and Chignet, R. (Eds) (1968). Social psychological research in developing countries. *Journal of Social Issues*, **24**, 1–289.

Deutscher, I. (1973). *What We Say/What We Do: Sentiments and Acts*, Scott Foresman, Brighton, Sussex.

Deutscher, I. (1977). 'Asking questions (and listening to answers): a review of some sociological precedents and problems, in Bulmer, M. (ed.) *Sociological Research Methods*, pp. 243–258 Macmillan, London.

Dixon, C. and Leach, B. (1981). *Survey Research in Less-Developed Countries: A Bibliography*, City of London Polytechnic, Department of Geography, London, mimeo.

Elder, J. (1973). Problems of cross-cultural methodology: instrumentation and interviewing in India, in Armer and Grimshaw (eds) *Comparative Social Research*, pp. 119–144, Wiley, New York.

Eldersveld, S.J. and Ahmed B. (1978). *Citizens and Politics: Mass Political Behavior in India*, University of Chicago Press, Chicago.

Fahim, H. (ed) (1982). *Indigenous Anthropology in Non-Western Countries*, Carolina Academic Press, Durham, NC.

Form, W.H. (1976). *Blue Collar Stratification: Autoworkers in Four Countries*, Princeton University Press, Princeton, NJ.

Frey, F.W. (1970). Cross-cultural survey research in political science. In R.T. Holt and J.E. Turner, *The Methodology of Comparative Research*, pp. 173–294, Free Press, New York.

Frey, F.W. *et al.* (1969). *Survey Research on Comparative Social Change: A Bibliography*, MIT Press, Cambridge, Mass.

Goldstone, L. (1977). Improving social statistics in developing countries. *International Social Science Journal*, **29**, 756–771.

Halsey, A.H. (ed.) (1972). *Trends in British Society Since 1900*, Macmillan, London.

Hauser, P.M. (ed) (1964). *Handbook for Social Science Research in Urban Areas*, UNESCO, Paris.

Henry, F. (1967) The survey research design: some practical problems. *Anthropologica*, **9**, 51–57.

Holt, R.T. and Turner, J.E. (Eds) (1970). *The Methodology of Comparative Research*, Free Press, New York.

Horowitz, I.L. (Ed) (1967). *The Rise and Fall of Project Camelot*, MIT Press, Cambridge, Mass.

Hursh-César, G. and Roy, P. (Eds) (1976). *Third World Surveys: Survey Research in Developing Nations*. Macmillan of India, Delhi.

Kearl, B. (ed) (1976). *Field Data Collection in the Social Sciences: Experiences in Africa and the Middle East*, Agricultural Development Council Inc., New York.

Leach, E.R. (1967). An anthropologist's reflections on a social survey. In D.G. Jongmans and P.C.W. Gutkind (Eds) *Anthropologists in the Field*, pp. 75–88, Van Gorcum, Assen, Netherlands.

Lindblom, C. and Cohen, D.K. (1979). *Usable Knowledge: Social Science and Social Problem Solving*, Yale University Press, New Haven, Conn.

Marsh, C. (1982). *The Survey Method: The Contribution of Surveys to Sociological Explanation*, Allen and Unwin, London.

Merritt, R.L. and Rokkan, S. (Eds) (1966). *Comparing Nations: The Use of Quantitative Data in Cross-National Research*, Yale University Press, New Haven, Conn.

Mitchell, J.C. (1967). On quantification in anthropology. In A.L. Epstein, (Ed) *The Craft of Social Anthropology*, pp. 17–45, Tavistock, London.

Moore, F.W. (Ed.) (1961). *Readings in Cross-Cultural Methodology*, HRAF Press, New Haven, Conn.

Morgenstern, O. (1963). *On the Accuracy of Economic Observations*. Princeton University Press, Princeton, NJ.

Moser, C.A. and Kalton, G. (1971). *Survey Methods in Social Investigation*, Heinemann, London.

Murthy, M.N. (1978) The use of sample surveys in national planning in developing countries. In N.K. Namboodiri (Ed.) *Survey Sampling and Measurement*, pp. 231–253, Academic Press, New York.

Neale, W.C. (1958) The limitations of Indian village survey data. *Journal of Asian Studies*, 17, 383–402.

O'Barr, W.M. *et al.* (Eds) (1973). *Survey Research in Arica: Its Applications and Limits*, Northwestern University Press, Evanston, Ill.

Peil, M. *et al.* (1982). *Social Science Research Methods: An African Handbook*, Hodder and Stoughton, London.

Przeworski, A. and Teune, H. (1970). *The Logic of Comparative Social Inquiry*, Wiley, New York.

Ralis, M., Suchman, E.A. and Goldsen, R.K. (1958). Applicability of survey techniques in Northern India. *Public Opinion Quarterly*, 22, 245–250.

Rimmer, D. (1982) Official statistics. In M. Peil *et al.* (Eds) *Social Science Research Methods: An African Handbook*, pp. 47–58, Hodder and Stoughton, London.

Robinson, W.S. (1950) Ecological correlations and the behavior of individuals. *American Sociological Review*, 15, 351–357.

Rokkan, S. (Ed.) (1968). *Comparative Research Across Cultures and Nations*, Mouton, The Hague.

Roy, P. and Fliegel, F.C. (1970). The conduct of collaborative research in the developing nations: the insiders and the outsiders. *International Social Science Journal*, 22, 505–523.

Rudolph, L. and Rudolph, S.H. (1958). Surveys in India: field experience in Madras State. *Public Opinion Quarterly*, 22, 235–244.

Schuman, H. (1982). Artifacts are in the mind of the beholder, *American Sociologist*, 17, 21–28.

Speckmann, J.D. (1967). Social surveys in non-western areas. In D.G. Jongmans and P.C.W. Gutkind (Eds) *Anthropologists in the Field*, pp. 56–74, Van Gorcum, Assen, Netherlands.

Srinivas, M.N., Shah, A.M. and Ramaswamy, E.A. (Eds) (1979). *The Fieldworker and the Field: Problems and Challenges in Sociological Investigation*, Oxford University Press, Delhi.

Szalai, A. and Petrella, R. (Eds) (1977). *Cross-national Comparative Survey Research: Theory and Practice*, Pergamon, Oxford.

Triandis, H.C. and Berry, J.W. (Eds) (1980) *Handbook of Cross-Cultural Psychology. Vol. 2: Methodology*, Allyn and Bacon, Boston.

Trow, M. (1957) Comment on 'Participant observation and interviewing' by Becker and Geer. *Human Organisation*, 16, 33–35.

Ward, R.E. (ed.) (1964) *Studying Politics Abroad: Field Research in the Developing Areas*, Little, Brown, Boston.

Warwick, D.P. and Lininger, C. (1975) *The Sample Survey: Theory and Practice*, McGraw-Hill, New York.

Warwick, D.P. and Osherson, S. (Eds) (1973) *Comparative Research Methods*, Prentice Hall, Englewood Cliffs, NJ.

World Fertility Survey (1980). *Annual Report 1980*, International Statistical Institute, World Fertility Survey, Voorburg, Netherlands.

Zarkovich, S.S. (1975). *Statistical Development*, Cairo University Press, Cairo.

SECTION II

RESEARCH STRATEGY

Social Research in Developing Countries
Edited by M. Bulmer and D.P. Warwick
© 1983, John Wiley & Sons, Ltd.

CHAPTER 2

RESEARCH STRATEGY

MARTIN BULMER AND DONALD P. WARWICK

Empirical social research requires a research *strategy*, a plan in terms of which particular studies are carried out embodying ideas about the task of social research, the research design to be used, and the choice of particular methods of data collection (Bulmer, 1977, p. 5). This section is concerned primarily with exploring the appropriateness of different kinds of methods for research in the Third World, with the main focus upon social survey research. Under what conditions should which methods be used for which kinds of data collection? What does one get out of one approach that one does not get out of another? These issues were raised briefly in Chapter 1, but will now be developed more fully here.

A Third World social researcher intending to carry out a social survey can turn to a standard textbook on survey research methods (such as Babbie, 1973; Moser and Kalton, 1971), written on the basis of experience in North America or western Europe. Conditions in developing countries, however, may modify some of the procedures and assumptions made in standard texts; this section aims to consider the extent to which this is necessary. Consideration of alternative research strategies raises the question of the extent to which social surveys are suitable at all for social investigation in developing countries. This point was touched on in Chapter 1, and is alluded to again in Chapter 4 by Stycos and Chapter 6 by Peil. As Peil emphasizes, social investigation is influenced by the environment in which it is done, and this cannot be ignored when the differences from industrial societies may be such as to undermine the fundamental assumptions on which the research method rests. The contributors to this section focus primarily upon the social survey, but in doing so raise issues about the appropriateness of other research strategies.

The sample survey is a standard tool of social research, and the one most commonly in use. It is a method of collecting information about a human population in which direct contact is made with those being studied, who are asked questions set out upon an interview schedule or questionnaire. A census is a survey in which information is gathered from, or about, all members of a population. In a sample survey, a fraction of the population is sampled to represent the whole, which is a much more efficient procedure than a census. Surveys provide a means of answering questions such as:

Who does *what*?
Why — what are the *reasons* for certain kinds of behaviour?
How?
How well?
With what effect?

One very important principle in social research is to determine at the outset for what purpose data are being collected. This is especially important in developing countries, not only to avoid trivial or unnecessary inquiries, but also because of the expense involved. One way in which this question can be answered is to ask for whom research is being carried out. This is not only a matter of who is sponsoring the research (a government department, or a university, or a research institute, for example) but who is going to use the research when it is completed. Users will include *policy-makers*, who may want to know about development trends, the nature of particular social and economic problems and the effectiveness of government programmes. They will include *development planners* and other change agents, who need information about the population and target area in terms of the characteristics, attitude and behaviour of those whom they are seeking to affect or reach. Another group of users are *international donors*, who frequently commission studies to evaluate programmes that they have sponsored, or simply to explore an area that is of interest to them. They may include *pressure groups* seeking information to support their case for particular policy positions and action. The audience for research includes *citizen groups* concerned with the interests of particular segments of the population, such as farmers or industrial workers. A principal audience is made up of *other researchers* either in the investigator's own or related fields. The study of development is increasingly an interdisciplinary area of academic work, and sharp lines cannot be drawn around the field for which a particular study is relevant. *Students* constitute yet another constituency, where research may have instructional benefits (Kearl, 1976, pp. 185–186).

There are also different types of research, oriented to different users. Intelligence and monitoring, of which the census is a prime example, provides demographic, social and economic data for policy-makers and development planners, primarily of a factual kind. Public-opinion polling is also of this type. Action-research uses research as an integral part of planned social change to study the effects of such change as it happens, oriented to users who are policy-makers or planners. Specific problem-oriented research is oriented to the same type of user and is designed to provide the answer to practical, operational problems. Strategic social science research is grounded in an academic discipline, but is oriented toward a socially problematical issue, without being aimed necessarily at providing a solution to it. Basic social science research is concerned with advancing the state of knowledge within a particular discipline, without necessarily having any practical end. It is also the basis of a social science education (Bulmer, 1978, pp. 8–9).

Censuses

The population census is the most comprehensive type of research exercise in the developing, as in the developed, world. It involves the complete enumeration of a population, within the boundaries of a state, simultaneously (or nearly simultaneously), using a massive army of specially recruited enumerators (often government officials and teachers working on a part-time basis). The census aims to produce a 100 per cent count of the population, with information on the restricted number of demographic, economic and social variables which it is possible to include in the census schedule (for a review of census coverage, see United Nations, 1972). In terms of representativeness, a census appears to be very nearly perfect, and for certain purposes seems to make available the optimum type of data. One of its main purposes is to provide a repository of data which can be drawn upon by policy-makers in government in the interval (usually 10 years) between one census and the next.

Gil and Omaboe in Chapter 3 of this book describe the formidable organizational problems of conducting a full census, using Ghana as an example. The cost of such an inquiry is very large. The cost of the 1973 Nigerian census, for example, is estimated at £20 million, or approximately 36 p per head (Mabogunje, 1976, p. 209). Some of the problems of censuses as sources of social data stem from their size and scale. For example, though the objective is to obtain complete coverage, in practice for several reasons (varying between urban and rural areas) complete coverage is very difficult to achieve. In countries like India where the census has to be spread over 2–3 weeks (rather than held on a single night) there may be some duplications or omissions due to movement of population during that period.

It is always desirable to make the census questionnaire as simple and brief as possible. Clarity and straightforwardness of questions is essential. Even so, it is very easy to devise questions which, inadvertently, produce meaningless results. In Britain, the 1961 census included a question on nationality which produced valueless results due to the complexity of British nationality law. In developing countries, census questions on economic activity are particularly prone to error, due to the lack of a sharp distinction between the money and subsistence economy, and in some cases the lack of a clear dividing line between employment, underemployment and unemployment (Jain, 1970). This is discussed further in connection with social surveys, p. 32–6.

Census-taking, because of its compulsory nature and the uses to which data are put for political apportionment, also has ethical and political dimensions. Such matters are considered more fully in the last section of the book, but should be mentioned here, since in a few cases they have influenced the validity of census-taking. The most striking case has been that of Nigeria, where the first census after independence, in 1962, was declared invalid by the government and a recount was carried out in 1963. The reasons for this debâcle were connected with regionalism in the country, and allegations that the census totals in certain regions had been artificially inflated to increase that region's representation in the federal parliament. The precise rights and wrongs of the matter are cloudy (Mabogunje, 1976: Udo, 1968; Yesufu, 1968) but the possibility that the census may become a matter of political controversy in societies divided along regional, ethnic, linguistic or religious lines has implications for the quality of data collected.

Social surveys

The census is a fact-finding inquiry for the government. Some large social surveys, like the Indian National Sample Survey described below in Chapter 9, are also done for the government. Social surveys are, however, of varying types which may be carried out for different audiences. At the other extreme to the census stands the small-scale academic survey contributing to basic research aimed at an audience of other academic colleagues. Most survey research in developing countries, however, falls some way between those two extremes, and usually incorporates some analytical element as well as having a policy purpose. Research on family planning, for example, though aimed at practical policy problems, seeks to find the determinants of fertility and identify variables that are susceptible to manipulation in the policy process.

Answers to the central question: 'Why are we collecting these data?' (see Casley and Lury, 1981, p. 17) thus depend on for whom the data are being collected and what type of research is being undertaken. Another key question to ask is: how is the research designed? Sample surveys differ in their research objectives; a broad distinction may be made between *descriptive* and *explanatory* surveys. Descriptive surveys seek to arrive at precise measurement of social phenomena: the census is the ultimate descriptive survey. Explanatory surveys, on the other hand, aim to test hypotheses or develop theory in relation to particular problems, whether theoretical or practical (Warwick and Lininger, 1975, pp. 46–56). The research strategy adopted for any particular study is thus the outcome of a series of choices made by the investigator or built into the sponsorship or specification of the research.

This book places primary emphasis upon social survey research, but it is not intended to treat this method in isolation from other methods. A later section, on methodological marriages, explicitly considers the relationship between surveys and other methods. Chapter 3, by Gil and Omaboe, discusses the role of the population census. The census is a complete survey of a population, carried out simultaneously at one point in time. Censuses are usually carried out every 10 years to provide bench-mark data on population and social conditions. A great advantage of the census is that it can provide data on small geographical areas of a country, which cannot be gathered by sample survey methods.

Social surveys, however, have a number of advantages compared with the census. They are very much less expensive, because only a fraction of the population is sampled and thus fewer staff and a smaller organization is required. To give two examples of the scale of a census, the Indian census employs nearly 1 million enumerators to gather data in the field (Jain, 1970). The recent Chinese census of 1982 employed 6 million enumerators. Surveys are also quicker in collecting and analysing data. Whereas the production of census data takes a matter of years, survey data *can* be available within a matter of months. A major advantage of the social survey, considered in detail in Section V, is that interviewers can be much more intensively trained than census enumerators, and so can be expected to produce higher quality data. Moreover, the greater training of field staff and smaller size of the study permits well-trained interviewers to use more complex questionnaires to investigate complex attitude questions and subjects not suitable for inclusion in the census. The length of interviews can be considerably greater than what is feasible in a census, a good example being the Indian National Sample Survey discussed in Chapter 9. Finally, a sample survey imposes much less than a census upon public goodwill, and is less likely to arouse opposition or accusations of invasion of privacy.

The sample survey can also be contrasted with methods based on intensive fieldwork (also known generically as 'participant observation'). In participant observation, the investigator participates intensively in a group and interviews members of the group informally. (For an example of these methods from a developing country, India, see Srinivas, Shah, and Ramaswamy, 1979). The advantages of one method tend to be the disadvantages of the other. Survey methods are an appropriate means of gathering quantitative data where the information sought is fairly specific, and where the researcher himself has considerable prior knowledge of the range of responses likely to be obtained. Intensive fieldwork is more appropriate for building up a qualitative, contextual, picture of life in a group, for observation of behaviour and public events; or for the indepth study of values and belief systems where prior knowledge of their variability is limited (Havens, 1964).

The survey has the advantage of providing extensive quantitative data relatively cheaply. Broad generalizations can be made from a relatively small number of observations as long as probability sampling methods are used (see Section III). This contrasts with the much more limited generalizability of data from case studies using participant observation methods. However, a method such as the social survey which relies so heavily upon verbal statements by respondents has a very large possibility of producing biased data, as a result of both intentional and unintentional distortion of information by respondents. This problem is discussed further in Section V on field research.

As noted earlier the social survey is a western product which cannot be straightforwardly exported to the developing world. Basic data needed for survey research may be lacking. Available sampling frames are often inadequate. There are considerable regional variations. Both field staff and respondents are unfamiliar with standard attitude measures and have difficulty in interpreting them. Responses to questionnaire items are strongly influenced by the culture of the respondent, with resulting problems of translation from one culture to another. Trained personnel are scarce, and rarely combine field experience with academic knowledge. Data-processing equipment is often limited or antiquated.

Employment surveys

Moreover, concepts and terms which are familiar from use in the industrialized countries cannot automatically be transferred for use in survey work in a developing country. Employment and unemployment provide a useful example in terms of which to consider the conceptual and methodological problems of conducting surveys and censuses in the Third World. For all of its centrality as a policy concern, it is by no means clear just what 'employment' means, especially in rural areas of the developing countries. With each new hundred pages of answers, we are less sure about the questions. The confusion is reflected in the very language used to guide research in this field. In the early 1960s economists and labour market researchers readily accepted the conventional western notions of employment and unemployment and organized data collection around them. When it became clear that these concepts missed or misrepresented a serious underutilization of labour in the developing countries, the notion of underemployment came to the fore. Then, in 1968, Gunnar Myrdal published a long and devastating critique of the origins, assumptions, and uses of these established concepts and the research which they generated. His solution, which he recognized as still inadequate, was to speak of labour utilization (participation, duration, and efficiency). This approach was adopted, often implicitly, by others, even though it had no major impact on the labour market research conducted in most of the developing countries. But as one scans the current literature, and particularly the categories actually used in data collection, there is little doubt that the traditional triad of employment–underemployment–unemployment is still the guiding paradigm. Ironically, even the critics of the conventional approach use its terms in their criticisms (see, for example, Jolly, 1973, p. 23).

The difficulties with the standard notions of employment and labour use are both conceptual and methodological. The two are linked, for ambiguous or irrelevant concepts invariably lead to problems of measurement, not least in census questions which aim to be simple and unambiguous. The concept 'unemployment', for example, may make little sense in many developing countries.

Unemployment in the statistical sense refers to a situation in which a person has no substantial source of earned income, is looking actively for work, will accept a job at the going wage, and has been unable to find work. In the context of a developed country, this means quite simply, that a person has lost his job and is looking for another job.... This concept has little applicability outside the context of an economy wherein the vast majority of the population is obliged to sell its labor to others on a regular basis. In Africa south of the Sahara the entire rural labor force, and the vast majority of the urban labor force, does not sell its labor to others on a regular basis (Weeks, 1973, p. 61).

More than any other writer, Gunnar Myrdal has criticized 'employment', 'unemployment' and related concepts for a basic ethnocentrism in their pre-supposition and approach. He observes (1968, p. 2220):

The fundamental difficulty lies in the analytical framework that has guided these inquiries. In general, these studies have been led to ask the kinds of questions Western economists would wish to investigate in their own countries. At the same time, however, it is often acknowledged that Western categories cannot be transferred intact to a South Asian environment.... The texts of these documents contain lengthy discussions of the special properties of the economy in question and of the adjustments in the Western concept of unemployment deemed appropriate to its circumstances.... But the essential point is that the contrast in institutional conditions is basic–so basic that an entirely fresh approach is needed if the fundamental issues affecting the labor force are to be grasped. They cannot be embraced by an imported conceptual kit to which marginal adjustments have been made . . . this approach simply invites a succession of frustrating experiments with further adjustments. When one variation on the Western theme fails to be satis-factory, another is devised.

The straightforward application of modern western economic ideas to the Third World assumes a fluid labour market, a rational outlook toward life on the part of potential members of the labour force, abundant opportunities for full-time remunerated employment, an adequate flow of information about such possibilities, few or no barriers to geographical mobility (such as debt bondage), and a widespread propensity to 'look for work'. Myrdal, among others, shows how each one of these assumptions is violated in the developing countries, especially in rural areas: Two issues — reasonably complete know-ledge and labor force mobility — are inextricably interlocked in the con-ventional Western mold of thought with its volitional approach to employment. The absence of one of these foundation stones is sufficient to destroy the Western approach. In South Asia, both foundation stones are often missing (1968, p. 1025).

Beyond the overarching problem of ethnocentric bias and the conceptual irrelevance which it often spawns, there are more circumscribed difficulties with the concepts and approaches used in conventional labour market research. Some of the strongest criticisms of studies on rural labour markets stem from their failure to relate guiding concepts to essential features of rural life. Rather than beginning with the work patterns actually found in rural areas and developing approaches based on this analysis, researchers commonly start with stock labour force concepts and try to squeeze rural experience into their confines. As a consequence notions such as employment and underemployment became a procrustean bed into which highly complex and often elusive work phenomena must be compressed.

Inseparable from the previous point is the very basic question of the appropriate unit of analysis for rural work. Following the western labour market paradigm, with its premise of individual rationality, most studies have focused on *individual* employment, unemployment, or underemployment. The statistical rates as commonly reported are for individuals above a specified age, for the prevailing models do not allow them to be calculated in any other way. This approach makes a great deal of sense in the urban labour markets of industrial nations where individuals are the key actors and decision-making rationality is not an unreasonable assumption. But in many rural areas of the developing countries the choice of individuals as the sole unit of analysis can be inappropriate and misleading. If, as many have observed, work is organized on a shared basis and incomes, where they are earned at all, are pooled, the family, clan, or kinship group may, depending on the circumstances, be the most suitable unit of analysis. This point has long been recognized in studies of income and expenditure, where the concept of family income is widely accepted, but not in research on employment.

Not only does the conventional paradigm rely on concepts which are irrelevant or ill-fitting, but it distracts attention from phenomena that are crucial to an understanding of rural development. Foremost among these is the question of debt bondage and somewhat more voluntary but long-term labour contracts, particularly evident in South Asia (Bardhan, 1977, p. 65; Myrdal, 1968, p. 1024). In these contexts, work cannot always be regarded as 'voluntary' in the western sense of the term, and relationships are not captured by conceptual frameworks distinguishing between 'working' and 'looking for work'.

The uncritical application of western concepts in labour force surveys in developing countries makes use of terms often totally unsuited to the life circumstances of those studied. Consider the following questions taken from the Nairobi City Council Home Interview Survey of some years ago.

Q3(a). What is your occupation and where do you work? (Please describe briefly. If unemployed, state clearly. If you are not normally in employment or if you are a student, please state this clearly. Write in housewife.)

Occupation ————————————————————————————————

Types of industry or profession ——————————————————

Enter name and address of work place, school or college —————————

(If informant is in employment, ask *3(b)* and *(c)*.)

Q3(b). Are you self-employed? ——————————————————————

A wage earner? ——————————————————————————

A casual worker? ————————————————————————

Other? ————————————————————————————————

Q3(c). Which of these categories does your income fall in? (Remember to include any income from rents or land or property):

(*Pounds*)

    0–100
    101–200
    201–300
    301–600
    601–900
    901–1200
    1201–2400
    2401–3600
    3600+

Such questions are typical of a survey instrument, and could have been taken from examples given in a standard textbook. In the context in which they are administered, however, the questions were less than adequate.

The question *(3(a))* 'What is your occupation? . . .' makes the usual western assumptions about labour markets. But there are many workers in Nairobi, particularly in the informal sector, for whom the question as put is not very meaningful. They simply do what they can to earn a living.

Question *3(b)* makes the common mistake of assuming that the respondent understands the conceptual categories of the researchers. To ask a very poor man in Nairobi if he is 'self-employed' or a 'casual worker' imputes a middle-class cognitive framework that is often simply not there. The definition of what constitutes being 'unemployed' was apparently left to the respondent to determine. For the last question, the instructions for obtaining accurate estimates of income were inadequate. Moreover, the income brackets were unwisely chosen, since the first two (£200 or below) include 60 per cent of heads of households in the city (Whitelaw, 1974, pp. 591–592).

A further problem with this sort of questioning is that many people simply do not understand what this kind of research is about. A substantial majority of respondents in rural areas may have no idea of what such a survey is or what it is for. This point is sometimes glossed over in discussions of research projects in developing countries, particularly if, as often happens, the respondents do not refuse but give answers that are quite haphazard.

The survey cited was conducted in an urban area. Carrying out employment surveys in rural areas of the developing world is even more hazardous in terms of using western categories. The very terms 'work' or 'working', which appear in almost every survey of this type, carry connotations of being employed by a recognizable employer to do some specific task. Yet for many cultivators and other rural residents such concepts make very little sense. If a farmer spends 18 hours a day working vigorously at half a dozen different tasks, the idea of 'are you working' borders on the insulting. If he understands this to mean 'are you working for someone else for pay' and replies 'no' the approach will miss a large part of rural economic activity. Another stock-in-trade of the employment survey is the concept of 'looking for work'. By definition, the unemployed are those who are not working, are looking for work, and would accept a job at the prevailing wages if it were offered to them. While the notion of 'doing something to look for work' has meaning in an urban labour market where there are employment offices and other sources of information, it may be totally devoid of meaning in rural areas.

These conceptual and methodological problems are not new. Several writers (Batty, 1971; Lydall, 1977; Raj Krishna, 1972; and Richards, 1977) propose a shift to multiple measures of employment or labour utilization, usually based on modifications of the conventional concepts. And a few, such as Weeks (1973), suggest that the entire debate about unemployment is so ideologically loaded and misguided that it should be abandoned in favour of a direct attack on poverty. Beneath this surface confusion about the very questions to be asked are conceptual ambiguities with profound implications for theory, method, and policy. The extended discussion of this example shows how the design of survey research in the developing world — both at the conceptual level and in terms of questionnaire design — has to consider carefully the local context and to what extent, and how, standard western procedures can be employed.

Fertility surveys

Some of the more general problems of adapting survey methods to the Third World may be considered by looking at the example of research on fertility, discussed in the Chapters 4 and 5 by Stycos and Hauser, and also considered later in Chapter 21 by Choldin, Kahn, and Ara and Chapter 26 by Warwick. A very popular form of survey instrument for family planning investigations in the Third World has been the so-called KAP (Knowledge–Attitude–Practice) Survey. These surveys have typically asked questions about respondents' knowledge of family planning methods, their attitudes towards family limitation and their birth control practices. A review of such studies by Berelson *et al.* (1966) draws a number of conclusions from such data, for example:
(1) On the whole, married couples in the developing countries want fewer children than they will have under present fertility conditions — enough

fewer to make a demographic difference if actuality were made equivalent to desire.

(2) Substantial proportions of people in developing countries want no more children now — from nearly half to three-quarters.

(3) Substantial proportions of married couples approve family planning in principle, express interest in learning how to control their own fertility, say they would do something if they had appropriate means, and want the government to carry on a programme along these lines (pp. 657–660).

If true, these conclusions have major implications for demograpic trends in the developing world. Other evidence cited by Berelson — that the *practice* of family planning in the developing world varies from very low to moderately low — suggests that the attitudinal data cannot be taken entirely at face value. Knowledge of contraceptive methods, moreover, ranged from very low to moderate in developing countries surveyed (Berelson *et al.*, 1966, pp. 660–661). In Chapter 5, Philip Hauser discussed the response errors to which such surveys are prone, suggesting that not sufficient attention is given to the relation between verbal responses and actual behaviour.

Empirical evidence is contradictory. Hermalin *et al.* (1979) found good correlations in Taiwan between KAP data and subsequent behaviour. Kar and Talbot (1980), however, report a mixed picture, while Kar and Bhatia (1969) found very little correlation between KAP data and subsequent behaviour. It seems plausible to argue that the validity of KAP data depends on the socio-economic and educational conditions of the respondents at the time of the study. Respondents who are above the subsistence level and reasonably well-educated (as in Taiwan) will often be in a better position to understand the survey and its specific questions; to think about the future; and to act on their intentions. For the very poor, the survey may mean little, the idea of planning the future may seem preposterous, and the possibilities of implementing one's desires on birth control or anything else may be scant (Warwick, 1982).

Detailed studies of the reliability and validity of such data from KAP fertility surveys suggest that there is more consistency in responses to factual information than to questions about desires, ideals and attitudes. Items like number of children in the family, number of pregnancies experienced by the wife, age, religion, language and occupation yield more reliable results than questions about knowledge of contraceptive methods, ideals of reproduction and attitudes toward family planning programmes and abortion (Mukherjee, 1975). Responses to items such as professed desire for additional children may fluctuate erratically over a period as short as a few months. To some extent, respondents appear to be unsure of the number of children that they want, throwing major doubt upon Berelson's first two conclusions quoted earlier. It seems reasonable to conclude that information from KAP surveys on desired family size 'is so liable to error and uncertainty that it can be confusing and misleading if used for policy formulation and implementation' (Mukherjee,

1975, p. 141). Other evidence throws doubt on Berelson's third conclusion for much the same sorts of reason. While there is apparently a high degree of readiness to accept family planning, and a high level of initial interest, this is not translated into continuing contraceptive use by the majority of the population (Gustafson *et al.*, 1967).

The purpose of this critique is not to suggest that survey research in developing countries is either impossible or so beset by problems as to produce worthless results. The point, as Stycos clearly explains in Chapter 4, is to pay attention to problems of response error, reliability and validity in advance of carrying out research, in order to ensure that the results are not vitiated by extraneous influences. Survey research on a sensitive subject such as fertility *is* possible in developing countries, as Stycos demonstrates, but it cannot be undertaken without careful prior thought and a recognition of the ways in which research practice will deviate in the developing world from the certainties and blueprints of western textbooks.

Cautions about surveys

A particular danger into which western social scientists in the developing world may fall is that of neglecting the methodological implications of doing research cross-culturally (for a review, see Warwick and Osherson, 1973). Without proper understanding of the sociocultural context in which they are working, their frames of reference and those of their respondents may be entirely at variance. The same problem can occur even when the researcher and respondent are citizens of the same country, mainly because of class and educational differences: 'Members of the educated elite in many non-industrial countries have had little experience with, and little understanding of, the peasant villagers in their lands' (Roy *et al.*, 1976, p. 49). These problems arise most acutely in translating research instruments from one language to another, discussed in Section IV on data collection. The existence of such problems shows the need for caution in using survey methods in developing countries, which is one major purpose of this book. The relation between, and complementarity of, survey methods and participant observation arises from the existence of these problems, and are considered further in Section VI.

Even more intractable problems can arise because of the social situation in which research is conducted. Emily Jones in Chapter 20 suggests that verbal responses are sometimes given not to communicate reality but rather to influence the interviewer. Problems of this type are considered extensively in Section V on research in the field. Again, the debate with the merits of participant observation is joined, since intensive methods may pose fewer problems (in the long run, at least) of the acceptance of the researcher by those being studied. They may also be more suited to researching the intrinsic and less visible components of village life which do not easily yield to survey questioning, for example religious practices, kinship relations, the nature of social control, land or leadership disputes, and so on: 'Case studies and community studies have often been, and should continue to be, the pioneering pieces of research in developing nations, providing a basic understanding of behavioural conditions, insights and hypothetical hunches for more general testing in surveys' (Roy *et al.*, 1976, p. 46). A different view is provided by Whyte and Alberti in Chapter 23, and by Warwick in Chapter 22.

References

Babbie, E.R. (1973). *Survey Research Methods*, Wadsworth, Belmont, Cal.

Bardhan, K. (1977). A survey of research on rural employment, wages and labour markets in India. *Studies in Employment and Rural Development No. 39*, International Bank for Reconstruction and Development, Washington DC.

Batty, I.Z. (1971). Effectiveness of employment in rural areas: a study sponsored by the Government of India, Government of India, unpublished Ms, New Delhi.

Berelson, B. *et al.* (Eds) (1966). *Family Planning and Population Programs*, University of Chicago Press, Chicago.

Bulmer, M. (Ed) (1977). *Sociological Research Methods*, Macmillan, London.

Bulmer, M. (Ed.) (1978). *Social Policy Research*, Macmillan, London.

Casley, D.J. and Lury, D.A. (1981). *Data Collection in Developing Countries*, Clarendon Press, Oxford.

Gustafson, H.C. *et al.* (1967). Educational efforts in the implementation of rural family planning programs in East Pakistan. *Demography*, **4**, 81–89.

Havens, A.E. (1964). Methodological problems of sociological survey research in Colombia. *America Latina*, **7**, 87–95.

Hermalin, A.I. *et al.* (1979). Do intentions predict fertility? The experience of Taiwan, 1967–74. *Studies in Family Planning*, **10**, 75–95.

Jain, S.P. (1970). Some problems of Indian censuses. In A. Bose *et al.*, (Ed.) *Studies in Demography*, pp. 104–17, Allen and Unwin, London.

Jolly, R. (1973). Economic development and labour use: a comment. *World Development*, **1(12)**, 23–24.

Kar, S.B. and Bhatia, S.A.K. (1969). Motivational correlates of family planning among government employees. *Journal of Family Welfare*, **16**, 3–17.

Kar, S.B. and Talbot, J.M. (1980). Attitudinal and non-attitudinal determinants of contraception: a cross-cultural study. *Studies in Family Planning*, **11**, 51–64.

Kearl, B. (Ed.) (1976). *Field Data Collection in the Social Sciences: Experiences in Africa and the Middle East*, Agricultural Development Council Inc., New York.

Lydall, H. (1977). Unemployment in developing countries. International Labour Office, Geneva, World Employment Programme Research, Working Paper.

Mabogunje, A.L. (1976). The population census of Nigeria, 1973. In J.T. Coppock and W.R.D. Sewell (Eds) *Spatial Dimensions of Public Policy*, pp. 207–226, Pergamon, Oxford.

Moser, C.A. and Kalton, G. (1971). *Survey Methods in Social Investigation*. Heinemann, London.

Mukherjee, B.N. (1975). Reliability estimates of some survey data on family planning. *Population Studies*, **29**, 127–142.

Myrdal, G. (1968). *Asian Drama: An Inquiry into the Poverty of Nations*, Pantheon, New York (3 vols).

Raj Krishna (1972). Unemployment in India. Presidential Address to Indian Society of Agricultural Economics.

Richards, P. (1977). Underemployment and basic needs satisfaction. World Employment Programme Research, Working Paper, International Labour Office, Geneva.

Roy, P. *et al.* (1976). The survey setting. In G. Hursh-César and P. Roy (Eds) *Third World Surveys*, pp. 42–90, Macmillan of India, Delhi.

Srinivas, M.N., Shah, A.M., and Ramaswamy, E.A. (Eds) (1979). *The Fieldworker and the Field: Problems and Challenges in Sociological Investigation*. Oxford University Press, Delhi.

Udo, R.K. (1968). Population and politics in Nigeria. In J.C. Caldwell and C. Okonjo (Eds) *The Population of Tropical Africa*, pp. 97–105. Longmans, London.

United Nations (1972). *United Nations Handbook on Population and Housing Census Methods*, United Nations, New York.

Warwick, D.P. (1982). *Bitter Pills: Population Policies and Their Implementation in Eight Developing Countries*. Cambridge University Press, Cambridge.

Warwick, D.P. and Lininger, C. (1975). *The Sample Survey: Theory and Practice*. McGraw-Hill, New York.

Warwick, D.P. and Osherson, S. (Eds) (1973). *Comparative Research Mehtods*, Prentice Hall, Englewood Cliffs, NJ.

Weeks, J. (1973) Does employment matter? In R. Jolly *et al.* (Eds) *Third World Employment: Problems and Strategy*, pp. 61–65, Penguin, Harmondsworth.

Whitelaw, W.E. (1974). An economist's view of survey research in Africa: observations on Tarzan, fascism, the measurement of attitudes and non-parametric techniques. *African Studies Review*, **17(3)**, 587–596.

Yesufu, T.M. (1968). Politics and economics of Nigeria's population census. In J.C. Caldwell and C. Okonjo (Eds) *The Population of Tropical Africa*, pp. 106–116. Longmans, London.

Social Research in Developing Countries
Edited by M. Bulmer and D.P. Warwick
© 1983, John Wiley & Sons, Ltd.

CHAPTER 3

POPULATION CENSUSES AND NATIONAL SAMPLE SURVEYS IN DEVELOPING COUNTRIES

B. GIL AND E.N. OMABOE

Periodic population censuses and special large-scale sample surveys are of importance even in countries where systems for the collection of population statistics on a current basis are well established, for they provide information that cannot in all cases be provided by current statistics. In developing countries, where current population statistics are often lacking, they are of even greater importance. In most of these countries the registration of births and deaths and records of migration and other demographic events are fragmentary and incomplete at best. As a result censuses and national sample surveys often constitute the only reliable source of population statistics.

Although periodic large-scale inquiries can to a certain extent replace the collection of statistics on a day-to-day basis, this by no means ensures that their results will be more satisfactory. High-quality information can be obtained only by qualified staff using special methods and procedures. In contrast, the improvement of current data collection depends largely on the quality of public administration and the level of education of the population; but these factors change only slowly and statistical information may often be needed to plan their improvement.

Even though the prerequisites for a satisfactory system of current statistics may be lacking, however, it is possible to create the conditions that will enable a successful census to be carried out.

While a developing country may not be in a position to maintain an efficient vital statistics registration system, it can make a special effort to carry out a census or large-scale sample survey. If available resources are pooled the conditions for a successful population census can be met with proper organization and planning.

In this chapter some of the underlying problems of population statistics collection in developing countries will be discussed and an attempt made to outline the main prerequisites for overcoming them. The considerations are

Reprinted, by permission, in abridged form from *International Labour Review* (Geneva), **92 (3)**, **September 1965**, 169–183. © 1965 International Labour Organization.

based primarily on the experience gained from the 1960 population census of Ghana, but wherever possible the experiences of other West African countries are drawn upon. The information provided may, however, have a much wider geographical application than the West African subregion.

Problems of data collection and processing

Statistical organization and experience

The absence or inadequacy of a national statistical organization is the first and often the major handicap. In countries with established statistical organizations it is often found that the development of the latter lags behind that of the state administration in general. The statistical organization was in the past often accorded low priority and was staffed mainly with officers from the administrative and clerical grades, as in most countries technical staff were either non-existent or could not be attracted. Geographically, the activities of the statistical organizations were restricted to the capital, one or two officials being appointed or attached to large provincial centres during censuses or major surveys. While the general administration in the provinces leaned heavily on the traditional institutions, sometimes integrated with the modern local government system, this has not been the case with statistical organizations. In recent years, however, they have undergone a certain expansion.

Special problems arise in the case of the field staff required in addition to those at the head office and provincial headquarters. A population census requires a large field staff for a short period. The situation is unlike that in other countries in that there is often a lack of trained labour offered; there are no educated housewives who would be willing to undertake short-term part-time work, and there are very few unemployed clerical and related workers who could be called upon to carry out an enumeration. Consequently, the recruitment of thousands of enumerators, supervisors and senior field officers and their training are among the difficult problems to be tackled.

There appears to be no other major source for the recruitment of such a large population census staff than the general civil service, and among the civil servants the most appropriate sources — according to Ghana's experience — are the teachers and social welfare and community development officers. There are several reasons why this is so. In terms of numbers alone the above two sectors of the civil service are the only major source that can satisfy the requirements of the census. Moreover, the educational background of their members can easily be determined and a good selection made; since they are used to teaching, they have little difficulty in learning. These two categories of the civil service possess other advantages in that they cover the entire country, know how to deal with the local population and are normally relied upon and respected by the rural community. These are very important attributes in countries where most literate people are concentrated in the towns and where certain other types of civil servants who have to carry out government decisions and enforce the law do not always enjoy the confidence of the large illiterate classes of the population.

Transport and communication

In most developing countries only main trunk roads are developed and telephone connections exist only with the larger localities; even in these, communication is restricted to the postal agency or local administration office. In the interior of many countries modern means of transport and communication are non-existent; foot-trekking is often the only means of travelling. The problem of conveying large numbers of enumerators at fixed dates, even if only to their bases (central locality in the area) can be solved only with great difficulty. Even more difficult is the maintenance of regular communication with the enumerators once they are dispersed throughout the country. Yet unless these two requirements are satisfied the census enumeration is doomed to failure.

The population

The population itself can perhaps create the most complex problem in two respects: general attitude and understanding of census concepts. The often uncompromisingly hostile attitude of the population towards any type of registration or inquiry is well known. This attitude is related partly to the degree of illiteracy and partly to certain historical events, and a favourable political and social atmosphere is very often an exception. Apart from the general attitude of the population, ignorance of elementary statistical concepts can be no less obstructive and frustrating, since misinterpretation can produce wrong results as surely as an unfavourable attitude. For example, misunderstanding as to who should and who should not be counted can result in considerable underenumeration or overenumeration. Lack of knowledge on how to obtain information on age — even if only approximately — or misunderstanding of place of birth or economic activity, can produce biased results in the same manner as premeditated misstatements or refusal to give information. In small-scale inquiries reliance for obtaining accurate information is placed on the trained enumerator rather than on the understanding of the population. Consequently, in such surveys meticulous selection and training of staff is the main aim. However, in large-scale surveys and censuses proper selection of staff is not always possible and funds for adequate training are limited. Hence mass education of the majority of the population itself as to the meaning of the concepts of the questionnaire may be of considerable assistance in obtaining the correct information in the shortest possible time. The resultant shortening of the interview in itself may increase the chances of a fuller and more accurate response. In some cases time saved on such basic items as place of birth and age through preparation of information in advance of enumeration could be utilized to obtain better answers on more complicated items such as type of activity and occupation.

The main prerequisites for a successful operation

It is not possible to prescribe universal remedies to overcome the difficulties and obstacles mentioned in the previous paragraphs. Political, social, economic, topographical and other conditions vary from one country to another, and even within countries. Consequently, the details of a plan have to be worked out to fit specific conditions. Nevertheless, the general principles, prerequisites and basic requirements can be indicated.

The meeting of these requirements cannot in itself, however, guarantee success. A census is a complex operation and its success depends on the interplay of so many factors that the likelihood of failure is ever present. The only positive assertion that one can make in the circumstances is that, without fulfilling the prerequisites listed below, a census can hardly succeed. Miracles rarely, if ever, occur in census taking.

Active participation of the government

Normally, after the cabinet decides that a census is to be taken, it delegates the authority and responsibility to an appropriate agency, and with that the major task of the cabinet is completed. In countries where statistical organizations are well established and where census-taking is an accepted procedure such delegation of responsibility has proved most appropriate. However, in countries where such conditions do not exist, the cabinet itself may have to retain part of the responsibility and actively participate in the census. The nature of this top-level authority, the extent to which it should participate in and take over the responsibility for the general direction of the census operation, etc., will depend on the particular conditions in the country concerned. It will also depend on the scope of the statistical inquiry and on the efficiency of the existing statistical organization and the general administrative machinery of the country.

Public support and understanding

It has already been pointed out that public support and understanding are equally important to ensure a good census. The two factors are interrelated: the better the population understands the objectives and concepts of the census the more willing it is to cooperate.

The scheme of a census education campaign can be summarized as follows:

Objectives
(1) Winning the support and cooperation of the population
(2) Making the population understand the aims, techniques and concepts of the census

Contents
(1) Technical and specialized for the more educated circles
(2) Quite extensive and partly specialized for the census field staff and campaign leaders
(3) Elementary and more general information for the general public.

Communication media
(1) Radio talks and technical papers
(2) Radio talks, popular writings and lectures
(3) Visual aid — films, newspaper advertisements and pictures, posters, etc., radio newsreel and radio announcements; rallies and other community gatherings.

Agents
(1) The press
(2) Broadcasting service
(3) Information services
(4) Other publicity departments, e.g. community development
(5) Chiefs
(6) Leaders of political, professional, religious and other social organizations
(7) Schools — teachers and pupils.

In the light of recent experiences in certain African countries the main task of census campaigners and, in general, the 'first commandment' for census planners, is to keep the census free of controversy. While ideal conditions of complete political, social and economic harmony can hardly be imagined in modern societies, unless the census is a national project overriding political, religious, social and other interests and controversies its chances of success are slight. If this aim cannot be achieved a postponement is the best solution.

Planning and organization

The carrying out of a modern statistical inquiry requires the preparation of technical and organizational plans and above all the institution of a system of supervision and control to ensure that they will be efficiently implemented. Both the preparation of plans and their implementation presuppose the establishment of an appropriate organization and the training of staff.

Setting up of statistical organization

The problem of statistical organizations in developing countries has already been mentioned. Even if these exist they are either in their elementary stages of growth or in the initial stages of formation. In any case they are not yet fully equipped — apart, perhaps, from a few exceptional cases — to undertake a population census. Consequently, a special organization has to be built up and its major problem is staff.

The lack of middle-grade staff in central statistical offices often leads to a certain waste of higher-level skills. In some of the developing countries the demand for professional and administrative skills is being satisfied (partly through local training schemes or foreign assistance) while the supply of middle-grade personnel in supervisory and technical fields is lagging behind. It often happens, therefore, that graduates have to carry out jobs normally done by supervisors, trained technical staff and experienced statistical clerks. Lack of these latter categories constitutes a serious problem in the building up of a statistical organization in developing countries.

The establishment of a census field organization presents somewhat different problems. The main task of the field staff is the preparation and taking of the census. These are short-term operations, and in the existing conditions secondment is the best solution. An integration of the census field organization with the existing state administration — regional, district, etc.— is, according to experience in Ghana, not only desirable but indispensable. The Ghana Census Office found in the regional and district administration a source of manpower, knowledge of administrative and organizational techniques and local experience. All these are valuable assets in setting up a countrywide field organization, although appropriate administrative and training arrangements have to be made as well. The latter task fell to the Census Office.

The structure of the field organization will naturally depend on the existing administrative structure of the country and the stage of development of its institutions; consequently very few generalizations can be made. A few rules can, however, be laid down with respect to the training of the field staff.

In developed countries with a long tradition of census-taking a concentrated training scheme for 3 to 5 days preceding the census day is an accepted procedure. Senior officers are trained 2 or 3 weeks ahead of the census day, middle-grade (supervisory) personnel 1 or 2 weeks ahead and enumerators during the week preceding the census enumeration. Moreover, in the advanced countries a better selection may provide better candidates, and accordingly training requirements can be easily determined.

In developing countries such a selection of staff, it at all possible, will often be very limited. The level of intelligence, education and experience of the potential enumerators will vary widely, and consequently the training should be more systematic, extend over a longer period and precede the enumeration by a much longer interval. In Ghana the period covered 5 months during weekends: a concentrated 3 to 4 days' course was held for senior officers, an extended one (over 8 weekends) for supervisors and a similar one (over 11 week-ends) for enumerators. The advantages of the system were as follows: ample time for review and adjustment of training content and system; possibility of using a smaller number of instructors and hence the better-qualified ones; possibility of better direct control from headquarters; adequate time for field exercises; improvement of selection system if the number of candidates is large enough.

There are also disadvantages, as, for example, higher rate of dropouts, memory lapses and above all higher cost of training. Consequently, a compromise between the two extremes might in certain conditions give better results. For example, a shorter period consisting of three sessions of 2 days each and within an interval of 3 to 4 weeks preceding enumeration should give good results if sufficient instructors are available and a systematic curriculum is adopted.

Plans and documents

These extend over a variety of fields and cover mainly enumeration, processing and publication, namely the questionnaire and other enumeration documents, geographical documents, training manuals and processing procedures. Only two will be briefly mentioned: the concepts and definitions of the questionnaire, and geographical breakdown.

The questionnaire, its concepts and definitions

Chronologically, the questionnaire is the first document to be tackled. Apart from the normal processes a questionnaire and related documents have to undergo in a statistical inquiry (for example, drafting and testing) there is one aspect that in a developing country has to be given special attention: simplicity of concepts and unambiguity of their definitions. In certain social sciences (for example, in sociology and ethnology) the study of different environments may require different sets of concepts. Although in population studies there is need at times for adaptation of certain internationally accepted concepts, as a rule international comparability should be preserved, preference being given to those concepts which deviate the least from international standards. Two examples will be cited from the Ghana census, namely birthplace and household.

In Ghana 'hometown' (that is, place of origin of the family) is a better-known concept — in fact a far more deeply rooted one — than 'birthplace' (of the individual), which is sometimes different from the hometown. Yet for the purpose of studying internal migration the comparison between place of birth and that of residence (or of enumeration in the census) is a conventional method (though not the best). Moreover, the concept of 'birthplace' is unambiguous, while that of 'hometown' may lead to different interpretations — depending, for example, on whether the population group being inquired about follows the pattern of matrilineal or patrilineal inheritance. In the Ghana census much explanatory work had to be done to avoid confusion between 'birthplace' and 'hometown', but on the whole the 'birthplace' concept was successfully adopted.

The other example relates to 'household', which is an internationally accepted concept though there is not as yet a uniform and universal definition. In Ghana — and in Africa in general — the concept of 'family' is more deeply rooted, while that of 'household' is hardly known. Long discussions preceded the adoption of the concept of 'household' by the Ghana Census Office in the postenumeration sample survey. Fears for its misinterpretation and even doubts as to its meaningfulness in African (rural) society were strongly voiced by certain academic circles. In fact, at the beginning of the census preparations a compromise was proposed, namely that the concept of 'household' would be used only in urban areas, i.e. in those societies undergoing a process of industrialization and urbanization. At a later stage, however, the results of pilot studies made in various regions and discussions held during training courses with senior census field officers induced the Census Office to apply the 'household' concept to the whole country. The definition recommended by the United Nations, however, required a slight modification. The Ghana definition referred to persons 'sleeping under the same roof and eating from the same pot'. Obviously, such a concept required careful handling and it was not used in the 100 per cent census enumeration but only in the 5 per cent postenumeration sample survey; the interviewing staff had to be specially trained and cautioned against misinterpretation, and control checks were applied in the first days of the survey to ensure uniformity of application.

In general, the guiding principles in the choice of concepts were countrywide and interregional applicability, international comparability, and unambiguity and simplicity (at the expense, if necessary, of more refined concepts requiring more elaborate definitions and methods for their measurement).

Geographical breakdown

Maps covering the whole country, even the most remote and undeveloped areas, with clear boundary descriptions, appear to be indispensable to ensure complete coverage and avoid double enumeration. Lists of localities in rural areas or of streets and neighbourhoods in towns are definitely insufficient to control enumeration; there is a large number of localities with similar or even identical names, and in towns houses have often been laid out in a haphazard fashion.

In addition to serving purposes of enumeration control, the division of the country into small geographical units such as enumeration areas of about 1000 persons each and supervision areas of about 10 000 persons each (aggregates of about ten enumeration areas) is also useful for data compilation and analysis. Further refinements can be obtained by aggregating these units into socioeconomic or statistical areas based on certain relevant criteria. In the last two decades the detailed geographical breakdown of statistical data has given new directions to demographic research. Small-area statistics are becoming increasingly useful for local administration and planning.

It is true that the carrying out of a field survey in a developing country for the purpose of a geographical division as explained above and the preparation of the relevant maps is a gigantic undertaking which frightens the census planner. Some of the obstacles which have to be overcome have been described above. There is a lack of basic maps and other documents for such a survey; there are terrain and transport difficulties; and there is an insufficient number of trained and experienced staff. Nevertheless, if a census planner considers the geographical project a necessity, ways and means can be found to carry it out with success as part of a national census or national sample survey. In Ghana the geographical project divided up the country into 6788 enumeration areas and 736 supervision areas, prepared the corresponding numbers of maps with boundary descriptions and other relevant information, one map for each of 8000-odd enumerators and supervisors. The field survey involved five geographical teams (of six persons each) recruited and trained by the Census Office. The drawing of maps and processing of other data required some 50 drawing assistants, draughtsmen and clerks and lasted about 8 months. After the census enumeration the redrawing of the enumeration area maps on a smaller scale and their publication (as supplements to Volume II of the *Census Report* and to the *Special Report on Large Towns*) employed some 15–30 drawing officers — photolithography and clerical staff — for about 4 years. Its total cost was £45 000, i.e. about 8.5 per cent of the total census expenditure.

Needless to say, the field survey was quite a daring undertaking and required a big effort at the time of census preparation when each of the projects demanded manpower, transport and head office supervision. It was by no means a smooth operation and there were a number of critical moments. However, its final success is a proof of its applicability on the African continent.

Supervision and control

Work measurement and quality control are integral parts of a modern census programme. Their application varies widely even in statistically advanced countries. In some of these countries much reliance is placed on the enlightened respondent and trained census official. There is also an assumption that partial and occasional checks meet the requirements of control, an assumption which is obviously wrong. In developing countries the low educational level of the respondent, the less experienced enumerator, the novelty of census techniques and concepts, and other shortcomings render scientific supervision and control indispensable prerequisites for a good census.

In applying a system of controls in developing countries the same basic principles have to be followed as in advanced countries, with perhaps slightly different emphasis on certain elements or sectors of control. The main objectives are universally known: economy of expenditure, keeping within the timetable and, above all, statistically acceptable quality of information. In the given conditions in the developing countries work measurement and the establishment of standards of output are of great importance. These objectives can be as easily attained as they can be missed.

Quality control is even more important and at the same time also more difficult to exercise than the work-measurement system of supervision. Whereas lower output results merely in higher costs, low-quality work can produce unusable results, and consequently the total amount expended may be lost. The difficulties in exercising quality control derive from the lack of experienced supervisory staff and from the fact that the system, and particularly the sampling procedure connected with it, is almost a novelty and not always convincing either to the controllers or to the controlled.

In this respect also the Ghana census experience can offer examples of quality control with varying degrees of success. For purposes of enumeration control the supervisors were taught the basic devices of sample control in checking coverage completeness of enumeration) and some quality of response and recording (filling out of questionnaires). Some of the supervisors, however, in the desire to ensure 100 per cent accuracy, carried out 100 per cent checks of certain sectors of enumeration work. The time spent on the 100 per cent checks was, of course, at the expense of other supervisory duties, which had to be neglected because of lack of time. Some other supervisors did not appear to have carried out any sample check at all because they did not attach importance to such a method of control.

Another example, this time of a successful application of quality control, can be given in the processing sector, in the field of coding. The quality control, called here 'coding verification', was built into the original programme as an integral part of the system. Initially it was 100 per cent verification, but when the operator reached the required standard of quality only a 10 per cent verification was carried out. For reasons mentioned before, this verification did not appear to be satisfactory in all cases; consequently, a reverification of a subsample of the verifiers' work was introduced to keep the verifiers themselves under control. This latter reverification was carried out by the more reliable among the supervisory staff and proved to be quite effective in respect of what was aimed at. On the whole, this dual control system appears, from the results obtained, to have worked very efficiently.

To ensure the best results, quality control in developing countries should be based primarily on what is known as 'independent control'. By this system, two persons working independently of each other carry out the same operation and another person in a higher position of responsibility compares the two results. For various reasons this method would be perhaps the only reliable one in certain sectors of statistical work in a developing country. It can, however, prove to be very costly, particularly when 100 per cent verification has to be carried out, which means in fact a repetition of the whole work.

Conclusion

Past censuses in Africa have failed not only because of lack of cooperation on the part of the population, but also because little time and insufficient attention were given to the planning and organization of the censuses. The chief census officer, usually a member of the colonial administrative service, headed the existing administrative organization, which was used for enumeration and processing. Even recently, although special census and statistical departments have been set up in some of the African countries and the role of planning and preparation has been recognized, the administrative side still received more emphasis than the statistical principles and techniques.

In view of the difficulties of adopting modern techniques and procedures some census takers often adopt the 'short cut' approach and apply unscientific methods which, in their opinion, are more appropriate for the prevailing conditions. Among these one may cite 'group enumeration' (as opposed to enumeration on the basis of data supplied by individuals), enumeration by broad age groups or by broad occupational classes, and the general limitation of the census to a few items only. In some other countries modern techniques of sample surveys are being applied instead of complete censuses. In such cases a severe limitation is placed on the scope of analysis and the approach does not entirely overcome the existing difficulties of data collection.

References

K.M. Barbour and R.M. Prothero (Eds) (1961) *Essays on African Population* Routledge & Kegan Paul, London; see particularly the article by T.E. Hilton, Population Mapping in Ghana.

B. Gil and K.T. de Graft Johnson (1964) *General Report* (Vol. V of the 1960 Population Census Report), Government Printing Office, Accra.

E.N. Omaboe (1959). Counting the People in Ghana *Economic Bulletin*.

Social Research in Developing Countries
Edited by M. Bulmer and D. P. Warwick
© 1983, John Wiley & Sons, Ltd.

CHAPTER 4

SAMPLE SURVEYS FOR SOCIAL SCIENCE IN UNDERDEVELOPED AREAS

J. MAYONE STYCOS

The social sciences may be viewed as ranging on a continuum where demography and cultural anthropology fall towards the two extremes, with sociology placed somewhere in between. Demography has its historic roots in economics, statistics, and biology and has emphasized the statistical analysis of vital events (births, deaths, and population movements) in the light of broad biological and social characteristics (age, marital status, occupation, residence, race, etc.). It has traditionally relied upon census and vital statistics data. Cultural anthropology has its roots in archaeology, ethnology, and history and has emphasized the non-quantitative analysis of the total social system. It has ordinarily relied on the data collection of individuals studying in small, preliterate communities for extended periods of time. Sociology has occupied a middle position, employing techniques and data similar to both these fields, but more recently has tended to rely increasingly on the sample survey.

The growing focus of attention of the social sciences on the under-developed areas of the world is accelerating convergence in both the theory and the method of the various disciplines. The anthropologist finds the analysis of complex civilizations not entirely amenable to traditional small-community-centred techniques, and he increasingly utilizes data and methods usually associated with demography and sociology (see Firth 1954 and Richards, 1938).

Demographers have found themselves handicapped by the absence or deficiency of census data and vital statistics in underdeveloped countries and have been turning to techniques usually associated with the other two disciplines. Moreover, partly as a result of the recent failure to predict rapid population gains in western society and a growing suspicion that western demographic history may offer few sound bases for prediction of trends in underdeveloped

Reprinted, by permission, from R.N. Adams and J. Preiss (Eds) (1960). *Human Organisation Research*, pp. 375–388, Homewood, Ill.: Dorsey Press © 1960, The Dorsey Press.

regions, demographers have taken an increasing interest in sociological and anthropological theory (Davis and Blake, 1956; Lorimer, 1954; Stycos, 1955b). American sociologists, who previously engaged in survey research almost exclusively within the United States, have been applying this instrument to other cultures and raising many questions as to its applicability with semi-literate peoples. In a more applied field, public health specialists with a traditional reliance on epidemiological theory and techniques have increasingly been turning to all three fields for assistance on both a methodological and a theoretical level (Paul, 1956; Paul and Miller, 1955).

Interest in the sample survey in underdeveloped areas is of major interest to all the fields considered, and this common denominator is the subject of the present chapter. Because the author has had considerable experience with sample surveys of human fertility and because the various disciplines share an interest in this substantive area, the major illustrations will stem from such studies. Furthermore, research on human fertility provides an unusually good test for the utility of the survey. The kind of data necessary for scientific analysis in this field has usually been volunteered by a respondent only after long acquaintance with a field investigator — or to such professional confidants as physicians and priests. If the survey technique seems feasible and productive of valid data in this area, we should be sanguine about its utility in a wide variety of fields.

Feasibility of the sample survey

The writer has been involved in five completed investigations of human fertility in two Caribbean islands, Puerto Rico and Jamaica, as well as in two under way in Haiti and Italy. In every case we were told by at least some of the local experts: 'It can't be done here. Our people will not consent to such personal questions by strangers.' In my opinion there is a good deal of exaggeration in both lay intellectual and professional circles concerning people's resistance to the survey approach on such topics. The anthropologist, because he usually works alone and lives in the community of study, naturally has plenty of time to build up rapport and proceed by gradual stages in his questioning. He is virtually compelled to do so, since he becomes a resident of the community and subject, to a certain extent, to their norms of politeness. For many purposes this technique has been very successful. But both because it has been successful and because it is traditional, some anthropologists have tended to regard it as *necessary*.

Furthermore, the middle-class and upper-class members of an underdeveloped society, especially the intellectuals, usually know no more, and often less, about their own lower classes than an American does about his. Among the largely mistaken notions projected into the lower class are exaggerations of its 'exclusiveness' and of its resistance to the 'invasion of privacy'.

To my knowledge no anthropologist has presented data on the proportion of his potential respondents who refused to cooperate in one way or another. However, a handful of American and British surveys provide useful points of comparison on refusal rates. In a recent publication Stephan and McCarthy (1958) cite refusal rates for nine sample surveys conducted in the United States. Sample sizes ranged from 1036 to 3630; some of them were of the fixed-address type and others quota-control. The (unweighted) mean of the proportions who refused to be interviewed in these surveys is 7.6 per cent. Although the range is from 0.4 to 13.0, only two showed rates below 5 per cent. Moser (1958) presents data from three British surveys for which the average refusal rate is about 5 per cent. Wilson (1950) reports an initial refusal rate of 10 per cent among those contacted in a survey in France, but this dropped to 5 per cent after additional efforts were made.

By way of contrast we may consider the refusal rates in the five Caribbean fertility surveys. With one exception the questions were of a much more delicate nature than were those in the American or British surveys cited above. All required marital and extramarital histories and asked for attitudes on birth control; two elicited data on frequency of sexual relations. The average educational level of respondents was much lower than that in the American or European samples. The Caribbean surveys had longer questionnaires than most of the others, ranging from averages of $1\frac{1}{2}$ to 6 hours. There was no overlapping of interviewing personnel between the surveys, and none used a quota-control system. Yet the average refusal rate was only 2 per cent, with four of the five rates falling under 2 per cent. Since such rates compare very favourably with survey experience in more developed areas, it would seem that surveys in the underdeveloped area, at least as judged by the Caribbean examples, present no special difficulties.

Let us speculate concerning the causes for the low rates of refusal. First of all the general role played by the interviewer makes sense to most respondents. They have enough familiarity with middle-class occupational patterns to know that asking questions and writing down answers is both typical and respectable. In this regard the survey researcher has an advantage over the anthropologist, whose role may be much harder to understand. Thus, in comparing anthropological and survey techniques in work among the Navajo, Streib (1952) found that the direct-survey approach was not only entirely feasible but that it had advantages in structuring the investigator's role in a meaningful way. With the direct approach '. . . from the outset of the research the investigator is busy at a clearcut task of asking questions and writing down the replies . . . when one pursues a more orthodox anthropological approach before initiating the survey . . . one's role definition is not so apparent.' As stated by a Navajo, 'We wondered what you were doing around here. Now I know that you have a job to do like other people.' It is of interest that the refusal rate among the Navajo was only 2 per cent (Streib, 1952).

While the general role of the investigator is understandable, it might be thought that suspicion of or objections to his specific aims might provoke hostility and lack of cooperation. In fact, while such reactions appear initially, they dissipate rapidly.

The attitude of the typical lower-class person in the Caribbean with respect to the upper classes is mixed. On the one hand, there is fear and suspicion — fear of the superior knowledge and power of this class and suspicion (through no little experience) that this knowledge and power may be utilized to the disadvantage of the relatively helpless lower-class person. But there is also admiration, awe, and envy of these same characteristics. Running through both attitudes is curiosity, since, among the rigidly stratified societies, the lower class has an opportunity to interact with higher-status individuals in only highly limited situations. Most critics of the survey method exaggerate the former attitudes and minimize or ignore the latter. My experience has been that, once the field worker cuts through the initial fear and suspicion, the favourable attitudes come to the fore and result in *greater* cooperation than might be expected in less stratified societies.

What kinds of suspicions are encountered and how they are dealt with are treated at some length in another publication. (Back and Stycos, 1959) We might mention, however, that the most frequent, and most difficult, kind of resistance to the survey is communal rather than individual. For example, a rumour sweeps the community that the interviewers have come to take away babies, and a crowd forms to menace the team. Such situations occurred a few times in Jamaica and, although dangerous, were always handled successfully. The task was always more difficult, however, than if an individual had been involved. In some instances this can be minimized by a 'hit-and-run' method, where a team of interviewers moves in and out of an area before gossip can spread. Moreover, it does not take long to localize the 'head' man or woman among the lower class of the community, and these individuals, flattered by a recognition of their importance, can almost invariably be talked into quelling the resistance and introducing a benign rumour. Since the initial rumours tend to be rather farfetched and wild, it often requires only the presence and brief explanation by a respectable, sober-looking interviewer to dispel it.

Once these rather wild rumours have collapsed, cooperation is generally marked. In the first place, it requires considerable courage to say 'no' to a higher-status person. But it goes beyond this. The respondent is flattered by the attention and by the novel notion that her views are of interest to a middle-class person. This is especially true if a sampling technique has been used, since the respondent is among a select group being consulted. She is curious about both the interviewer and the kind of questions to be asked. Above all, as indicated in the following comment, the experience of being treated as an equal is highly gratifying: 'Her husband told me that what we are talking is good talk and nobody has ever spoken to them like that before and made them feel like human beings instead of cattle' (interviewer's notes, Jamaica).

By way of contrast the upper-class person finds it less novel and certainly no honour to be speaking with someone of the same, or even lower, class level. She is more likely to feel it an imposition on her time and an invasion of her privacy and is more likely to translate these views into verbal or other action to expel the interviewer.

Should our optimism about survey feasibility be confined to the Caribbean? The writer has been associated with another projects which leaves one with the same impressions. It was carried out by the Bureau of Applied Social Research and involved interviews in the Near East and Middle East on such topics as mass media and politics. The generalizations of the field director are strikingly similar to those we have expressed above.

When we set out to do our studies in the Arabic world, some experts predicted that such a broad-scale public opinion survey could not be carried our because people would never admit our interviewers into their homes, much less answer questions. . . . Our studies proved these experts wrong. We were able to move into areas where the concept of survey research was utterly unknown (including the Bedouin tribes of the desert) and find that there, as is apparently true in all parts of the world, people are flattered to be asked their opinions and delighted to have a sympathetic captive audience (Carlson, 1958, p. 225).

Reliability and validity of survey data

Thus far we have demonstrated only that it is entirely feasible to get semi-literate peoples of other cultures to consent to being interviewed by strangers on intimate topics. This says nothing about the reliability and validity of the results. We may divide the problems in this area into two broad classes— those referring primarily to the interviewer and those referring primarily to the respondent.

Neither the demographer nor the anthropologist has been traditionally concerned to any great extent with middlemen in data collection. The statistics used by most demographers come either directly from the registrations of birth and deaths or from census publications based on interviews over which the analyst exercises little control. The anthropologist usually gathers his own data singlehanded or works closely with one or two other professionals or semi-professionals. In survey research, on the other hand, the sociologist is in a direct relation to non-professional middlemen, who filter data from respondents and pass it on via interview schedules. Strangely enough, we know very little about interviewers and the interviewing process. A milestone was reached with the volume by Hyman *et al*., (1954) but it represents the first mile only. Typically the sociologist relies on rule-of-thumb assumptions in screening, training, supervising, and evaluating interviewers. But the utility of rules of thumb, since they are based on relatively unsystematic experience, is usually limited to highly circumscribed situations. When the situation — for example, the culture — changes, they may prove to be of limited utility. Let us mention just a few of the staff problems facing the survey researcher in the foreign area.

1. Since one of the prerequisites for interviewing is literacy, often including some formal education, the typical interviewer in the underdeveloped area is much further removed in status from his respondents than is the case in the usual western survey.
2. The personality characteristics generally considered desirable for an American interviewer may be the ones least useful to a foreign interviewer.
3. Since the underdeveloped areas have relatively rigid systems of social stratification and since status tends to be ascribed rather than achieved, social and biological characteristics which are of minor relevance in the United States may be of crucial importance in the foreign situation. Sex, age, marital status, caste, religion, nationality, language, and colour are among the characteristics which can be of decided relevance.
4. The motivations of the interviewer are more varied. In the typical American survey, the interviewer is not especially emotionally involved with the project, the project directors, or the data collected. The non-American interviewer, since he is relatively well educated, is acutely selfconscious of his country's position.
5. The necessity for *objectivity* in data collection and analysis is not fully appreciated, even by many professionals. Lloyd and Susanne Rudolph (1958) note that '. . . many Indian social scientists quite explicitly believe that social science should not be value-neutral, but should serve a moral purpose . . . a neutral social science becomes at best a luxury which they cannot afford, and at worst a species of immoral deception or hypocrisy. The clinical stance, in their view, favors the status quo.' In our fertility research we found it difficult to dissuade interviewers from becoming family-planning propagandists with their respondents. 'All these poor people need is a little information,' they argued, 'Why would it hurt to give it to them?' The last two problems mentioned are aggravated by a tendency on the part of survey researchers to hire individuals who feel that the post of interviewer is beneath their status. Many of the underdeveloped areas have a surfeit of 'unemployed intellectuals', small armies of university-trained persons which the economy has not yet been able to absorb. Such individuals take the post as a temporary economic expedient, or because of its university prestige, but really feel that the requisites of the position tend to demean them. In consequence, they use various techniques for 'fancying up' their assignments, among which are reading in abstruse meanings in the data, arguing volubly about fine theoretical points, the role of social science, etc.

How have we dealt with these problems? Other publications (Back and Stycos, 1959; Stycos, 1952; 1955a) have discussed specific training techniques at some length, but we can profitably pull together a few generalizations based on our screening and training procedures.

1. The initial pool of candidates for interviewing posts is provided by local experts, and from this pool the American study directors make the final selections. We attempt to get a pool three to five times the size of the staff needed.
2. We believe that the most desirable interviewing staff is one that is homogeneous from an educational standpoint and that clusters around the high school-graduate level. Although less-educated persons learn more slowly, for sustained motivation, stamina in the field, and lack of preoccupation with problems of status, they have, in our experience, a slight edge over college-trained individuals.
3. We devote more time in training than is usual in the United States and emphasize somewhat different aspects. Objectivity gets special attention. The nature of scientific inquiry is discussed; bias is made the *bête noire* which haunts research projects and is ridiculed by means of demonstration interviews in which the effects of non-objective interviewing are exaggerated.
4. The needs of the interviewers to be creative and to be critical are channelled away from the interviews themselves by means of requiring regular field reports, separate comments on each interview, group discussion sessions during fieldwork, and evaluation questionnaires asking for criticisms and suggestions on the conduct of the training and administrative aspects of the project. These have proved to be of great value in themselves.

Another major source of error in surveys stems from the respondent, and we may divide the errors into those which are intentional and those which are unintentional. An example of the former is seen in the case of a survey of the African Baganda (Richards and Reining, 1954), in which highly inconsistent data on family size was given by a number of respondents. It turns out that the Baganda do not like to count their children, fearing it will bring bad luck. It is considered bad manners to question a woman on the number of her children. Again, in Southern Rhodesia a sample survey in 1948 (Shaul, 1954) showed surprisingly low death rates. This is attributed partly to the fact that 'Africans believe that if anything bad is spoken of the departed his spirit will be annoyed and seek to be revenged. It may be that reporting a death to the Government is likely to be resented. . . .'

There is, however, nothing unique about respondents being unwilling to give valid information on certain topics. Every society has such taboos, and, rather than appear uncooperative, respondents may prefer to volunteer misleading information. Recent surveys indicate that Americans are more willing to give information on sex than on income. This does *not* mean that we cannot get valid information on income by the survey technique, *if this taboo is known in advance*. The problem in underdeveloped areas is that the survey researcher usually lacks such advance information. The obvious solution is that surveys requiring standardized, structured techniques should always be preceded by pilot or exploratory investigations employing relatively unstructured methods. Once the nature of the taboos is known, methods for eliciting information in a more structured fashion can always be devised. In both Puerto Rico and Jamaica our surveys were preceded by intensive exploratory investigation, which enabled us to avoid direct questioning in especially sensitive areas. As just one example, in the Jamaica survey we had to prelist several thousand households prior to interview to determine whether there were any women in the household exposed to the risk of conception. Since a high proportion of conceptions occurs as a result of the union of non-cohabiting couples, we were faced with the problem of determining in 5 minutes whether or not an unmarried girl was having regular sexual relations with a male outside the household. We had also determined, understandably, that a direct question of this kind would not produce valid responses, but we had established from earlier investigation that 'dating' almost invariably implied sexual relations among the lower class. We therefore asked every unmarried woman whether or not she had a boyfriend. The technique was successful, and the assumptions proved correct.

In any investigation, of course, we expect a certain amount of invalidity. The significant questions become 'how much?' and 'who?' In the Jamaican survey, at the completion of each interview, the fieldworker evaluated the degree of validity of the information given by the respondent. In addition, we used such internal measures as whether the respondent said he had heard about or believed in certain non-existent events; and such external checks as a comparison of actual behaviour, as judged by official records, with behaviour reported by the respondent.

A much more serious problem stems from unreliable responses produced by non-intentional 'errors' on the part of the respondent. Again I would argue that the real culprit here is instrument error — a product of insufficient preliminary knowledge of the conceptual apparatus of the people being surveyed.

One of the commonest types of unreliability occurs with respect to numerical questions of fact — age, number of children, births, etc. I would maintain that unreliability has stemmed not so much from deliberate falsification as from differing concepts of 'age', 'children', etc. In Richards and Reining's (1954) study mentioned above, one of the commonest sources of error was the respondents' failure to include as 'children' grown-up sons and daughters: '. . . one very cooperative respondent . . . omitted two grown sons and three daughters who were absent, because, he said, "he was not used to counting them like that" '. In India, there is good evidence that subjects tend to forget female births, presumably because they are of less importance (Mahalanobis and Das Gupta, 1954).

A second source of unreliability refers to questions eliciting opinions. American surveys have disclosed that large portions of the public will cheerfully give opinions on issues of which they have no knowledge, including fictitious ones. We should expect no less of populations in underdeveloped areas, but there is again the added problem that we can rarely predict which issues are meaningful and which are not. It might be assumed, for example, that attitudes toward the United States would be a universally meaningful area for questioning. Yet, when we sampled groups of Arab Bedouins and asked 'What questions would you like to ask about the United States?' we occasionally received such responses as 'What is it?' 'Where is it?' 'Is it within walking distance?' Or we might assume that mothers the world over here an opinion on the ideal number of children. But where there is little awareness of an alternative to accepting what God or fate sends, the question may not be very meaningful. Among the Bahaya 'to ask a woman how many children she would like is meaningless'; and among the Baganda, when surveyed women were asked how many children they would like to have, 'the question was frequently met by a refusal to answer or it produced giggles and pained surprise' (Richards and Reining, 1954) American pollsters are turning increasingly to the use of 'filter questions', which ascertain the degree of knowledge about a topic before asking for opinions on it. Such techniques should be emphasized in foreign areas, again after careful exploratory work. In Haiti, where we suspect that attitudes on family size are relatively uncrystallized, we are using photographs of Haitian families of different sizes and economic status to serve as the stimulus to comments, followed by increasingly structured questions. There is no reason why this technique, if successful, cannot be further standardized for use in surveys.

Another problem concerns what might be termed the 'situational opinion'. American experiments have shown that opinions expressed in group situations may be quite different from those expressed privately. Nevertheless, the usual assumption of the survey researcher is that the individual private opinion is the more meaningful one. But where the family, the neighbourhood, or the clan are more important units of social organization, a 'public opinion' may be equally or more meaningful. When questioning Sinhalese women on ideal family size, for example, Ryan (1952, p. 359) noted: 'The sample of mothers . . . offered evidence that many women are torn between the community valuation of the large family and a personal desire for restricted numbers. . . .' It was sharply evident to the interviewers that infinite numbers of children were an unqualified blessing in situations where several women were present. Such situations can cause high unreliability of response. The question as to which response reflects the 'true' attitude is meaningless. Both are 'true', and under such circumstances the researcher must make an effort to elicit both or be aware that he is confining his data to one area only (Dean and Whyte, 1958). Our Caribbean studies seem to indicate that what appears to be the unreliability of response is often a measure of ambivalence in situations of competing norms (Hill, Stycos, and Back, 1959, pp. 74–83).

Finally, we should note that reliability data should be *used*. Ordinarily, such data are cited only to show that the particular study has higher or lower reliability on various measures than other studies have or that the data tend to be of 'good' or of 'poor' quality. Actually the nature of the unreliability and the characteristics of those persons who seem especially reliable or unreliable can be of considerable substantive interest. In Jamaica, where the survey questionnaire embodied a number of items which could be used to measure consistency and veracity of the respondent, we were able to show (Stycos, Back, and Mills, 1957), for example, that unreliability was correlated with conservatism in the sphere of family planning. If those desiring small families and those favourable toward family planning had been the more unreliable respondents, then the generally favourable implications of our findings for programmes of fertility control would have been subject to serious doubt. Parenthetically, we should note that panel data on our lower-class Jamaican respondents indicate that reliability on such items as age, education, and number of children is now lower than that which is found in a number of comparable American surveys (Back and Stycos, 1959). The Cornell Methodology Project in India also found high reliability and validity in a sample survey in India (Ralis, Suchman, and Goldsen, 1958).

Finally, I should like to mention that, aside from the various quantitative measures of reliability and validity, our general experience leaves us with no impression of special problems with respect to intentional errors on the part of respondents. Once the initial fear and suspicion of the interviewer is overcome, our impression is of greater frankness and sincerity than is encountered in the American cross-section. The average subject is not out to pull the wool over the eyes of the field worker, to mislead and confuse him. More typically the *respondent* is confused by the unusual procedures and the assumption that he knows something about the topic under consideration, that he has an opinion worth voicing, and that he has made up his mind. If this be true, unreliable data provide no indictment of the survey method as such; indeed highly *reliable* data in such circumstances would be suspect. Rather, they suggest that much more care needs to be taken in preparing the survey, in measuring and interpreting reliability and validity, and in improvising more flexible survey techniques.

Conclusion

I have attempted to demonstrate, largely by illustrations from fertility investigations in the Caribbean, that research on relatively intimate topics among semiliterate populations is amenable to survey techniques. Special problems are raised with respect to interviewing personnel, reliability, and validity. Regarding the former, special attention to methods of screening and training of interviewers seems indicated. Respondent error is more likely to be unintentional than intentional, and while careful attention to questionnaire construction — primarily by means of preliminary broad-gauge investigations — and to analysis of the sources and nature of unreliability seem essential, there is little reason to doubt that the survey technique can be highly productive of valid data. The convergence of interest of demographers, anthropologists, sociologists, and public health workers in underdeveloped areas leaves no doubt that the survey will be increasingly employed in the study of complex foreign societies. It is equally clear that each of these disciplines can contribute to an improvement in data-collection procedures by means of the sample survey.

References

Back, K.W. and Stycos, J.M. (1959). *The Survey under Unusual Conditions: Methodological Facets of the Jamaica Human Fertility Investigation*, Society for Applied Anthropology Monograph no. 1, Ithaca, New York.

Carlson, R.O. (1958). To talk with kings. *Public Opinion Quarterly*, **22**, 224–229.

Davis, K. and Blake, J. (1956). Social structure and fertility: an analytic framework. *Economic Development and Cultural Change*, **April**.

Dean, J.P. and Whyte, W.F. (1958). How do you know if the informant is telling the truth? *Human Organisation*, **17** (**2**), 34–38.

Firth, R. (1954). Census and sociology in a primitive island community. In *Problems and Methods in Demographic Studies of Preliterate Peoples, Proceedings of the World Population Conference, Paper VI*, pp. 105–227. United Nations, New York.

Hill, R.J., Stycos, J.M. and Back, K.W. (1959). *The Family and Population Control*, University of North Carolina Press, Chapel Hill, NC.

Hyman, H.M. *et al.* (1954). *Interviewing in Social Research*, University of Chicago Press, Chicago.

Lorimer, F. (Ed.) (1954). *Culture and Human Fertility*, UNESCO, Paris.

Mahalanobis, P.C. and Das Gupta, A. (1954). The use of sample surveys in demographic studies in India. In *Problems and Methods in Demographic Studies of Preliterate Peoples, Proceedings of the World Population Conference, Paper VI*, pp. 105–227, United Nations, New York.

Moser, C.A. (1958). *Survey Methods in Social Investigation*, Heinemann, London.

Paul, B.D. (1956). Social science in public health. *American Journal of Public Health*, **November**.

Paul, B.D. and Miller, W.B. (1955). *Health, Culture and Community: Case Studies of Public Reactions to Health Problems*, Russell Sage, New York.

Ralis, M.E., Suchman, E., and Goldsen, R. (1958). Applicability of survey techniques in Northern India. *Public Opinion Quarterly*, **22**, 245–250.

Richards, A. (1938). The village census in the study of culture contact. In *Methods of Study of Culture Contact in Africa*, Oxford University Press, Oxford.

Richards, A. and Reining, P. (1954). *Report on Fertility Surveys in Buganda and Buhaya*. In F. Lorimer (Ed.) *Culture and Human Fertility*, UNESCO, Paris.

Rudolph, L. and Rudolph, S. (1958). Surveys in India: field experience in Madras State. *Public Opinion Quarterly*, **22**, 235–244.

Ryan, B. (1952). Institutional factors in Sinhalese fertility. *Milbank Memorial Fund Quarterly*, **October**.

Shaul, J.R. (1954). Some problems of sampling African population characteristics. In *Problems and Methods in Demographic Studies of Preliterate Peoples. Proceedings of the World Population Conference, Paper VI*, pp. 105–227, United Nations, New York.

Stephan, F.F. and McCarthy, P.J. (1958). *Sampling Opinions*. Wiley, New York.

Streib, G.F. (1952). The use of survey methods among the Navaho. *American Anthropologist*, **54**, 30–40.

Stycos, J.M. (1952). A report on interviewer training in another culture. *Public Opinion Quarterly*, **16**, 236–246.

Stycos, J.M. (1955a). Further observations on interviewer training in another culture. *Public Opinion Quarterly*, **19**, 68–78.

Stycos, J.M. (1955b). *Family and Fertility in Puerto Rico*, Columbia University Press, New York.

Stycos, J.M., Back, K.W. and Mills, D.O. (1957). *Prospects for fertility reduction in Puerto Rico*, Conservation Foundation, New York, mimeo.

United Nations (1954). *Problems and Methods in Demographic Studies of Preliterate Peoples. Proceedings of the World Population Conference, Paper VI*, pp. 105–227, United Nations, New York.

Wilson, E.C. (1950). Adapting probability sampling to Western Europe. *Public Opinion Quarterly*, **14**, 215–223.

Social Research in Developing Countries
Edited by M. Bulmer and D.P. Warwick
© 1983, John Wiley & Sons, Ltd.

CHAPTER 5

THE LIMITATIONS OF KAP SURVEYS

PHILIP M. HAUSER

This chapter is an extract from a long review of Bernard Berelson et al. *(Eds),*
Family Planning and Population Programs *(University of Chicago Press, 1966).*
It is concerned with so-called 'KAP surveys' in the family planning field, social
surveys designed to elicit the knowledge of (K), attitudes toward (A) and practice
in the use of (P) contraception by respondents in the developing world. KAP
surveys are further discussed in Chapter 26.

Utilization of the sample survey

Probably in no other field in social action has the sample survey been more
widely utilized as a tool for policy formulation and programme design as in
family planning programmes. Much in Berelson's volume is based on the
results of such surveys. Moreover, the sample survey may be expected to play
an even greater role as the programmes mature and as they are increasingly
employed as one instrument for the evaluation of the action programmes. It is
of considerable importance, therefore, to examine the manner in which the
sample survey has been employed in the field.

The most comprehensive summary of surveys used in studies in fertility is
that in Berelson's chapter, 'KAP Studies on Fertility'. As he indicates, over
twenty KAP studies 'of some substance have been done in as many countries
since the 1960 Conference on research in family planning' (p. 655). Berelson
points out that his discussion concentrates on 'the place of KAP studies in
furthering family planning programmes — that is, on their applied or professional contributions rather than their basic academic ones' (p. 655). He refers
readers to Mauldin's (1965) article for consideration of the 'basic or academic'
aspects of these surveys. Berelson proceeds to summarize what the KAP
studies cover, what was learned, and how the studies are used.

Reprinted, by permission, from P.M. Hauser (1967). Family planning and population programs:
a book review article. *Demography*, **4**, 402–405. © 1967, Population Association of America.

Since Berelson does not discuss the problem of the reliability and validity of the survey findings, it is in order briefly to summarize Mauldin's analysis. Mauldin acknowledges 'in a general way that verbal and non-verbal behavior often are not closely related' (1965, p. 9) and reports the results of studies showing high unreliability of responses to the types of questions asked in KAP surveys. He comes to the conclusion that the surveys are, nevertheless, useful: 'The above comment on indications of low reliability on some questions and lack of validity on others should not obscure the fact that much useful information has been obtained from such surveys. And much more useful information can be obtained' (1965, p. 10).

In the judgement of this writer, KAP surveys, along with many other sample surveys, have exhibited two major deficiencies. First, they have, in general, failed to include adequate efforts to study the reliability and validity of their data; and, second, they have failed to make adequate efforts to obtain measurements of the 'intensity' of the opinions or attitudes reported. This is not the place for a detailed and prolonged examination of the problems posed. It must suffice, first, to point to the literature on response error which these surveys have sadly ignored, and, second, to suggest alternative and equally plausible, although quite contradictory, interpretations of some of the more important KAP findings to those generally given.

The Bureau of the Census over the past 15 years has published a series of studies (US Bureau of the Census 1960, 1963a, 1963b, 1965) on response error in the census and in census-conducted sample surveys which report surprising magnitudes of response error on questions which are relatively simple compared with most of those on KAP schedules. One would suppose that the results of this research would lead to intensive studies in response error in all surveys and, in fact, in all collections of data based on interviews — communication between an enumerator and a respondent. Surprisingly enough, this has not been the case in sample surveys in general and KAP surveys in particular. It is to be hoped that the time is not far off when professional readers of survey results will simply refuse to read publications which do not include full appendixes that permit analysis of response as well as sampling error. Unfortunately, this time has not yet arrived and, in consequence, it is a moot question whether surveys do not mislead as much as they inform. The danger of being misled may, of course, be much more expensive if the surveys are used for programme design and administration, for practical matters, than solely for the acquisition of knowledge.

To illustrate the danger of uncritical use of KAP survey results, let us examine the interpretation generally given to findings on 'interest in learning fertility control' and suggest a quite different possible interpretation. Berelson regards as 'quite remarkable . . . the essential equivalence of interest in learning' (1966, p. 660) reported in KAP surveys — interest manifested by approximately 70 per cent of the respondents. He states that 'whenever asked, substantial proportions of married couples approve family planning in principle, express interest in learning how to control their own fertility, say that they would do something if they had appropriate means, and want the government to carry a program along these lines' (1966, p. 660).

Berelson, and family planners generally, interpret 'interest in learning' as reported in the surveys as evidence in effect, of a market for family planning. This is, in the judgement of the writer, a questionable interpretation for two reasons — the first methodological and the second empirical. Methodologically, in the absence of a measurement of response error, the burden of proof of the validity of this interpretation must be carried by Berelson and the other family planners. Moreover, the gap between 'interest in' and doing something about it remains unstudied. The generally accepted interpretation is methodologically naive in the sense that in an analogous situation it would be the equivalent of a market research organization concluding that a 70 per cent affirmative response to a question of whether the respondent would like to have a jeep constituted a measurement of the market for jeeps. The marketeer, perhaps more sophisticated than the KAP surveyor, also obtains a measurement of purchasing power to evaluate effective demand. The KAP survey has not done the equivalent, even though techniques are available for doing so. For example, it is possible in various ways to measure the 'intensity' of the interest.

The empirical reason for questioning the general interpretation of the 'interest in learning' finding is to be found in the contrast between 70 per cent response of 'interest' and the relatively low percentage response to opportunities provided to learn. This gap, one would think, would be interpreted, among other things, as a credibility gap — that is, it should presumably arouse suspicion about the meaning of the response to 'interest in learning.'

As an alternative interpretation it is possible to say that the 70 per cent response does not signify 'the essential equivalence of interest in learning' but, rather, is a measurement of the 'essential equivalence' of politeness in response to an unmeaningful question in a society in which culture dictates the avoidance of a negative response. Or, it is possible that 'the equivalence in response' is, in Park's words, the result of a 'purely scholastic exercise in which the answers to all the questions are already implicit in the conceptions and assumptions with which the inquiry started' (Park, 1952, p. 125).

Similarly, alternative interpretations can be given to the KAP findings on 'ideal' family size. This question, in a society characterized by a pre-Newtonian mentality — a society in which the number of children is determined by nature, spirits, or God — may be a meaningless question. It should not be too surprising therefore that the response to this question is highly correlated with actual or 'completed' family size; the ideal tends to be what has actually occurred (Berelson, 1966, p. 658). The fact that the 'ideal number' tends to be lower than the 'completed' number may again reflect the respondent's sensitivity to what the interviewer wants rather than something meaningful to the respondent. It is quite possible that many of the responses in KAP surveys are efforts at politeness to meaningless queries or forced responses to questions to which the respondent really has no answer either before or after the question is put.

KAP surveyors would do well to read the Bureau of the Census publications to which reference has been made above and Chapter 18 of this book by Mitchell, and the bibliography which it contains, to appreciate the range of response error which is possible, especially in cross-cultural surveys; and to insist on the inclusion of response error measurement as an integral element of all surveys. KAP surveys, as other surveys, cannot evade the obligations to evaluate the reliability and validity of response.

It is necessary to state that this critique is not to be interpreted to mean that all the findings of KAP surveys are questionable and useless. There are some types of information, especially inventory types of information, which probably have relatively high reliability and validity. For example, reports on knowledge about contraceptive methods, which reveal very low levels of knowledge, are in all likelihood both reasonably accurate and useful. Even on such matters, however, studies of response error are needed.

By reason of the fact that the cost of being misled by erroneous data may be especially high in action programmes, it is astonishing that Berelson closes his paper with the following observation:

If there is one key recommendation that emerges from this quick review of the KAP survey as a servant of family planning programs . . . it is that we must find quicker, and more efficient ways to tie the KAP studies into administrative actions. That probably means shorter interviews and faster analysis and reporting of central findings; in administrative work at least, there is such a thing as misplaced precision (1966; p. 668).

The only justification for such an observation may lie in the fact that KAP survey results, erroneous or not, have helped to persuade prime ministers, parliaments, and the general population to move in a desirable direction and have provided family planning programme administrators with 'justification' for budgets and programmes. This role of the sample survey should not be minimized, but neither should it be confused with the goals and procedures of science. Berelson's hurry is readily understood and is to his credit. The problems posed by excessive population growth are grave and cry for the most rapid possible resolution. Berelsons are needed and are to be commended, but their advice on the conduct of surveys should not necessarily be heeded.

Definitely to be heeded, however, is the direction for the improvement of surveys pointed to by Stephan (1966) and by Chandrasekaran (1966), among others.

Stephan in his paper (the only methodological critique in the volume), points out, in his usual judicious and competent manner, that 'published reports of recent pilot studies and demonstrations are helpful, but they do not suffice to guide present and future programs' (Stephan, 1966, p. 712). He stresses the fact that 'there is no standard pattern for family planning pilot studies and experiments' (p. 713). He points to the need for more basic research and the directions for improvement of research, including survey research, rather than to the need for short cuts in present inadequate methods (pp. 719–720).

More of the critical and analytical approach to the use of the survey of the type displayed by Chandrasekaran is also badly needed. In his paper he points to the 'difficulties in framing the questions and in obtaining accurate responses' and to the prevalence of 'response errors' and 'interviewer bias' (Chandrasekaran, p. 547). He deals with the 'need for using probes to increase the accuracy of information' (p. 549) and the need for more 'sophisticated techniques like attitude scales and projective techniques' (p. 552). He, like Stephan, also raises basic questions about the evaluation of the success of action programmes.

References

Berelson, B. et al. (Eds) (1966). Family Planning and Population Programs, University of Chicago Press, Chicago.

Chandrasekaran, (1966), Recent trends in family planning research in India. In B. Berelson et al. (Eds), Family Planning and Population Programs, University of Chicago Press, Chicago.

Mauldin, W.P. (1965). Fertility Studies: Knowledge, Attitudes and Practice, The Population Council, Studies in Family Planning no. 7, New York.

Stephan, F.F. (1966). Demonstrations, experiments and pilot projects: a review of recent designs. In B. Berelson et al. (Eds), Family Planning and Population Programs, University of Chicago Press, Chicago.

Park, R.E. (1952). The city as a natural phenomenon. In R.E. Park, Human Communities, Free Press, Glencoe, Ill.

US Bureau of the Census (1960). The Post-Enumeration Survey, 1950. U.S. Government Printing Office, Bureau of the Census Technical Paper no. 4, Washington, D.C.

US Bureau of the Census (1963a). The Current Population Survey Reinterview Program, U.S. Government Printing Office, Bureau of the Census Technical Paper no. 6, Washington, DC.

US Bureau of the Census (1963b). Procedural Report on the 1960 Censuses of Population and Housing, U.S. Government Printing Office, Bureau of the Census Working Paper no. 16, Washington, D.C.

US Bureau of the Census (1965). Response Errors in Collection of Expenditure Data by Household Interviews: an experimental study, U.S. Government Printing Office, Bureau of the Census Technical Paper no. 11, Washington, DC.

Social Research in Developing Countries
Edited by M. Bulmer and D.P. Warwick
© 1983, John Wiley & Sons, Ltd.

CHAPTER 6

SITUATIONAL VARIABLES

MARGARET PEIL

Guides to research methods usually give the impression that they are universal — becoming a participant observer or conducting a survey is the same task whether carried out in a multinational corporation in Argentina or among Indian peasants. While this is a convenient assumption for the authors of texts and for lecturers on methods, it is a long way from reality. Not only must methods be chosen which suit the data to be gathered, they must also be tailored to the sources of these data. This chapter will discuss the ways in which research is influenced by the environment in which it is done. The possibility of doing research and the success of the techniques used are often strongly affected by local or national structural and cultural variables. These vary not only between countries but also within them — between rural and urban areas and between regions with differing historical or political backgrounds. Thus, it is best to consider training in research methods as providing only a very rough outline of how researchers actually behave in the field. Even personal reports of 'how it was done' (such as Adams and Preiss, 1960; Srinivas, Shah, and Ramaswamy, 1979 or Wax, 1971), while providing useful pointers, are likely to miss vital points which must be faced on a new project.

As a first principle, one needs as much knowledge about the local situation as possible before venturing into the field. This poses many problems, especially in countries where statistics are grossly inadequate or non-existent and in areas which have been little studied. This may be a circular problem; research is needed because so little is known, but there is so little information that the project cannot be adequately planned and carried out. As a bare minimum in an unfamiliar area, it is necessary to read about the geography, history, politics and culture of the people to be studied and/or about the historical development of the institutions on which the research will focus. Structures and norms do not appear in a vacuum, but develop gradually in reaction to external and internal pressures. For example, people's ideas of what an educational system ought to be and do are the result of the historical development of education in their country, reports in the mass media on the arguments of politicians and educators over the role of education, the use the local and national labour market makes of educational certification and the individual's own educational and occupational experiences.

Seeking appropriate background knowledge often requires crossing disciplinary boundaries; the economist should try to understand the social and political background just as the sociologist must take into account geographical and economic factors; both will find it useful to consult data provided by economists and/or psychologists (Williams, 1974). But there are also many research topics, especially in developing countries, where little scholarly information is available or where it is out of date and/or misleading. Daily newspapers and informed local people are important sources of supplementary information. Using a wide variety of sources will alert the researcher to conflicts of opinion which can be important in shaping a project. It is important for novices to learn that 'fact' is a variable which only a broad knowledge allows them to explore.

Most social science research projects are carried out in the 'home' area of the researchers, who therefore assume that they have all the background information needed. However, even experienced sociologists often forget how heterogeneous most societies are. Expectations and behaviour can vary considerably even from one organization or neighbourhood to another of the same type, and generalization from one's own experience to the whole of society can be dangerous. For instance, Williams (1974, p. 145) comments that in Brazil, 'very few statements which one might make concerning the socialization of lower class children would hold for the upper-middle, even in the same city'. Workers at one factory often have more autonomy in organizing their work or stronger feelings about their union than workers doing the same jobs at a nearby factory. Residents of some housing blocks in China take much more pride in their buildings than others living only a short distance down the street; this will be reflected in their social relations even though both groups conform to the same regulations and hold identical positions in their society.

Researchers who have grown up in one sector of society must beware of assuming that they know all about other sectors or even about their own; there are probably many things you do not know about your own family because you have not seriously questioned them. Even behaviour which looks familiar may have different meaning to those involved than it does to the observer. Research is a process of acquiring knowledge, and assuming understanding at the beginning can seriously handicap the project. If you do not question, you will never discover your misconceptions.

Access

It often takes as long to get the necessary permissions to carry out research as to complete the fieldwork. Governments and other sponsors or gatekeepers must be convinced that the project will not threaten their position or conflict with their interests. Respondents must be informed that permission of the appropriate authorities has been given and their own consent must be sought. All this can involve complex political manipulation and calling on numerous influential contacts for strategic personal intervention. The lower the status of the researcher and the more conflict-prone the environment, the more difficult this process is (Form, 1976, pp. 278–294). Financial sponsorship will not be discussed here, but many of the problems of obtaining this are similar to the task of securing the aid of gatekeepers (government, managers, trade unions and other officials who could forbid access to respondents). Lastly, approaching respondents themselves must be considered.

Gatekeepers

Government, in the form of politicans, bureaucrats and/or the military, is the most important gatekeeper in most countries, though its degree of interest in and control over research varies considerably. In some countries, this is the only source of funds for research. In many, national and/or local authorities must give written permission for field projects. Research by non-citizens is often subject to stricter regulation than that of local people, but some governments are more worried about the potential opposition of local academics than the gathering of data by foreigners who will not spread their findings locally. Ethical considerations have led to increasing regulation of research on human subjects, unfortunately often without distinguishing between medical and social science research as a source of danger.

Governments also vary considerably in how much of their data is available to scholars. The United States Freedom of Information law has considerably widened access to government data in a country which was already quite open. Other countries may use an Official Secrets Act, a 20 or 50-year limit on archives, or put other bureaucratic barriers in the way.

Research is generally much more closely controlled in authoritarian than in democratic countries, but regulations have increased considerably in the latter over the last decade. It also varies with the topic; politically oriented projects will be subject to more control than studies of agriculture or manufacturing productivity. But an insecure government may see the potential for political disruption in a wide range of topics; civil servants could expose corruption, the squatters' plight could proclaim discrimination in resource distribution and ethnographic studies could stimulate intergroup conflict or a selfconscious resistance to outside influences.

Few bureaucrats, politicians or military men have any training in research and few are likely to see the results as of much potential benefit to themselves. It is well to remember that many cultures do not value knowledge and the ability to make rational decisions based on detailed information to the same extent as Americans do. In many societies it is assumed that an experienced man can make the right decisions by instinct; detailed knowledge based on empirical research could be a distraction, with the additional danger of mistakes. Thus, the suspicion of research inherent in most open societies is multiplied in others where the scientific method is less established or where those in power have more to lose than to gain from such studies.

In addition, academic researchers are often suspect as more liberal than the government, or the individual in it who is making the decision. This usually means ideologically to the left, but in some countries academics may be seen as ideologically less radical, not providing sufficient support for government initiatives or questioning their utility. It may fall to the scholar's lot to discover that peasants strongly oppose government attempts at coercive collective farming, or other populist attitudes which the government would prefer to ignore. It may be seen as easier to forbid the research than to suppress the results.

Even after permission has been obtained, the political climate of a country often limits systematic data collection. Turner (1975, p. 99) found that some respondents were pleased that a political survey could be done in Argentina (in 1973), saying that it would have been impossible in Cuba. However, others refused to answer questions about people in power because it might get them into trouble.

Other gatekeepers may cause similar problems. Firms are often very suspicious of requests to study their workers. If industrial relations are bad, the managers may see researchers as spies to whom the workers will complain. If they are good, managers fear that researchers may suggest new demands that workers might make. Many managers feel that their authority is increasingly questioned by trade unions and government, and wish to isolate their workers as much as possible from outside influences. Within the office or factory, they must be seen to be in charge. Outsiders over whom they have no control are not welcome. Similarly, trade union officers are often in a competitive situation, walking a tightrope between the demands of their members, competitors for their posts, managers and the government. An outsider who goes about asking questions is unlikely to improve their position and may well complicate it.

Academics who are suspicious of strangers or want to reserve a field or topic for themselves can make it very difficult for an outsider to do research. Jayaraman (in Srinivas, Shah, and Ramaswamy, 1979) reports on the vigorous attempts made by a group of Australian anthropologists to prevent his study of a community where one of their number had been working for some years, and the delays this caused. While a community can be overstudied (one African village was the site of five independent studies in 3 years), it is generally better for the development of our disciplines to cooperate with colleagues in our own and related fields rather than attempting to maintain a monopoly over a topic or site. Human behaviour is very complex, and a variety of approaches can explore the field in more depth than any single researcher. In general, objections to outsiders are more often based on academic insecurity or ideology than on possible interference with scholarly goals.

On the other hand, outsiders sometimes rush in without finding out what research is going on locally, and may do considerable damage by giving the impression that 'research' can be seriously inadequate in conception, repetitious, methodologically weak and/or likely to be a nuisance (at best) to the authorities or the general public. They then go away, oblivious of the havoc they have wrought. Local academics must bear the brunt of resentment raised by these outsiders, and are likely to be suspicious of further proposals from anyone whose work they cannot vouch for.

Manipulating the system and gaining access to documents or potential respondents are often accomplished through the use of sponsors, individuals who are personally acquainted with the gatekeepers and who will intercede for the researcher. The higher the level of sponsorship which can be mobilized, the better the chance of overcoming resistance. Personal relationships can be as useful in a supposedly universalistic society as in a particularistic one; the researcher whose social networks can supply an appointment with the appropriate official, or even the name of the official most likely to provide the information needed, has a considerable advantage.

Form (1976, p. 292) recounts how his Indian student spent considerable time seeking support from local research institutes. He obtained letters of introduction to researchers at these institutes and discussed his work with them. While they generally approved, no one was initially willing to support his approach to factory management. This was a case where an untried researcher was away from his base and no one wanted to take responsibility for his actions. Should he cause trouble, they did not want to be associated with his work. This is a reasonable precaution on the part of potential sponsors, but can cause considerable difficulty for a researcher who is eager to begin fieldwork.

The characteristics of the preferred sponsor will vary with the nature of the task, the inherent status of the researcher and official attitudes toward research and toward outsiders. Full professors can usually mobilize higher level sponsorship than graduate students, but they need it less because their own status gains them entry to many offices. Non-nationals are often given a more cordial welcome than nationals of equivalent status, either through courtesy to the stranger or in response to the implied flattery of being sought out by someone from a distance. A highly privatized society or institution will require higher level sponsorship than a more open society or organization. A project which makes relatively few demands on time or other resources will face fewer hurdles than a project with greater demands.

An alternative approach to seeking the aid of outside sponsors is to approach middle or lower level individuals within the organization. Their support will be essential if the work is to be carried out, and they may be able and willing to help the researcher gain a hearing at the top. Part of the resistance of senior gatekeepers to research is the fear that it will cause conflict among their subordinates; a willingness of intermediate officers to cooperate reduces this worry. Middle-level staff will be aware of how the system works. They know who really holds power in the organization and whether these are best approached directly or indirectly. They can give advice on modifications which may be necessary if the plan is to gain approval.

Power relations are important at every stage of a project, but especially at the beginning. One aspect of this is the deference due to officials, which is expressed differently from one country or organization to another. In asking for research access, we are expecting people to give us time and information. An arrogant manner can turn a willing informant into a reluctant and unreliable one, but in other societies a too deferent manner will signal incompetence to carry out the work.

Students and even experienced researchers often assume that once top authorities have given their permission everyone lower in the hierarchy will fall into line, but this will depend greatly on the nature of the local hierarchy and the extent of authority and autonomy at each level. In practice, officials like to think that they are important enough to have the project explained to them and their cooperation requested. The more officious or less secure among them can cause considerable trouble if they are not treated with sufficient deference, whereas a supervisor who sees the project as enhancing his position can make the whole process far easier than it would otherwise be. Even when relationships are established, they cannot be taken for granted. Form (1976, p. 291) points out that in a 'highly personalistic environment, verbal agreements remain binding only when personal relationships are constantly reinforced'.

The nature of the organization is also relevant to gaining access to an institution and conducting research within it. Stinchcombe (1965, pp. 153–169) has pointed out that organizations reflect the conditions under which their type was founded. For example, the building industry fosters dispersed authority through subcontracting to craft specialists. New, high-technology industries have much greater expectations of change than industries which were founded 50 or 200 years earlier, and place more emphasis on staff departments and flexibility in moving into new products and processes. The relative isolation of mines, for example, gives them much more importance in their local community than is possible for an employer located in a large, heterogeneous city. Long-established industries like the railways and docks have to take their history of management/labour relations into account, whereas factories which have been operating for only a few years will still be building up a code of 'custom and practice'. Firms which employ mainly young, single women and expect a high turnover (a characteristic of the electronics industry in Malaysia, for example) will provide a different environment than firms which expect career commitment of a labour force for which they provide training and incentives (as is common in Japan).

Other types of organization, such as hospitals or prisons, pose somewhat different problems of access than factories, but many of the same principles apply. Hospital administrators can use potential interference with treatment as an all-purpose excuse to deny access. Prison warders do not want meddling with their system of control and may have something to hide. Before approaching an organization, it is important to consider carefully how the research can be useful to its goals and how the intrusion of research can be minimized.

Access to a community is often easier than access to an organization. We all have some experience of moving into a new community and the bureaucratic constraints of an organization are stronger than those of natural communities. This does not mean that local leaders might not try to impede research into their communities, but that openness to outsiders is such that this is more difficult to do, especially if participant observation is used rather than the more obvious formal interviews.

Respondents

When all the official permissions have been given, it is still necessary to get the cooperation of research subjects. This may be easy or difficult, depending on the influence which sponsors and gatekeepers have and are willing to exercise, the history of research in the area and consequent attitudes toward it, local culture as it relates to privacy and attitudes toward strangers, the relative sophistication of respondents in handling new situations and the ability of the researcher to demonstrate that the study will have positive (or at least not negative) results for the individuals concerned. Wax (1971) shows how the ways of acquiring useful contacts with individuals vary from one project to another even for the same anthropologist working in a single country.

Respect for or suspicion of sponsors can make the difference between willing cooperation and complete refusal to participate, though usually the response is somewhere in between. Many people want nothing to do with research sponsored by the government because they fear it will lead to increased taxes, trouble with the police or other unwelcome attention to their activities. Guaranteed confidentiality may not be enough to overcome justifiable mistrust of government intentions. Sponsorship by a university is usually preferable, even though the money comes from government, because most people see universities as benign institutions.

While few peoples have been as exposed to research as the Indians of the American south-west, increasing numbers of people even in remote areas have either been in contact with someone carrying out research or heard about such projects through the mass media. What they experience or hear will affect participation in future projects by themselves and their families. If they have been seriously inconvenienced, think of research as a Camelot adventure (Sjöberg, 1967, pp. 141–161) which may harm themselves or their community, or see it merely as a questionable exercise and a waste of time, it should hardly be surprising if they try to avoid researchers. If, on the other hand, social science research has a good name, as having results favourable to people like themselves, cooperation is easier to get.

The culture and relative sophistication of potential respondents must be taken into account in getting their agreement to cooperate as well as in deciding which methods to use. Some societies have positive roles for outsiders, whereas others find affiliation difficult to arrange. If strangers are generally perceived as intruders or enemies rather than as guests (Levine, 1979), it is likely to take considerable time to build enough confidence to produce reliable data. In addition, societies vary considerably in their norms of privacy. One indication of this is housing. If houses are walled and care is taken to hide household activities from passersby (as in France, for example), privacy is likely to be considered more important than in societies where much of life takes place in full view of the neighbours. Privacy is likely to be less important where large households are the norm (often involving extended families), or in crowded, mixed-tenancy houses, than in areas featuring mainly small, nuclear family households.

Suspicion of outsiders is likely to be greater in rural areas where almost everyone is illiterate than in heterogeneous cities, but it may be easier to establish friendly contacts in the former than in the latter. Once rural community members have accepted a researcher, they may be more cooperative than city dwellers, who are used to outsiders and have many sources of diversion. Subjects with relatively wide experience often know something about research use and abuse and are likely to be more cynical about the return it is likely to give them than people who know little of the wider world. In some developed countries it is getting increasingly difficult to enlist the cooperation of the general public in research; some see it merely as someone making a living at their expense.

Local norms about paying informants may lead to systematic manipulation of researchers, with regular demands for money and services before any further information will be provided. This is yet another situation where local knowledge is essential. There will be norms about whether it is customary to pay for information and, if so, how much. The researcher who pays highly for what others would get for nothing deserves to be, and often is, treated as a sucker.

The discussion so far has been phrased in terms of males, as women researchers are as yet a small minority. They face the same problems as their male colleagues, but also some difficulties peculiar to their sex. Most of the gatekeepers are male, and these sometimes treat women researchers as incompetent minors or potential sex objects; at best many are uncomfortable in the presence of a woman carrying out what is usually a male role (see Daniels in

Sjöberg, 1967). Women have an advantage in approaching other women in purdah, but for other types of respondents their usual low status in comparison to men can make it difficult to get cooperation.

Many societies segregate the sexes and some consider women who move freely outside the house to be morally loose. This poses problems for the researcher. If she is single, people think she should have either a husband or some other male protector. Madan (in Sjöberg, 1967, p. 173) reports that one sociologist had to take her mother with her because the villagers would not accept her without a chaperone. If a woman is already married, she will be asked why she is not at home with her husband instead of gadding about doing research. Women often face questioning from leaders and others in the community about personal details which would not be of concern if they were male. There have been some extremely able women researchers (especially among anthropologists), but sex must be taken into account when planning and carrying out the work.

However, in the long run women may have wider access than men if they can gain exemption from societal norms as to their role. While a man sometimes finds it difficult to observe and interview women without arousing suspicion as to his intentions, women have often been able to study what goes on in the world of men by using the role of researcher to take on the status of 'honorary male'. Regardless of who is doing it, research usually focuses on either men or women and thus misses important sources of societal variation. A woman who manages to study a topic largely concerned with males may deliberately exclude women from her study, only to find out later that they too have important roles to play (Gupta in Srinivas, Shah, and Ramaswamy, p. 110).

Samples

Given the constraints of time and money and a lack of information on the population, many samples are much less representative than they are assumed to be even though considerable care has been taken in the choice. Problems of variability and comparability should always be considered. The standard approach to sampling suggests that random, stratified or quota samples can be drawn up by following certain principles. This assumes knowledge of the population being studied, which is often possible in developed countries where regular censuses of population, households, schools and businesses provide detailed information on various aspects of the society. But in many countries such statistics are rudimentary, out of date or unavailable. As an extreme example, estimates of the Nigerian population in 1980 varied from 60 to 120 million and the population of towns and cities was similarly subject to guess-work. There was very little data on the characteristics of the population, which was assumed to be undergoing considerable change.

In addition to such data inadequacy, sampling is often rendered difficult by a lack of maps, street plans and directories which could be used as a sampling frame; by the unorganized development of squatter settlements and lack of all-weather roads to isolated villages. In many countries, small firms tend to be unknown to authorities and hard to find even if listed, so they are under-sampled. Formal sampling in rural areas is complicated when farm ownership is widely dispersed, in irregular and unsurveyed packages which are subject to conflicts over tenure.

Within an institution, other sampling problems arise. Managers and other officials are often unable to provide much information on workers or members of their organizations; they may even be vague about their number. Only a minority of firms in less bureaucratized countries have efficiently organized personnel offices. Recreation and welfare associations often lack up-to-date lists of members and do not distinguish between active and inactive members. Lists of voters vary in usefulness with the proportion of the population which registers to vote and the recency of this registration. Telephone subscribers may include only a small proportion of the population, which biases such a list toward the wealthy.

It is often useful in urban studies to have information about the spatial distribution of the population. Cluster sampling is used as a convenient method of including an adequate number of respondents having selected character-istics. Stratification by class or economic status is based on cluster sampling in areas having high, medium and low-cost housing; migrants are sought in areas frequented by newcomers; religious or ethnic groups may be clustered in their own areas. This works well in towns which have such residential differentiation, but not all towns follow such a pattern. Migration status, religion or ethnicity may have little effect on where a person lives if the town is growing rapidly and housing is hard to find. The location and quality of urban housing tends to reflect economic status (with constraints for race and family size), but countries vary in the extent to which housing is used as an expression of economic success or conspicuous consumption. Custom and sentiment also affect housing choice. Some people continue to live in a family house because they prefer the old neighbourhood even though they could afford something better; others cannot afford or resist moving to a smaller house. Where extended family households are common, members of varying economic status often share the same house.

It may be fairly simple to make a list of residents of a village, but one must consider whether to include those who are away on a temporary or longer-term basis, or who have recently arrived on a visit. Some houses may be owned by people who live in town and only use them on holidays. It may be difficult to distinguish households if people who consider themselves united for some purposes (such as in their use of the compound) divide into smaller groups for other purposes (meals, for instance). Urban households may also be indeter-minate, with members coming and going, so the distinction between *de facto* and *de jure* population (those actually in the house and those who are usually there) is important. Hannerz (1969, p. 49), for example, discusses the variability of membership of households in the Washington, DC ghetto.

Given financial and time constraints on the size of sample, certain groups may be omitted because they are considered culturally or theoretically less important; the consequences of this should be considered carefully. Cornelius (1975, p. 14) omitted women from his sample because controlling in sex in addition to numerous other variables would have been too difficult and because, 'among most Mexicans, politics is still regarded as "men's business", and that women are, in general, less likely than men to have . . . participated in some forms of political activity'. But failure to sample women means that such stereotypes are perpetuated. Women have often been ignored in studies in the past, and studies which aim at comparability tend to concentrate on men because there are no 'baseline' data on women. Similarly, it is so conventional to study either the elites of the poor that too little attention is given to middle level people.

The possibility of generalizing from the sample is constrained by the heterogeneity of the population and the breadth of the sample. Too often studies of one village or town are treated as if they represent all villages in the area or all towns in the country. But size, centrality, history, economic base and many other factors mean that each place is to some extent exceptional. Whenever possible, at least two or three places should be sampled. If the results are similar for all of these, generalization may be justifiable.

Sampling can be complicated by the need for comparability, especially across cultures. To what extent are people with 10 years of schooling in a largely illiterate society equivalent to those with the same amount in another society where education is more widespread? Malawska and Peyre (in Szalai and Petrella, 1977, p. 157) show that repeating a year at school varies in effect on the individual depending on how common this is and when the repeating usually takes place (early or late in the educational career). If standards of living vary considerably (as between Lima and an Andean village or between the poor of Calcutta or Buenos Aires), to what extent are individuals having similar income or similar occupational positions really comparable? Teune (in Szalai and Petrella, 1977, pp. 119–120) points out that many international studies are based on samples from one region of each country, which are then generalized to the country as a whole (regional samples, or even samples of a single city, are treated as if they were national samples). In such a situation, there is no measure of intranational variance and observed international differences may be the result of selective sampling.

In the field

Carrying out a research project poses problems of the method(s) to be used, the relevance of personal characteristics and the variability of language use.

Personal capacities will obviously be important, but there are also structural and cultural variables which should be considered.

Methods

The method used for data collection varies with the topic, training and inclination of the researcher, but the usefulness of various methods is also affected by the situation in which the research takes place. Given an identical topic, it may be possible to use official records in one place but necessary to collect one's own data in another. Telephone or postal surveys are possible in some countries but not in others; interviewing or observing members of the public is fairly easy to do in some places but either difficult or unrewarding in others.

Generally, the quantity or quality of data-gathering by government is better in developed than in Third World countries for the obvious reason that the latter have inadequate funds and trained personnel for the task. The problems which arise in using African statistics have been discussed by Rimmer (in Peil, Mitchell, and Rimmer, 1982); while many Asian and Latin American countries have a more advanced capability, many of the same problems must still be taken into account. For instance, Tannenbaum is reported as saying, 'Statistics are the poetry of Latin America' (cited by Randall, 1975, p. 137). Figures are juggled to avoid or enforce tax collection, to encourage investment, to stigmatize political enemies and demonstrate one's own political success, to avoid accusations of incompetence and demonstrate the necessity of one's job, or because demands are made for figures which simply do not exist (Randall, 1975, p. 137). Thus, it is best never to accept a set of figures at face value without investigating the conditions under which it was produced and possible sources of conflicting figures.

Countries also vary in the statistics which are thought worth gathering. For example, Sweden maintains computer files with considerable personal detail about all its citizens, which is used to support the welfare system. The British public would object to the collecting of some of this information as an invasion of privacy.

Economic data tend to be the easiest to get (though quality varies considerably from place to place and over time), and there are many unofficial sources of political data, such as newspapers and journals. Sociological data, on the other hand, are often not collected or are available in a form which does not answer the research questions being posed. This makes it necessary for sociologists to collect their own data, usually through observation and/or interviewing. Where observation is rendered difficult by the nature of the topic, the privatization of the group being studied or the length of time available, surveys are often used.

Telephone surveys are increasingly popular in countries where a majority of families have a telephone. Drawing a random sample of telephone numbers is a simple task for a computer, and respondents over a wide area can be contacted quickly, with little time wasted between one interview and the next. This cuts down costs considerably. While people who refuse to be interviewed can hang up, many people have less objection to talking with a stranger over the telephone than they would admitting someone into their homes. This is especially true in neighbourhoods with a high level of crime.

However, since only a few countries have a sufficiently widespread use of telephones to make this method practicable, postal surveys are a more widely used form of contact at a distance. However, these often have a very high non-return rate, either because the postal system is inefficient or because the recipients see no reason why they should take the time to reply. Both of these methods suffer from increased problems among low-income respondents. These are least likely to have telephones or adequate arrangements for getting letters, and many will not be well enough educated to handle a questionnaire unaided. There will also be problems among the foreign-born population, who may not understand what is wanted of them.

These methods are also more suited to individuals than to organizations. Officials of organizations are required to fill in forms for the government; they are less likely to pay attention to a questionnaire received from a private individual or research institute because there is no compulsion to reply. This partly varies with the pressure of such requests. If little research is being done locally, so that officials receive few such requests, and if they find the topic interesting, they may cooperate. If they get many requests and see the project as a nuisance, they will not. School principals may fill in a questionnaire if the accompanying letter assures them of Ministry of Education support for the project (or managers may do the same for projects supported by a businessman's organization). On the whole, it pays to contact organizations personally. ✓

Several of the authors in Srinivas, Shah, and Ramaswamy (1979) report that ʰeir attempts at formal interviews were unrewarding. Compared to the richness of data from observation, they found respondents uncooperative and answers stereotyped. Several reasons are given for this, which must be taken into account when survey methods are being considered. The most important is that illiterates are often intimidated by the interview situation. Many have little self-confidence when confronted by a prestigious interviewer (university student or other educated, middle-class, secure individual). Form (1976, p. 275) reports that interviewing Indian factory workers took twice as long as interviewing workers in Italy, Argentina or the United States. This was seen as partly a problem of illiteracy, but also of a lack of experience in dealing with impersonal questioning by a stranger.

However, he does not report that the answers were unusable; I would argue that the difference between Form's graduate student and those who reported trouble with interviews in Srinivas' *et al.*'s book is training. Far too many people attempt formal interviewing who are unaware of the problems which it poses. It appears that all of these saw research as essentially long-term observation. Some were not even clear about what they intended to observe until they had been at the task for some time, and most lacked confidence in interviews though they felt constrained to attempt them. They were similar to many British students, who have heard about all the difficulties of surveys as part of their methods courses but have never participated in a well-organized interviewing programme.

Properly organized interviews will usually provide usable data. It does not seem to have occurred to the Indian students to make the situation less formal by not putting a table between themselves and the interviewee, by talking informally at the beginning to put them at their ease, or to use a less structured approach with open questions which would encourage respondents to talk at length about topics which interest them rather than being pushed rapidly from one closed question to the next. It is better to interview a small number of people adequately rather than to be so rushed that no one feels secure enough to cooperate. Questions should always be phrased in simple language, suitable to the person being interviewed. Similarly, an interview can be conducted while eating a meal, drinking in a pub or giving someone a lift. Over time, these can add to a considerable body of quantitative or qualitative data.

Personal characteristics

Fieldwork can also be affected by the social position, marital status, sex, age and religion of the researcher if these characteristics are considered important in the society studied. Class or caste often complicates the researcher–subject relationship. Caste can pose many difficulties in India, but most researchers appear to overcome them (Srinivas, Shah, and Ramaswamy, 1979). Scholars are often more liberal than the people they study, who may take offence if caste distinctions are ignored. Seshaiah (in Srinivas, Shah and Ramaswamy, 1979, p. 244) points out that it may be difficult initially for an Indian to study a casteless society, because they are unprepared for a different form of clues to status. Similarly, someone who has grown up in a class-conscious society may be continually looking for signs of class distinction and miss other subtle forms of differentiation in a society in which class is not very important.

Researchers are usually of middle or upper-class origin, whereas the people they study are often lower class. They must learn new words and symbols which have meaning in this sector of society. The group studied may resent them as outsiders and accuse them of 'putting on airs' because they do not follow local conventions. This often comes as a surprise to students who have assumed that their own society is relatively homogeneous. Students of urban background working in rural areas also find that the culture is more varied than they expected. Sheth argues (in Srinivas, Shah, and Ramaswamy, 1979, p. 168) that an open attitude often overcomes barriers of class or caste. People do not want the researcher to be something he is not, but many enjoy an opportunity to interact on familiar terms with someone from a different sector of society.

The fact that graduate students are unmarried at an age when most other people in the society are married can cause difficulty. People without much education usually marry early, and find it hard to understand why an 'adult' should have no spouse. Srinivas, Shah, and Ramaswamy, (1979, p. 26) points out that anthropologists who go into the field as a husband and wife team often have an advantage in that they can pool their efforts and contact all members of the community, while upholding family life in a style the community approves of. He faced extended questioning about still being a bachelor, and found that he was not trusted to talk with young women in the village. However, he argues that a solitary researcher is forced to make friends in the community and spend full time on the project whereas a couple inevitably use each other for support and are less reliant on the community for companionship.

Other sources of differentiation, such as religion, race or ethnicity, or political ideology can interfere with fieldwork because they make people suspicious. Some communities will emphasize background characteristics which are unimportant in others. In the early days of a project, researchers often find that they are answering more questions than they ask, because people are trying to place them within the local hierarchy and give them an acceptable role. In a largely ascriptive society, where everyone knows everyone else, who the researcher is is important. But even in more universalistic societies people prefer categoric interaction if personal ties cannot be established. For this, they need to know which categories the researcher fits. There is seldom a role of 'someone who studies us', though over time the researcher may create one.

In so far as conflict is structured differently and deference expressed differently from one society to another, researchers may find that they have unwittingly overstepped the bounds of what is acceptable or fallen short of what is expected. Conflict may not be recognized as such because competing parties are so polite (as demonstrated, for example in James Clavell's *Shogun*, 1975). It may be difficult for an outsider to guess whether friendly banter indicates cordiality or conflict, or whether a person showing polite deference to someone in authority has regard for his hierarchical superiority, fears open opposition or is scornful of his abilities and actively seeking to undermine his position.

Each culture and subculture has its own clues in language and behaviour, which outsiders often find difficult to interpret. For example, cultural variance in the use of time and space can cause misunderstanding. Someone coming from a society where time is important may misinterpret habitual lateness in others for whom arriving precisely when agreed would be grossly impolite. Most societies have a norm for arrival, but some treat time very loosely and expect outsiders to maintain equal flexibility. Graduate students in particular often worry about the passage of time and thus miss many things to which they could profitably put the time they are 'wasting'. Missed appointments have various meanings: Have the proper preliminaries been observed? Is too much being asked of the informant?

Cultural differences in the use of space can be observed by watching people of different backgrounds in conversation. In making oneself understood and conveying respect for another person, distance between speakers, position (standing or sitting), hand and arm movement and volume are as important as the words used (Argyle and Trower, 1980). In some societies, people kiss when they meet, or men walk down the street holding hands. In others, greeting is expressed through a bow or handshake; touching another person who is not a close relative may be unacceptable. How is anger expressed in this society — in facial expression and gesture as well as in tone of voice? How is a person notified that he has been accepted? Should inferiors look superiors in the eye or keep their eyes down when addressing superiors?

Language

Language is most obviously a problem when working outside one's own country, but multiethnic countries often require some competence in more than one's mother tongue. Even within a monolingual community there are often differences in the meaning and use of words from one sector to another. The underclass often has a jargon of its own, as do occupational groups (machinists, economists). Elderly people may use words common in their youth, whereas adolescents pick up new words from the mass media, often with very imprecise meaning. Pronunciation often varies according to the geographical origin of the speakers or their education.

Subjects base their opinion of researchers on how they speak and behave. If speech is only partly comprehensible, it is often greeted with a glazed look and avoidance of the speaker. People tend to look down ethnocentrically on those who cannot speak 'properly' and judge harshly those who contravene local norms of behaviour even if this is due to ignorance. Thus, a researcher with limited knowledge of the local variant may be seen as (intentionally or accidentally) impolite and disrespectful and may also be laughed at behind his back. On the other hand, an outsider who has been accepted by the community may be forgiven mistakes in grammar and pronunciation which would be unacceptable from an insider because he is given credit for 'trying' in comparison to outsiders who ignore the local language or dialect.

Most important, a thorough knowledge of the local language is useful for understanding the connotations of words. The basic ability to follow a conversation is not enough to pick up the nuances, the way words are being used to express meaning. One reason why survey responses may seem stereotyped is that interviewers reduce answers to the least common denominator rather than recording precisely what the respondent said. This is especially likely to happen when answers are translated from the local to the national language.

Conclusions

It makes little sense for an American sociologist to apply open-ended interviews to Mexican businessmen or projective tests to Argentine students if he does not at the same time understand enough of the language and culture to know when he is being 'turned on'. Similarly, field observations can become easily transformed into travelogues unless the full force of comparative social history and intensive involvement is brought to bear on the subject of analysis (Horowitz, in Sjöberg, 1967, p. 213).

Comparative research is becoming increasingly important in the social sciences. But it will miss much of its potential contribution if situational variables are ignored. All people are not 'just like us'; few of them are. Our quest for generalizations leads us to focus on points of similarity, but account must be taken of points of difference. Whether research takes place at home or in distant lands, it will be improved by a lively awareness of the way these variables affect access to the field, sample selection, the methods used and the character of the data collected.

References

Adams, R.N. and Preiss, J.J. (Eds.) (1960). *Human Organization Research: Field Relations and Techniques*, Dorsey Press, Homewood, Ill.

Argyle, M. and Trower, P. (1980). *Person to Person: Ways of Communicating*, Harper and Row, London.

Clavell, J. (1975). *Shogun*, Hodder and Stoughton, London.

Cornelius, W.A. (1975). *Politics and the Migrant Poor in Mexico City*, Stanford University Press, Stanford, Cal.

Form, W.H. (1976). *Blue-collar Stratification: Autoworkers in Four Countries*, Princeton University Press, Princeton, NJ.

Hannerz, U. (1969). *Soulside*, Columbia University Press, New York.

Levine, D.N. (1979). Simmel at a distance: on the history and systematics of the sociology of the stranger. In W.A. Shack and E.P. Skinner (Eds), *Strangers in African Societies*, pp. 21–36, University of California Press, Berkeley.

Peil, M., Mitchell, P.K., and Rimmer, D. (1982). *Social Science Research Methods: An African Handbook*, Hodder and Stoughton, London.

Randall, L. (1975). Lies, damn lies, and the Argentine GDP. *Latin American Research Review*, 11, **1**, 137–159.

Sjöberg, G. (Ed.) (1967). *Ethics, Politics, and Social Research*, Routledge and Kegan Paul, London.

Srinivas, M.N., Shah, A.M., and Ramaswamy, E.A. (Eds.) (1979). *The Fieldworker and the Field: Problems and Challenges in Sociological Investigation*, Oxford University Press, Delhi.

Stinchcombe, A.L. (1965). Social structure and organizations. In J.G. March (Ed.) *Handbook of Organizations*, pp. 142–193, Rand McNally, Chicago.

Szalai, A. and Petrella, R. (Eds.) (1977). *Cross-national Comparative Survey Research: Theory and Practice*, Pergamon, New York.

Turner, F.C. (1975). The study of Argentine politics through survey research. *Latin American Research Review*, 10, **2**, 73–116.

Wax, R.H. (1971). *Doing Fieldwork: Warnings and Advice*, University of Chicago Press, Chicago.

Williams, M.T. (1974). Social psychology and Latin American studies. *Latin American Research Review*, 9, **1**, 141–153.

SECTION III

SAMPLING

Social Research in Developing Countries
Edited by M. Bulmer and D.P. Warwick
© 1983, John Wiley & Sons, Ltd.

CHAPTER 7

SAMPLING

MARTIN BULMER

The selection of individuals (or other units) who are to be those studied in a particular investigation — usually in a survey, to be interviewed personally — is a most important issue. The idea of *sampling* from a population, rather than enumerating the whole population, was introduced early in the twentieth century and has now become the standard method of selecting for study a *representative* cross-section of a larger population. Representativeness is ensured by the use of *probability (or random) sampling*, in which each member of the population has a known and non-zero chance of selection. By these methods, rather precise estimates of population values can be obtained by studying only a very small fraction of the total population. There are excellent introductions to the principles of sampling in standard texts (such Moser and Kalton, 1971, pp. 61–210; and Warwick and Lininger, 1975, pp. 69–125) as well as more detailed treatments (such as Hansen, Hurwitz and Madow, 1953; Kish, 1965; Yates, 1949).

Survey research in developing countries presents a paradox so far as sample design is concerned. Some of the most advanced applications of sampling methods have been carried out in the developing world, starting with Mahalanobis' work in India in the 1940s, and his pioneering introduction of the National Sample Survey as early as 1950, the first national general social survey in the world. Its progress is reviewed in Chapter 9. More recently, the World Fertility Survey has involved a very sophisticated cross-national sample design and a major commitment of resources to demographic sampling work in the Third World (Verma *et al.* 1980; World Fertility Survey, 1975).

Yet in many third world countries, sampling according to standard principles poses formidable problems: Sampling text books were not written with the developing countries in mind. There are usually no sampling frames, no central registry of all citizens, no census tracts with home addresses, no comprehensive directories of who's where. If any of these exist, they are likely to be unreliable except possibly in some rural areas (Kearl, 1976, p. 37). As Zarkovich points out in Chapter 8, the conditions are unfavourable by definition. There is no

91

tradition, no previous experience on which to base decisions, and so on.

The practical difficulties to which this gives rise may be illustrated by a contrasting experience of sample design in three societies, Syria, Nepal and Somalia (Bergsten, 1980). In Syria, the Central Bureau of Statistics maintained lists of dwelling units derived from the census, which could be updated. People lived in defined villages, so that for the settled population, sampling was a manageable task. (The nomadic Bedouin, who would have presented formidable sampling problems, were not included in the study.) By contrast, Somalia posed much more difficult problems. Where maps were available they did not accurately locate villages. Lists of villages were available, but did not always agree with the maps. People did not necessarily live within a village. Houses were unnumbered, paths unnamed and housing congested. Sampling nomads presented particular difficulties, complicated by the splitting of families for grazing, men with camels being away for months at a time. The plan was to sample nomads during the dry season using watering holes as the primary sampling units. The author wryly comments that 'the lifestyle of the nomad certainly does not lend itself to the efficient carrying out of demographic surveys' (Bergsten, 1980, p. 73).

In Nepal, basic information for constructing a sampling frame was sparse. Villages are remote and isolated, maps and communications are poor and most villages could be reached only on foot. In the summer monsoon season, the few existing roads are unusable and flights difficult. These conditions are totally different from the usual circumstances of conducting a household survey in Western Europe or North America, which are assumed or described in standard textbooks. As the experience in the three countries indicates, conditions may vary considerably between different parts of the world but in most cases sampling will involve departure from well-codified textbook norms.

Resource limitations

Efficiency in the design of sample surveys is commonly defined as the achievement of a given level of accuracy for a certain cost (Moser and Kalton, 1971, pp. 64–74). The design of samples is then treated as a question of reconciling the objectives of accuracy and cost to decide upon an optimum design. Thus, for example, decisions on how many stages to incorporate into a design, or what degree of clustering to use in selection of primary sampling units, are conditioned by their implications for sampling error on the one hand and the budget of the investigation on the other.

A basic limitation of surveys in less developed countries is that resources are very scarce, and the technical infrastructure taken for granted in industrial countries wholly or partly lacking. As Zarkovich points out in Chapter 8, in this situation the design is imposed more by the circumstances of the work than by the sampler's knowledge of skill. Designing sample surveys becomes more a study of limitations and their sampling implications than an exercise of principles and type of work leading to an optimum design in developed countries. A good deal of work is being done to improve conditions and standards, particularly through training research workers and statisticians (see Zarkovich, 1975), but limitations of resources and infrastructure are likely to constrain survey research in the Third World in the foreseeable future.

Limitations of sampling frames

Textbooks of survey methods take for granted the availability of adequate sampling frames. In Britain, for example, the electoral register (listing individuals age 18 and over entitled to vote) and the rating records (a list of dwellings maintained for tax purposes) are the two most commonly used frames. For multistage surveys, extensive information is available about the location of the population in areas of different sizes (such as parliamentary constituencies, wards and parishes) and many characteristics of the population of such areas can be identified from the census.

In developing countries, such extensive information is either not available at all, or where it is available is subject to considerable degrees of error. In practice, the two types of difficulty merge into one another, since incomplete or inaccurate information (for example, a sampling frame that does not cover the population it purports to cover) is often as misleading or more misleading than no information at all. The absence of sampling frames for individuals has been noted in the Somalian and Nepalese examples earlier. Robert Mitchell in Chapter 18 documents the poor quality and non-comparability of sampling frames used or compiled in a variety of Asian surveys. It is a common experience to find that no frame exists for the study of a given population, or it cannot be economically prepared. In the World Fertility Survey, for example, a pre-existing list of individual women has never been used in any country to identify those available for interview, because usually such lists have not been available, or if available they are not up to date or individuals are not traceable in the field (Verma, 1977, p. 104).

In some circumstances, it may be possible to use the records of the decennial census as a sampling frame. Apart from problems of invasion of privacy which this involves (and which in industrialized countries prevents this use of the census), census data on the location of individuals rapidly becomes out of date for sampling purposes, and is of doubtful value for much more than 1 year in any decade. Moreover, in most less-developed countries, such data is not published and so is only available to government researchers who can gain access to it.

In some countries, such as India, village authorities maintain population records, either of vital events or as a population register. These record systems potentially offer a means of sampling, but are seriously deficient. A review by

Lipton and Moore (1972, p. 52) shows that these records tend to be rather unreliable. For various reasons, they are incomplete and not a sound guide either for sampling or basic population counts.

Land records, particularly relating to revenue, appear to be a more promising source. In much of Asia they have been of great importance as land tax has been the principal means by which state and peasant came into contact. In many areas, such as most of India, the state has recruited people at village level to perform administrative functions and maintain land records. The most complete records exist for India and Pakistan, where they contain detailed information on ownership and use. Such records are not available in other states with shifting cultivation or pastoralism, or in much of Latin America, where land has not been taxed and the local power structure is different (Lipton and Moore, 1972, p. 47).

Such records, even where apparently complete, may be unsatisfactory due to inertia or deliberate distortion on the part of those maintaining them. Officials are paid little for their work on maintaining the records and have little incentive to update them. Deliberate distortion (either overstating or understating land ownership or use) occurs because of the use for tax purposes of the records. The investigator using the records for a village study needs to be wary (Lipton and Moore, 1972, pp. 48–51).

These cautions should not be taken to mean that probability sampling in the Third World is not possible. They do indicate, however, that sampling at the final stage from a list of individuals which provides adequate coverage is the exception rather than the rule. Alternatives have to be used which are less common in industrial societies, except for the study of special populations.

Alternatives to pre-existing frames

If pre-existing frames are inadequate, various alternatives have to be used. For example, for studies in rural areas, in particular, considerable reliance may have to be placed on aerial photography or mapping. Even in urban areas, such methods may be superior to reliance on inadequate or out of date census figures. R.C. Mitchell (1973), for example, has described the use of aerial photography to select a sample in a study of Ibadan, Nigeria. Wishing to draw a random sample from an area in which dwellings were haphazardly scattered and unnumbered, he used aerial photographs to make the selection. The method to use involves dividing the map of the area to be studied into a matrix of grid squares, each square is numbered in 'serpentine' fashion, and finally every *n*th grid square is selected from a random start, the skip-interval being determined by the sampling fraction (J. Ascroft in Kearl, 1976, p. 37).

The use of maps to select samples is more common, and is complementary to census-taking activities which usually require the preparation of adequate maps for the whole country (see Mabogunje, 1976). For the first and second stages of multistage surveys, available maps must be used, using selection processes based on grid squares on the map. When such squares have been randomly selected, then an attempt must be made to identify the area on the ground and (usually) list the population resident in that area for final-stage sampling. Maps may also be used for sampling purposes at the village level. If a village has been selected at an earlier stage, the investigator may find it more practicable to construct a simple map of the area from which to draw a probability sample, then to attempt to list the whole population. Such maps can be drawn to an acceptable standard without professional surveying experience, to provide a sample frame of dwellings (Lipton and Moore, 1972, pp. 43–46).

A particularly important point to establish (in rural surveys particularly) are the geographical boundaries of units: 'There have been many examples of surveys which have been badly damaged by failure to ensure that the boundaries of the units in the frame were precisely known and identifiable' (Casley and Lury, 1981, p. 74). A failure to include in the frame all parts of a settlement (for example, dwellings outside the main village) results in an incomplete frame and bias in the resulting sample drawn.

Area sampling

One type of sample design which is common in developing countries is an area sample. One type of list which is commonly available is a list of villages or settlements in a country, compiled for census or tax purposes. Provided this list is reliable and complete, it can be used to select a probability sample. In Frey's (1963) study of Turkish peasant attitudes, he sought a sample of all Turks 16 years and over resident in settlements of 2000 persons or less. The sample design was a two-stage cluster design, the first stage unit being villages and the second-stage unit villagers. The 1960 national census provided a list of all 35 000 villages in the country, together with their location and population. From this list, 458 villages were selected, stratifying by region and proximity to an urban centre, with probability proportionate to size.

Frey's team, at the second stage, explicitly rejected available village-level listings (of voters, and of residents, kept by central government and the village headman) as adequate sampling frames. Instead, in nine-tenths of villages these lists were used as a starting point, from which deletions (for the dead or those who had moved out) and additions (for those who had moved in, come of age, been missed, etc.) were made, with the help of village leaders and knowledgeable people. In one-tenth of the villages, no list was available, and a list had to be compiled from scratch by the interview team. In either case, the list created was used to generate a random sample of individuals age 16 and over for the second stage (Frey, 1963).

Such a multistage area sampling procedure is used in the Indian National Sample Survey, described in Chapter 9. The notable characteristic of such designs is that they narrow down the geographical area to be studied at the earlier stages. In preparation for the final sample selection, the fieldwork team prepares lists of the households or individuals to be sampled at the last stage.

A similar procedure has been adopted for many of the national studies forming part of the World Fertility Survey. There the main stages of the sample field operation have been:

(1) Creation of an area sampling frame (mapping).
(2) Listing of dwellings and/or households in areas selected at (1) (listing).
(3) Collection of fertility data on a 'large' sample drawn from (2) (the household schedule sample).
(4) Listing of household members at (3) to identify women eligible for the individual interview.
(5) The individual interview itself with women of childbearing age residing in households.

The experience of this very large project has shown that probability sampling can be carried out successfully in less developed countries.

The WFS has found an overwhelming majority of the countries to have available census enumeration districts, along with maps and some idea of population size, which are more or less suitable area units for selecting a strict probability sample of the required type. It is true that often the available materials fall short of the ideal; for example . . . area maps available may not be accurate, or data on population of the areas may be outdated. Nevertheless, in spite of these shortcomings the picture on the whole has been very encouraging . . . One of the most important conclusions to emerge from the WFS is that it is feasible to conduct surveys based on strict probability samples in most developing countries (Verma, 1977, p. 105).

The limitations of probability sampling

All sample design involves error, which may be divided into sampling and non-sampling error. Sampling error is the difference between a sample estimate and the population value that would have been found by a 100 per cent census conducted with identical procedures. In the absence of a complete enumeration, sampling errors are due to the inherent variations among population units. Provided that probability sampling methods are used to select the sample, sampling errors can be calculated statistically to provide estimates of population values from sample values (Moser and Kalton, 1971, pp. 61–78; Warwick and Lininger, 1975, pp. 82–94).

Non-sampling errors are errors arising from other causes which lead to the measurement of a value being distorted and rendered inaccurate. Such errors very frequently arise from procedural deficiencies in the conduct of sampling or other stages of an inquiry. For example, the exclusion of units in the population from the sampling frame will lead to bias in the sample which is a source of non-sampling error in the survey results. In contrast to sampling error, non-sampling error is very difficult to detect and estimate. Many of the later sections of this book are concerned with various sources of non-sampling error.

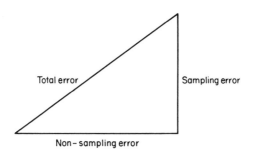

Fig. 7.1

Total error may be represented by a triangle (Figure 7.1). All social inquiry involves error, and the basis of sound design is to try to minimize error so far as possible. It is apparent from Figure 7.1 that reducing sampling error alone will be inadequate to reduce total error, and the reduction in total error will be less than the corresponding reduction in sampling error. Reduction in error requires attention to both sampling and non-sampling errors, and attention to sampling errors alone (for example, by increasing sample size) yields diminishing returns.

This is particularly likely to be the case in surveys in developing countries, where control of non-sampling errors depends on a number of factors such as well-defined concepts, adequate operational definitions, clear cut instructions to field staff, literacy, knowledge and cooperation from respondents, living conditions, background, experience and workload of field staff, transport and communication, adequacy of supervision, and other factors 'over which the survey statistician has minimal or no control at all' (Murthy, 1978, p. 246). The extent and seriousness of non-sampling errors, discussed by Michael Ward in Chapter 10 and Robert Mitchell in Chapter 18, as well as throughout sections IV and V of this book, suggest that they may be greater than sampling errors. Ward cites a West African study which suggests they are four times as great. An Indian study suggests they may be six times as great in magnitude as sampling errors (Casley and Lury, 1981, p. 87).

In development research in academic disciplines such as sociology, anthropology and political science, non-probability sampling is more common than probability sampling due to 'indefinite populations, unavailable sampling frames, small budgets, lack of time, inexperienced personnel, pressure for results and the like' (Hursh-César and Roy, 1976, p. 194). Probability sampling on a national scale such as that used in the Indian National Sample Survey or the World Fertility Survey is more readily undertaken by relatively well-funded governments or international bodies.

Research planning, however, often offers choices between different kinds of sample design. Non-probability, judgemental or purposive samples may be drawn in a variety of ways, such as quota samples, volunteer samples, chunk samples and snowball samples. All are significantly cheaper than true probability designs, which can be very expensive, but none have the theoretical basis which permits the estimation of population parameters from the sample values. The use of the method rests on the hope that units are uniformly distributed and so the resulting sample will be 'typical'. In practice, however, this is rarely the case. For example, a quota or 'chunk' sample selected in a market place is most unlikely to be representative of a population, since systematic bias is built into the geographical location in which people are found (see Moser and Stuart, 1953).

However, the likely extent of non-sampling errors in surveys in developing countries has led some commentators to question the absolute value of probability sampling *per se*. This view is most strongly expressed here by Michael Ward in Chapter 10, though it is also implicit in Section VI on methodological marriages. Ward argues that smaller-scale qualitative case studies may yield just as useful data as attempts at large-scale probability samples which yield unsatisfactory data (he cites income and expenditure surveys as an example).

Certainly, there are circumstances in which non-probability sampling may be preferred. If the objective is not to obtain a representative sample but to study a few cases, identify problems or generate hypotheses, then it is certainly appropriate. Where a sampling frame is unavailable and cost considerations preclude the creation of one, random sampling may be ruled out. Non-probability sampling is also appropriate when describing systems or institutions of which there are only a few, so that statistical procedures are not called for — for example, in studies of a single village, firm or government department.

It can also be argued that in a homogeneous population or under assumed conditions of homogeneity, non-probability sampling is acceptable. When you describe one unit, you describe all units. In a study of agricultural enterprise in Nigeria, this was explicitly used as a justification for judgemental sampling. There tended to be a uniform degree of capitalization in traditional farming, labour still represented the dominant input and adoption of agricultural innovations had been fairly uniform. The possibility of extensive variation in resource endowment and enterprise combination was much reduced, and the departure from probability sample selection was justified (Kearl, 1976, p. 44). How far conditions of homogeneity exist is, however, an empirical question in each case, and cannot be treated as a blanket justification for the use of non-probability methods in sample selection. Those who adopt such methods have to recognize that they are substituting intuitive judgement for scientifically measurable probability. Sampling errors cannot be calculated from the sample, and the potential magnitude of sampling bias is unknown.

References

Bergsten, J.W. (1980). Some sample survey design problems in Syria, Nepal and Somalia, *Proceedings of the Section on Survey Research Methods*, pp. 72–74, American Statistical Association, Washington DC.

Casley, D.J. and Lury, D.A. (1981). *Data Collection in Developing Countries*, Clarendon Press, Oxford.

Frey, F.W. (1963). Surveying peasant attitudes in Turkey. *Public Opinion Quarterly*, **27**, 335–355.

Hansen, M.H., Hurwitz, W.N. and Madow, W.G. (1953). *Sample Survey Methods and Theory. Vol. I. Methods and Applications. Vol. II. Theory*, Wiley, New York.

Hursh-César, G. and Roy, P. (eds.) (1976). *Third World Surveys*, Macmillan of India, Delhi.

Kearl, B. (ed.) (1976). *Field Data Collection in the Social Sciences: Experiences in Africa and the Middle East*, Agricultural Development Council Inc., New York.

Kish, L. (1965). *Survey Sampling*, Wiley, New York.

Lipton, M. and Moore, M. (1972). *The Methodology of Village Studies in Less Developed Countries, IDS discussion paper no. 10*, Institute of Development Studies, Falmer, Sussex.

Mabogunje, A.L. (1976). The population census of Nigeria 1973. In J.T. Coppock and W.R.D. Sewell (Eds) *Spatial Dimensions of Public Policy*, pp. 207–226, Pergamon, Oxford.

Mitchell, R.C. (1973). Using aerial photography to select samples. In W.M. O'Barr *et al.* (Eds) *Survey Research in Africa: Its Applications and Limits*, pp. 100–106, Northwestern University Press, Evanston, Ill.

Moser, C.A. and Kalton, G. (1971). *Survey Methods in Social Investigation*, Heinemann, London.

Moser, C.A. and Stuart, A. (1953). An experimental study of quota sampling. *Journal of the Royal Statistical Society A*, **116**, 349–405.

Murthy, M.N. (1978). Use of sample surveys in national planning in developing countries. In N.K. Nambooditi (Ed) *Survey Sampling and Measurement*, pp. 231–253, Academic Press, New York.

Warwick, D.P. and Lininger, C. (1975). *The Sample Survey: Theory and Practice*, McGraw-Hill, New York.

World Fertility Survey (1975). *Manual on Sample Design*. The International Statistical Institute, The Hague.

Verma, V. (1977). Sample designs for the World Fertility Survey. *Bulletin of the International Statistical Institute*, **46(3)**, 101–117.

Verma, V. *et al.* (1980). Sample designs and sampling errors for the World Fertility Survey. *Journal of the Royal Statistical Society A*, **143**, 431–473.

Yates, F. (1949). *Sampling Methods for Censuses and Surveys*, Griffin, London.

Zarkovich, S.S. (1975). *Statistical Development*, Cairo University Press, Cairo.

Social Research in Developing Countries
Edited by M. Bulmer and D.P. Warwick
© 1983, John Wiley & Sons, Ltd.

CHAPTER 8

SOME PROBLEMS OF SAMPLING WORK IN UNDERDEVELOPED COUNTRIES

SLOBODAN S. ZARKOVICH

Introduction

Many projects are going on at the present time in various parts of the world which have as their aim assistance to underdeveloped countries in starting the work on application of sampling methods or preparing programmes for some specific activities in this field. A prerequisite for successful planning of these projects is an adequate picture of the problems which arise in sampling work under the conditions in these countries. This paper is an attempt to point out some of these problems without pretending that either the field is exhausted or implying that the problems mentioned were properly dealt with.

Limitations in resources

The first thing which strikes a sampler from developed countries when he starts studying conditions for sampling work in an underdeveloped country is the paucity of resources available. This fact has a considerable bearing upon basic aspects of sampling. The ideal of optimum designing will be mentioned here as a typical example. When we speak about optimum designs in developed countries, where a variety of means and tools are available, we always have in mind a large number of designs. The underlying assumption of an optimum design is the possibility of choice from among a number of alternatives. If some designs are neglected or some resources used more and others less, our preferences are not due to the non-availability of alternatives but to the requirements imposed by the optimum philosophy. We fix the size of the sample at a certain level although there is no difficulty, in principle, in using any

Reprinted by permission of the publisher and the author from *Bulletin of the International Statistical Institute*, **3**, (1960), 249–255. © 1960, International Statistical Institute.

smaller size and very often a number of larger samples as well. In some types of statistics we use clustering of elementary units and fix the average size of clusters but we are free, if optimum considerations are neglected, to use whatever we want within a wide range of cluster sizes. The same is true with the number of stages of selection, number of the enumerators to be used, the size of primary units, the number of strata, etc.

It will be very often found that in underdeveloped countries the possibilities for the choice are seriously limited in almost any respect. The following illustration is more or less the model of the situation. The example refers to the sample census of agriculture which was taken in Basutoland in 1949–50 as a substitute for the complete enumeration census (Douglas and Tennant, 1952). The study of the conditions revealed that sufficiently accurate data on areas and yields, which were basic survey information, could be obtained only by applying the objective methods. This was the first limitation as to the methodology to be used. As a further stage it was found that ten Europeans were the only staff available to carry out the measurements as crew leaders. This was another limitation because of which the size of the sample had to be fixed in accordance with the possibilities of the available ten persons. A further fact bearing on the design was that measuring the areas of fields could start shortly after ploughing and last until the late stages of crop growth, i.e. the survey could be extended over a period of 7 months; in this way an upper limit was placed on the size of the sample. Later is was also seen that a two-stage design was the only practically feasible one. Finally, it became clear that within the period of time available, each crew could only cover two primary units with the second-stage sampling fraction which was also determined by the average work load possible within the time left at disposal on each primary unit.

Similar examples of the restrictions imposed on sampling work in underdeveloped countries are numerous today and very well known. What is important for us here is the meaning of these limitations.First of all, under these conditions the design is imposed more by the circumstances of the work than by the sampler's knowledge and skill. Designing sample surveys becomes more a study of limitations and their sampling implications, than an exercise of principles and type of work leading to an optimum design in developed countries. Quite often the only frame available is lists of villages. For most types of interview surveys this immediately means a two-stage design. Since no information on villages is available at all it further means equal probabilities of selection. It also often means unbiased estimates because nothing else can be used in the process of estimation. The creative function of the sampler is largely reduced here; the possibilities given to him for combining and choosing from among a variety of solutions are meagre; the optimum design philosophy can be applied in a reduced amount only.

Obviously enough, efficiency becomes a serious problem under such conditions. In some of the countries involved surveys were taken in which totals for a large number of characteristics had to be estimated from a design where primary sampling units were selected with equal probabilities from lists of highly variable villages. Another typical design often followed is the selection of a small number of primary units due to lack of enumerators and transport and a consequent increasing of the number of second-stage units. The low efficiency of such surveys causes many problems and also leads to moral difficulties for the samplers. They are aware that the designs they adopt are considered inefficient compared to the cases discussed in books based on western conditions, and in order to improve them from this point of view as far as possible, they deviate sometimes from theoretically sound procedures. Cases will often be found such as the use of substitutes for 'not-at-homes' and refusals, measuring areas under particular crops over a long period in order to give data on harvested areas, using substitutes for the fields already harvested in crop cutting work, cutting the immature crop, etc. By doing so the difficulties encountered with low efficiency and low precision are broadened because of biases in data.

Accuracy limitations

The study of statistics is basically a product of western development. In a country which was not influenced by this development statistical work will be confronted with more or less serious troubles: those resulting from limitations in resources; and those connected with accuracy limitations. The latter will be our concern in this section.

It was pointed out that in developed countries respondents, in general, understand statistical jargon; concepts and definitions used in questionnaires and instructions convey to most people a more or less definite meaning; units recommended for expressing answers belong to the vocabulary the people are using; collaboration with various statistical inquiries is a part of the tradition of these countries; respondents understand the need of collecting data and often use statistics themselves for various purposes, etc. In underdeveloped countries, however, it may be quite different. For example, in many parts of the world the people have no idea whatsoever of various units used in statistics. Asking for areas harvested and yields are rather vague questions. The difficulties in getting answers to some common questions in statistics are sometimes incredible. A report from Africa reads:

For the general African population, individual ages have little significance and 15 and 50 could mean exactly the same. The African appreciates the small baby, the small boy, the child, the adult, the old. He can picture them in his mind's eye. Therefore, the problem was to give the questions to the African in a pictorial form, in a form he could appreciate (Martin, 1949).

These people are afraid of the consequences collection of statistical data might have on their taxes and other contributions they are obliged to make. They are often superstitious and believe statistics might be connected with magic forces.

There is nothing that the Bedouin hates more than for a person to come to him and ask him his name, or the name of his father, or brother, or wife, or son. Or for a person to ask him what tribe he belongs to and how many children he has, or his relationship to this or that person. He also hates to reply to you if you ask him what about the location of his tent or whence he has come or where he is going (Aref, 1947).

In East Africa there is a belief that counting people will do harm to somebody; in some tribes the mother will never say the number of children she has borne; in many other provinces a male enumerator will never be allowed to talk to the women, etc. (Goldthorpe, 1952; Harvie, 1950; Martin, 1949, 1953; Seng, 1949; Shaul, 1952; Shaul and Myburgh, 1948; 1949).

The obvious tendency on the part of the sampler in such conditions is to try to avoid situations where the accuracy of his data depends upon respondents. A remarkable result of this tendency is the appearance of objective methods as they are known, first of all, in agricultural statistics and practised in estimating areas and yields. On the other hand, the conditions for sampling work in underdeveloped countries gave a considerable impetus to the study of errors and biases. One should not forget, however, that the idea of interpenetrating samples appeared in a country with serious accuracy limitations, that considerable work was done in India in studying errors and biases of yield statistics based on crop cutting, that the role of pilot surveys was better understood in view of the conditions in underdeveloped countries, etc.

Accuracy limitations lead to the paradoxical situation in which underdeveloped countries have to apply more complicated methods than those used in developed countries. A glance at the objective methods in agricultural statistics is enough to realize this problem. In yield statistics the size of plots has an important bearing on the results. So does the type of crop, the size of fields, the moment at which cutting was performed, the care in carrying out the work, etc. In area statistics, the result depends upon the accuracy of measurement of each particular leg and each particular angle. Personnel of a rather high standard is thus assumed in many activities. Since no previous experience is available as to the most adequate procedure and solution concerning a large number of items which determine or influence the accuracy, considerable amount of experimentation is needed as a prerequisite for reliable data. Planning such experiments and analysing the results obtained again requires specialized professional personnel who are not often available even in developed countries. This is the first paradox of sampling in underdeveloped areas which we would like to mention.

The second is connected with expenditure. If objective methods have to be applied, it means the use of rather expensive tools. First of all, it assumes an availability of instruments for measuring distances, angles, weight, volume, etc.; special transportation is then needed because little use can be made of public transport; teams of field workers are indispensable because workers on their own need backup provisions, etc. There is no need to comment on how costly this system of work is in comparison with mail surveys or reporting system as used in some developed countries. The same is true with the experimentation costs, extensive control of all the operations, the need for longer training, etc. Generally speaking, we have the feeling that sampling in under-developed countries involves some additional expenditure as compared to practices in more developed countries, and this is what we call the second paradox of the use of sampling in underdeveloped countries.

The size of the sample

It is a widely known fact that there is a good deal of confusion involved in thinking of the size of the sample and the aimed-at precision in many surveys taken in underdeveloped countries. However, someone from an under-developed country may easily say that the same is true with sample surveys in highly developed countries.

The size of the sample is, in principle, a well-defined problem in the case of a single variable and the magnitude of sampling error stated. In modern surveys, however, with a large number of characteristics on the programme and the estimates intended to satisfy entirely unspecified uses, fixing up the size of the sample is very arbitrary. The items involved are usually differently distributed, and any fixed size of the sample produces errors scattered over a wide range of magnitudes. There is a way of thinking that the precision should be defined for some basic items, while the others are estimated with the precision obtained. The application of this idea leads to a difficulty of ranking the importance of various items in the absence of any specification of future uses and the precision in which the users might be interested. In addition to this, at the present time we are producing estimates for the country as a whole and a number of provinces. In the case where the latter is more or equally important as the former, the existence of such a rank list would not help much because the characteristics dealt with are usually differently distributed by provinces with the result that the precision of provincial estimates for 'important' items will again vary considerably. We have a feeling that in this situation the size of the sample is more a matter of convenience (such as 1 or 10 per cent) or routine (3–5 per cent is usually discussed in books and often applied in past surveys) than of real justification. It is difficult to believe that in surveys with many items on the programme and the estimates presented by, say, ten provinces, 1 per cent more or less in the precision of estimates changes substantially the usefulness of data.

The existence of an established tradition, justified or not, is missing in underdeveloped countries and it leads to serious troubles while determining the size of the sample in a survey. The aimed-at precision which is used in sample surveys in western countries cannot be achieved in most cases because of the limitation in resources or accuracy. If because of these reasons the estimates by provinces have the precision of the order of 12 per cent on average, the question arises whether 15 or 20 per cent would not also represent a satisfactory precision. Samplers would welcome this possibility.

Here we come back to the question of the purpose of surveys with many items on the programme. There is a feeling that in underdeveloped countries the estimates should, in principle, be less precise than in developed countries. For justification one says that in developed countries figures are often used as a basis for action whereas in underdeveloped areas they are not supposed to give more than a general orientation about the field concerned. This problem is certainly a metastatistical one which can be easier discussed in terms of a concrete situation. In any case, however, the question remains as to what should be the precision of estimates intended for general information? In an underdeveloped country the yield of a crop for the country as a whole was estimated with a precision of 4 per cent; provincial estimates were between 10 and 20 per cent. We asked for reasons of fixing the size of the sample at the level selected and the answer given was the question: what are the arguments against this size? We disagreed entirely in evaluating the situation. The same type of disagreement we found elsewhere too and this is just the reason to believe that very little guidance, if any, is available in this field.

The role of the theory

Is the knowledge of the theory necessary for designing sample surveys in underdeveloped countries? This question arises automatically after the limitations in resources are pointed out. As a matter of fact, almost all the designs of surveys conducted in various underdeveloped countries that we have a chance to see were very simple from the theoretical point of view; the theory used did not cross narrow borders of a rather elementary course on sample surveys and it gives the impression that nothing else is needed.

This impression is definitely misleading. The situation in any underdeveloped country is hardly every such that the design to be used is determined in all its details; the conditions are rarely, if at all, such that no action whatsoever can be taken to secure more choice and more freedom in planning. If the list of villages is the only frame available with the number of qualified enumerators fixed and a period of 1 month at disposal for carrying out the field work, it would be in general a very poor design if every enumerator were assigned two primary units (because of difficult transport) and instructed to do as intensive subsampling as possible. As drastic as the restrictions may be in such a case they still leave a good deal of choice and bring about a number of questions. What is the optimum second-stage sampling fraction within the fixed number of primary units? What are the components of variation between and within primary units? Would it not be better to start training more enumerators many months in advance of the survey, and by these means increase the number of primary units instead of running the risk of a survey with insufficiently precise data? How about an investment in more cars? Would it not be more efficient to increase the number of stages, particularly in agricultural statistics for purposes of yield data? A large number of similar questions could be asked assuming the conditions stated. Each of them represents a more or less worthwhile alternative in designing the survey. Which one is the more efficient? The answer may require long studies and possibly pilot surveys which can be planned properly and analysed only by a person with a complete knowledge of the theory. The theory is thus the only guidance in an objective study of relative merits of various alternative solutions and no substitute can be found for it. Such a study may result in a simple design which has the quality of being the most adequate at a given moment only if accepted after a full review of theoretical possibilities within the conditions given. In this respect there is no difference between a developed and a underdeveloped country.

After reviewing the accuracy limitations, however, we have to say that the sampler working in underdeveloped countries has to be, in some respects, better equipped with theory than his colleague in a developed country where without previous pilot surveys and special provisions for securing acceptable accuracy, such as intensive field checking and the like, the results are not likely to lose their practical usefulness. Favourable social background, previous experiences, trained and experienced field personnel, and many other factors act as if intensive studies of errors were conducted and adequate measures were applied to eliminate errors. In underdeveloped countries, however, the inaccuracy may be catastrophic if the problem of non-sampling errors was not studied systematically before the survey was taken. The conditions are unfavourable by definition; there is no tradition; there is no previous experience on which to base decisions, etc. Accordingly, any major decision has to be preceded by experiments and studies. In addition, various phases of the execution of the work have to be accompanied by some checks with the aim of determining to what extent the expectations were achieved and what is the magnitude of errors left over. Responsibility for this work assumes an indispensable knowledge of some theories that are usually only roughly dealt with in a formal training in the theory of sample surveys. Besides, it requires a knowledge of a large variety of experiences from various surveys which can be useful in later work as an indicator of tools and measures to be applied when faced with corresponding problems. This is an additional knowledge which in underdeveloped countries has to supplement the theory of sample surveys in its classical formulation.

References

Aref el Aref (1947). Justice among the Bedouins. Jerusalem, 1953. In S.W. Dajani

(Ed.), The enumeration of the Beersheba Bedouins in May 1946. *Population Studies*, I, 301–380.

Douglas, A.J.A. and Tennant, R.K. (1952) *Basutoland Agricultural Survey 1949–50*. Basutoland Government, Masern.

Goldthorpe, J.E. (1952). Attitudes to the census and vital registration in East Africa, *Population Studies*, 6, 163–171.

Harvie, G.H. (1950). A sampling census in the Sudan. *Population Studies*. 4, 241–249.

Martin, C.J. (1949). The East African population census, 1948: planning and enumeration, *Population Studies*, 3, 303–320.

Martin, C.J. (1953) The collection of basic demographic data in underdeveloped territories. *Bulletin of the International Statistical Institute*, 34(3), 17–27.

Seng, Yon Poh (1949). Practical problems in sampling for social and demographic inquiries in underdeveloped countries. *Population Studies*, 3, 170–191.

Shaul, J.R.H. (1952). Sampling surveys in Central Africa. *Journal of the American Statistical Association*, 47, 239–254.

Shaul, J.R.H. and Myburgh, C.A.L. (1948) A sample survey of the African population of Southern Rhodesia, *Population Studies*, 2, 339–353.

Shaul, J.R.H. and Myburgh, C.A.L. (1949). Provisional results of the sample survey of the African population of Southern Rhodesia, 1948. *Population Studies*, 3, 274–285.

Social Research in Developing Countries
Edited by M. Bulmer and D.P. Warwick
© 1983, John Wiley & Sons, Ltd.

CHAPTER 9

DEVELOPMENT OF THE SAMPLE DESIGN OF THE INDIAN NATIONAL SAMPLE SURVEY DURING ITS FIRST 25 ROUNDS

M.N. MURTHY
AND
A.S. ROY

Introduction

History and objectives

The absence of reliable and adequate statistics relating to production, consumption and other aspects of economic and social life in India had been felt for a long time. Since the advent of independence in India in 1947, the government became increasingly aware of this lacuna and recognized the urgent need for improving the quality and quantity of statistical data. As a consequence of this realization the Indian National Sample Survey (NSS) was set up in 1950 by the late Professor P.C. Mahalanobis with the active support of the late Jawaharlal Nehru, who was the Prime Minister of India at that time. The NSS was started with the objective of filling up the gaps in essential statistics by collecting comprehensive information relating to agricultural, demographic, economic, and social characteristics through continuing and country-wide integrated multisubject sample surveys.

Being a large-scale, continuing and nationwide multisubject sample survey, the NSS has evoked considerable interest regarding its survey design among professional statisticians and economists. The object of this paper is to give an account of the main aspects of the general sample design and the special techniques adopted to meet specific situations arising from time to time. Some

Reprinted with the permission of the editors of *Sankhyá* and the authors, and with abridgements agreed by the authors, from *Sankhyá: the Indian Journal of Statistics*, Series C, **37 (1)** (1975), 1–42. © 1975, Indian Statistical Institute.

of the salient features of the NSS are briefly described in the following paragraphs and others are discussed in detail in subsequent sections.

Geographical coverage

The NSS covers the entire rural and urban areas of the country with the exception of a few small tracts which are excluded from the scope of the survey mainly on operational and administrative considerations.

Rounds of survey

The NSS is a continuing survey in the sense that it is carried out in the form of successive *rounds*, each round covering several topics of current interest in a specific survey period. Each round is a distinct entity regarding its scope, sample design and programme which are determined by taking into account the requirements of the users, the resources available and the past experience, and with provision for, when considered necessary, complete or partial repetition of the units between successive rounds. Since 1958–59, each round has generally been of 1 year's duration spread over the agricultural year July to June.

Subjects of inquiry

The wide variety of inquiries so far conducted by the NSS can be broadly divided into three classes: socioeconomic (including demographic) inquiries, agricultural surveys and industrial inquiries with the first group concentrating on the household sector of the economy, the second on fields and the third on establishments. The subjects covered more or less regularly in the past few rounds are: household consumer expenditure; employment and unemployment; population, births, deaths; rural retail prices; and area and production of major cereal crops. Data on small-scale enterprises, professions and services, landholdings, debt, savings and investment, capital formation, housing condition, farming practices, economic condition of rural labourers, family planning and migration have also been taken in up several rounds of the NSS.

Methods of data collection

In the NSS the general approach has been to collect information relating to socioeconomic inquiries from a sample of households spread over a sample of villages and blocks, information on prices from a sample of shops and markets and data on crop particulars from a sample of crop fields. (Villages have an average population of about 700 in Indian rural areas; blocks are area subdivisions of urban areas with an average population of 800.) The data collection in the NSS is done by a team of permanent, full-time and well-trained investigators. They collect data on socioeconomic enquiries by the *interview method* by actually contacting the sampled households, persons, shops, etc. For crop survey, the investigators visit sampled fields and collect data by *physical observation* for area survey and by *measurement* (actually harvesting and weighing the crop in a sample area) for estimating yield-rate.

Generally the data collected from a sample unit are recorded in a *schedule* devised, for the concerned inquiry. The schedule approach is preferred to the questionnaire approach since the latter is not suitable when the literacy rate is not very high among the respondents and the items on which data are collected are not easily understood by the respondents, who mostly belong to the traditional sectors of the economy. The NSS enquiries usually consist of a large number of items many of which cannot be easily put in the form of simple questions; in this respect the schedule is more compact, flexible and suitable for tabulation than a questionnaire. Further, it is not generally possible at the time of preparing the questionnaires to visualize all possible cases that one might come across at the time of actual inquiry and to prepare standard questions covering all eventualities. Once the items on which information is required and necessary concepts, definitions and procedures are given, the investigator is in a better position to collect data by framing and asking questions suited to the exigencies of the situation instead of by asking a pre-specified set of questions.

Moving reference period

In the NSS, the *reference period* for socioeconomic household inquiries is usually the date of survey, or a week, a month or a year preceeding the date of survey. That is, the reference period is a *moving* one when the entire sample is considered because the canvassing of the sample is spread over a complete year. The moving reference period has two advantages over the fixed reference period: it entails less recall error and secondly it furnishes a better estimate of the seasonal and overall values of the characteristics. In case of crop surveys, the data are collected for crop seasons.

The length of the reference period varies, depending on the nature of the items. For example, it is *date of survey* for demographic particulars, such as age, sex and marital status, *a week* for employment and unemployment particulars, *a month* for consumer expenditure, particulars of enterprises, etc. and a *year* for incidence of births and deaths.

Periodic progressive estimates

The Indian economy, being largely dependent on agriculture, is subject to pronounced seasonal fluctuations, and hence the survey period of the NSS rounds has been made *one complete year* so that all the seasons are fully covered by the survey. Staggering the survey over a long period like a year has one more advantage — it requires a lesser number of investigators than would be required with a shorter survey period. Further, estimates can be obtained on the basis of samples surveyed in different subrounds in order to study the seasonal variations and to compute periodic progressive estimates.

Problems of sampling frame

Sampling frame

A sampling frame gives an enumeration of all the sampling units in the population along with their identification particulars (addresses, location particulars, or boundaries, etc.), so that each and every unit can be clearly identified in the field. A sampling frame should be accurate, free from omissions and duplications and up to date. The frame becomes more useful if, in addition to meeting the above basic requirements, it also contains relevant auxiliary information for each unit, which can be utilized at the stage of planning, sample selection and/or estimation for reducing the overall sampling error or reducing the cost for given sampling error, and for increasing the multiplicity of subjects or increasing the depth of investigation for given subjects when the total cost is fixed.

For most of the situations commonly met with in practice, the sampling frames can broadly be divided into two types: (a) list frame and (b) area or map frame. While the former is a list of units (not necessarily area units) with their identification particulars, the latter is a list or map of area units which are definite parcels of land and can be identified on the ground with the help of boundary particulars given in the frame or/and map. Examples of list frame are provided by a list of factories; a list of revenue villages with the maps of the villages, which are area units, is an example of an area frame. A village map showing boundaries of plots within it is a map or area frame.

Frames used in the NSS

One of the main requirements for efficiently designing a multisubject survey sample is a set of complete and up-to-date sampling frames equipped with information on suitably chosen auxiliary variables. Hence, it would be worthwhile to examine the sampling frames used by the NSS (or for similar surveys in India) and to suggest some ways for their improvement. In the NSS design the first-stage units are *area units* (that is, *villages* in rural areas and *blocks* in urban areas) and the second-stage units are *households* for socioeconomic enquiries and *plots* for crop surveys. So frames for the villages/blocks are required for the whole of India and frames of households and plots for the selected villages and blocks. A detailed discussion on the use of population census as a source of sampling frame for various surveys is given by Murthy (1969).

Rural frame of census villages

In rural areas of India, the census villages which are the smallest area units, having an average population of about 700, are the most common and convenient first-stage sampling units for any large-scale household enquiries or crop surveys. The rural frame used in the NSS is *the list of census villages* supplied by the decennial population census (the latest one being in 1971). The census publications give a complete list of villages, for each *tehsil* in the country, along with their idetification particulars as well as supplementary information on several items for each village, e.g., area, population, number of houses and households, number of literates, number of workers in nine different occupational groups such as cultivation, agricultural labour, trade, transport, manufacture, services, etc. The publications also give district maps showing the boundaries of component tehsils. (A *tehsil* is an administrative unit comprising on average 200 villages; a district is a larger unit comprising on average 7 *tehsils*).

This list of census villages is perhaps the only sampling frame for the whole of rural India mainly because no other complete list of villages (or similar area units) is available at one place or in published form. But apart from this compelling reason, the census frame is satisfactory in other respects also. First, the major part of the census frame relates to a fixed point of time, 1 March of the census year. Second, the concepts, definitions and procedures of census taking are fairly uniform throughout India and hence the census frame represents a uniform and consistent body of data. Third, the census gives a host of supplementary information which, if used with care and skill, can help in evolving an efficient sample design.

However, one should not get the impression that the census frame leaves nothing to be desired. Some drawbacks of the census frame of villages and in what ways they have been tackled in the NSS are briefly discussed here.

(1) The village list becomes backdated a few years after the census has been conducted. Between two successive censuses, some villages are declared as urban areas, some villages go out of existence due to natural causes such as floods or due to new construction of roads and projects, while some new villages come up from forests and vacant lands.

Fortunately, the extent of such changes in the population is quite small and does not affect much the survey results. Moreover, this is taken care of by making suitable adjustments to the extent feasible at the time of tabulation.

(2) Some of the villages are very big in area and population, and hence are difficult to survey within a reasonable time limit. A practical solution for this problem consists in subdividing a large village into several compact and identifiable subdivisions of nearly equal population content, and

conducting the survey in one of the subdivisions selected at random.

(3) In a few cases the census villages are artificially demarcated by temporary boundaries for census purposes and such villages tend to become unidentifiable with the passage of time. One procedure in such cases has been to take the revenue village corresponding to the census village as the unit of survey and then to make necessary adjustments during tabulation, taking into account the information such as the number of census villages comprising the revenue village.

(4) The census frame does not generally give figures for cultivated area, number of manufacturing, trading and transport establishments in the village. With these data, the census frame would have been more suitable for enquiries on landholdings and household and non-household enterprises. This lacuna in the census frame can be partially compensated by matching it with other frames (if available) showing village-wise data for the required characteristic.

Urban sampling frame of blocks

The urban frame is the list of census *enumeration blocks* demarcated during the decennial population census. These blocks, which are small subdivisions of towns and cities, are the smallest units with an average population of about 800 for which the census data (same as for villages) are published for the urban sector. Up to the 15th round (1959–60) of the NSS, the list of census blocks was the only sampling frame for the urban areas. But the census blocks were proving to be unsatisfactory due to the following reasons: (a) they are not well-demarcated area units with clear boundaries in many cases; (b) they are usually describe in terms of census house numbers which often get defaced or erased over a period of time. As a result, the census blocks become less and less identifiable with the passage of time and the risk of wrong coverage and undercoverage increases. The need for a better urban frame led to the initiation of the *urban frame survey* (UFS) in 1959–60.

Urban frame survey

The object of this survey was to demarcate the area of a city/town into urban blocks that would remain identifiable over a long period of time and that would minimize the risk of wrong and undercoverage mentioned earlier. To achieve these objectives, it was ensured tht the newly formed blocks (a) covered the *whole area* (as at the time of survey) of a town/city including vacant plots, (b) were compact area units, (c) were bounded on all sides by stable, well-demarcated and easily identifiable boundaries like streets, lanes, canals, big buildings, etc., and (d) contained 150 to 200 households. After demarcating the blocks (called UFS blocks) on field, a set of maps and schedules was prepared, the maps showing the locations and boundaries of the blocks and the schedules giving detailed description of the boundaries, and also estimating number of households, population and locality type code for each block. The UFS has been completed for about 2300 towns of India. Hence two sampling frames are used for the urban areas — the UFS frame for these 2300 towns and the census frame for the remaining 600 towns not yet covered by the UFS.

Sampling frame for second-stage units

The frames of second-stage units (households and plots) are prepared or collected by the investigators only for the sample villages and blocks. After arriving at a sample village/block, the investigator prepared a complete and up-to-date list of households residing in it. During this listing, he also collects for each household some information which can be utilized to increase the efficiency of household selection, estimation of parameters or/and analysis of results. The nature of information, to be collected, of course, depends on the subjects of enquiry of that round.

For crop survey, the frame is the revenue map of the village, or in its absence, a list of plots in the village. The map shows the survey numbers (identification), locations and boundaries of all plots in the village. The list gives the survey numbers and sometimes plot areas also. The investigator collects the map or the list from the village office, revenue officials, etc. Maps or lists of plots are available for about 96 per cent of villages. When neither map nor list is available, then a sample of households is selected from the household list, and plots possessed by them are surveyed.

General strategy of sample design

Basic sample design

The basic design of the NSS like that of many large-scale sample surveys, is built around a stratified sampling scheme with unistage or multistage selection in each stratum. India being a federation of states, each state is naturally taken as a domain of study and is divided into several strata of compact areas. Within each stratum, a two-stage or three-stage scheme is adopted for sampling of households and plots, which are the ultimate units for socioeconomic inquiries and crop area surveys. Details of stratification, sampling methods, etc. are given in the subsequent sections. The distinguishing features of the NSS design are being described below. Since the 4th round (1952), the design has been made partially self-weighting for one or more household inquiries of each round.

Multisubject integrated survey

The NSS is a prominent example of the multisubject integrated survey system. A multisubject survey is one in which several subjects of inquiry, not necessarily very closely related, are simultaneously canvassed in a single joint survey operation for the sake of economy, operational convenience, greater scope and better analysis. A multisubject survey is regarded as an integrated survey if the data on different subjects are collected from the same sample of ultimate stage units (*complete integration*), or from the same sample of higher stage units with different samples of ultimate units (*partial integration*) which may or may not be of the same type. Multisubject integrated surveys are generally recognized to be more convenient and economical than a series of non-integrated unisubject surveys, provided that the subjects of inquiry are not so numerous and diversified as to affect the quality of data. In fact, sometimes the NSS has adopted the completely integrated approach in respect of many interdependent household characteristics by canvassing an integrated household schedule which gives a complete account of various demographic and economic particulars for a common set of sample households. In most of the rounds, however, the strategy has been a partially integrated approach by having a *common sample* of villages and blocks within which sampling of households is done *separately* for different household enquiries. In both the cases, crop survey is conducted in the same sample of villages as selected for household enquiries.

The economy of this system stems from the fact that a sizeable portion of the total expenditure (that spent on overhead, organization, journey to sample points, camp-setting and preparation/collection of frames of households and plots) becomes common for the subject integrated. This considerable saving is utilized for increasing the sample size of first-stage units, thereby improving the efficiency of the design. Also this increase in sample at the first stage facilitates deeper stratification, taking into account information on several auxiliary characteristics. Further, integration of inquiries make the work of data collection more worthwhile since the investigator has to stay in the sample villages/blocks for a longer time, and this longer stay helps to obtain data of better quality and to reduce the idle-time of the investigators. A multisubject integrated survey gives a wide cross-section of the economy and helps to study the relationship among items belonging to different subjects of inquiry.

A detailed discussion of the advantages and problems of multisubject surveys can be found in Lahiri (1963). Murthy (1968; 1974) and United Nations (1964).

Use of parallel samples

An important feature of the NSS has been the use of the technique of parallel samples for the study and assessment of sampling and non-sampling errors in the survey results. The technique, also known as replicated sampling, and originally developed by Mahalanobis in the 1930s consists in drawing the total sample in the form of two or more parallel and independent samples, termed interpenetrating subsamples. This technique is discussed in detail by Lahiri (1958), Mahalanobis (1946) and Mahalanobis and Lahiri (1961).

Formation of strata

Approach to stratification

According to the basic principle of stratification, each stratum should be as homogeneous as possible with respect to the variable under study. Since a multisubject survey involves a large number of variables pertaining to different subjects of inquiry, the general policy in respect of stratification is to adopt a collective approach which aims at reducing the 'within stratum' variations of some key characteristics relevant to the parameters to be estimated. The pattern of stratification in the NSS has been so evolved as to cater to the needs of different inquiries canvassed in any particular round with emphasis, in some cases, on a few important inquiries of that round. In essence, the procedure consists in taking each state as a subpopulation (broad stratum) and in dividing it into several (two to six) regions (primary strata) within which the ultimate strata are demarcated.

Natural divisions and regions

From the very inception of the NSS, there has been a growing demand for reliable estimates, not only at the all-India level but also at the level of states and for regions within states. The NSS attempts to meet growing requirements for state and regional statistics by gradually increasing the sample size and improving the survey design. The regions are taken as primary strata. The regions have some distinctive geographical features and climatic conditions and this makes the regional estimates more meaningful and useful. Further, stratification is resorted to within the regions to reduce the variability of the regional, state and all-India estimates.

Stratification in rural areas

Rural strata are geographically compact areas formed by grouping contiguous *tehsils* of nearly equal population densities within the same natural division or region (from 1960). Districts, each of which is composed of *tehsils*, were grouped to form strata in rounds 1 to 3 and 9 to 13. However, grouping of *tehsils* which offers more flexibility is being consistently used since the 14th round. Since the 18th round, information on transport facilities between *tehsils* have been used so as to reduce difficulties of journey within a stratum. Further, strata populations (or some measures of population) are equalized to the extent possible to have equal allocation for different strata. This is done to facilitate using the strata as investigation zones with similarly phased programmes of work and approximately equal workload for each investigator posted in different investigation zones.

The rural strata are useful and effective for both household socioeconomic inquiries and agricultural surveys, since the regions have been formed on the basis of crop pattern and the strata within them are homogeneous with regard to topography and population density.

Demarcation of rural strata

The actual demarcation of strata boundaries is done in the following manner:
(1) A map of the state showing district and *tehsil* boundaries is procured.
(2) Region, state and NSS administrative block boundaries are drawn on it, for the conduct of fieldwork, most of the states are divided into two or three administrative subdivisions, called NSS blocks. As far as possible, strata are ormed within them.
(3) *Tehsil*-wise figures for population density, population (or any other size measure) and the names of main food crops are posed on the map for each tehsil.
(4) The transport facilities between every pair of contiguous *tehsils* classified as 'good' 'fair' and 'bad' are shown by colours.
(5) Sometimes two or three state maps showing different features are prepared on tracing papers to enable superimpositions, so as to identify the grouping which gives maximum homogeneity in respect of all the features.
(6) Making use of these plotted information, the actual grouping of tehsils is done according to the criteria laid down for stratification.

Stratification in urban arcas

Urban strata are formed by grouping towns situated in the same area (like a state, natural division or region) and belonging to the same population-size class. During the 16th to the 25th rounds, in each state, the towns with population less than 50 000 were grouped to form one stratum, and the remaining towns were grouped to form another stratum. The four big cities (Bombay, Calcutta, Delhi and Madras) formed separate strata in their respective states.

Allocation of samples

Since the 14th round the allocation to the states is based on a joint consideration of their rural population, geographical area, area under cereal crops and number of investigators. This mode of allocation had now stabilized with a minimum of 360 villages for most of the states. Allocation of urban blocks to the ultimate strata is done in proportion to their urban or non-agricultural population.

Selection procedure

Sampling of villages

There are three basic sampling schemes, simple random sampling (srs), systematic sampling and sampling with probability proportional to size (pps), and these have certain variations. In the first three rounds, when the 1941 census list of villages was used as the sampling frame, villages, the first stage units, were selected with pps with replacement, size being village population (whenever available) or village area (if population figures were not available). Simple random sampling was used for areas for which neither population nor area figures were available. In view of the smallness of the sampling fraction, there were not many cases of repetition of sample villages.

In rounds 4 to 7, *tehsils* were selected as first-stage units and villages as second-stage. The reason for this departure was to make use of the 1951 census frame. Collection of the whole frame of nearly 600 000 villages would have meant a delay of 2 or 3 years more. Hence, it was decided to select a sample of *tehsils* in the first instance, to collect the village frame (by copying) only for the sampled *tehsils* and select villages from these frames. *Tehsils* were sampled with pps with replacement (size being population in most cases and area in others) and the same scheme was also adopted for villages.

With the arrival of the complete 1951 census frame in 1954, switchover was made to the direct sampling of villages in the 8th round. This has continued since then. During the 8th to the 13th rounds, villages meant for both household enquiries and crop surveys were selected with probability proportional to population (ppp) and with replacement, whereas in the 10th to 13th rounds additional sample villages, intended for crop survey only, were selected with probability proportional to village area (ppa) and with replacement.

A major change in the 14th round was the reintroduction of equal probability sampling. This was done in order to effect full and economic integration of socioeconomic enquiries and crop surveys by having just a common set of villages for them without any additional sample for the latter. This scheme eliminated the two drawbacks of the previous scheme — (a) a separate sample for crop survey at the cost of socioeconomic enquiries; and (b) loss of economy due to partial integration. The effect of increasing the number of sample villages for socioeconomic inquiries on the efficiency of estimates has been beneficial, as for estimators of most of the parameters the between-village variance is more pronounced than the within village variance, particularly since the within-village variation is generally controlled through proper stratification and/or arrangement of households and fields.

Having opted for equal probability sampling, it was decided to have systematic sampling of villages in preference to simple random sampling since the former, with existing arrangement in the frame or with rearrangement, provides a more representative sample.

Sampling of households

While listing all the households in a sample village/block, the investigator collects some relevent auxiliary information about them, like household size, means of livelihood, land possessed, monthly consumer expenditure, number of self-employed persons, etc. and other characteristics meaningful for the concerned inquiries. This helps in preparing appropriate sampling frames for different inquiries and in increasing the efficiency of sampling at the second stage. The households of a frame are stratified and/or arranged by such auxiliary information before systematic sampling of households with a view to ensuring proper representation of the different sections of the population in the sample.

When an inquiry relates to a section of the population, the corresponding sampling frame is also limited to that section. For example, for an inquiry on trading enterprises, only those households which have this enterprise constitute the frame. This makes the frame compact and relevant.

Sample households for an inquiry are selected from the corresponding frame linear systematically with specified interval and random start in case of self-weighting designs and circular systematically (sample size being specified) in other cases. In some recent rounds of the NSS sampling for the three inquiries (on consumer expenditure and household enterprises; employment and unemployment; population, births and deaths) have been made in a joint manner. At first a sample (called combined sample) of 20 to 25 households is drawn after arranging all the households in six classes by their household size and means of livelihood. From this combined sample, a subsample of two to three households has been selected for the consumer expenditure, all the remaining households for population inquiry, and one-third of these for the employment enquiry. The selection was done systematically in such a manner as to avoid the selection of the same household for different inquiries.

Sample size and field work

Determination of sample size

A very natural question that arises is how has the sample size been determined for different inquiries in the NSS. Actually the question of fixation of sample size cannot be tackled in an isolated manner, but it has to be viewed in the context of the requirement of the users and the general strategy of the proposed survey design. In the NSS, a number of factors such as variabilities of different characters, the integrated nature of the design, emphasis on some selected items, operational conditions in different areas, existing field staff, etc. are considered while fixing the sample sizes, noting that a vast multisubject integrated survey like the NSS has its own complex pattern of cost and variance functions.

Considering all these aspects, an empirical approach has been adopted in the NSS to tackle the problem of sample size. The first few rounds were somewhat experimental in nature and a study of their results gave some useful ideas about the allocation of the all-India sample size (first-stage units) to the different strata as well as the allocation of second-stage units for different types of inquiries. Regarding the total sample size, the aim has been to have a large sample of first-stage units (fsu's) with a small number of sample second-stage units (ssu's) for any particular inquiry in each of them. The number of ssu's within an fsu varies from one inquiry to another, depending on the 'between-fsu' and 'within-fsu' variabilities and the emphasis given to an inquiry in a round. An idea of the sample sizes for the main inquiries is given in the following paragraphs.

It may be mentioned here that in the NSS, the sample of ssu's for all the inquiries (subjects) taken together is not very small in a sample fsu. From the viewpoint of sampling efficiency, a large number of sample fsu's goes well with a small number of ssu's per sample fsu. But from the point of view of cost-efficiency, which is of importance in practice, a too-small sample size of ssu's per sample fsu is not desirable. However in a multisubject survey, a very small size of ssu's per sample fsu for any particular subject of inquiry is perfectly justified if the size of sample ssu's per sample fsu for all the subjects taken together is not too small. Thus, in a multisubject survey it is possible to work with relatively smaller total sizes of ssu's or ultimate stage units for any particular inquiry, and hence tabulation time and cost get reduced.

With the increasing demand for reliable estimates at the state level and the regional level (a region being part of a state), the need for larger sample sizes has been accentuated. Hence consistent efforts have been made to maximize the sample size for a round subject to the field and tabulation resources allotted for that round and to gradually increase the resources over the rounds. The all-India central sample size has increased from 1833 villages in the 1st round (1950) to 8400 villages and 4640 blocks in the 25th round (1970–71).

Use of time-record schedule

A time-record schedule for keeping a complete daily record of time spent by an investigator on various operations of field work (like journey, camp-setting, listing of households, contacting persons, actual filling up of different schedules, copying of schedules, any other work) was used right from the first round of the NSS. These are utilized to study time requirements for various operations and plan the programme of work for a round.

Conclusion

A large-scale integrated multisubject survey like the NSS presents challenging technical, operational and administrative problems, which are to be kept constantly under consideration with a view to finding and developing solutions under the changing circumstances in respect of requirements of the users, field conditions and availability and type of processing equipments. The technical aspects of the survey design have been given in a number of publications as is evident from the list of references. The various aspects of fieldwork, such as training of investigators, data collection techniques and inspection and supervision of fieldwork, were discussed in detail at a seminar held at Calcutta in 1969 and the proceedings of this seminar (Murthy, 1971) includes the papers presented at the seminar and the conclusions arrived at.

In 1977 an economic census of establishments engaged in non-agricultural enterprises (like those engaged in manufacture trade, transport, construction, etc.) was conducted in India. Consequent to this, detailed surveys of non-agricultural enterprises were undertaken in the 33rd (1978–79) and 34th (1979–80) rounds of the NSS. The first-stage sampling units in these two rounds were enumeration blocks (EBs) — which also were *area units* like villages and blocks — formed during the economic census. The EBs were sampled with probability proportional to number of establishments in them according to the census. A sample of establishments was immediately selected, without going through households, from an up-to-date list of establishments prepared afresh for each sample EB.

References

Chowdhury, H.B. and Das Gupta, B.M. (Eds) (1960). Technical records of sample design, instructions to field workers and list of sample villages, urban blocks, NSS ninth round (May–November 1955), NSS Report No. 27, Government of India.

Lahiri, D.B. (1951). A method of sample selection providing unbiased ratio estimates, *Bulletin of the International Statistics Institute*, **33**, (**2**), 133–140.

Lahiri, D.B. (1954). Technical paper on some aspects of the development of sample design, NSS Report No. 5, Government of India, reprinted in *Sankhyá*, **14**, 264–316.

Lahiri, D.B. (1958). Recent developments in the technique of assessment of errors in nationwide surveys in India. *Bulletin of the International Statistics Institute*, **36**, (**2**), 71–93.

Lahiri, D.B. (1958). Observations on the use of interpenetrating samples in India. *Bulletin of the International Statistics Institute*, **36**, (**3**), 144–152.

Lahiri, D.B. (1963) Multi-subject sample survey system — some thoughts based on Indian experience, *Contributions to Statistics, Professor Mahalanobis Seventieth Birthday Volume*, pp. 175–220, Statistical Publishing Society, Calcutta.

Mahalanobis, P.C. (1946). Recent experiments in statistical sampling in the Indian Statistical Institute. *Journal of the Royal Statistics Society*, (A), 109, 320–378, reprinted in *Sankhyá*, **20**, (1958), 1–68.

Mahalanobis, P.C. and Sen, S.B. (1954). On some aspects of the Indian National Sample Survey. *Bulletin of the International Statistics Institute*, **34**, (2), 5–14.

Mahalanobis, P.C. and Lahiri, D.B. (1961). Analysis of errors in censuses and surveys with special reference to experience in India, *Bulletin of the International Statistics Institute*, **38**, (2), 401–433, reprinted in *Sankhyá*, **23**, (A), 199–204.

Murthy, M.N. and Nanjamma, N.S. (1959). Almost unbiased ratio-estimates based on inter-penetrating sub-sample estimates. *Sankhyá*, **21**, 381–392.

Murthy, M.N. (1962). *Technical Paper on Sample Design, NSS Fourteenth Round* (July 1958–June 1959), NSS Report No. 70, Government of India.

Murthy, M.N. and Sethi, V.K. (1965). Self-weighting design at tabulation stage. *Sankhyá*, **27**, (**B**), 201–210.

Murthy, M.N. (1968). On designing and conducting multi-subject household enquiries with reference to a permanent survey organization. *Sankhyá*, **30** (**B**), 367–382.

Murthy, M.N. (1969). Population census as the source of sampling frame in India, *Sankhyá*, **31**, (**B**), 1–12.

Murthy, M.N. and Roy, A.S. (1970): A problem in integration of surveys — a case study. *Journal of the American Statistical Association*, **65**, 123–135.

Murthy, M.N. (Ed) (1971). *Proceedings of the Seminar on Data Collection Techniques in the National Sample Survey*, Department of Statistics, Government of India.

Murthy, M.N. (1974). Evaluation of multi-subject sample survey systems. *International Statistics Review*, **42** (2), 173–191.

Nanjamma, N.S. (1963). Technical paper on sample designs of working class and middle class family living surveys, 1958–59. *Sankhyá*, **25** (**B**), 359–418.

Roy, A.S. and Bhattacharya, A.K. (1968). *Technical Paper on Sample Design, NSS Nineteenth Round* (July 1964–June 1965), NSS Report No. 125, Government of India.

Sengupta, J.M. (1964). On perimeter bias in sample cuts of small size. *Sankhyá*, **26** (**B**), 53–68.

United Nations (1964). Recommendations for the preparation of sample survey reports. *Statistical Papers Series C, No. 1, Rev. 2*, New York.

Social Research in Developing Countries
Edited by M. Bulmer and D.P. Warwick
© 1983, John Wiley & Sons, Ltd.

CHAPTER 10

MISSING THE POINT: SAMPLING METHODS AND TYPES OF ERROR IN THIRD WORLD SURVEYS IN IDENTIFYING POVERTY ISSUES

MICHAEL WARD

Introduction

The fundamental problem of development policy is how to raise the living standards of the vast majority of the population in low-income countries who earn less than the average income per head, yet social researchers face major problems in studying such people. Those groups in whom policy-makers should be most interested — the unemployed, illiterate, abandoned, malnourished, ill-housed or unsheltered, sick, etc. — are rarely included or identified in any official records or surveys.

The inadequacies and incompleteness of national lists and registers arise for many administrative, political and financial reasons. This precludes their use either as a direct basis for administrative policy decisions or as a relevant national sampling frame on which to base specific surveys relating to these development concerns. Even before it starts, a random sample drawn from an inadequate national sampling frame is not only biased to an unknown extent (and usually in the worst direction) but it also generates point estimates that are essentially irrelevant to the real problems under investigation. No amount of subsequent manipulation, however statistically sophisticated, can compensate for such inadequacies. Technical precision combined with the careful and faithful conduct of a random sample survey cannot ensure that the resulting statistics are right, relevant or useful for policy.

This chapter therefore focuses on three important interrelated questions:

(1) To what extent are random sampling methods relevant and feasible in investigating many important policy issues in developing countries?

(2) What is the nature and relative magnitude of the sampling and non-sampling errors to be expected in social surveys using random sampling?
(3) To what extent do the benefits of non-random, deliberately selective purposive sampling outweigh its disadvantages for certain types of policy research?

Because of the anticipated reduction in total survey error, it may be justifiable to adopt a purposive sampling approach to many subjects of enquiry where the variables concerned are difficult to locate and identify. Examples are drawn from a budget and an employment survey to illustrate this issue.

Survey methods and random sampling

The simplest and most common form of statistical inference is concerned with making certain statements about the presumed nature of a population on the basis of a sample. To provide a better guide as to their validity, these statements are usually accompanied by some numerical measure of their assumed reliability in relation to the (unknown) true population values.

In this context, probability sampling is described in most textbooks (Moser and Kalton, 1971, for example) as a statistical procedure for selecting units from a population or universe on some basis of chance. Simple random sampling— which is usually taken as a sort of 'ideal' model— is more narrowly defined as a method of choosing such population units in a way that gives each unit of the group an equal chance of selection which, in theory, should remain the same throughout the selection process. Priority ranking in terms of need or identifying special or important groups according to predetermined criteria cannot be considered.

The benefits of probability sampling are described in lay terms (with heavily implied value judgements) as substituting 'fair' methods for 'foul' ones. It avoids adopting prejudiced selection procedures like 'first come, first served', 'last in, first out' and 'personal judgement'.

The literature is full of instances showing serious bias in samples composed of individuals chosen because they were presumed to be representative of the population. But there is no guarantee that in actual operation, a random survey — which is only one of the many samples that, hypothetically, could have been taken — will provide an any more truly 'representative' reflection.

In many developing countries the target population cannot be correctly or comprehensively delineated because survey investigators are compelled to use inappropriate and incomplete lists such as out-of-date population census records, telephone directories, electoral registers, electricity or water subscribers, etc. as the basic sampling frames for their inquiries. These lists predetermine the nature of the stratification procedures possible. The sampling errors do not apply and the appropriate survey population parameter can not be estimated from its related function in the sample. Two specific examples may be chosen to illustrate these points.

The first is the 1973 Fiji household income and expenditure survey (Fiji, Bureau of Statistics, 1974) which was based on a random selection of households living in six principal urban centres. The principal objective of the survey was to determine the general pattern of expenditure of different urban families and to use the results to provide expenditure weights for a new Consumer Price Index.

Although the 1966 Fiji Census of Population was considered inappropriate as a sampling frame because of changes in the households' structure, it was nevertheless used as a benchmark for estimating population in 1973. A list of electricity consumers, supplemented by a registered list of squatters, that is, dwellers in unauthorized structures, were combined to form the sampling frame. The 795 households actually comprising the sample were selected from a possible total of 6625 listed urban households (the subsequent 1976 Census showed 34 048 households in these towns).

The selection was made using a table of random numbers. The approximate 10 per cent sample contained all ethnic groups and all income levels. Although the sample frame excluded several of the smaller towns, the official report alleges that the survey represented more than 80 per cent of all urban households.

The survey was carried out over a period of 5 weeks from 1 October to 4 November 1973. Within the separate areas chosen for the survey, the 795 selected households were grouped in such a way that each group provided information for a fortnight only.

The actual scope of the survey, however, was less than planned due to non-response and incomplete coverage. It was hoped that by spreading the enumeration and allowing a consistent spread of reporting units over peak and lean spending periods, a better overall control of the survey through closer supervision and attention to detail would be achieved. Unfortunately, the evidence suggests that enumerator fatigue set in towards the end of the exercise. The official report states:

due to the size of the sample, a test of randomness showed that there were no defects in the use of such a sampling technique, and there was no evidence to show that such a procedure affected the main results of the survey. There is no reason, therefore, to believe that the figures obtained from this survey are not representative of urban households in general (Fiji, Bureau of Statistics, 1974)

Not all households were covered by the survey frame. The ethnic groups in Fiji have different consumption patterns (the diets are but one example of the dissimilarities) and there are significant income inequalities between racial groups as well as within races. The list was clearly deficient. Not only is squatting illegal (and so most squatters would not be registered) but many urban houses, for a variety of reasons, were not connected to electricity. Furthermore, there is an obvious possibility of confusion in this example between the 'household' and the 'house' or 'dwelling-unit'. It is difficult not to conclude that, despite the best of intentions, this random survey was biased from its outset. In addition, the example raises another general point that, in a large number of surveys, the primary sampling unit— in this case the household — is used as a basis for generating estimates relating to other units (for example, individuals) that were not randomly selected, and since households are not of equal size and age/sex composition this is a potential source of misinterpretation.

The second illustration is taken from an ILO survey of informal sector activities in Jakarta in 1977 (International Labour Organization, 1977). The frame was compiled from existing outdated and inaccurate population lists supplied by the authorities. The survey itself was based on a sample of about 4500 heads of enterprises permanently resident in Jakarta. The official lists were particularly deficient because many of the urban poor are not legal residents and it was assumed (incorrectly) that those who lived and worked in the city were quite distinct from those who lived and worked in the countryside (whereas many informal operators in the city are not permanent residents but come from the surrounding villages). For the most part, informal sector operators are engaged in unlicensed and other irregular and unregistered activities. Official sources of information will often fail, therefore, to detect these very groups whom the government is attempting to identify — the homeless, unemployed, illiterate, itinerant and casual workers. The usual terminology employed in a formal conventional survey of the informal sector, such as enterprise, income, profit, employer, etc., is not only meaningless but also has no real meaning for the respondents. Furthermore, over time, for example as between day and night, weekday–weekend, winter-summer, harvest–planting, etc., both the sample population and the target population varies considerably but not always in the same way.

In practice, it is rarely possible to select a random sample from the desired target population because a suitable sampling frame does not exist and it is not easy to construct one. The sample, therefore, has often to be selected from some other related population assumed to contain the same characteristics it is desired to investigate. Valid probability statements, however, can only be made about sample populations and their estimated parameters on the basis of random samples and their associated derived statistics. Statements about the real target population (such as the poor and other similarly deprived groups who are not easily identifiable) are not valid in a relative frequency probability sense unless the target population is the same as the sampled population— or so close to it as to make little difference in practice. Even if the sample can be taken from the desired target population, this will provide no guarantee that the resulting information will be accurate and reliable if the variables are not directly observable and objectively measurable — for example, income, wealth, transfer payments, etc. At best the sample would generate unbiased estimates of what would be the reported and recorded (but not necessarily the 'true') income levels. In other words, however accurate and representative a sample may be of the target population and however 'complete' the responses, it will fail to obtain satisfactory and reliable information about that population if the nature of the survey inquiry methods give rise to responses at variance with reality. It is well known that conventional large-scale household survey inquiries lead to biased estimates of incomes, particularly at the lower and upper ends of the distribution.

Survey errors of interpretation and analysis are always present. The theoretical possibility of drawing incorrect conclusions from misleading results and thus making wrong decisions cannot be avoided. In statistical terminology these are usually referred to as type I and type II errors. Such errors arise when a statistician rejects a given hypothesis when it is in fact true (error of the first kind) or when he accepts that hypothesis (as opposed to some alternative) when the alternative is true (type II error) (Figure 10.1).

In practice the universe and the action proposed on the basis of the survey results are selected in such a way that the type I error is the one that statisticians are most interested in avoiding. But any reduction in one type of error is balanced by a compensatory increase in the second kind of error. To resolve this dilemma in practice, statisticians use prior information about the state of the universe to try and avoid type I errors occurring.

In the conduct of continuous, integrated multipurpose and highly complex

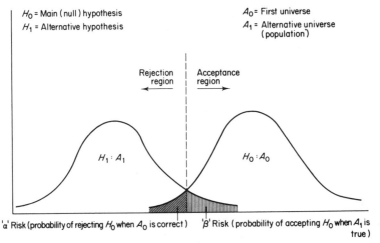

H_0 = Main (null) hypothesis
H_1 = Alternative hypothesis

A_0 = First universe
A_1 = Alternative universe (population)

Rejection region ←

Acceptance region →

$H_1 : A_1$

$H_0 : A_0$

'α' Risk (probability of rejecting H_0 when A_0 is correct)

'β' Risk (probability of accepting H_0 when A_1 is true)

Figure 10.1

socioeconomic sample surveys in developing countries, there are *prima facie* reasons for suspecting that the type II errors (and the risk of making them) are relatively higher because of the changing nature of the reference universe and target areas of interest in 'rotating' not only samples and respondents but also schedules and survey modules.

All these factors affect the feasibility and relevance, whatever theoretical advantages may be claimed, of undertaking a random sample survey in a socioeconomic context. What may be justifiable in the case of small, controlled, scientifically measurable experiments carried out in an observable, defined and restricted area, for example, plots of land where a specific crop is being cultivated, is not necessarily applicable to large-scale household surveys.

Sampling and non-sampling errors

Suppose a random sample *is* feasible and there are no problems of matching the survey objectives to the existing sampling frame, would such an enquiry generate the necessary information desired to clarify policy issues? The answer, in many cases, is 'no', mainly because insufficient attention is paid to the total survey error.

In surveys — or, more specifically, sample design — the total error concept tends to get ignored. Statisticians, of course, give much thought to possible non-response errors and operational difficulties but it is always a question of, having already chosen a specific sample design, finding the best way to limit these so-called 'uncontrollable errors'. Rarely is there any scientific consideration of the total error and overall cost–benefit ratio in relation to the information required. The relationship between sampling error, non-sampling error and total error can be represented diagramatically (Figure 10.2).

Reduction in one type of error without reduction in the other type will not significantly reduce total error. Thus to reduce sampling error markedly (Figure 10.3) only reduces total error by a much smaller amount (Blalock, 1972). Clearly, the relative size of the (uncontrollable) non-sampling error

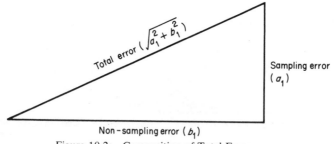

Figure 10.2:   Composition of Total Error

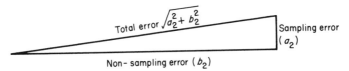

Note: The impact on total survey error is minimal where non-sampling errors are substantial, as is likely in most developing countries.

Figure 10.3:   Effect of a Reduction in the Sampling Error on Total Error

compared with the (controllable) sampling error is critical. If the reduction in sampling error is achieved by a big increase in the sample size and its complexity then the non-sampling error can rise rapidly and the resulting total error will be very large.

Put more formally, the total error can be defined as the mean square difference between a survey estimate and the true population value. The mean square difference is chosen rather than the absolute difference because it is an easier mathematical concept to use; i.e. in principle it can be 'minimized' in a simple fashion. The (unknown) total error is made up of several distinct components, some of which can be controlled and estimated while others are less susceptible to easy identification and control:

Total error = sample error + non-sampling error + sample bias + non-sampling bias + interaction factor between sampling and non-sampling errors

The interaction term is often assumed, incorrectly, to be non-existent. Since there is no easy way of separating the non-sampling error from the bias, these are normally lumped together. But, in practice, the distinction may be intuitively apparent — given knowledge about the way the survey was conducted within a certain context and time-span and some familiarity with the actual interviewing process.

It is argued that non-sampling errors can be reduced by holding the same responding units unchanged over time (in which case non-sampling errors associated with boredom and fatigue increase rapidly) and by using the same cadre of trained and skilled permanent enumerators for all surveys. The interdependent interaction term is likely to be greater, however, the larger and more complex the survey.

Nevertheless, the 1973 Fiji survey indicated quite clearly that trained enumerators can also contribute to deteriorating response levels over the progress of the survey. The survey process itself aggravates non-sampling errors. If the sampling variance (error) is expected to be much less than the non-sampling error then the survey can be conducted using a smaller sample size and a more intensive type of enumeration procedure and, possibly, a simpler schedule of enquiry. But evidence suggests that the total non-sampling error is considerably greater than the pure sampling error at most levels of interest (Gibril, 1979; UNRISD, 1980).

Many survey statisticians argue, therefore, that the easiest method of increasing the reliability and precision of a survey is to improve the method of enumeration rather than, as is usually advised, to increase the sample size. In any survey where the survey error is likely to be large, it is essential to use better qualified enumerators rather than increase the survey's size and complexity.

There are many methods for dealing with total survey errors and incomplete data, some theoretical and some quite subjective and judgemental. In the case of developing countries non-sampling errors have many different facets. Usually the main concern is not so much with non-response but with wrong-response and socially conditioned responses.

Non-sampling errors can make nonsense of any survey data. This is particularly true where the evaluation of conceptually complex and definitionally difficult socioeconomic variables such as income, wealth, transfers, etc. are concerned and there is a difference in technical and lay perceptions of these terms. Conventional household income and expenditure surveys provide clear illustrations of the unrepresentativeness of poor and deprived groups and their levels of living. The quality of the data can suffer through bad selection; incomplete, inadequate and non-response; measurement errors as well as processing errors; and each source of error is different in type, direction and magnitude. In surveys with different strata, the frequencies of various characters of the population are represented by the relative frequencies in the strata subsamples and these may be very biased, particularly at the extremes.

In matters of practical development policy it is not sufficient to know that, in a theoretical long-run average sense in which similar samples are repeated, the results will centre around a point estimate that is not particularly useful for understanding poverty and its causes.

The purposes and limits of estimation

Policy interest needs to focus on the extremes, on specific segments of the population, particularly on poverty bands and subsistence groups and not on those better-off people centred around the arithmetic mean. The population median estimate, or better still the mode, and estimates of specific partitions of the distribution are the statistics most required. This is more than merely a survey reporting issue. Nearly all key official indicators in developing countries are based on arithmetic mean estimates and so major policy issues concerned with poverty, unemployment and generally unregistered informal activities are imperfectly understood. In other words, because of the underlying skewness of incomes (from different sources), of asset ownership, output concentration and employment distribution, very little is known about the impact of policy on the nature and structure of these high priority socioeconomic variables, and sophisticated mathematical manipulations of the basic data, like log transformations, do not deal with the basic issues. Arithmetic mean estimates are convenient but rarely representative. When employed in economic analysis as aggregate measures such as gross domestic product (GDP) *per capita*, doctors per 1000 population, etc., they often provide misleading indications of the changes taking place, even if they are the best approximate estimates.

There is an additional problem; although statisticians dutifully avoid the compelling attractions of speed, convenience and cheapness in survey enquiries and resolutely pursue their task of applying scientific sampling techniques, there is always a chance that a single selected survey will produce an extreme sample that is unrepresentative and which therefore generates unrealistic sample statistics. This is much more likely when the underlying distribution is highly skewed although relevant stratification — where possible — offers some protection. Furthermore, in probability sampling, it is axiomatic that information relating only to the selected unit(s) is obtained; it is assumed the unit cannot give reliable and unprejudiced information about other units which can only be deduced in total. Both official ('confidentiality') and statistical censoring techniques prohibit the use of any such knowledge gained about units not drawn in the sample for the purposes of general estimation in that particular sample.

Finally, the means obtained from different samples may differ widely from the true population parameter in skew distributions (even where the probabilities of selection with a given sample size appear very similar) if just a few extreme upper population values are omitted.

The importance of relationships compared with incomes

In the field of dynamic policy analysis, governments are usually more interested in relationships and socioeconomic linkages than in distinct 'atomistic' values (Moore, 1979a) from which such relationships must be derived implicitly by quantitative analysis. In the conventional approach, the sample survey statistician is able to ascertain 'what' and 'how much' but rarely 'how' and 'why' and this leaves the general level of understanding of the problems fairly bereft. From the start, the sample surveyor gets off on the wrong foot because units, definitions and classifications must be predefined. Inherent in these is a conceptual view of the universe, a perception of reality that probably conforms to a given hypothesis or theory of the world. In a sense, the scope of the analysis, if not restricted, is clearly predetermined. Perhaps, more important, since all large-scale samples cover multiple purposes, these may not be representative in respect of certain important characteristics which researchers wish to study, especially in those cases where the characteristics are not easily quantifiable. Sampling designs can only be 'optimized' for specific domains of enquiry and not for all purposes at the same time.

What then are the alternatives? Of course, politicans can make their own reasoned (or otherwise) guesses or rely on the professional judgement and experience of their civil servants. This may turn out to be inefficient and worthless and even positively dangerous. Another possibility would be to adopt some form of carefully selected, purposive survey design where the investigator selects the target groups and problems in which there is policy interest. This means going straight to the heart of the question, using supporting evidence and information to guide the direction of enquiries.

Although probability sampling is still regarded as the fundamental tool in survey procedures, it is an approach under question, especially by Bayesians who have no place for random methods and chance approaches in their theory. There is increasing pressure from Bayesians who argue that selection probabilities do not matter to utilize *a priori* information to formulate an *a priori* distribution of the parameters to facilitate the determination of the subsequent actual *posterior* distribution of those parameters, even if this must include personal and subjective elements. Such prior information can be used although, in practice, Bayesian techniques have been rarely applied. Varying the probabilities of selection of certain units in different strata is the standard common alternative. Where costs are important this is vitally necessary. An estimator not only needs to be unbiased, his sampling distribution must also be concentrated as closely as possible about the respective parameter to be estimated; in other words, the values of the various estimates in the sampling distribution should vary as little as possible around the true parameter value. The answer may lie, therefore, in making more selective choices using qualitative indepth surveys. This approach comes not by way of default but simply because it possesses intrinsic merit. It can also be utilized in conjunction with existing conventional methods.

It is important to make the point that errors in data, while obviously objectionable in the abstract, may not be particularly important in relation to particular analytical issues. This immediately suggests a strong argument (if arguments are needed) in favour of a close integration of statistical and analytical work. The statistician working in isolation would presumably regard errors of the same absolute size as being equally important whereas analytical work in relation to a particular issue might well demonstrate the contrary.

The benefits of non-random, purposive sampling

The simple graph in Figure 10.4 depicts fairly clearly the fundamental dilemma confronting the survey statistician and the need to select an effective tradeoff between two conflicting sources of error arising from the adoption of alternative inquiry techniques and the undertaking of surveys of different size.

In developing countries, non-sampling errors are especially important, particularly in the area of socioeconomic distributional analysis by regions or

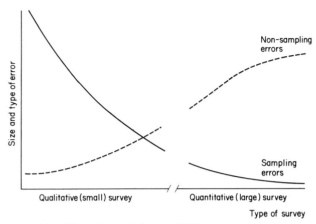

Source: Adapted from Market Research Society (1979).

Figure 10.4:   The relative size of sampling and non-sampling errors in different surveys

classes. They are usually of a higher level of incidence because of problems of contact and communication. This is not only a matter of transportation difficulties and literacy or comprehension problems but also a question of social custom and activity patterns. Many respondents, even if they are literate, are unable to understand the purpose of the survey because the issue is outside their experience and so they cannot relate to or identify with the question concerned.

The merits and defects of a qualitative, investigatory approach to socioeconomic issues of policy concern should not really be discussed in relation to the more conventional quantitative method of survey enquiry as if they can be regarded as alternative techniques. Although they usually refer to quite different and specific types of investigation, it is, however, easier to identify their characteristics by comparing the two approaches.

Qualitative surveys may, in fact, be large scale as well as small scale but, in general, this approach involves limited size, deliberate, selective (purposive) sampling techniques. It is often associated with a prespecified quota design that is meant to reflect (or be closely representative of) the target group and problem area under investigation. The method is thus subjective and rational in the sense of being directly focused on a specific population (the poor, old, sick, etc.) or issue. For the most part, indepth techniques of questioning and eliciting responses (as well as presurvey problem analysis) are employed. Non-formal, flexible and unstructured methods of enquiry are adopted to maximise respondent cooperation even though they are frequently mistrusted as reflecting the interviewer's prejudices and views.

Although this method makes widespread use of prior knowledge and

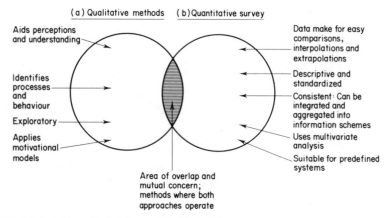

Source: Adapted from Market Research Society (1979)

Figure 10.5:   Qualitative and Quantitative Survey Methods

information in determining the most accurate selection of target groups, deciding an appropriate sample design, ensuring representative data are collected and the critical analysis of data and survey results, the approach itself is relieved of making any basic assumptions about the problem area. It is not usually specifically tied by an inflexible methodology such as is imposed by a rigid preset sample questionnaire, sample design or survey procedure and administrative organization. As such, it can be opportunistic and exploratory, particularly in problem identification and even problem solving (Figure 10.5).

Comparative features of qualitative and quantitative research

A relative comparison of the two main approaches can probably best be seen from the list of survey features shown in Table 10.1. It should also be pointed out that there is a distinction between informal and formal methods of questioning and between qualitative and quantitative survey procedures although, in practice, they are usually linked respectively (Figure 10.6). The approach, however, is not without its serious drawbacks and these have to be weighed against the probable reductions in non-sampling errors associated with interviewer effects, response bias, data collection, field survey organization, reporting, inadequate sampling frame, etc. Non-sampling errors will tend to be higher the more difficult and expensive it is to identify and contact subsets of the population (unregulated enterprises, illiterate, homeless, orphaned, alien, immigrant, etc.).

Unrepresentative sampling may be a problem where informal sampling is used or an informal questioning approach is adopted. Thus the disadvantages of qualitative surveys are mainly concerned with the selection and hence, it is

Survey design

Quantitative   Qualitative

	Quantitative	Qualitative	
Structured, formal	I Most general conventional approach	II Usually part of a larger general survey	Usually random
Unstructured informal	Pilot presurvey, *ad hoc*	Purposive, selective	Usually NON-RANDOM (probability sampling has little relevance)

Questionnaire design

Sample design

Figure 10.6:   Survey Design, Questionnaire Design & Sample Design

argued, unrepresentative nature of the sample selection. Inevitably, the results will be biased and possibly very unreliable and, therefore, unusable in formulating policy. That the approach is subject to (unknown) sampling errors seems, in practice, to be less important especially when compared with the potential standard errors associated with (so-called random) surveys actually conducted. The sort of two-stage survey samples with stratification commonly carried out by official statistical offices may have a low design efficiency. The link is loosened if the selection of first-stage units (villages, towns) is based on probabilities proportional to population size and then applied to an analysis of households rather than individuals. Problems may also arise when selections are related to the head of household and/or his occupation as a basis for describing household activity patterns.

Table 10.1   Comparative features of qualitative and quantitative research

	Qualitative	*Quantitative*
(1) Survey size	Small (30–200)	Large (100+)
(2) Sampling method	Quota/purposive, non-random	Random
(3) Coverage	Typical of specific groups (modal)	Representative (arithmetic average)
(4) Data collection techniques	Unstructured/flexible	Structured/rigid
(5) Enumeration	Interviewer perception and initiative crucial	Interviewer precise discipline crucial
(6) 'Questionnaire'	Adaptive; responsive	Rigid, inflexible
(7) Enquiry method	Indepth	Uniform, formal

Table 10.1 Comparative features of qualitative and quantitative research (*contd.*)

		Qualitative	Quantitative
(8)	Analysis process	Innovative, exploratory, individual, many varied research techniques	Established, deductive standardized
(9)	Report content	Soft, impressionistic data	Hard, precise data
(10)	Report style	Interpretative narratives with illustrative quotes	Comparative but non-interpretative commentaries on statistical tables
(11)	Focus and approach	Multidisciplinary, but only a few well-specified objectives	Single and multidisciplinary, more general
(12)	Perceived uses	Understanding and insight of prescriptive value	Facts of descriptive value
(13)	Characteristics	Normative/implicative; different investigatory tools utilized to build up an integrated research collage; more sensitive; often involves carefully selected case studies some of which (in particular areas such as agriculture) involve surveys of a long duration	Positive; wide-ranging, 'general purpose' scope; relatively unselective in terms of narrow objectives; expensive; usually time and resource consuming
(14)	Advantages	Enables people to investigate problems outside traditional boundaries of enquiry Important where direct measurement of characteristics and understanding of behaviours and attitudes is difficult. Searches out the meaning, causes and relationships of phenomena, i.e. the similarities and differences; reduces non-sampling and total sampling errors; generally quick and relatively inexpensive	Precise quantification with estimates within defined limits Makes for easy comparisons Visible techniques Representative (and thus enables estimation at population level)

NB: The comparison shows that qualitative methods are most useful in the investigation of reasons for different kinds of behaviour and the better understanding of the interrelationships between various phenomena. The techniques should therefore enable policy-makers to improve and develop policy with greater relevance in specified problem areas.

The use of purposive sampling methods, linked to a qualitative approach, can be illustrated by the method of selection of poor people from a skewed distribution of income earners or asset holders (Figure 10.7a). If two or three people are selected from the income bands $O-Y^1$ or Y^1-Y^2, their pattern of consumption behaviour will not be very different from that of anyone else in those 'fractile' or fixed income groups. Hence their behaviour will be to a large extent 'typical' if not 'representative', even though they have not been randomly selected. This is because their low level of income or ownership of assets severely restricts the scope of their behaviour and the variations possible. People in the income band $O-Y^1$ have only that amount of income to allocate; people from $Y^1\,Y^2$ have slightly more (that is, $0-Y^2$), but comparatively little to allow them to purchase much else than their essential requirements. This probably explains, in part, the apparent stability of observed Engels coefficients amongst poor households in various developing countries. Clearly, the same argument cannot be applied to similar-sized groups or income levels at the top end of the distribution as these people have a wide variety of alternatives for allocating their purchases (or not buying at all) once their main needs have been met.

The strength of the selective sampling approach increases as the income bands and/or groups are more narrowly limited and defined. In Figure 10.7(b) the selection of a single person chosen from an even narrower income range such as Y^1-Y''' (as opposed to having two people chosen from a range twice as big such as Y^1-Y^2) becomes even more representative and homogeneous. The unit is then 'typical' according to the definition specified. The method seems particularly suitable where survey objectives are fairly limited.

In practice, especially in developing countries where transport, organization and communications are difficult, it is known that non-sampling errors contribute enormously to bias and unreliability in survey results. For example, even

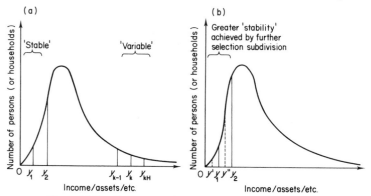

Figure 10.7:   Skewness and selection representitivity

in good quantitative research it has been shown that less than two-thirds of field interview checks have been properly conducted with the right person in the right place in the right manner with no discrepancies in approach. Taped field interview checks usually confirm this observation (Pool and Pool, 1971). It is recognized that interview methods and the systematic and consistent nature of recording of field information is influenced by the day itself, the time of day, location of the interview, the nature of the weather, etc.). Tape recordings were used in Fiji in the World Fertility Survey to assess field interviews as a means of enumerator, etc. quality control during fieldwork.

In qualitative research, assuming that one is using well-trained and experienced social scientists who clearly understand the survey's objectives, non-sampling errors can be reduced to a very low level. Data is collected from respondent's own expressions and in a free atmosphere. Responses are looked at from several points of view. Monotony, fatigue, etc., which are well-known sources of error in questionnaires, are minimized by involving respondents in informal interviewing.

Such a skilled qualitative researcher continuously sifts and checks the data collected. The representativeness of informants can be assessed directly and allowances made for strengths of opinion, deception and social pressure. Sampling errors in properly conducted qualitative research can be reduced by careful prestratification, pairing and matching (against 'control' groups). The reduction of the standard error by accurate matching may be equivalent to increasing the sample size several-fold.

It seems obviously wrong to chose a sample design with a large number of respondents simply because it has a low sampling error. In many situations, the higher sampling errors in qualitative research can be reasonably traded off for its much lower non-sampling error (see Figure 10.4) quite apart from the other benefits obtained from a better understanding of specific problems and areas. Indeed, in a controlled commercial experiment it was found that a qualitative study produced essentially the same results at about half the cost of a more conventional quantitative survey at least ten times as large; in addition, the qualitative survey provided extra benefits of insight into market conditions (Market Research Society, 1979).

Belief in qualitative research and its usefulness increases as users become more familiar with it; unfortunately, most government statistical offices have not been prepared to adopt this approach despite its obvious and practical advantages of cheapness and speed. They have therefore been unable to judge whether the benefits of qualitative research outweigh any reservations about sample size or the absence of statistical scientific method.

The methods are hardly ever used even in areas of social policy where the government is attempting to provide community services (education, health, welfare, roads, etc.) designed to satisfy people's needs. The reasons are many, but perhaps the most important is that, paradoxically, public sector managers individually are more responsible but have less direct responsibility for public decisions (which are usually taken in committee). This official decision process is much more rigid and institutionalized. It must be possible to prove the results of research to others and to show that such information has been obtained 'objectively'. The approach of public sector officials is thus primarily quantitative. They fail to recognize that a qualitative survey can do much more than simply fill out and complement some conventional statistical enquiry but provide real, usable information in its own right.

In terms of financial cost, use of resources and speed of delivery of results, as well as depth of perception, the qualitative research approach using a rational selection procedure of respondents is undeniably superior to an officially conducted random sample survey of the conventional kind. The main question remaining, however, is whether the information collected is useful, 'reasonably' representative of the group and problems to which the survey is intended to refer, and whether such surveys produce data sufficiently reliable for policy purposes. These matters can only be assessed subjectively and from first-hand experience of the difficulties of carrying out empirical enquiries. Unfortunately, for the most part government statistical offices have been unwilling to allocate their scarce resources to experiments with techniques of this kind, so it is difficult to assess their effectiveness by any results to date. The methods proposed seem worthy of official trial as well as further development in academic research.

References and bibliography

Asrat, D. (1980). Some notes on the typology for survey organisations in developing countries and data availability, reliability, comparability, timeliness and cost. *Food Supply Analysis Group*, Oxford.

Blalock, H. (1972) *Social Statistics*. McGraw-Hill, New York.

Casley, D. (1975). Problems in estimation of crop areas and crop yields. *International Statistical Institute Conference, Paper 15*, Warsaw, September 1975.

Chambers, R. (1980). Shortcut methods in information gathering for rural development projects, *Agricultural Sector Symposia*, World Bank. (Also Institute of Development Studies Discussion Paper, 1981)

Fiji, Bureau of Statistics (1978). *An analysis of data collected in the 1976 Census (religion; school attendance, etc.; household and family size)*. Census Occasional Paper No. 2, Suva, Fiji.

Fiji, Bureau of Statistics (1974). *Fiji Household Income and Expenditure Survey, 1973*, Suva, Fiji.

Gibril, M.A. (1979). *Evaluating Census Response Errors; A Case Study for the Gambia*, OECD Development Centre Studies, Paris.

Government of Jakarta, Census and Statistical Office (1972). *Hasil Survey Fasilitas Perpasaran DKI Jakarta 1972*, DCI, Jakarta.

Howes, M. (1979). Stratifying a Rural Population: trade-offs between accuracy and time. *Conference on Rapid Rural Appraisal*, Institute of Development Studies, Sussex.

Hindess, B. (1973). *The Use of Official Statistics in Sociology*. Macmillan, London.

International Labour Organisation (1972) Asian Region Team for Employment Promotion (ARTEP): *Manpower and Related Problems in Indonesia*, Bangkok.

International Labour Organization (1977) *Survey of Informal Sector Activities; The Study of Jakarta*, Geneva.

Jellenik, L. (1977). Surveys and sensitivities, appearance and reality; a case study approach to the investigation of the urban poor in Jakarta, *Development Statistics Seminar*, Institute of Development Studies, Sussex.

Kish, L. (1965). *Survey Sampling*, Wiley, New York.

Kruskal, W. and Mosteller, F. (1979). Representative Sampling III; The Current Statistical Literature. *International Statistical Review*, **47**, 3.

Market Research Society, (1979). Qualitative research — a summary of the concepts involved. R and D Sub-committee on Qualitative Research, *Journal of Market Research*, **21**, 2.

Moore, M. (1979a). Beyond the tarmac road; a (nut)shell guide for rural poverty watchers. *Conference on Rapid Rural Appraisal*, Institute of Development Studies, Sussex.

Moore, M. (1979b). Denounce the gang of statisticians, struggle against the sample line, unite the researching masses against professional hegemony. *Conference on Rapid Rural Appraisal*, Institute of Development Studies, Sussex.

Moser, C.A., and Kalton, g. (1971). *Survey Methods in Social Investigation*, Heinemann, London.

Murthy, M.N. (1977). *Sampling Theory and Methods*, (2nd impression) Statistical Publishing Society, Calcutta.

Neyman, J. (1934). On the two aspects of the representative method of stratified sampling and the method of purposive sampling. *Journal of the Royal Statistical Society*, **97**.

Oyeke, Chike S. (1976). *A survey report based on tape recorded interviews during the 1974 population census of Sierra Leone*. Demographic Unit, Fourah Bay College, Freetown.

Pool, J.E. and Pool, D.I. (1971). The use of tape recorders to ascertain response errors in a KAP survey, Niger, West Africa. Conference Paper, Population Association of America, **April**; Abstract in *Population Index* No. 37/3.

Scott, W. (1978). *Measurement and Analysis of Progress at the Local Level, Volume I, An Overview*, United Nation Research Institute for Social Development Report No. 78.1.

Sethuraman, S.V. (1976) *Jakarta, Urban Development and Employment*, ILO, Geneva (World Employment Programme Study)

United Nations (ESCAP). (1966). *Problems and methods of collecting statistics of distributive trades for household and small-scale enterprises*, Document E/CN.11/ASTAT/SDT/L.4, ESCAP, Bangkok.

United Nations Research Institute for Social Development (1980) *A Development Monitoring Service at the Local Level*, Geneva.

Ward, M. (1979). *Poverty Policy; Relevant Survey and Sampling Procedures*, UN Statistical Institute for Asia and Pacific, Tokyo.

Ward, M. (1982). *Data and Development Policy*, Institute of Development Studies

Williams, K. (1978). Populations at risk and social planning, *Social Statistics Bulletin*, **1**, (5), UNICEF (East Africa).

Yates, F. (1960). *Sampling Methods for Censuses and Surveys* (3rd edition), Charles Griffin and Co., London.

SECTION IV

DATA COLLECTION

CHAPTER 11

DATA COLLECTION

MARTIN BULMER
AND
DONALD P. WARWICK

Introduction

Are there unique or special problems that arise in collecting and analysing census or survey data in the developing countries? A good case could be made that the problems encountered in those countries are not so much unique as more frequent, more severe, and more intractable than those elsewhere. There is probably not a country in which at least a few respondents will fail to understand the nature of a sample survey and perhaps the entire idea of social research. The distinctive feature of survey research in the developing countries is not the presence of this difficulty but its prevalence and severity. Where in the United States the number of respondents who simply do not understand he survey would be less than 1 per cent of the total sample, in the rural areas of some developing countries the figure might be closer to 10 or 15 per cent. And because the designers of social surveys typically assume that most respondents will understand what the method is about, data are only rarely collected and reported about the full extent of non-comprehension.

This and the next section consider problems in the collection and analysis of data in the developing countries, including operational difficulties in the field. This section takes up the design of questionnaires and their suitability for eliciting certain kinds of data and then discusses a few aspects of data analysis. The following section will discuss problems of interviewing and field organization in sample surveys. The material presented does not attempt to summarize the general practices and norms of data collection and analysis. These are already well treated in existing texts on research methodology, survey research, and demography (Cox, 1970; Moser and Kalton, 1971; Shryock and Siegel, 1976; Warwick and Lininger, 1975; Kpedekpo, 1982). Instead the emphasis is on questions that are particularly salient, if not totally unique, in the Third World.

Goals and strategies

There are two basic goals in the design of survey and census instruments: to obtain relevant information, and to ensure the reliability and validity of the data collected. To obtain relevance the investigators must specify the precise types of data required in the study and then design the questionnaire or interview schedule accordingly. Securing reliable and valid data is an objective requiring attention at every step in the research, from the initial conceptualization of the question under investigation to the final analysis of the information collected. Much of this and the next section of the book are concerned with these questions.

Data collection in survey research involves a series of strategic decisions; these are represented simply in Figure 11.1. The alternatives posed by these decisions are well-described in general terms elsewhere (Warwick and Lininger, 1975, pp. 128–130). In surveys conducted in the developing coun-

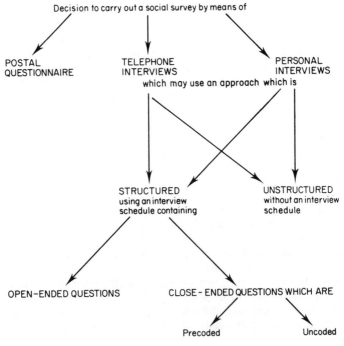

Figure 11.1:   Decision steps in data collection by social survey

tries, however, it is essential to be aware from the outset of the constraints common to those settings. The first concerns the extent to which this methodology will be understood by respondents and otherwise be viable in the field. It makes little sense to launch an ambitious survey if a substantial number of respondents in rural areas will misunderstand the purposes of the research, fear government repression if they cooperate with the study, or otherwise be ill-disposed to cooperate. It would be equally unwise to carry out a study that posed substantial risks to the health and perhaps the lives of the interviewers, a genuine possibility in areas of civil conflict, smuggling operations, or malaria infestation.

Other strategic decisions concern the specific means to be used in data gathering. In recent years telephone interviewing has become a favourite mode of contact for certain kinds of surveys in North America. But this is obviously an option only in societies with high telephone penetration and even there only in circumstances where respondents are prepared to accept this intrusion as legitimate. Thus, while telephone interviewing does enjoy reasonable, though not universal, legitimacy in the United States, it is far less common in western Europe. In most developing countries it is not an option worth considering unless the population to be sampled (a) has telephones; (b) has them listed under their own names; (c) is willing to answer the telephone for purposes of a survey; and (d) is willing to communicate the necessary information in this way. Areas fulfilling these conditions are rarely encountered.

Postals surveys are likewise suitable only when the population is nearly 100 per cent literate, when everyone has a recognizable address that is accessible to the samplers, when the postal service is reliable, and when potential respondents are accustomed to completing and returning structured questionnaires. In most developing countries none of these conditions is met, and even in the industrial countries there are serious problems with response rates in postal surveys (Oppenheim, 1966). A study carried out in one developing country came up with a response rate of only 17 per cent (Kumar and Pareek, 1966).

Further strategic decisions have to do with the amount of structure used in questionnaires. In rural areas of many developing countries there are competing considerations about structure. From the standpoint of respondents, many of whom will not be accustomed to condensing their thoughts into preformed categories, the open-ended format will often be preferable. But that format is also the most risky and difficult to control unless field personnel are skilled at interviewing and are thoroughly familiar with the purposes of each open question. Often the most fruitful alternative is to use a combination of open and closed responses, beginning with the former and moving slowly to the latter, perhaps with selected probes. (Warwick and Lininger, 1975, Chapter 6). The choice between closed and open questions further depends on the subject matter of the survey, the attitude of respondents toward the content of given questions, and other characteristics of the respondents, such as education and familiarity with surveys. Particular problems arise in adapting items developed in the industrial countries to the conditions commonly found in the Third World, one example of which is discussed in Chapter 27, by Kleymeyer and Bertrand. The question of linguistic equivalence, which arises both within and across countries, also bears directly on the problem and is given attention in this section.

Opportunities and constraints

The discussion of strategic decisions raises a question that should be confronted early in designing a census or survey: what can be done *here*? Some of the greatest mistakes in social research derive from faulty assumptions about the feasibility of conducting certain lines of research in a specified area. And some magnificent opportunities are often lost by applying the wrong strategy in circumstances where other possibilities would have been perfectly viable. The most common, though not the only, form of misapplied methodologies is seen when structured surveys are carried out in areas that are psychologically, culturally, or politically unprepared for them. The cost is not only a bungled survey, but a lost opportunity for research of a more subtle and indirect kind, such as informal interviewing or limited observation.

One of the questions that should be raised before any survey or census goes to the field is the extent to which the method as a whole and specific parts of the study will be understood by respondents and 'gatekeepers' controlling access to respondents. Researchers should ask themselves candidly during the design stage just what percentage of the respondents are likely to understand the survey itself, whatever its content. If this question cannot be answered on the basis of earlier work or other reliable information, it will typically be better to begin with a pilot study than a full-blown field operation. One of the difficulties with the Knowledge–Attitude–Practice (KAP) surveys discussed by Warwick in Chapter 26 was that investigators often assumed on the basis of no experience that respondents *anywhere* would be open to questions about fertility and would understand the surveys containing those questions. This kind of optimism may be heartening to research sponsors, but it is ultimately counter-productive for serious inquiry.

The point about pretesting applies as much to specific parts of a questionnaire or interview schedule as to the survey as a whole. If the researchers really do not know how well key sets of questions will work in the field, they should take the time to find out before they move into the main part of their data collection. Experience to date has shown that clusters of questions, and sometimes even single items, that are not well understood by respondents may create problems of validity not only for themselves but for the entire survey. And if the damage is serious enough the experience may preclude future surveys in that general region.

Questionnaire design

It is often suggested that question wording is more an art than a science. To some extent this is true. Unlike probability sampling, where fairly precise scientific measurement is possible, there is more scope for judgement and less certitude about the effects of varying designs. But there is systematic research on the effects of question wording that takes the field somewhat beyond the realm of art, and considerable practical experience suggesting proven means of avoiding bias in many situations (Schuman and Presser, 1981). Payne's much admired text *The Art of Asking Questions* (1951) is, despite its name, a good synthesis of both art and science in this field. Warwick and Lininger (1975, pp. 140–148) also suggest a number of guidelines that can help to avoid some of the more gross errors and sources of bias in questionnaire design. They propose specificaly that eight questions be asked of items in an interview schedule:

(1) Are the words used in the questions simple, direct, and familiar to all respondents?
(2) Is the question as clear and specific as possible?
(3) Do items try to cover more than one point within the same question?
(4) Are any of the questions leading or loaded? Do they use emotionally charged words or threats to self-esteem?
(5) Is the question applicable to the respondents of whom it will be asked?
(6) Will respondents answer the question in biased ways, such as saying 'yes' to items without regard to their content, or giving answers that are socially acceptable rather than the respondent's own views?
(7) Can the question be shortened with no loss of meaning?
(8) Does the question read well?

Some problems with question content are particularly salient to surveys in the developing countries and are discussed by authors in this section. One problem that should be faced more openly than it has in the past is the extent to which the respondent has an adequate frame of reference for answering the question. A major drawback to the typical KAP survey (see Chapter 26) was that it assumed that respondents had attitudes and opinions when they may have had neither. While specialists on opinion research have long been concerned about the danger of assessing opinions when they are not present before the interview, investigators still design surveys on the assumption that most if not all respondents have previously thought about the matters covered. If there is a single lesson from the sad experience with KAP surveys, it is that the extent to which attitudes and opinions are present should itself be a topic of research rather than be assumed. Among respondents with little or no formal education, low income, and minimal exposure to urban influences the chances of measuring opinions that do not and never have existed are very high. In such circumstances, and in general, it is better to determine whether and to what extent the respondent has thought about the matter at hand than to be left with data whose very meaning is in doubt.

Other difficulties arise from the sensitivity of the subject matter covered in the questionnaire or interview schedule. Some questions may be offensive or embarrassing for certain respondents. Such might be the case with items on marital status in Latin American countries where legal marriage is favoured but a large proportion of the population is not legally married. Other questions may be embarrassing, among them items asking about sexual attitudes and behaviour in a family planning survey. Still other items, such as those probing attitudes toward the government or political behaviour, may arouse fear among respondents unaccustomed to discussing such matters with strangers. There are no clear rules to guide the researcher in this area, but both prudence and ethical responsibility suggest the need for careful attention to the meaning of questions not only on paper but to the population being studied. And, while it is often difficult to predict every kind of adverse reaction, careful pretesting and checking with informed observers can forestall some of the most common antipathies and *faux pas*.

Sensitivity likewise has a positive dimension. As Pareek and Rao (1980) point out in their review of cross-cultural surveys and interviewing,

> The language used in the interview should reflect the interviewer's acquaintance with cultural norms. In many cases, word usage makes a pronounced difference in creating the proper climate for communication. This is particularly important in sensitive areas, such as sex. Knowledge of local terms used for sex organs, copulation, menstruation, etc., can help make the interview culture-relevant. (1980, pp. 127–129).

The same point applies to local terms for land and land tenure arrangements, irrigation systems, crops, weights, and even government agencies and their subdivisions. In heterogeneous countries such as Indonesia there may be several dozen regionally specific ways of calculating land holdings; without a working knowledge of local concepts and phrases the field interviewer will have great difficulty holding a meaningful discussion with farmers about agricultural matters.

Additional problems are caused by asking questions that are hypothetical, excessively complex, or outside the normal experience of respondents. Hypothetical questions asked of individuals who are unaccustomed to think in conditional terms have a notoriously high unreliability. When asked to comment frankly on the validity of such items in a national sample survey in Peru, interviewers often reported that poor people were embarrassed or confused, even though they sometimes gave an answer. (This information was gathered by Donald Warwick in 1970 as part of a consultancy for the Technical Office of Manpower Studies (OTEMO) of the Government of Peru. To evaluate the validity of the survey in general and of specific items he spent considerable time at the end of each day interviewing the interviewers about their experiences in the field. These discussions produced some valuable and illuminating information about the progress of the survey. It is a simple technique that might well be applied to any survey in the developing countries, particularly if there are doubts about whether respondents understand the survey or particular items.) Similar difficulties arise when the questions pose unreal alternatives: 'Asking people to tell what they would do, for example, if they had much more money ignore(s) the real constraints of subsistence living on small parcels of poorly irrigated land, and may only encourage the respondent to ask the interviewer to give him money' (Herzog *et al.*, 1976, p. 284). Other questions may be outside the respondent's experience. Asking poor villagers about their aspirations for their son's education or future occupation and then giving as alternatives 'university' or 'doctor' may be totally unrealistic in light of the actual opportunities open to the family. These issues are discussed further below.

Some of the major complications in questionnaire design are highlighted by attempts at translation. In Chapter 14, Iyengar observes that in 44 per cent of all nation-states, three-quarters or less of the population speak the dominant language. The common assumption in many textbook discussions of survey methods that all respondents speak a single language simply does not hold (Deutscher, 1973, 1977). Moreover, in adapting survey methods for use in developing countries, the tendency to translate standard English-language survey items into a local language gives rise to a whole host of problems of its own (Anderson, 1967). These problems will be considered at some length, since they are central to data collection.

It has been argued that in developing countries those who are responsible for the design and interpretation of measurement are linguistically incapable of either. Typically, measurements are framed in English or another foreign language, translated into a major regional language, and further translated into local dialects. Quite commonly, the individual interviewer makes on-the-spot local adaptations of regional languages. Whether individual interpretation (and the non-random biases therein) are permitted or not, what happens is that no one but the field workers and a few local project staff really know what is being asked or replied in the field. Since they may not speak English or be fluent in the regional language, their observations are passed upward through intermediaries. Issues become lost and meanings twisted in the process (Herzog *et al.*, 1976, p. 285)

This comment is made by scholars with Latin American and Indian experience, but can be generalized. Similar problems are encountered in interviewing respondents who have no written language at all. Frey faced this problem in interviewing Kurdish-speaking people in eastern Turkey. Bilingual, specially trained interviewers who were skilled at simultaneous translation between Turkish and Kurdish were used satisfactorily, but some control over the interviewing process was relinquished by those in charge. (Frey, 1973, p. 240).

Lexical equivalence

The most obvious translation problem faced in social research is that of lexical equivalence: how can one render the question as asked in the original language in the same words when asked in a different language? An early solution to this problem was either to allow bilingual interviewers to translate simultaneously during the interview, or to use bilingual translators to translate from one language to another. This approach was not satisfactory, as bilinguals may use their native language differently from monolinguals, and the procedure provided no independent check upon the translation accomplished. A different method, that of 'back-translation', is therefore more commonly used. The interview schedule is translated from the original language to the local language. It is then translated independently, by another translator, back from the local language into the original language. (The procedure is described by Iyengar in Chapter 14). The results are then compared to identify and correct semantic errors in translation.

The process of back-translation does ensure literal accuracy in translation and identifies inaccuracies, but it can lull the investigator into believing equivalence has been achieved when it has not. Howard Schuman has observed, on the basis of a study in Pakistan, that 'wording can be equally meaningful to both parties without the meaning being shared' (Schuman, 1966, p. 218). Deutscher (1968) gives various examples of situations in which respondents answers, but one is not sure of the question to which they are replying. And Flay, Bull, and Tamahori point out in Chapter 13 that back-translation can instil a false sense of security. Some concepts do not have equivalents in the local language and even when they do the exact meaning may be quite different.

Conceptual equivalence

This discussion directs attention to the broader problem of conceptual equivalence or equivalence in meaning. Do the concepts used in a particular study — whether these are theoretical terms such as 'anomie' or 'solidarity' or terms with more direct empirical reference like 'income' or 'household' — transfer unambiguously from one society to another? A good example is the notion of 'looking for work', a concept widely used in studies of unemployment across the world. While 'looking for work' may be a generally meaningful phrase in the urban areas of industrial countries (though some say that it has limitations even there), what meaning does it have, however accurately translated, for the peasant in a subsistence economy? Does it make any sense to put questions about 'looking for work' to poor farmers who, in an effort to stay alive, are already farming, fishing, cutting firewood, doing chores for others, and selling a few items at the nearby market? What the concept really means is 'are you doing anything specific to find a paid job in some recognizable place of business'. For subsistence farmers who may already be working 12 or more hours a day questions about looking for work may seem implausible, if not insulting. Yet they are regularly asked on employment surveys in the developing countries.

Concepts differ in their salience within a culture, and also in their research-ability through a census or survey (a point discussed by Mitchell in Chapter 18). Considerable knowledge of the local culture is needed to ensure conceptual equivalence (Nagt_r1977). To acquire such knowledge the investigators may have to spend weeks, months, or sometimes longer in attaining the kind of qualitative understanding that will permit questionnaires and interviews to be workable across the sites covered. In social science research dealing with somewhat abstract concepts, particular efforts will have to be made to ensure that the concepts themselves are meaningful in all locations, and that their empirical manifestations are equivalent.

A strong argument can be made that in translation the first priority should be conceptual equivalence rather than lexical comparability. This point is exemplified by the concept of 'opinion'. Wuelker observes in Chapter 12 that the ability to form and express opinions is confined to relatively small sections of the population. If this is true, the assumption in many western surveys that most respondents will hold a salient opinion on a given issue would be called into question (Blumer, 1948). Survey instruments seeking to elicit the 'opinions' of respondents in the developing countries may therefore produce meaningless results by adopting a framework that is culturally inappropriate. The resulting problems are discussed by several authors in this and the next section.

Equivalence in measurement

Troubles with conceptual equivalence may emerge very sharply when investigators try to establish equivalence in measurement from one site to another. If a concept is known to differ in its specific meaning across cultures, or between language groups in the same culture, how can it be measured in an equivalent way? One way of proceeding is to find out exactly what the concept does mean in each group, whether through ethnographic observation, exploratory interviewing, or other means. Another is to identify a general theme that is common to two or more groups and then organize the questions around that theme. But that strategy would still have the drawback of leaving out the features that are different across the groups. In short, a researcher can never assume that a question that is an adequate measure of a concept in one society can be used willynilly in another, even if the language is the same ('lift' and 'boot' may have quite different meanings in the United States and the United Kingdom). There is a middle ground between rigid universalism and total relativism in designing survey questions, and that ground must be sought. The quest for equivalence will require painstaking conceptual analysis, genuine familiarity with each research setting, extensive pretesting, and perhaps items that ostensibly differ in content but reflect generic similarities (Warwick and Osherson, 1973). Chapter 13 illustrates some of the practical challenges in establishing equivalent measurements for a survey of Polynesian and Pakeha automobile assembly line workers.

Some have sought to evade the constraints of cultural diversity by adopting supposedly 'culture-free' projective tests. The most obvious candidates are the Rorschach inkblot technique, the Thematic Apperception Test (TAT), the draw-a-person test, and various sentence completion or word association tests (Holtzman, 1980). Optimists in the field have long felt that such devices would obviate the most obvious difficulties seen with questionnaires, particularly their heavy reliance on culturally embedded words and phrases. But experience with projective techniques suggests that they may bring their own set of problems when applied in the developing countries. In India, for example, the fundamental assumption that respondents will discern figures in inkblots or identify three-dimensional figures from two-dimensional stimuli, may be incorrect.

Instances are not rare in the rural areas of India where people have not seen their own photograph in the whole of their lives. A test like TAT implies that the subject must be able to identify with the characters presented. This becomes difficult if the subject's habit or experience of appreciating his own photographs or image in the mirror is absent, which is certainly the case with most of our tribal peoples. In some tribes as well as some villages a prejudice is still there that a photograph reduces the longevity and health of the man whose photograph is taken (Misra, 1961, p. 190).

Speaking more generally of projective techniques in cross-cultural research, Holtzman (1980, p. 266) concludes:

Most techniques rely upon verbal behavior for response and many use culture-bound stimuli such as pictures or words. Maintaining the equivalent meanings of these methods across cultures can be difficult, especially when the linguistic and cultural differences being studied vary markedly. Even an otherwise 'meaningless' inkblot has culturally different connotations that obscure the meaning of personality interpretations unless they are taken into account. In techniques like the TAT, which involve a content analysis of verbal response, the language in which the response is given may be confounded with the way that the personality is expressed.

Holtzman cites research showing that in their responses to the TAT, bilingual Frenchmen showed different 'personalities' according to whether their replies were in French or in English. Thus one would be seriously misguided to hope for a solution to the problems of cross-cultural equivalence from the straight-forward adoption of projective devices.

Questions about equivalence of measurement arise as well when semiprojective techniques are included within the framework of a sample survey. In a national survey in Peru the investigators included a translated version of Hadley Cantril's 'ladder scale of aspirations'. In this technique, after the respondents are shown a picture of a ladder they are told that the top is the best possible life they can imagine while the bottom is the worst possible life. They are then asked three questions: where are you now? where were you 5 years ago? and where will you be in 5 years? Various problems arose with this method in the Peruvian survey. Some respondents in rural areas looked at the picture but did not see a ladder. Others understood the task in general, but had trouble with the hypothetical nature of the questions. A peasant in southern Peru seemed to grasp the question about 'where are you now' and pointed to one of the upper rungs to indicate his position. But when asked 'where were you 5 years ago' he motioned to the horizon and said: 'In Ayacucho [an Andean city]'. Another problem came up with older respondents. When asked 'where will you be in 5 years' some pointed upward as they replied: 'In heaven'.

It should be clear by now that there are no gimmicks or quick solutions for the nettlesome problems of cross-cultural equivalence. And in one sense what we refer to as 'problems' may really be opportunities for exploring the rich diversity of nuance and meaning in human societies. If groups really do have different ways of thinking about and reacting to sexuality, land tenure, politics, and other matters, then the differences are not just a nuisance standing in the way of research efficiency, but a vital challenge to research effectiveness. The general strategy we have already suggested of using the means at one's disposal to explore both similarities and differences is thus not just a matter of removing 'obstacles' but of practising sound social science. Exploring cultural diversity across settings, trying out items in each setting, and doing what is possible to understand, rather than only collect, data are all steps to be recommended not just on the grounds of better technique, but of better comprehension. As Herzog et al., (1976, pp. 289–290) point out, even satisfactory measurement is impossible

unless we have a culturally adept design in the hands of thoroughly and thoughtfully trained interviewers guided by regular and empathic supervision that motivates and rewards competence for performing tasks that are conceptually within their grasp as well as their respondents. In short, recognising the limitations on survey measurement, we must take elaborate precautions in preparing, conducting, and analysing surveys. Competent pre-testing is one step toward obtaining sensitive and sensible measurement in unfamiliar cultural settings.

Equivalence of response

Finally, cross-cultural surveys must pay close attention to equivalence of response. A survey question that is well-translated and renders a concept accurately in another language may elicit non-equivalent patterns of response from different social or linguistic groups. This problem shades over into the questions of interviewing discussed in the next section, but it also has distinct cultural and linguistic components. In Chapter 18 Mitchell shows that respondents in different cultures may show differential loquacity, even within the same country or city. Studies in Malaysia indicate that Chinese have a higher proportion of 'no answers' to fixed choice items than do Indians. The reason may be the greater reticence of the Chinese compared to the relative loquacity of the Indians. Different response styles, discussed later, can also influence the results of the same survey items administered to different groups.

Reliability, validity, and relevance

Two very important general criteria to be satisfied in designing data collection instruments are reliability and validity (see Chapter 1). Reliability refers to the extent to which a research instrument gives a consistent or reproducible result. One field in which reliability has been examined has been research on family planning. So-called KAP fertility surveys were discussed in Chapter 5 and are the main topic of Chapter 26. An examination of published KAP surveys shows that inconsistent patterns of response on certain items were particularly characteristic of female respondents,. the main group sampled in such studies (Maudlin, 1965a; 1965b; Stoeckel and Choudhury, 1969). In Dacca, one survey showed that a fifth of men and a quarter of women who knew about contraceptives denied this knowledge, while one-fifth of men and one-third of women who used contraceptives denied that as well (Green, 1969). Responses to attitude questions on family planning also appeared to be quite unreliable. A likely reason for denying the knowledge and use of contraceptives is a social setting in which positive responses would be perceived by respondents as unacceptable. Unreliability on attitude and opinion measures may stem from the lack of a frame of reference on such matters or on questions, such as those dealing with ideal family size, that are often meaningless to respondents, especially women.

A study by Mukherjee in Haryana, India, showed that the usual KAP approach to fertility studies is too simple for the problem at hand (Mukherjee, 1975, 121). This research suggested that many dimensions of attitudes toward preferred family size must be isolated and investigated separately. A few questionnaire items were insufficient to tap the complex attitude structure seen among respondents. The same study concluded that data from the usual surveys on desired family size are so contaminated as to be misleading if used for policy formulation and implementation.

Hauser in Chapter 5 points out the severe limitations of using such survey data for making inferences from attitudes to behaviour. Items assessing 'interest in' contraception do not necessarily indicate that the practices of the respondent will change. Much will depend on the immediate circumstances in which individuals and families find themselves, such as culturally based pressures for large families (Mamdani, 1972; Warwick, 1982 especially Chapter 7). Moreover, data on 'ideal' family size elicited by survey items may be meaningless in a society in which the number of children is thought to be determined by nature, spirits, or God. It is quite possible that many of the replies to KAP surveys are efforts at politeness or forced responses to questions about which the respondents have no real opinion.

Oscar Alers (Chapter 15) provides a further assessment of the reliability of survey techniques with particular reference to different types of attitude questions. His careful comparison rightly counsels against the outright rejection of survey data on the grounds of unreliability, and examines some of the reasons for inconsistency on successive applications of the same item to the same respondent. The message is rather that unreliability is a besetting problem which must be anticipated in the design stage, in the construction of research instruments, and in data collection in the same field. Much of the technical literature on questionnaire construction is concerned with establishing the reliability of items, but the solutions proposed often pay little attention to the sociocultural sources of inconsistency. The discussion here suggests that especially careful attention be given to this question when surveys are carried out in developing countries, and that the entire question of reliability be set in the larger social context of research. In the rural areas of many countries one will do more to improve reliability by designing surveys that are meaningful to respondents from the outset than by focusing excessively on the wording of single items.

The validity of survey responses is inherently more difficult to establish than their reliability. Hauser argues (Chapter 5) that KAP surveys lack validity because stated intentions are not matched by corresponding behaviours. On the question of contraceptive usage, what people say they do and what they actually do, do not always coincide. But even there the problem may not be invalidity in some disembodied technical sense ('we don't have very good items') but a poor theory about the links between attitudes and behaviour. For over 40 years social psychologists have known that attitudes and stated intentions do not always lead to the behaviours they imply. It is not necessarily a sign of poor items that women who say they are interested in contraception do not flock to family planning clinics when such services are offered. With a more accurate theory of human behaviour one might well predict just that outcome, particularly if the women find themselves locked into a system that rewards high fertility and punishes sterility. This point is closely related to the discussions of 'construct validity' raised almost three decades ago by Cronbach and Meehl (1955). Their argument is that validity is not established by any simple correlation, such as that between stated intentions and behaviours, but by the pattern of relationships one would expect in that situation on the basis of a guiding theory.

Since many developing countries lack adequate registration systems for births and deaths, they may rely on sample surveys for estimating short-term demographic trends. Yet such surveys often fail to provide valid counts of the number of people or events they are supposed to measure. Mauldin (1966, p.

639) concluded that 'single retrospective surveys cannot be depended upon to provide valid or reliable estimates of births and deaths'. Such surveys tend to undercount vital events, but without consistency over time or among different groups. There is similar evidence from the experience of a number of countries (reviewed in Lunde, 1976). For example, in the Indian National Sample Survey of 1953–54 (its design is described in Chapter 9), Som (1973, pp. 88–89) estimated that one out of five infant deaths and one out of seven infants alive at the time of the survey were missed in questions requiring recall over the previous 12 months. He also found, not unexpectedly, that the rate of omission varied directly with the time that had elapsed since the event occurred.

In survey work depending on recall, steps can be taken to minimize these problems by considering how serious memory decline is likely to be. It varies with the salience of the event. A different form of question may improve the response, as Blacker and Brass show in Chapter 16. Instead of asking for the number of children ever born, respondents were asked three separate questions about the number still living with the mother, the number living elsewhere and the number who have died. The discussion in Chapter 16 is a careful review of the problem of response error in demographic surveys, and the measures that may be taken to try to reduce such errors.

A more fundamental problem faced in some kinds of recall question is whether the answer to the question was *ever* known to the respondent. This may apply either to factual questions of a retrospective kind, or to attitude questions about the respondent's state of mind at some point in the past. As we have seen, such questions are fraught with difficulty, and liable to several types of response error. These were referred to earlier by Michael Ward in Chapter 10 and will be considered further in Section V.

This brief discussion of reliability and validity of survey data collected in developing countries is filled out in several of the following chapters, notably by Mitchell in Chapter 18. The issues to be faced are serious, and underline the point made in Section III on sampling that non-sampling errors are at least as serious as sampling errors in survey work in developing countries.

References

Anderson, R.B.W. (1967). On the comparability of meaningful stimuli in cross-cultural research. *Sociometry*, **30**, 124–136.

Blumer, H. (1948). Public opinion polls and public opinion polling. *American Sociological Review*, **13**, 342–349.

Cox, P.R. (1970). *Demography*, Cambridge University Press, Cambridge.

Cronbach, L.J. and Meehl, P.E. (1955). Construct validity in psychological tests. *Psychological Bulletin*, **52**, 281–302.

Deutscher, I. (1968). Asking questions cross-culturally: some problems of linguistic comparability. In H.S. Becker *et al*., (Eds), *Institutions and the Person*, pp. 318–341, Aldine, Chicago.

Deutscher, I. (1973). *What We Say/What We Do: Sentiments and Acts*, Scott Foresman, Brighton, Sussex.

Deutscher, I. (1977). Asking questions (and listening to answers): a review of some sociological precedents and problems. In M. Bulmer (Ed.) *Sociological Research Methods*, pp. 243–258, Macmillan, London.

Frey, F.W. (1973). Surveying peasant attitudes in Turkey. In D.P. Warwick and S. Osherson (Eds) *Comparative Research Methods*, pp. 227–247, Prentice Hall, Englewood Cliffs, NJ.

Green, L.W. (1969). East Pakistan: knowledge and use of contraceptives. *Studies in Family Planning*, **39, March**, 9–14.

Herzog, W. *et al.* (1976). Problems in measurement. In G. Hursh-César and P. Roy (Eds) *Third World Surveys*, pp. 246–298, Macmillan of India, Delhi.

Holtzman, W. (1980). Projective techniques. In H.C. Triandis and J.W. Berry (Eds), *Handbook of Cross-Cultural Psychology, Vol. 2, Methodology*, pp. 245–278, Allyn and Bacon, Boston.

Kpedekpo, G.M.K. (1982) *Essentials of Demographic Analysis*, Heinemann, London.

Kumar, V.K. and Pareek, U. (1966). Response behaviour of behavioural scientists. *Interdiscipline*, **3**, 75–80.

Lunde, A.S. (1976). *The Single-Round Retrospective Interview Survey*, University of North Carolina, Department of Bio-Statistics, Population Laboratories, Scientific Report Series no. 24, Chapel Hill, NC.

Mamdani, M. (1972). *The Myth of Population Control*, Monthly Review Press, New York.

Mauldin, W.P. (1965a). Application of survey techniques to fertility studies. In M.C. Sheps and J.C. Ridley (Eds) *Public Health and Population Change*, pp. 93–118, University of Pittsburgh Press, Pittsburgh.

Mauldin, W.P. (1965b). Fertility studies: knowledge, attitude, and practice. *Studies in Family Planning*, **7, June**.

Mauldin, W.P. (1966). Estimating rates of population growth. In B. Berelson (Ed.) *Family Planning and Population Programs*, pp. 635–654. University of Chicago Press, Chicago.

Misra, H. (1961). Use of psychological techniques in social surveys in India. *Indian Journal of Social Work*, **22**, 189–192.

Moser, C.A. and Kalton, G. (1971). *Survey Methods in Social Investigation*, Heinemann, London.

Mukherjee, B.N. (1975). Reliability estimates of some survey data on family planning. *Population Studies*, **29**, 127–142.

Nagi, M.H. (1977). Language variables in cross-cultural research. *International Social Science Journal*, **29**, 167–177.

Oppenheim, A.N. (1966). *Questionnaire Design and Attitude Measurement*, Heinemann, London.

Pareek, U. and Rao, T.V. (1980). Cross-cultural surveys and interviewing. In H.C. Triandis and J.W. Berry (Eds) *Handbook of Cross-Cultural Psychology, Vol. 2, Methodology*, pp. 127–179. Allyn and Bacon, Boston.

Payne, S.L. (1951). *The Art of Asking Questions*, Princeton University Press, Princeton, NJ.

Schuman, H. (1966). The random probe: a technique for evaluating the validity of closed questions. *American Sociological Review*, **31**, 218–222.

Schuman, H. and Presser, S. (1981). *Questions and Answers in Attitude Surveys*, Academic Press, New York.

Shryock, H.S. and Siegel, J.S. (1976). *The Methods and Materials of Demography*, Academic Press, New York.

Som, R.K. (1973). *Recall Lapses in Demographic Inquiries*, Asia Publishing House, New York.

Stoeckel, J. and Choudhury, M.A. (1969). Pakistan: response validity in a KAP survey. *Studies in Family Planning*, **47**, **November**, 5–9.

Warwick, D.P. (1982). *Bitter Pills: Population Policies and Their Implementation in Eight Developing Countries*, Cambridge University Press, New York.

Warwick, D.P. and Lininger, C. (1975). *The Sample Survey: Theory and Practice*, McGraw-Hill, New York.

Warwick, D.P. and Osherson, S. (1973). Comparative analysis in the social sciences. In D.P. Warwick and S. Osherson (Eds) *Comparative Research Methods*, pp. 3–41, Prentice Hall, Englewood Cliffs, NJ.

Social Research in Developing Countries
Edited by M. Bulmer and D.P. Warwick
© 1983, John Wiley & Sons, Ltd.

CHAPTER 12

QUESTIONNAIRES IN ASIA

GABRIELE WUELKER

Is public opinion research feasible in Asia?

There seems to be some justification for doubting whether research methods elaborated in the west are in fact suitable for South-East Asia. Asian peoples require an entirely different approach from that indicated in dealing with the peoples in countries to which industrialization came earlier. Since the number of illiterates in these parts of the world is still large, relatively few people are able to find things out for themselves and, accordingly, the ability to form their own opinions and express them is confined to comparatively small sections of the population.

Naturally, then, new methods have had to be devised for market and public opinion research in Asia; and thanks to these it is possible to secure results as objective as those in western countries. In the developing countries, however, it is far from sufficient merely to collate the results of interrogation. There is much more need for a thorough knowledge of the economic and social structures of those lands. This is a region where fieldwork and scientific research must go hand in hand.

Research as a supplement to fieldwork

In drafting a questionnaire it is essential to have a knowledge of social psychology and to be familiar with the sociological structure of the population concerned and with its level of education and vocational training. Occupational and wage structures also vary from one country to another. Areas with a high proportion of unemployment may have among their unemployed a considerable percentage of university graduates who have not yet been able to find employment in their country. Or people with a college education may be doing work for which a much lower standard of education would be sufficient. Other points to be taken into consideration in Asia include the ethnic situation, the

Reprinted from *International Social Science Journal* (1963), **XV** (**1**), 35–47. © 1963, UNESCO.
Reproduced by permission of UNESCO.

status of women and the relationship between different generations. These few examples of the points that have to be taken into account when conducting market and public opinion research in Asia show that fieldwork needs to be supplemented by research, and also make it even clearer what a mistake it would be to try to carry out empirical social research entirely from a foreign base. The complex nature of the radical changes that are taking place in the countries concerned, and the rapidity with which their social, political and economic transformation is being effected, call for close cooperation between the market and public opinion research workers in the western institutes and in their newly founded Asian equivalents.

Drafting the questionnaire

When a survey is commissioned from a non-Asian source, the general scheme may be elaborated in a foreign country; but the wording of the questionnaire and the selection of fields to be covered by the questions must be decided jointly with the appropriate institute. The questionnaire has to be adapted to the level of the group to be interviewed. For instance, an Indian knows much better than a foreigner what questions can be put to Indians and in what way; and the same will apply to Japanese or Burmese. The final decision about the questionnaire must therefore be left to the national institutes concerned. They know best how to strike the right note.

This is comparatively easy in a country where only one language is spoken, or at any rate where there is one language for official purposes. But it becomes difficult in countries where the population is not ethnically uniform. And this applies to most South-East Asian countries. Where several languages are in use, the questionnaire must be translated into those languages, or the results will not be representative. And the interviewers must, of course, be multi-lingual, or familiar with all the different dialects, in order to win the confidence of the people they question. Care must also be taken to ensure that the local translators produce an accurate version of the questionnaire and do not make what they regard as judicious changes. In many cases it is advisable to arrange, without the translators' knowledge, for a translation into a dialect or local language to be retranslated into English or into the official language of the country, as a further check.

When the first exploratory tests come in, the national institutes study them to discover whether the questions were put properly and whether they were answered frankly. Not until this has been ascertained is the full-scale survey launched.

Representative methods of selection

A representative cross-section of the whole population of a country or of a particular region can be arrived at either by random sampling or by the quota method. The aim of both systems is to represent the whole population on a reduced scale. The quota system is practicable only where statistics are available to show how the whole population or part of it is divided into age groups, occupation groups, etc., and among localities of different sizes and various districts.

The different proportions of certain structural features (age and occupation groups, etc.) within particular areas are then reduced to a smaller scale which varies according to the size of the sample desired, the aim being to arrive at a representative cross-section of the population, small enough to be interrogated. These reduced percentages are then given to the interviewers as their quota — in other words, each interviewer must find and question a range of persons corresponding to the quota.

Censuses have been carried out in a number of Asian countries in the last few years. The statistics thus obtained relate chiefly to the town populations, however. In Europe and other parts of the western hemisphere, it is essential to cover, for market research, for instance, a cross-section of the entire population, because there are very few products of which the consumers are confined to certain areas, or localities of a particular size; but in Asia the position is different.

Inquiries among retail traders and wholesale firms in Asia have revealed, for example, that the market for many durable goods, and consumer goods as well, is very largely in urban areas. Similar conclusions emerge from public opinion surveys. The persons and strata who influence public opinion are found chiefly in the towns. Thus, the quota method is indicated more often than is sometimes supposed by market researchers unacquainted with Asia. Where the random sample method is adopted, the theory of probabilities is taken as a mathematical basis, or the investigators make use of its conclusions by employing established formulae.

This method obeys one fundamental rule — that every sampling unit must have a possibility, an equal chance, of being included in the sample.

This sampling unit can be defined in a great variety of ways. It may be every household on the local register of population. In that case the sample might be formed by taking every hundredth household, or on the basis of random number tables. The number of households to be selected will be determined by the probability figures.

Again, the sampling unit may be arrived at by dividing a map of the region — usually a very large-scale one — into areas of an agreed size. Once the whole region has been thus divided, a random selection of areas can be made by the method described above. Here again, the procedure — also known as area sampling — assumes that the fundamental rule of random sampling is observed, in other words that every street, square, etc., in the area as a new sampling unit, has an equal chance of being selected. These new sampling units may also be called the starting points, one of them being allotted to each interviewer as the area he is to cover (starting-point method).

The last-mentioned method is the one preferred for surveys in Asian countries. If the prescribed procedure is closely adhered to, it has certain advantages over the quota system. For one thing it dispenses with the often wearying search for statistical material; for another thing it avoids the risk of inaccuracy on the part of the interviewers. By careful methods of selection and properly contrived samples, it becomes possible to assemble opinions which are genuinely representative of the population concerned.

Practical problems

The theoretical and technical preliminaries for empirical social research in the developing countries appear to be comparatively evident. Yet there are numerous practical problems which may considerably hamper such research unless due allowance is made for them (see Jones, Chapter 20). In the first place, in such countries where the government or governmental system is not always firmly established, the approval, or at least the consent of the authorities must usually be obtained before a start can be made. In many cases the statistical frame, generally regarded in western surveys as an essential prerequisite for ensuring that the sample interrogated is truly representative of the total population, is either incomplete or unreliable, while in some countries it simply does not exist. However, statistics are generally available for large population centres, or for particular social categories or occupations. And the occupational categories covered are precisely those most calculated to influence current public opinion. This is particularly true in those parts of the world where the trend of national policy is determined by the upper classes, so that the reaction of such groups to an important international political event will be representative of the population as a whole.

Empirical social research is naturally affected by political factors as well. In countries where political minorities exist, their attitude towards the government has to be taken into consideration. If these minorities are not held in very high esteem — like the Chinese in a few South-East Asian countries — they will show a marked reluctance to answer political questions, for fear of making themselves politically unpopular. If their numbers are large (for instance, the Chinese make up 85 per cent of the total population of Singapore) and they play an important part in the country's social and economic life, they cannot be disregarded. The more authoritarian the government of a country, the more the replies of those interviewed may be expected to 'chime in' with the official policy.

The vast area covered by countries such as India, Indonesia and the Philippines, and the primitive character of their communications, set further difficult problems for those embarking on sample surveys. The climate, too, has a far-reaching influence on the zeal of interviewers and interviewed. In tropical climates activity is at a low ebb. And during the monsoon period, with its heavy daily rainfall, travel becomes virtually impossible.

The completion of a survey may also be delayed if the investigator does not know the dates of religious feasts or public holidays. In Muslim countries, for example, there would be no point in attempting a survey during Ramadhan, the month of fasting, when the faithful neither eat, drink nor smoke between sunrise and sunset. During this period they are liable to become so weak that no extra physical effort can be expected of them.

Disagreeable surprises also lie in wait for any interviewer who is insufficiently acquainted with the manners and customs of the country. For example, in some countries age is an important factor, and it would be quite contrary to polite usage for a young man to put questions to an older one — even if the younger man were the better educated of the two — unless he held some official position entitling him to do so.

Any attempt at sending out non-Asians to interview Asians would be a fiasco. Asians are far too polite to tell a foreigner anything he might not like to hear, and a European will always receive rose-tinted answers to his queries for fear of offending him.

In the towns of South-East Asia the clans and family groups cling together so much that it would be almost impossible for a non-Asian to distinguish between the various dwelling units and households and devise a proper sample survey.

These difficulties should not be overrated, however, for the governments of the Asian countries are beginning to recognize the value of market and public opinion research and to give it their approval. Moreover, it has been found that in many of those countries human relationships have remained more natural and unspoilt than in the west. Mutual trust still plays a bigger part than amid the rush and agitation of the industrialized countries. If the interviewer manages to inspire confidence, all classes of the community will answer his questions with alacrity. Furthermore, the clearcut social structure and the infrequency of intermingling of the different classes make it possible to achieve the desired purpose with smaller samples than in the west. Preliminary investigations in selected towns in Cambodia and Thailand provided information which, after careful evaluation, proved to be applicable to the whole of the country.

Personnel

If due allowance is made for the practical difficulties, they will not prove insuperable. But for the time being the shortage of trained personnel, both western and Asian, is a serious handicap. Few western experts are well versed in the principal South-East Asian languages, and English or French brings one into contact only with persons or groups who are not really typical of their own countries, and have been away from them for more or less long periods or no longer feel quite at home in them.

The accuracy and completeness of the results depend to a great extent upon the ability of the interviewer. In these countries it is therefore most important to give the interviewers a thorough training and to supervise them carefully. A supervisor should come and check, on an average, one interview in every five. Moreover, every questionnaire should include control questions, as a means of checking the correctness of replies. And for each interview the exact time at which it began and ended should be noted, together with the date.

Social Research in Developing Countries
Edited by M. Bulmer and D.P. Warwick
© 1983, John Wiley & Sons, Ltd.

CHAPTER 13

DESIGNING A QUESTIONNAIRE FOR POLYNESIAN AND PAKEHA CAR ASSEMBLY WORKERS

BRIAN R. FLAY,
PATRICK E. BULL
AND
JOHN TAMAHORI

Recently, we were asked to design a questionnaire to assess the attitudes of clock staff in a New Zealand manufacturing plant toward aspects of their employment situation. The questionnaire was part of a comprehensive study of labour turnover involving biographical data drawn from the company's application form and supervisory ratings on attendance, standard of work, personal conduct, and a decision as to the reemployment of any terminated staff. The study also involved establishing monthly reports within the company of labour turnover ratios by plant sections, reporting indices of stability and conservation, establishing the mathematical definitions of the various labour wastage curves, and an inquiry into the exact costs of turnover.

Approximately 71 per cent of the company's employees were Polynesian, 46 per cent being from Samoa and the Cook Islands and 25 per cent being Maori, with the remaining 29 per cent of the staff being mainly Pakeha — that is, New Zealanders of European ethnic origin.

The attitudes to be assessed by the questionnaire included sections on pay and hours, training, supervision, the specific nature of the work, the perceived promotion possibilities, the perceived involvement in company decisions, the social nature of the work, the social facilities provided in the plant, and attitudes in relation to employment stability. In the analyses we expect these separate areas of concern to relate to a general construct of job satisfaction.

Reprinted from 'Designing a Questionnaire for Polynesian and Paketia Car Assembly Workers: by Brian R. Flay, Patrick E. Bull, and John Tamahori, *Journal of Cross-Cultural Psychology* (1976), **7**, (**2**), 235–241. © 1976, Western Washington State College. Reprinted by permission of Sage Publications.

Our questionnaire development rationale contained four general constraints. First, as the data were expensive to collect, a questionnaire that could be self-administered was suggested. However, since it was expected that some workers might need assistance to complete the questionnaire effectively, it was designed to be administered in a pseudointerview situation. The actual administration involved a pseudointerviewer of the same racial group, handling a racially homogeneous group of four to six respondents. In addition, the questionnaire was to be translatable into Pacific languages. Second, it was felt that the questionnaire should concentrate on establishing the staff's subjective feelings about pay, conditions, social interaction, training, supervision, and so on, rather than the objective information which could be obtained from the company's records and interfirm comparisons. The third stipulation defined was that the information recovered should not merely satisfy our curiosity but should have the potential to lead to effective executive action. Last, the data should be obtained in a form amenable to analysis by techniques such as principal components, discriminant analysis, and various regression techniques. This meant that the items should have continuous response scales that either formed a normal distribution or could be transformable to one, and that there should be more than one question relating to the same general area of information.

In addition to these self-imposed constraints, there are rules inherent in cross-cultural psychology that we applied as the questions were developed. Initially, we were guided by the rules developed by Brislin, Lonner, and Thorndike (1973, p. 33):

(1) use short, simple sentences of less than 16 words.
(2) Employ the active rather than the passive voice.
(3) Repeat nouns instead of using pronouns.
(4) Avoid metaphors or colloquialisms. Such phrases are least likely to have equivalents in the target language.
(5) Avoid the subjunctive mode (for example, verb forms with 'could' or 'would').
(6) Avoid adverbs and prepositions telling 'where' or 'when' (such as, frequent, beyond, upper).
(7) Avoid possessive forms where possible.
(8) Use specific rather than general terms (for example, the specific animal, such as cows, chickens, pigs, rather than the general term 'livestock').
(9) Avoid words which indicate vagueness regarding some event or thing (such as 'probably' and 'frequently').
(10) Avoid sentences with two different verbs if the verbs suggest different actions.

These rules all appear sensible, but it was surprisingly difficult to satisfy them simultaneously when writing questions for factory floor staff. Under these rules, a question may go through four to ten rewrites before acceptance. As an example, the development sequence of a question that was aimed at establishing the staff's evaluation of amount of training they received for their specific job went through eight stages, as follows.

Development sequence of a question

First attempt

'How much time have you had being trained here?' Left open, this question asks for objective information on the amount of time allocated for training, rather than for the respondent's subjective assessment of the adequacy of the training he received. The question in this form lacks the directness required.

Second attempt

'How much time have you had being trained here? (1) much more than I expected to get; (2) a little more than I expected to get; (3) about what I expected; (4) a little less than I expected to get; (5) much less than I expected to get.' Here the stem is still asking for objective information, but the answers try to make this subjective by forcing a comparison with expectations. Further, the responses were too long and complicated for easy comprehension.

Third attempt

'Compared with what I expected to get, the training I received here was: (1) far too much; (2) a bit too much; (3) just right; (4) a bit too little; (5) far too little.' Here we had a direct question, but the complicated expectation comparison was transferred to the stem. This relation may not be easily handled by some of the sample.

Fourth attempt

'Regarding the training programmes here, I think they should be: (1) increased a lot; (2) increased a little; (3) left as they are; (4) decreased a little; (5) decreased a lot.' This stem was regarded as awkward and contained the subjunctive 'should', which was difficult to translate.

Fifth attempt

'I would like to see the training programmes given here: (1) increased a lot; (2) increased a little; (3) left as they are; (4) decreased a little; (5) decreased a lot.'

This alteration reduced the awkwardness but did not eliminate the subjunctive. So we altered the stem in the sixth version.

Sixth attempt

'I wish the amount of training given here was: (1) increased a lot; (2) increased a little; (3) left as it is: (4) decreased a little; (5) decreased a lot.' This question was probably adequate for the person whose natural language was English. It failed however, to meet the cross-cultural criterion of being in the active voice, and so more easily translated.

Seventh attempt

'I think the amount of training given here is: (1) far too much; (2) a bit too much; (3) just right; (4) a bit too little; (5) far too little.' Here we decided that the form of the stem was correct but we found that the English vernacular used by some of the staff could disturb the scale properties of the responses. The phrase a 'bit too much' could be taken to mean a more extreme value than the phrase 'too much'. In the vernacular, 'a bit too much' can mean that a situation is beyond the bearable level, whereas 'too much' might mean that it is more extreme than it should be but still tolerable. Thus, questions must be examined in respect to the local idiom.

Eighth and final attempt

'I think the amount of training given here is: (1) too much; (2) quite a lot; (3) just right; (4) not much; (5) too little.' This was the question that was finally used.

There are also points concerning vocabulary, response modes, instructions, order of questions, and translation problems that became apparent during the development and piloting of the questionnaire. Words·such as organized, occasion, responsibility, opportunity for advancement, constant, increase, decrease, and praise created problems for some of the respondents. In the future, it should be possible to control for this problem by utilizing school spelling lists or some definitive basic English reference. It was also found to be better to keep the prose as concrete as possible because abstractions, such as 'the *value* of friendship', tend to be culturally specific.

The response mode in the pilot questionnaire consisted of circling the chosen response. The interviewers believe that a tick in a box placed adjacent to the responses would be more readily understood.

A conviction developed, as work progressed, that responses are only valid in this situation where every point on a scale is verbally labelled so that its meaning is clearly distinguishable from all other points on the scale. For example, respondents would have difficulty if, on the scales presented above, the second and fourth points existed but were not verbally defined. Lane (1975) has reported that Likert and semantic-differential types of scales are inadequate in the New Zealand cross-cultural environment. A suggestion has been made that physical forms of response, such as the selection of cards or placing marbles in cans, might be desirable (Ah Sam, 1975), but this form of response makes group administration difficult. With these considerations in mind we persevered with verbally defined, alternative-choice items.

It seemed crucial to personalize the explanations and instructions given to the respondents and to solicit their cooperation by indicating the purpose for which the information was being collected. This situation was facilitated in the study by the earlier decision to collect the data by pseudointerviews.

On a scientific basis, it was decided to order the questions randomly. This probably increased the difficulty the respondent had in reading the questions, and we would now group together the items that deal with a similar content area. People with a low level of education may not have the flexibility to move randomly from questions on one subject area to questions on another. Order effects may or may not be induced by grouping items together, but it appears likely that such grouping will increase reading comprehension by establishing a meaningful cognitive set.

Last, a series of observations arose from the translation process. Retranslation back into English by someone other than the original translator is necessary to ensure that the meaning has been retained. However, a failure to back-translate exactly does not necessarily mean that the translation was in error, as the connotations of words may be different in other languages. For example, the word 'indifferent' retranslates from Cook Island Maori as 'couldn't care less', but in Maori it lacks the negative connotations of the English form and so seems to be a correct translation. When translating a five-point scale, it is often better to translate the intermediate responses first. In general, the lesson learned was that it is necessary to work with the translator at all stages.

As back-translation checks could lead to a false sense of security (Brislin, Lonner, and Thorndike, 1973, pp. 41 ff.), it was also felt necessary to pretest the questionnaire to check that it was producing meaningful results in relation to the purpose for which it was designed. Pretesting was done on six people who were to act as the pseudointerviewers, and then the questionnaire was piloted on a sample of 60 workers. On the basis of this pilot run, the length of the questionnaire was reduced and some minor alterations were made to the questions and scales.

The points outlined in this chapter were formulated as we developed a questionnaire to collect part of the data needed to analyse labour turnover in a New Zealand manufacturing plant. They emerged both from a consideration of principles developed by academics and from an extremely diverse team of people considering and debating problems encountered during the questionnaire's development. They have been written into this article as points for consideration, rather than as established facts, with the aim of assisting occupational psychologists who are developing questions for a multicultural environment.

References

Ah Sam, U. (1975). Personal communication to the authors, University of Auckland, Department of Psychology.

Brislin, R.W., Lonner, W.J. and Thorndike, R.M. (1973), *Cross-cultural Research Methods*. John Wiley, New York.

Lane, R.H. (1975). *Culture conflict and inter-generation, problems among European, Cook Island and Samoan adolescents and their families in Otara and Tokaroa*, Presented at the annual conference of the New Zealand Psychological Society, Wellington.

Social Research in Developing Countries
Edited by M. Bulmer and D.P. Warwick
© 1983, John Wiley & Sons, Ltd.

CHAPTER 14

ASSESSING LINGUISTIC EQUIVALENCE IN MULTILINGUAL SURVEYS

SHANTO IYENGAR

Introduction

The problem of measurement equivalence is of vital importance to comparative research. Unless it can be demonstrated that the indices used in one particular context are applicable to other contexts, comparison is of little value. (Frey, 1970, pp. 243–248, 284–288; Przeworski and Teune, 1970, pp. 114–141). The problem is of special concern to studies that deal with heterogeneous populations. In cross-national research, measurement equivalence is difficult to achieve due to variations in political structure and process along with other cultural and socioeconomic differences. Because of these differences, operational measures of the same concept may have to vary across nations if equivalence is to be achieved. Political participation in the Soviet Union, for instance, cannot be assessed through indicators used in the United States (such as voting frequency and campaigning). The difference in political structure between the two nations necessitates the use of indicators specific to each nation. Since few if any countries have completely homogeneous populations, the problem is also pertinent to single-country studies as illustrated by the current debate in the United States concerning racial biases in intelligence testing.

One barrier to measurement equivalence which applies to both cross-national and single-country studies is linguistic diversity. In this research note, the effects of multilingualism on attitude measurement are discussed, and two methods involving the use of bilingual respondents are used to assess equivalence.

It must be emphasized that linguistic diversity is by no means a rarity. According to a recent tabulation, 44 per cent of all nation-states may be

Reprinted with permission from *Comparative Politics* (1976), **8 (4)**, 577–589. © 1976, *Comparative Politics*.

classified as linguistically heterogeneous in that less than 75 per cent of their populations speak the dominant language (Rustow, 1968, pp. 94–96). Clearly, the problem of achieving measurement equivalence across languages has widespread relevance.

Multilingualism and linguistic equivalence

Since research in the multilingual context entails measurement in more than one language, measurement equivalence is, in part, a function of linguistic equivalence. Measurement equivalence is not completely reduced to linguistic equivalence, since linguistic differences generally coincide with other cultural differences. As a result, the extent to which linguistic differences affect measurement independently of other cultural differences cannot be precisely specified.

In analogy with the approach of Adam Przeworski and Henry Teune (1970), pp. 114–117), linguistic equivalence is defined as validity within languages; but it is operationalized as reliability across the languages concerned. (Anderson, 1967). Validity within languages implies that indicators measure what they intend to measure in each language (Blalock, 1968). Validity thus requires that questions in one language be translated into another language in such a way as to retain their meaning. Where 'systemic interferences' are serious, very non-literal translations may be needed to achieve validity. At the opposite extreme, where the linguistic groups are perfectly matched on all characteristics other than language, validity would be determined simply by the accuracy of translation.

This indicator–concept linkage is, however, difficult to evaluate empirically in any language. Hence, linguistic equivalence is operationalized using the criterion of reliability across languages. Two types of reliability are to be examined: internal consistency and test–retest stability (Bohrnstedt, 1969).

Testing for internal consistency requires that responses to sets of indicators of the same concept be compared across languages. If two languages are being used, each may be considered a method of measurement; and reliability can be expressed as the level of consistency in the responses obtained from the two methods. If the attitude of political efficacy is being measured, for example, indicators of political efficacy phrased in one language should elicit a similar response pattern as the same indicators phrased in some other language. As Przeworski and Teune have put it (1970, p. 117):

> The similarity of the structure of indicators is the criterion for establishing the equivalence of measurement instruments. The similarity of structure can be defined in terms of the pattern of intercorrelations among indicators. If the indicators for particular systems, hypothesized to belong to the domain of the same concept, are intercorrelated with each other in the same way in each system, the structure of the indicators is said to be the same.

Linguistic equivalence can thus be assessed by comparing correlations among sets of indicators purporting to measure the same concept in different languages. To the extent that language does not affect responses, the magnitude of these correlations will be similar in the different languages. The greater the similarity between the sets of correlations, the higher the level of equivalence.

The second test of reliability assesses the extent to which language affects the stability of responses. Can responses to the same item be made to change by manipulating the language of the instrument? Obviously, this relationship can only be examined using bilingual respondents. Bilinguals are given the same instrument twice, with the second administration following the first by approximately 8–9 weeks. Randomly picked respondents take the first and second administrations in different languages. Comparing the amount of change on the part of these respondents with the change shown by respondents who take both administrations in the same language indicates the level to which stability is dependent on language — the greater the difference in stability between the two groups, the lower the level of equivalence (Converse, 1970).

To summarize, linguistic equivalence has been operationalized using two methods. The first considers the extent to which different respondents answer the same questions consistently in their respective languages. The second method considers the extent to which respondents answering the same questions at two time points in different languages are more or less stable than respondents answering the same questions at two time points in the same language.

Previous research

With few exceptions, political scientists have neglected to investigate the effects of language differences on attitude measurement. There is some work, however, on the methodology of translation. Though various techniques have been suggested to improve the quality of translations, (see Brislin, Lonner, and Thorndike, 1973, pp. 32–58; Schuman, 1966), empirical tests of equivalence between translations and the original version of the instrument are rare and there are very few references to the use of bilinguals as a means of gauging linguistic equivalence. (Frey, 1970, p. 278).

Fortunately, ethnolinguists and anthropologists have accumulated a considerable body of research dealing with bilingualism (Deutscher, 1968; and Hymes, 1970). Some of this work relating to typologies of bilingualism is pertinent here, and may be briefly reviewed. Two types of bilinguals have been identified — the coordinate and the compound. The former uses the two languages interchangeably while the latter, though competent in both, separates the conceptual categories of each language. As Bruce W. Anderson has states (1967, p. 136): 'If the bilingual uses a sort of "common" set of concepts which link his two languages together, we term him a coordinate bilingual. If on the other hand, such a link is absent and he uses the languages more or less independently, we term him a compound bilingual.'

A further distinction refers to the context in which the language is acquired. Wallace Lambert *et al*., (1958) have differentiated between fused and separate contexts of acquisition, the former referring to the situation where both languages are acquired within the same environment, the latter to learning that occurs in varying contexts. The fused context has been found to be related to coordinate bilingualism, but the relationship is slight (see also Lambert, 1959).

These distinctions are of considerable import to the search for linguistic equivalence. Using a sample of compound bilinguals, Susan Ervin (1964) was unable to obtain equivalent versions of certain personality tests. Anderson (1967) cites a study in which equivalence was achieved when coordinate bilinguals were used as respondents. In short, it is important for the researcher employing bilingual respondents to identify the types of bilinguals included in the sample.

Finally, tests of equivalence based on bilinguals may not be applicable to monolinguals. In certain cases, it has been found that bilinguals and monolinguals use the same language differently (Lambert and Moore, 1966). Furthermore, bilingual ability may entail greater familiarity with concepts the researcher is investigating. For example, in the Telugu language there is no conversational term for the political party. As a result, speakers of Telugu who are also familiar with English are more likely than monolingual Telugu speakers to respond to questions of partisanship.

The database

The data analysed here stem from a larger study of political socialization in the state of Andhra Pradesh in India. A questionnaire was prepared in English and translated into Telugu. Back-translation, through bilingual officials of the Andhra Pradesh Department of Education, was the method used to prepare the Telugu version.

The sample consists of 101 respondents, drawn from two junior colleges in the same city. Respondents were randomly selected from the four highest classes. All the respondents are bilingual, and many are trilingual. While Telugu is the mother tongue for most, all the respondents speak English in school, since it is the medium of instruction. In terms of the compound–coordinate distinction, respondents are mainly compound bilinguals who have learned the languages in separate contexts, since Telugu is spoken at home and English is used at school. The two schools from which the sample is drawn are known for relatively high standards of English, and the competence of the respondents in English can be safely assumed.

The questionnaire was administered during the 4th week of June 1973, and again during the 1st week of September. Using random allocation, 60 respondents took the 1st round in English and 41 answered in Telugu. For the 2nd round, the English version was given to 49 respondents, while 52 answered in Telugu. Four groups may be identified: (1) respondents who took the English version twice; (2) those who took the English version first and then the Telugu; (3) those who answered first in Telugu and then in English; and (4) respondents who answered the Telugu version twice. For purposes of assessing equivalence, the English–English and Telugu–Telugu groups are combined ($n=63$) and compared with the English–Telugu and Telugu–English respondents ($n=38$). As pointed out earlier, respondents taking the questionnaire in different languages were randomly selected. Because some of the respondents chosen to take a different version of the questionnaire at the second administration expressed reluctance to do so, this group is smaller than the group taking both rounds in the same language.

Since most respondents are compound bilinguals, and given the research cited previously, the barriers to achieving equivalence are increased. Furthermore, respondents are children so their grasp of the languages will naturally not be as firm as that of adult bilinguals. It is also well known that politics and government are extremely non-salient stimuli, especially to children. Recent work on children's political opinions has shown them to be quite unstable (Vaillancourt, 1973). In short, the nature of the respondents and the stimuli to be used combine to make this analysis a rigid test of linguistic equivalence.

Equivalence will be assessed with respect to three sets of variables. The first relates to the respondents' political knowledge and comprises five indicators: does the respondent know the names of the prime minister, chief minister, and governor of Andhra Pradesh, and the governor's chief adviser, and can the respondent identify the capital of Andhra Pradesh? It can be hypothesized that equivalence comes relatively easily in this set, since language is not likely to affect responses to such specific, factual items.

The second set of items consists of five evaluations of the prime minister and governor: do they perform good work, do they help the people, and is the prime minister hardworking? Though these are relatively specific questions, they require the respondent to express an opinion. It can be hypothesized that their level of equivalence will be lower than that obtained for the political information questions.

Finally, the third set consists of four 'diffuse' questions making up a political trust scale: can the government be trusted, does it help all segments of society, does it pass only good laws, and do politicians keep their promises? Given the abstract nature of these questions, the level of equivalence is expected to be lowest here.

Analysis and results

The first test of equivalence requires computation of correlations between the items in the three sets. For each set, three matrices of correlations are computed corresponding to the entire sample and to the English and Telugu subsamples. Since all the items meet the ordinal level of measurement, Maurice Kendall's tau-*b* may be employed as the measure of association. Among the ordinal correlations, tau-*b* is the most stringent since it is reduced by the presence of 'ties' on either of the two variables being correlated (Kendall, 1970).

In order to assess whether the relationships between indicators are affected by the language of the instrument, the correlations obtained from the Telugu and English subsamples are compared with their counterparts in the parent sample. Instead of using the norms of statistical significance, the following arbitrary threshold is adopted to specify subsample–sample differences: a correlation in one of the subsamples is considered different from the parent correlation only if it differs from the latter by at least one standard error of the parent correlation. For example, a tau of 0.24 with a standard error of 0.10 is obtained for the entire sample. The corresponding tau for the Telugu subsample is 0.35. Since the difference exceeds the standard error, it it concluded that the relationship is not independent of the language of the instrument (Kendall, 1970, pp. 60–63). Obviously, the greater the number of obtained differences within each set of indicators, the lower the level of equivalence.

As a further aid to comparison, the average difference between the Telugu and English correlations is computed for each set. The higher this difference, the lower the level of equivalence.

The interitem correlations are only presented for the first administration responses, since responses to the second may be affected by the change in language. Since Telugu respondents at the second administration (*T*2) include respondents who answered the English version at the first administration (*T*1), differences between the Telugu and English responses at *T*2 may be a result of the manipulation of language.

Table 14.1 presents the correlation matrices for each of the three sets of items within each language and for the entire sample. Before examining these matrices, it is to be noted that the Telugu and English respondents at *T*1 are not noticeably different with regard to the background characteristics of age, class in school, sex, and religion. Therefore, variations in the response patterns of the two groups may not be attributed to such compositional differences.

The intercorrelations among the political information items are consistent across language. None of the differences between the two subsamples and the parent sample meets the threshold specified here. The average difference between the Telugu and English subsamples is only 0.06. As expected, responses to these items are similarly related in both languages.

Table 14.1 Pooled and within-language correlation Matrices at $T1$

Set 1 — Political information

	Entire sample (N = 101)				English subsample (N = 60)				Teluga subsample (N = 41)			
	(1)	(2)	(3)	(4)	(1)	(2)	(3)	(4)	(1)	(2)	(3)	(4)
(1) Who is the prime minister?												
(2) Who is the governor?	0.14				0.14				0.12			
(3) Who is the chief minister?	0.07	0.40			0.10	0.43			0.04	0.35		
(4) Who is Mr Sarin?	0.31	0.12	0.20		0.33	0.13	0.19		0.26	0.09	0.23	
(5) Where is the government of Andhra Pradesh?	0.04	0.09	0.22	0.34	0.05	0.16	0.24	0.34	0.10	0.02	0.14	0.34

(Average difference between Telugu and English correlations = 0.06)

Set 2 — Evaluations of prime minister and governor

	Entire sample (N = 101)				English subsample (N = 60)				Teluga subsample (N = 41)			
	(1)	(2)	(3)	(4)	(1)	(2)	(3)	(4)	(1)	(2)	(3)	(4)
(1) Prime minister works hard												
(2) Prime minister does good work	0.55				0.55				0.37			
(3) Prime minister helps the people	0.53	0.52			0.52	0.52			0.40	0.49		
(4) Governor does good work	0.41	0.36	0.45		0.40	0.65	0.45		0.26	0.38	0.47	
(5) Governor helps the people	0.18	0.40	0.47	0.62	0.18	0.40	0.47	0.61	0.08	0.28	0.49	0.53

(Average difference between Telugu and English correlations = 0.11)

Set 3 — Political Trust

	Entire sample (N = 101)				English subsample (N = 60)				Teluga subsample (N = 41)			
	(1)	(2)	(3)	(4)	(1)	(2)	(3)	(4)	(1)	(2)	(3)	(4)
(1) Politicians keep promises												
(2) Government can be trusted	0.15				0.13				0.18			
(3) Government helps all people	0.15	0.21			0.22	0.08			0.01	0.37		
(4) Government only makes good laws	0.22	0.19	0.30		0.33	0.14	0.11		0.07	0.28	0.58	

(Average differences between Telugu and English correlations = 0.24)

The measure of association used is tau-b. Since pair-wise deletion of missing data was used, the N for each correlation is not identical. Subsample correlations which do not meet the operational norms of equivalence are underlined.

The correlations among the second set of items also reveal a high degree of consistency. Three of the ten correlations based on the Telugu responses differ from their parent correlations compared to only one of the correlations based on the English responses. The primary source of these differences in the Telugu subsample is the evaluation of the prime minister as hardworking, since all three differences involve this particular item. Overall, the average difference between the Telugu and English correlations for the second set of items is 0.11, only somewhat higher than the difference for the political information items.

Unlike the other two sets, the correlations among the political trust items in the English and Telugu subsamples are markedly different from those based on the whole sample. Four of the six correlations from the Telugu responses and two of the six from the English responses do not meet the operational criterion of similarity used here. Furthermore, the average difference between the correlations in the two subsamples is 0.24, indicating that responses to the trust items are affected by the language of the instrument.

The evidence contained in Table 14.1 warrants the conclusion that the political information items are similarly related in both languages. All of the comparisons between the subsample and sample correlations meet the criterion of equivalence. Similarly, 16 of the 20 comparisons in the second set of items meet this test of equivalence. In the case of the political trust items, however, half of the comparisons fail to meet the norms of equivalence.

The second test of equivalence compares the amount of response stability shown by the group which takes both administrations in the same language (the 'constant' group) with the stability of the respondents who take the administrations in different languages (the 'switched' group).

Responses to the information items are no less stable for the switched group. Even smaller differences are obtained in the second set. The political trust items provide the only sizeable differences. It may be hypothesized that the increased instability on the part of the switched respondents is due to the abstract nature of the political trust items. Stability on these items calls for well-developed and firm attitudes toward government. For most children, however, government is a non-salient stimulus, as noted earlier. Repeated exposure to a remote stimulus tends to reinforce the respondents' uncertainty, especially when the stimulus is presented in different languages. The more remote the stimulus, the greater the impact of language on response stability.

To summarize, changing the language of the instrument does not affect the stability of responses to the political information items. Similarly, evaluations of the prime minister and governor are no less stable when language is varied. The stability of responses to the political trust items, however, is distinctly reduced when the language of the instrument is changed.

Conclusion

Before drawing any conclusions, it is to be emphasized that the findings of this study may not be applicable to other multilingual settings. As previously noted, it is impossible to incorporate all the possible relevant cultural variables into the study design; and therefore the results obtained here may have been influenced by such unknown factors.

Bearing in mind the problem of cross-cultural generality, the results reported here are encouraging because they suggest that linguistic equivalence of conventional, self-administered, specific survey items is not difficult to achieve, even when children are used as respondents. In the case of the more diffuse and abstract items, however, the problem seems formidable. It would seem essential, therefore, that the survey researcher working in a multilingual society ascertain in advance what effects language differences have on survey responses. Items that do not meet the norms of linguistic equivalence may be modified, replaced, or deleted. The procedure used here to assess linguistic equivalence is relatively inexpensive and simple to carry out. Hopefully, it will prove useful to others.

Finally, it is to be stressed that even though this report suggests the adequacy of conventional survey items (if they are specific in content), it is necessary to obtain comparable data on the performance of other types of survey items, such as semantic differentials, self-anchoring scales, open-ended questions, and 'semi-projective' tests before firm conclusions can be reached regarding optimal strategies of measurement in cross-cultural and multilingual research.

References

Anderson, B.W. (1967). On the comparability of meaningful stimuli in cross-cultural research *Sociometry*, **30 (June)**, 124–136.

Blalock, H.M. Jr. (1968). The measurement problem: a gap between the languages of theory and research. In H.M. and A. Blalock (Eds) *Methodology in Social Research*, pp. 5–27, McGraw-Hill, New York.

Bohrnstedt, G.W. (1969). Reliability and validity assessment in attitude measurement, In G.F. Summers (Ed) *Attitude Measurement*, pp. 80–99, Rand McNally, Chicago.

Brislin, R.W., Lonner, W.J., and Thorndike, R.M. (1973). *Cross-Cultural Research*, Wiley, New York.

Converse, P. (1970). Attitudes and non-attitudes: continuation of a dialogue. In E.R. Tufte (Ed) *The Quantitative Analysis of Social Problems*, pp. 168–189. Addison-Wesley, Reading, Mass.

Deutscher, I. (1968). Asking questions cross-culturally. In H. Becker *et al.* (Eds) *Institutions and the Person*, pp. 318–341. Aldine, Chicago.

Ervin, S. (1964). Language and T.A.T. content in bilinguals. *Journal of Abnormal and Social Psychology*, **68 (May)**, 500–507.

Frey, F.W. (1970). Cross-cultural research in political science. In R.T. Holt and J.E. Turner (Eds), *The Methodology of Comparative Research*, pp. 243–288. Free Press, New York.

Hymes, D. (1970). Linguistic aspects of comparative political research. In R.T. Holt and J.E. Turner (Eds), *The Methodology of Comparative Research*, pp. 295–342, Free Press, New York.

Kendall, M. (1970). *Rank Correlation Methods*, Griffin, London.

Lambert, W.E. *et al*. (1958). The influence of language-acquisition context on bilingualism. *Journal of Abnormal and Social Psychology*, **56 (March)**, 239–244.

Lambert, W.E. *et al*. (1959). Linguistic manifestations of bilingualism. *American Journal of Psychology*, **72 (March)**, 77–82.

Lambert, W.E. and Moore, N. (1966). World association responses. *Journal of Personality and Social Psychology*, **3 (March)**, 313–320.

Przeworski, A. and Teune, H. (1970). *The Logic of Comparative Social Inquiry*, John Wiley, New York.

Rustow, D. (1968). Language, modernisation and nationhood. In J.A. Fishman *et al*., (Eds) *Language Problems of Developing Nations*, pp. 94–96, John Wiley, New York.

Schuman, H. (1966). The random probe. *American Sociological Review*, **37**, 218–222.

Vaillancourt, J-M. (1973). Stability of children's survey responses. *Public Opinion Quarterly*, **37**, 373–387

Social Research in Developing Countries
Edited by M. Bulmer and D.P. Warwick
© 1983, John Wiley & Sons, Ltd.

CHAPTER 15

RELIABILITY OF SURVEY TECHNIQUES IN HIGHLAND PERU

J. OSCAR ALERS

Introduction

There has been a question among social scientists as to whether the technique of the interview survey, hitherto utilized primarily among the developed peoples of the European tradition, can meaningfully be used in the under-developed areas of the world. Beginning in July 1963, I spent 6 months in the highland Peruvian estate of Vicos. Between 1952 and 1965, the former Hacienda Vicos was the site of a research and development programme under the auspices of the Cornell-Peru Project. (For background information, see Alers, 1966; Holmberg, 1961; the collection of articles in Holmberg *et al.*, 1965; Vázquez, 1952; and Chapter 23 below). My research involved collecting the data necessary for an analysis of social and attitudinal factors in the economic development of the community. The principal instrument for this purpose was a structured interview schedule, which was used in interviewing virtually all male heads of household who had been enumerated in a census of the community completed earlier in the year. Perhaps to an even greater extent than most of the underdeveloped peoples of the world, however, the Indians of Vicos are as a whole illiterate, diseased, disadvantaged, and depressed; thus I could not be certain that the responses given in the interviews were meaningful.

The immediate purpose of the present study was to assess the reliability of the responses obtained in Vicos in the 1963 survey and thereby to determine the use to which the data might legitimately be put in later substantive analyses, but I also anticipated that the outcome of the attempt to make a formal survey under the rather extreme conditions prevailing in Vicos would be of interest to others at a time when this technique is being increasingly used in the under-developed areas of the world. To assess response reliability, I studied the responses of the same Vicosino subjects to the same questions in three succes-sive interviews at three separate points in time, noting the relative proportion of responses that remained consistent.

Reprinted with permission from *Rural Sociology* (1970), **35** (**4**) 500–511. © 1970, *Rural Sociology*.

Table 15.1   Data sets and number of units sampled

Data sets	Number of units sampled		
	Subjects	Items	Responses
Pretest (A_1)	20	20	400
Test (A_2)	20	20	400
Test (B_2)	30	10	300
Retest (B_3)	30	10	300

Design

In the United States during the spring of 1963, I developed a first draft of the interview schedule in English. Later, after consulting with several *mestizos* and Indians in Vicos, I prepared a revised final draft and translated it into Spanish. The Spanish version was in turn translated into local Quechua by two Vicosinos and three *mestizos*, one of whom was the anthropologist of the Cornell-Peru Project stationed in Vicos. Ten persons were selected as interviewers, four native Vicosinos and six *mestizos* resident in the community over a period of years.

The sampling design for the three interviews was as follows (see Table 15.1): For the first interview, the pretest (set A^1), 20 subjects were chosen at random from the population of 334 male heads of household in Vicos, with the probability of selection proportional to the number of subjects in each of the ten administrative zones into which the community is divided. (Consultations with local experts had indicated that there might be important differences in various characteristics among these zones.) Pretest interviews were carried out during October and the 1st week of November, and they pointed up the need for a number of revisions in the schedule. It was found, first of all, that the schedule was much too long, with a mean length of 170 minutes, or almost 3 hours. Although this length was in part due to the fact that the interviewers were not yet completely familiar with the schedule, I decided to omit about 25 per cent of the questions for the subsequent interviews. Identical questions, however, were asked of the subjects in all three interviews.

The second, or test, group of interviews (from which sets A^2 and B^2 were selected) was conducted with 98 per cent of the male heads of household living in the community at the time of the survey and constitutes the principal source of data for the survey as a whole. These 326 interviews were completed during December 1963 and the first 2 weeks of January 1964. One effect of interviewer training and schedule revision was the reduction of the mean length of these interviews to 71 minutes.

As in the pretest, the final or retest subjects (set B^3) were selected at random, with probability proportional to the number of subjects in each of the ten administrative zones. For the retest, however, a slightly larger sample was selected — 30 subjects, or 9 per cent of the male heads of household in the community. Interviews with the retest subjects were begun in the last week of December 1963 and completed in mid-January 1964. No records were kept of the length of these interviews (the interviewer did not have access to a time-piece) but, as will be seen later, the retest interviews were designed as a brief follow-up of the test interviews and their mean length certainly did not exceed 15 minutes.

Because it was not feasible to include every response to every question in the study of reliability, a sample of questions also had to be selected. Local testimony and the literature on survey research suggested that differences in the level of reliability might be expected according to the types of questions asked and their placement in the interview, and that the sample of quesitons accordingly should be stratified by these variables. The items were therefore classified as coming early or late in the interview, with the dividing point occurring about halfway through the interview, both in the number of questions completed and in elapsed interview time. Each question was also classified as open or closed, and as calling for fact or opinion, as these terms are understood in survey research. Each item in the interview schedule was then cross-classified on these two points, yielding four question types: open factual, open opinion, closed factual, and closed opinion.

For analysis of data from the pretest interviews, 20 items were chosen at random from the total population of 194 questions contained in the interview schedule, with the probability of selection proportional to the number of items in each of the six categories created by dividing the items according to question type and placement within the interview. The same 20 items were selected for each subject. For the retest, the procedure varied in that only ten items were selected per subject and it was not required that the items be identical for each. With only ten questions to be asked, the retest interviews were of course quite brief. For the pretest sample (set A^1), there is a corresponding sample of test subjects (set A^2) who were asked the same questions, and for the retest sample (set B^3) there is again a corresponding sample of test subjects (set B^2) who were asked the same questions (although these were embedded among other items in the test interview). Four sets of data were thus distinguished for the study of reliability.

However, because of the limited sample size and several methodological difficulties encountered in collecting the data, the present study of reliability should be regarded as tentative and exploratory. This qualification will be developed further in the final discussion following the presentation of results.

Results

The analysis focused first on a comparison of the consistency of responses of groups of subjects, and then on a comparison of shifts in the values of response pairs by individual subjects (that is, on 'turnover tables').

In making the first analysis, I proceeded as follows: For the pretest-test comparison (A^1 versus A^2), I divided the responses to each item at the midpoint of the distribution for the combined pretest and test responses; thus, the same cutting point was used for both pretest and test responses. I divided each of the response distributions into only two categories to avoid the difficulties involved in comparing the reliability of responses to a question which had only two response categories in its original form with, for example, the reliability of responses to another question which originally had six response categories. For the test-retest comparison (B^2 versus B^3), I followed the same procedure for the items sampled for these two groups, except for those items that originally contained seven or more response categories. These were omitted from the analysis because the questions involved had such a large number of categories that they could not easily be dichotomized or otherwise made comparable to the bulk of the items. (This involved a total of only 22 responses. Purely by chance, none of the sampled items in the pretest–test comparison contained more than six response categories, and the problem therefore did not arise for this comparison.) In order to make the appropriate comparisons, I classified each of the responses for each set according to whether it fell into the first or the second category of the dichotomized items, and calculated the overall percentage of responses falling into each of the two categories. Because there is no significant difference between sets A^1 and A^2 or between sets B^2 and B^3 in the percentage of their responses falling into each of the two response categories, we may conclude that percentage comparisons between groups of subjects are likely to be reliable. The relevant data are given in Table 15.2.

These data show that the percentage of responses in each of the two categories is virtually the same for the pretest set and the test set, and that this is also the case for the comparison between the test set and the retest set. When I calculated the distribution of responses for set B^2 on the 20 items common to sets A^1 and A^2, I found that 59 per cent of the 588 responses fell into the first category, which is virtually identical to the percentages falling into that category from sets A^1 and A^2. Percentage comparisons between groups of subjects

Table 15.2 Percentage distributions of responses, by response category and data set

Response category	Pretest (A_1) ($n = 357$)	Test (A_2) ($n = 356$)	Test (B_2) ($n = 234$)	Retest (B_3) ($n = 242$)
		Data set		
	------- per cent -------			
First	60	57	52	53
Second	40	43	48	47

Table 15.3   Number and percentage of consistent responses, by data set, question type, and interview phase

Data sets and question types	Interview phase					
	First half		Second half		Total	
	number	*per cent*	*number*	*per cent*	*number*	*per cent*
Pretest–test:						
Open factual	55	79	46	68	101	73
Closed factual	24	67	19	53	43	60
Closed opinion	20	56	62	57	82	57
All questions	99	70	127	60	226	64
Test–retest:						
Open factual	41	68	15	48	56	62
Closed factual	12	48	13	41	25	44
Closed opinion	18	72	49	52	67	56
All questions	71	65	77	49	148	55

therefore attained a much higher level of reliability than might have been expected in the Vicos research setting.

In measuring the reliability of individual responses, I divided all but a few items at the midpoint of their distributions in order to equalize the probability of obtaining a consistent response over different items. The exceptions consisted of those items in the test-retest comparison that contained seven or more response categories, which in this case were scored as consistent only if the paired responses were identical; that is, they were not dichotomized. These items contained a more limited and workable number of response categories than those that were omitted from the group–retest analysis. As a byproduct of this procedure, the criteria for consistency for the individual test–retest pairs were somewhat more rigorous than for the pretest–test comparison.

Overall, the data show that for all items in the interview, comparing the pretest with the test results, 64 per cent (or 226) of the total of 354 response pairs were reliable, whereas in the test–retest comparison, only 55 per cent (or 148) of the total of 268 response pairs were found to be reliable (Table 15.3). When the data are broken down by question type, the open factual items are the most reliable in the survey — a finding that is generally consistent for both the upper and the lower halves of the table — and, more broadly, the open questions are more reliable than the closed questions. (This finding is bolstered by the fact that, in one respect, it is actually contrary to expectations, since theoretically there are two potential sources of error for the open questions — response error and coding error — and only the former applies for the closed questions). In the pretest–test comparison, the factual questions are generally more reliable than the opinion items, but this is not the case for the corresponding test–retest responses. Another conclusion is concerned with the effect of item location within the interview. With the exception of the closed opinion items in the upper half of the table, responses obtained during the first half of the interview were consistently more reliable than those obtained during the second half.

Thus, at the level of the individual response, it would seem that there may be some truth in the observation that the use of closed items is likely to be especially inappropriate for survey research in developing areas such as Vicos, and that what is needed is open-ended questions that will allow the subject to respond in his own words. This implies that the interview schedule as a whole was imperfectly tuned in on the cognitive frame of reference of the Vicosinos. The open questions permitted the subjects to respond to a greater extent in terms familiar to them and in categories of their own conception, as the closed questions did not, a fact which perhaps accounts for the observed difference in results between the two types of items.

These data also indicate that, even in the best of circumstances, the level of reliability in Vicos did not exceed 79 per cent. This may be due to general limitations of the survey method itself, which perhaps should not be expected to produce data that are 100 per cent reliable (Kendall, 1954). Alternatively, however, this figure may represent a ceiling for the community at the present stage of its development. The results for Vicos appear to be poorer than the results obained by Back and Stycos (1959, p. 27) on factual items in Jamaica, which in turn generally appear to be somewhat poorer than those of three surveys conducted in large urban centres of the United States, although the date are not exactly comparable across the three cultures. The difference between Jamaica and the United States revealed in this study was attributed primarily to differences in education and in rural–urban residence. Vicos is an almost completely rural farming estate and its inhabitants still have very little formal education, conditions which may account for the presumably lower ceiling for the community on the factual questions.

If in addition the community has a lower ceiling on the closed questions, as seems likely, the cause may be, in part, its lower level of education, for educational testing procedures frequently rely on closed questions, and a formal education may thus tend to increase one's ability to handle this type of question.

The observed decline in reliability over the length of the interview seems very likely to be due to the effects of fatigue. The interesting point about this finding, however, is that the decline is also quite substantial for the open factual questions, (Richardson, Dohrenwend, and Klein, 1965), that is, for the very items that are the most reliable of the survey. Thus, it appears that part of what is gained in reliability by asking an open question is lost again over the length of the interview because of fatigue. The reasons for this is probably related to the greater inherent difficulty of responding to an open than to a closed question. To the latter, the subject can respond simply by choosing one of a limited set of alternatives presented to him by the interviewer, without providing his own frame of reference or otherwise giving much thought to the choice. The open question, by contrast, requires a more active effort on the part of the subject. These remarks would apply to any survey population, but they hold with even greater force for the Vicosino, whose daily life has typically been a round of physical toil and psychic subservience. Unaccustomed as he is to performing any sustained intellectual task, either by vocation or by schooling, the Vicosino found the whole interview tiring and the items that required a greater degree of concentration even more exhausting.

Alternatively, however, the possibility must be recognized that the decline in reliability over elapsed interview time may be due to the statistical effect of regression, for the relatively high reliability of the open questions during the early part of the interview is such that the probability that it will decline is greater than the probability that it will increase or remain constant during the later part of the interview (Hovland, Lumsdaine, and Sheffield, 1949).

Discussion

Confronted with the generally poor reliability of the individual responses obtained in Vicos, one might conclude that the survey technique is indeed inapplicable to a population such as that of Vicos, and that the most prudent course of action would be to discard the results and write a book on why this technique will not work in the underdeveloped areas of the world. Alternatively, one might decide to retain the open factual items, which were the most reliable, and discard the closed questions (that is, almost 60 per cent of the items in the survey). Similar decisions might be made on the basis of the observed decline in reliability over elapsed interview time. But for several reasons, neither course should be followed.

Simply to discard all or a large part of the data would constitute a waste of time, money, and human effort. Further, to discard data is to assume that the results just reviewed should be taken completely at face value. Actually, in view of the differences in results between pretest–test and test–retest comparisons, it is legitimate to raise some questions as to the reliability of the method used to assess reliability. If the randomization of subjects and questions was effective (McGinnis, 1958) and if there were no other important variables that were not controlled, comparison of pretest and test response pairs should generally lead to the same results as comparison of test and retest response pairs. But the crucial point in this statement is of course the second premise. The data were collected under field conditions that were certainly at the opposite extreme from the ideal experimental conditions of the laboratory, which would have permitted the imposition of rigorous controls on the 'other important variables'.

The most competent persons available in the community were in the first instance selected as pretest and test interviewers. Because of the brevity of the retest interview, and because of the pretest subjects' resistance, encountered earlier, to a second interview, I decided that the members of the retest sample should be interviewed in their homes — often at considerable distances by foot over steep mountain trails — rather than at a central location as had been done with the pretest and test samples. Most of the pretest and test interviewers were no longer present in the community by the time of the retest and those who remained were unwilling to traverse the distance required to conduct an interview in the homes of the subjects. As a result, a new interviewer, in many ways less competent than the earlier interviewers, had to be hired to conduct the retest interviews.

Thus, there were several differences between the retest procedure and the procedure followed in the first two interviews which may have affected the results. The interviwer was different, he was less competent, and the location of the interviews was in or around the homes of the subjects, where they were more exposed to interference from their relatives and neighbours. The interview itself was much briefer and the ten questions that were asked were taken out of the context of the interview as a whole. In addition, when the retest began, the project was rapidly drawing to a close, and the training of the interviewer was therefore less thorough than that of the earlier interviewers. Another difference was that in the earlier interviews, conducted in the central plaza of the community, each schedule was checked carefully in the presence of the subject to make sure that all questions had been answered. The retest interviews, conducted in the subjects' own homes, could not be subjected to such careful checking, and they were later found to contain more unanswered questions.

A related point concerns the probable effect of interviewer training and skills on the results. Because the pretest constituted a training exercise for the interviewers, the responses elicited during the pretest may have been less stable than those elicited during the test when the interviewers had become more familiar with the interview schedule. Similarly, the retest interviews were also carried out by an inexperienced and relatively unskilled interviewer, who probably therefore elicited unstable responses from his subjects. These circumstances suggest that the test results, the final data of the study, may actually be more reliable than they would appear to be when measured by the techniques used in this study.

An additional point is that no controls could be exercised on the movements of the subjects between their first and second interviews. This fact, of course, made them vulnerable to the operation of intervening events and to the effects of contacts with their relatives and neighbours, some of whom had previously been interviewed and who may have exercised an influence on their responses. The operation of these factors could have led to genuine changes of response between the two interviews, which would therefore not be indicative of unreliability at all.

Finally, inconsistency of response between the first and the second interview may have been due to the stimulus of the first interview itself. That is, it may have been a function of practice effects, which are generally recognized as being quite common in restudies of this type (Anastasi, 1961, pp. 56–57). Thus, the initial interview may have stimulated the subjects to reconsider their opinions or to recall facts that had not occurred to them during the interview itself, but which they would report upon being reinterviewed.

The import of this discussion is not so much to question the rules by which reliability may be assessed as to indicate that in several respects they could not be applied with any degree of precision under the field conditions prevailing in the survey of Vicos. I place greater faith in the results of the pretest–test comparison than in those of the test–retest comparison, but when the results of the two are consistent in spite of procedural variations my confidence in them is increased. The two findings that are most stable in this sense are that open questions are more reliable than closed, and that responses given in the first half of the interview are more reliable than those given in the second half.

If, in view of this discussion, discarding all or a large part of the data collected in the Vicos survey would amount to overkill, there are several alternatives to simply going ahead and using data that have been shown to be deficient. First, the results indicate that individual shifts in response cancelled each other without affecting the overall reliability of responses for groups, and there is thus no obstacle to the use of the data for group comparisons, provided that the form of the reanalysed — comparison of percentage differences between groups — is not charged.

The high reliability of the grouped data also suggests the possibility that scales and indices, composed of several items, may be more reliable than single items. There is, in fact, what appears to be a consensus among survey analysts that single items are to be mistrusted because of the expectation that they will be unstable, and they are thus frequently combined with similar items in the construction of scales and indices in order to bolster the stability of measurement. Guttman (1954), who subscribes to this viewpoint, has alluded to the 'retest unreliability of each variable separately' and gone so far as to state that scale ranks 'are always highly reliable' (1954, p. 249), (For negative evidence, see McGinnis, 1953). Scale analysis — which often uses closed items — might thus provide a solution to the problem of the lower reliability of closed questions on a single-item basis and, more importantly, it may increase the general level of reliability of the data collected by means of the survey technique.

If the general decline in reliability over elapsed interview time also suggests that the responses obtained in late stages of the interview should be discarded, there is again an alternative course of action — namely, to use the location of an item in the interview as a control or the relationship observed between any two or more variables in whatever substantive analyses to be carried out. Persistence of the relationship between these variables in spite of such a control would constitute direct evidence that declining reliability over elapsed interview time is of little or no consequence for these variables.

References

Alers, J.O. (1966). *Population, attitudes, and development: the case of Vicos*. Cornell University, unpublished PhD dissertation, Ithaca, New York.

Anastasi, A. (1961). *Psychological Testing*. Macmillan, New York.

Back, K.W., and Stycos, J.M. (1959). *The Survey Under Unusual Conditions*. Society for Applied Anthropology, Ithaca, New York.

Guttman, L. (1954) The principal components of scalable attitudes. In Paul F. Lazarsfeld (Ed), *Mathematical Thinking in the Social Sciences*, Free Press, Glencoe, Ill.

Holmberg, A.R. (1961) Changing community attitudes and values in Peru: a case study in guided change. In *Council on Foreign Relations Social Change in Latin America Today*, p. 63–107 Vintage Books, New York.

Holmberg, A.R., Vázquez, M.C., Doughty, P.L., Alers, J.O., Dobyns, H.F. and Lasswell, H.D. (1965). The Vicos case: peasant society in transition. *American Behavioral Scientist*, 8 (**March**), 3–33.

Hovland, C.I., Lumsdaine, A.A. and Sheffield, F.D. (1949). *Experiments on Mass Communication*. Princeton University Press, Princeton, NJ.

Kendall, P. (1954). *Conflict and Mood: Factors Affecting the Stability of Response*: Free Press, Glencoe, Ill.

McGinnis, R. (1953). Scaling interview data. *American Sociological Review*, **18** (**October**), 514–521.

McGinnis, R. (1958). Randomization and inference in sociological research. *American Sociological Review*, **23** (**August**), 408–414.

Richardson, S.A., Dohrenwend, B.S. and Klein, D. (1965). *Interviewing: Its Forms and Functions*. Basic Books, New York.

Vazquez, M.C. (1952. La antropologia cultural y nuestro problema del indio: Vicos, un caso de antropologia aplicada. *Peru Indigena*, **2** (**June**), 7–157.

Social Research in Developing Countries
Edited by M. Bulmer and D.P. Warwick
© 1983, John Wiley & Sons, Ltd.

CHAPTER 16

EXPERIENCE OF RETROSPECTIVE DEMOGRAPHIC ENQUIRIES TO DETERMINE VITAL RATES

J. BLACKER
AND
W. BRASS

Introduction

Demographic enquiries have some special advantages for the evaluation of data collection techniques. The basic questions are mainly simple, requiring no elaborate definitions. The interrelations between the dynamic characteristics of populations (birth, death and growth rates, sex–age structures, family compositions, etc.) make it possible to apply checks of internal consistency with fair reliability in the absence of external gauges. Such studies come then at the easy end of the spectrum of error definition and explanation. On the other hand, the practical applications of retrospective methods have been largely among populations with low levels of education and familiarity with numerical specification. The nature of the errors as well as being important in their own context may also give pointers to situations where the questions are less simple but the respondents more sophisticated.

Retrospective surveys have been used extensively in developing countries in order to determine the components of population growth. Throughout most of Africa, Asia and Latin America the registration of births and deaths is either non-existent or seriously defective, so that special inquiries have had to be mounted to ascertain the fertility and mortality rates. Sometimes these enquiries have been incorporated in the national population census, but, except in the case of small countries with populations of less than a million, this has generally been done on a sampling basis — either by including the fertility

Reprinted in abridged form with the permission of the publishers and the authors from the authors' chapter in L. Moss and H. Goldstein (Eds) (1979), *The Recall Method in Social Surveys*, London, London University Institute of Education, pp. 48–61. © 1979, London University Institute of Education.

and mortality questions in a sample post-enumeration survey, or by means of a 'built-in' sample such that an expanded census schedule incorporating these extra questions is used in a probability sample of areas. Elsewhere, they have constituted independent sample surveys not directly connected with the census operation.

The results of these surveys have been subject to both sampling and non-sampling errors. This paper is concerned primarily with the non-sampling, or response, errors. This is not to imply, however, that the sampling errors are necessarily negligible. Indeed, one of the difficulties confronting demographers and statisticians is the fact that since births and deaths are relatively rare events, and since one is trying to estimate the rates to a high degree of accuracy, large samples are needed for demographic surveys. The figure of 100 000 persons has been cited as a minimum if any attempt is to be made to estimate age-specific rates (United Nations Economic Commission for Africa, 1974), and a recent analysis of sampling errors of a demographic survey conducted in Bangladesh in 1974 showed that, with this size of sample, the coefficient of variation of the current age-specific fertility rates ranged from 4–5 per cent for the 20–24 and 25–29 year-old age groups to nearly 20 per cent for the 45–49 year-old age group. Since these figures must be doubled to obtain the 95 per cent confidence limits, errors of this magnitude should not be swept under the carpet.

This paper is also concerned primarily with the response errors in the fertility data. Of the mortality data it can be said briefly that direct questions on deaths occurring during the 12 months preceding the survey or census are subject to errors which are at least as bad as, and generally substantially worse than, those of the fertility information. Indeed, in many cases such questions have had to be discarded altogether and mortality estimated by indirect methods and models, discussion of which is beyond the scope of this chapter.

Where the fertility questions are concerned, they can conveniently be divided into two categories: those concerned with lifetime fertility — i.e. the total number of children ever borne by the women up to the time of the survey; and current fertility — the number of children borne by her during the 12 months preceding the survey.

Lifetime fertility

In their simplest form, enquiries into lifetime fertility have been embodied in a single question on the number of children borne alive by the woman during her lifetime, a live birth generally being defined as one when the child cried. It has long been recognized, however, that the data obtained in answer to such questions are subject to errors, both of omission and of faulty inclusion. The omissions are generally thought to have been more serious, especially in the case of older women who, either because of misunderstanding or of memory

Table 16.1   Gambia — females aged 15 and over by number of census and MRC total numbers of children ever born

Census number of live births	MRC number of live births											Total
	0	1	2	3	4	5	6	7	8	9	10+	
0	63	10	5	—	1	1	1	1				82
2	8	55	10	—	1	2	—	—	—	1	1	78
2	1	9	49	3	1	—	1	—	—	—	2	66
3	1	5	13	26	4	1	—	2	1	1	1	55
4	1	—	—	3	24	5	1	1	1	1	1	38
5		—	1	5	5	22	6	2	2	—	2	45
6		1	—	1	3	9	25	7	3	1	2	52
7				1	—	3	12	22	3	1	3	45
8				1	2	3	1	5	17	7	1	37
9						3	1	1	7	8	3	23
10+							2	3	8	9	30	52
Total	74	80	78	40	41	49	50	44	42	29	46	573

Source: Gibril (1976), p. 69.

failure, are particularly liable to omit children who died in infancy, who have grown up and left the home, and who were born to another husband. Faulty inclusions, on the other hand, may arise in the case of adopted children, the children of relatives for whom the woman may be acting, perhaps temporarily, *in loco parentis*, children born to her husband by another wife, grandchildren, and stillbirths.

A recent demonstration of these errors has been provided by an interesting exercise conducted in the Gambia in connection with the 1973 census of that country. In the Lower River division of the Gambia, four villages (Keneba, Jali, Manduar and Kanton Kunda), comprising a total population of rather more than 2000 persons, have been kept under observation by the Medical Research Council since the 1950s. The populations of these villages have been enumerated annually and both births and deaths are recorded as they occur. Population registers of an unusually high degree of accuracy (for African populations) have thus been established, and it was possible to match these records against the 1973 census returns for the four villages (Gibril, 1976). As the three-pronged lifetime fertility questions were asked in the census, it was possible to compare the results of these questions for 573 women aged 15 and over for whom corresponding data were available in the Medical Research Council (MRC) records. The results are summarized in Table 16.1. If the MRC data are regarded as correct, the census succeeded in recording the correct parities for only 60 per cent of the women; for 18 per cent parity was understated and for 22 per cent it was overstated.

An alternative approach to the compilation of data on lifetime fertility is the use of pregnancy or maternity histories. Instead of simply asking questions on the numbers of children she has borne, the woman is asked to provide particulars, one by one, of each of her pregnancies or live births. The information normally recorded in this way is the outcome of the pregnancy (live birth or stillbirth), the date of the birth, the sex of the child, whether the child is still alive or dead, and, if dead, the date of death. This approach has the additional advantage that if the dates of birth of the children are correct it should be possible to reconstruct fertility rates for different periods in the past, and hence to throw light on fertility trends. The extent to which this objective has been realized will be discussed in a subsequent section; here we will confine ourselves to the question as to whether or not the true parity of the woman is recorded more accurately by the use of pregnancy/maternity histories than by questions on numbers of children born. On *a priori* grounds it might be expected that the additional probing required for the pregnancy history approach would help to eliminate some of the errors described above. But these expectations have not always been borne out in practice, and the empirical evidence is in fact conflicting.

Probably the first comparative exercise of this type was that conducted with the data obtained in the Mysore Population Study in India in 1951–52 (United Nations, 1961, pp. 234–238). In this study the information on some 2800 births obtained in the Household Survey (questions on numbers of births) and in the Fertility and Attitude Survey (pregnancy histories) were compared. Overall discrepancies of the order of only 1 per cent were found, and it was concluded that 'there was no important deficiency in the reporting of these data in either survey, at least so far as the younger women were concerned'. However, another study in Peru in 1969 showed that the use of pregnancy histories yielded consistently higher average parities than did questions on numbers of births (Marckwardt, 1973). The two investigations, however, were conducted on different samples of women, so that no matching was possible, and it was also found that a large part of the difference was attributable to the fact that the pregnancy histories were only compiled for those women who were present in the household at the time of the interviewer's visit and could thus answer for themselves; in the case of the questions on numbers of births, proxy answers were accepted from other members of the household when the women concerned were not present. It could therefore be argued that the differences may have been attributable not only to the faulty answers given by the proxy respondents, but also to lower-than-average fertility of the absent women.

It would seem that in general the form of the questions on this topic is of less importance than the quality, training and supervision of the interviewers. A good example of this has recently been provided in Bangladesh. Here, the Retrospective Survey of Fertility and Mortality which was part of the 1974 census operations covered a large sample of some 360 000 persons; an

Table 16.2   Bangladesh — mean live births per woman derived from 1974 Retrospective Survey and 1976 Fertility Survey

Age group	BRSFM 1974	BFS 1976
15–19	0.385	0.585
20–24	1.847	2.344
25–29	3.485	4.181
30–34	4.917	5.686
35–39	5.861	6.636
40–44	6.194	7.149
45–49	6.084	6.468

Source: 1974 — Bangladesh, 1977, Table 3.1 p. 66; 1976 — unpublished table

unmanageable number of 442 enumerators were employed who were poorly trained and poorly supervised. In contrast the Bangladesh Fertility Survey of 1975–76 covered a sample of only 6515 women of reproductive age, and used a field staff of 55 interviewers and 22 supervisors; the standard of both training and supervision was unusually high. While the 1974 BRSFM asked questions on numbers of births, the 1975–76 BES used pregnancy histories. The average parities obtained from these two operations are shown in Table 16.2. The BFS figures are consistently higher and reach a modal value of 7.149 births per woman, which in fact agrees closely with the total fertility rate estimated from the 1974 survey after various corrections had been made for response errors.

Reporting of siblings

Some further light is thrown on factors which affect reporting of children born, in this case by sibling, by the data from a small, closely controlled survey recently carried out by Ms Ahmad in several villages of North Pakistan. This is a very underdeveloped area where the aim was to study mortality and health problems in relation to cultural factors, particularly the differential treatment of the sexes. As part of the attempt to measure mortality, questions were put on the number of maternal siblings (births to the same mother) of each person in the sample of households, and of the numbers surviving. The data from the study are still being analysed but Ms Ahmad has given permission for the preliminary measures in Table 16.3 to be used for the present purpose.

The need for demographic consistency determines the structure of the true measures with considerable certainty. The mean number of brothers reported should be the same for males and females of a given age and the ratio of brothers to sisters must be about 1.05. Since we can be confident that fertility has changed little on average in this population the means should not vary much with age of respondents after these are old enough for the mothers to

Table 16.3   Northern Pakistan — mean number of siblings reported

Age group (years)	Males Number of reports	brothers	sisters	Females Number of reports	brothers	sisters
Under 10	2546	2.39	2.17	2460	2.55	2.32
10–19	1635	3.31	3.40	1356	3.41	2.94
20–29	1007	3.53	3.01	927	3.28	2.85
30–39	682	3.45	2.82	730	3.04	2.73
40–49	537	2.84	2.43	521	2.69	2.43
50–59	385	2.61	2.28	338	2.44	2.22
60–69	275	2.39	2.13	259	2.15	2.22
70 and over	245	2.24	1.96	176	2.14	1.89

have completed their childbearing (around 20 to 25 years of age of respondents). It is possible that selective mortality of children by the numbers of children born to mothers might effect the mean numbers of siblings, but it is very unlikely that this would be important in such a homogeneous community.

As can be seen the mean numbers of brothers and sisters reported deviate considerably from those expected. The three and a half brothers each reported by males aged from 20 to 40 can be shown from other evidence to be about right. The significant deviations are as follows.

(1) The mean numbers of siblings reported decrease greatly with age of respondent after 40 years. It seems certain that this is mainly due to the omission of dead siblings (the proportions surviving clearly become too high, the excess rising with age).

(2) When sampling error is allowed for there is no reason to query the reports for the under-20. Most of these were, of course, given by parents.

(3) At ages above 20 years sisters were more often omitted than brothers although the differential is small at older ages. Again this seems to be strongly connected with a greater failure to report dead sisters than brothers but the justification for this conclusion is complex and cannot be elaborated here. North Pakistan is a male-dominated society and there seems little doubt that the poorer memory for sisters reflects importance in the community.

(4) The reporting of sisters shows little difference by the sex of the respondent but brothers are better recorded by males. This finding is not easy to explain in simple terms but there may be opposing tendencies. Thus, the fact that the main respondent in households is usually the male head will be a factor predisposing towards greater omissions of siblings of his wife and other female dependants but women may have, in contrast, a more retentive memory than men of their dead sisters.

Even in this relatively simple situation with straightforward factual questions, the structure of retrospective reporting error is complex.

Current fertility

Questions on current fertility have generally taken the form of asking adult females whether they have borne a child during the 12 months preceding the census or survey. Occasionally, such questions have produced results which could be accepted without major modification; but more often they have been demonstrably in error. However, such errors have not necessarily rendered the results worthless. If it can reasonably be assumed that the errors are independent of the ages of the women, the age-specific rates so obtained will provide valuable information on the *shape* of the age-specific fertility distribution; corrections based on a comparison of the cumulated current rates and average parity can then usefully be made (Brass *et al.*, 1968). But sometimes even this assumption has been clearly invalid, and the whole shape of the fertility distribution has been distorted (United Nations, 1971).

In these circumstances improved results have sometimes been obtained by replacing the question on births in the last 12 months, with one on the date of the woman's most recent live birth; women bearing children during the preceding 12 months can then be extracted and tabulated separately during the processing. The improvements so effected in the data for Kenya (censuses of 1962 and 1969) have been described by one of the authors elsewhere (Blacker, 1971).

These changes have undoubtedly been in the right direction, but there is still a long way to go, particularly as regards the overall level of the reported rates. In the Gambia census of 1973 a correction factor of 28 per cent was used. Taperecordings and a matching exercise with MRC records provided valuable insight into the causes and nature of the errors. The principal findings can again be summarized under three headings.

Failure to ask the questions

In about one-third of the taperecorded interviews concerning eligible women, the question on the date of the most recent live birth was not asked. Yet in the majority of such cases entries were in fact being made on the census schedule, and it must be presumed that the enumerators were inferring the answers on the basis of other information, such as the age of the youngest child in the household. This procedure wold clearly lead to error if the woman had subsequently borne another child who had either died or was living elsewhere. In an attempt to forestall this error a check question had been included on the census schedule as to whether or not the last-born child was still alive. But this question also was not being put— this time in almost half the relevant interviews.

Mistranslation

In the process of translation from the English of the census schedule into the local African vernaculars, the question was becoming seriously garbled. In the first place in Gambian society it is more polite to talk about 'children' than about 'births'. Secondly, so unfamiliar are most Gambians with the concept of 'dates', that there is no word for 'date' in the two principal local languages (Mandinka and Wollof). Thus, instead of asking for the date of the last birth, enumerators tended to ask for the age of the woman's youngest child — a procedure which will lead to a similar misunderstanding and error.

Misdating

Due to the general ignorance of dates and ages, the dates of birth eventually recorded on the census schedules were subject to substantial errors. The matching exercise with the MRC records suggested that while much of this misdating was seemingly random, a systematic bias is also discernible: births occurring in the recent past (say the last 3 years) tended to be pushed back in time, while those in the more distant past (say 10 to 15 years before) tended to be brought forwards; the result is thus a heaping of births in a central period of some 3 to 9 years before the census.

Maternity histories

One method of combating the 'wrong child' error liable to arise from the first two findings above would be to require the dates of birth of *all* the woman's children to be recorded, not simply that of the most recent — or, in other words, to adopt the pregnancy or maternity history approach. But we shall still be left with the dating errors, and if the pregnancy histories are also being used to try to detect trends in fertility, false conclusions can be drawn all too easily. The possible distortions from such errors were pointed out by Brass (1971) who also devised techniques for detecting and adjusting dating bias. Potter (1975) proposed a model for the description of these biases. Briefly, his hypothesis is that when birth dates are reported by mothers there is a tendency to displace the furthest in the past towards the present; subsequent birth intervals are recorded reasonably accurately until within a few years before the survey when a compression occurs to correct the very recent events where memory is more accurate. On this model the number of births, and hence the level of fertility, are inflated at some time before the enquiry (say 5 to 10 years) giving a false impression of a downwards trend. If this is a consistent mechanism the results from recording maternity histories backwards in time from the most recent birth should be different from forward questioning. Madigan has carried out an experiment in the Phillippines splitting the sample of women into two and recording maternity histories forward in one half and backwards in the other. He has stated (oral communication) that the event misplacements do not appear to differ between the two orders of recording.

The inflation of the births reported in a period located a few years before the survey, as predicted by Potter, has been established in a number of maternity history enquiries but in most of these there has also been an understatement of recent births (not in accord with his model). In fact, patterns of the type suggested by the Gambia matching exercise described in the preceding section seem to be the most common. A good example is that of Bangladesh, where three successive surveys have all shown similar features. The heaping of births in the period 5–10 years before the surveys, combined with the deficits in the recent quinquennium, have stimulated substantial declines in fertility — a conclusion which many people would be all too glad to believe in. Unfortunately, the period of low fertility shown by one survey coincides with that of high fertility shown by the next which should shake the beliefs of all except those who see the figures with the eye of faith.

But there are counter-examples. A series of well designed and carefully controlled maternity history enquiries were carried out by the Dutch in western New Guinea in the early 1960s (Groenwegen and van de Kaa, 1964–67). The total histories recorded were about 19 000. It has been demonstrated (Brass, 1977) that the pattern of error in the dating of births was the reverse of that noted above as being common. That is, in western New Guinea, recent births were overstated and there was a 'valley' 5 to 20 years before. We do not know what respondent–interviewer interactions dictate these variations in the pattern of error.

Conclusion

The impression gained from the foregoing may well have been that the errors in the data are so large as to render them entirely worthless. Such a view, however, would be unduly jaundiced. By making various checks of internal consistency it is generally possible to sort truth from fiction and to correct the faulty parts of the data. At the same time, further research is needed into the causes of the errors: in particular the mechanism which produces the systematic bias in the dating of the births is imperfectly understood. The massive size of the errors which frequently occur even when the measures to be estimated appear simple and straightforward may serve as a warning against the ready acceptance of more complex and less easily checked information.

Meanwhile, progress clearly can be made only by ensuring that all the relevant questions are asked in the field, and that their correct meaning is conveyed to the respondent. This must be done by improved questionnaire design, particularly as regards the wording of the questions in the language of the interview, and by improved training and supervision.

References

Bangladesh, Census Commission, Ministry of Planning, and U.K. Population Bureau, Ministry of Overseas Development (1977), *Report on the 1974 Bangladesh Retrospective Survey of Fertility and Mortality*, Dacca and London.

Blacker, J.G.C. (1971) The estimation of vital rates from census data in Kenya and Uganda. In P. Cantrelle (Ed.), *Population in African Development*. International Union for the Scientific Stufy of Population, **1**.

Brass, W., *et al*. (1968). *The Demography of Tropical Africa*, Princeton University Press, Princeton, NJ.

Brass, W. (1971). The analysis of maternity histories to detect changes in fertility, Paper presented to the United Nations Technical Meeting on Methods of Analysing Fertility Data for Developing Countries. Budapest.

Brass, W. (1977). The assessment of the validity of fertility trend estimates from maternity histories. *Proceedings of the IUSSP International Population Conference, Mexico 1977. IUSSP*, **1**.

Gibril, M.A. (1976). *Some reporting errors in the 1973 Gambian census*, unpublished MSc dissertation, London School of Hygiene and Tropical Medicine.

Gibril, M.A. (1977), *The problem of identifying and measuring response errors from survey data*, unpublished background information paper, OECD.

Groenwegen, K. and van de Kaa, D.J. (1964–67), *Resultaten van het Demografisch Onderzock Westelijk Nieuw-Guinea*. Government Printing and Publishing Office, 6 vol, The Hague.

Marckwardt, A.M. (1973). Evaluation of an experimental short interview form designed to collect fertility data: the case of Peru, *Demography*, **10, 4 (November)**.

Potter, J.E. (1975). *The Validity of Measuring Change in Fertility by Analyzing Birth Histories obtained in Surveys*. University Microfilms, Ann Arbor, Mich.

United Nations (1961), *The Mysore Population Study*. New York.

United Nations Economic Commission for Africa (1971). Demographic surveys in Africa 1950–1970: some results and conclusions. In *Methodology of Demographic Sample Surveys*. New York.

United Nations Economic commission for Africa (1974). *Manual on Demographic Sample Surveys in Africa*. Addis Ababa.

SECTION V

INTERVIEWING AND FIELD ORGANIZATION

Social Research in Developing Countries
Edited by M. Bulmer and D.P. Warwick
© 1983, John Wiley & Sons, Ltd.

CHAPTER 17

INTERVIEWING AND FIELD ORGANIZATION

MARTIN BULMER

The most critical phase in social research is that during which data are actually collected. In censuses and surveys, this normally takes place by personal enumeration or face-to-face interview. Many problems arise at this stage of data collection. This section considers in particular the special problems of conducting research in the field in the developing world, and how the field worker may guard against the difficulties likely to be encountered.

This section is particularly concerned with types of non-sampling error, which have been briefly mentioned already. Earlier in the book, Leach's critique of survey research and Hauser's comments on the problems of interpreting KAP fertility survey data were quoted. Some further examples help to make clear the kinds of problem which can arise.

A common form of error in the Nepal Fertility survey [part of the WFS] is misreporting of current age and current duration of marriage. The Nepalese population presents a severe challenge to any effort to determine exact ages and dates, since it is clear that the majority of Nepalese do not keep a calendar and often do not know age, even approximately. In general, the respondents in the NFS were not able to recall their own date of birth or date of first marriage and instead the respondents, or the interviewers, estimated ages and marital durations, often with numbers divisible by two or five (Goldman *et al.*, 1979, p. 9).

In the Sudan, we have found that rural people usually respond quite freely on such subjects as age and education (except in the case of family size and distribution by sexes). Our interviewees never like to talk about the female side of their families, and they feel very embarrassed when asked about the number of girls they have, their ages etc. In some instances, they may not give the correct family size, being afraid of the 'evil eye' . . . The lowest response was to questions about livestock. Farmers *never* give the actual numbers of their animals. They are afraid of the 'evil eye' and they are also afraid of taxes, since they have to pay a certain tax for every animal (Kearl, 1976, p. 151).

In reviewing agricultural surveys in village India, it has been suggested that data reliability is low because 'questions are asked of the cultivator to which he does not know the answer; sometimes because the questions are not asked in the cultivator's terminology, sometimes because the cultivator has no means of knowing the answer; sometimes because the questions are not ones to which the cultivator normally gives consideration' (Neale, 1958, p. 394). There are other reasons also. Errors of recall occur. Respondents are often not particularly interested in giving accurate answers, despite showing courtesy to the interviewer. And cultivators have good reason not to tell the truth, with an eye to neighbours, landlords or government as potential recipients of the information.

A more extended discussion of the difficulties that may arise is found in Chapter 18 by Robert Mitchell and Chapter 21 by Choldin, Kahn, and Ara. The collection of data by social survey interview is particularly liable to the occurrence of non-sampling errors affecting the reliability and validity of the resulting information. Many, though not all, of the difficulties arise at the interview, in the way that the research is presented to the respondent, the respondent's perceptions of the interviewer, and the interaction between interviewer and respondent. The circumstances giving rise to the existence of error will now be discussed, followed by suggestions as to how data quality may be improved.

The general problem facing the interviewer

Background characteristics

The problem of non-sampling error may be conceptualized at a general level in terms of a model of the relationship between interviewer and respondent. Each bring to the interview certain background characteristics, such as sex, age, social status, language, which suggest group membership and group loyalties. Both interviewer and respondent may be influenced in various indirect ways by the background characteristics of the other. They provide cues to each about the other; for example, if the interviewer is white and the respondent black, the respondent may be influenced in his attitude to the interviewer and his behaviour, and therefore the results will be affected. Moreover, background characteristics are the source of many attitudes, perceptions, expectations and motives. If interviewer and respondent are widely divergent in their background characteristics, they are likely to have widely different attitudes and motives which make mutual misunderstanding more likely: 'They constitute a kind of subsoil in which many of an individual's attitudes, motives and perceptions have direct roots' (Kahn and Cannell, 1957, p. 183).

Psychological and behavioural factors

Psychological factors also play an important part in determining patterns of survey response. The respondent's sensitivity to the interviewer's attitudes is likely to be great and can readily bias the results. Behavioural factors, are the means by which predispositions and potentially biasing characteristics become operative. How interviewers ask questions, how respondents answer, how these answers are recorded, all determine to what extent the results of the interview are subject to error in practice.

A useful model for the interaction between interviewer and respondent has been suggested by Kahn and Cannell (1957), and is reproduced as Figure 17.1. This emphasizes how each of the three sorts of factor influence the outcome, both within that individual, and in interaction between the two individuals.

The ways in which bias can enter into the interviewer situation can be illustrated by looking in more detail at the behaviour of the interviewer. Errors may occur, in the first place, in asking the questions. The interviewer may shorten the question, or simplify the language, or suggest answers through changing question wording. Where the interviewer is required to translate questions into another language, the scope for error increases significantly. Errors also occur in probing, when the respondent does not give an adequate answer and the interviewer seeks a complete, relevant and accurate answer to the question. Here the background characteristics of the respondent are par-

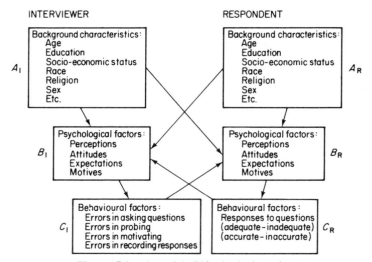

Figure 17.1: A model of bias in the interview

Source: Kahn and Cannell (1957, p. 194)

ticularly likely to influence the behaviour of the interviewer. In recording answers, errors take place. The interviewer may 'improve' the respondent's answers when writing them down, either to bring them more into accord with his or her expectations, or to render more coherent. Errors may occur, finally, in motivating the respondent. This may take the form of providing under-motivation, inappropriate motivation or insensitivity to the situation of the respondent.

The following discussion places more emphasis upon sources of non-sampling error arising from the background characteristics, attitudes and behaviour of the respondent, but these are the outcome of interaction with the interviewer. The interviewer is an active participant in the research process, whose presence may trigger a variety of reactions from the respondent. One initial problem for the respondent is in recognizing correctly what the inter-viewer wants, and behaving appropriately in the role of respondent.

A basic difficulty facing those undertaking social survey research in develop-ing countries is that the activity of social research, and the role of social researcher or interviewer, are not widely recognized, indeed are little known. In industrial countries, census-taking and extensive social survey interviewing are well-established. Since 1945, the social survey interview carried out by government, academic and commercial research organizations has become commonplace. Millions of such interviews are carried out each year in coun-tries such as Britain and the United States (see Bulmer, 1979, pp. 57–67). Moreover, the results of such researches are presented regularly in the mass media, most evidently in the form of political opinion polls (see Marsh, 1982, Chapter 6; Teer and Spence, 1973). The public thus has some familiarity both with the role of social researcher and with the results of such research. The citizen faced with a request for a research interview is likely to have some conception of what is being asked for.

In developing countries these conditions are generally not present. Social survey research is not well established, requests for interviews are rare, the results of such research do not percolate back to the general population, and problems of illiteracy and geographical and cultural difference between centre and periphery and between elite and mass render the average citizen quite ignorant of the activity of research or the role of social researcher or inter-viewer. Faced with a request for an interview, the scope of misunderstanding about what is required and what are the purposes of the inquiry are very wide.

A prime difficulty is the confusion that is likely to occur between the research organization and the administrative functions of government. Although in the distant past censuses were conducted for both enumeration and taxation (for example, Jesus was born in Bethlehem because Joseph had travelled there with Mary for the census), in modern times research activities and government action have been kept entirely separate. This, however, is not apparent to an uneducated peasant in rural Asia who is approached with a request for an interview. Interviewers are quite likely to be mistaken for tax collectors, police agents, government administrators, political party workers, relief officials or travelling salesmen. Both Chapter 19 by Hershfield *et al*. and Chapter 21 by Choldin, Kahn, and Ara document this kind of role confusion, and the serious consequences which it may have for the success of the interview. The problems are greater in rural areas, but exist potentially wherever the research role is an unfamiliar one to the general population (Pausewang, 1973).

Reviewing fieldwork experience in Turkey, Turan (1975) suggests several reasons why fieldworkers tend to be perceived as government agents. Apart from salesmen and occasionally politicians, officials are the most likely outsider to visit a Turkish village. Attempts to explain that his research had university sponsorship failed, because villages did not distinguish between an educational institution and the rest of government. The village school, which they knew, was government-run, and the teachers frequently helped with central government activities locally. Other factors contributing were the research team's use of government jeeps for transport, and expectations that the governing party of the time would send representatives to listen to villagers' problems. Many villagers thought the interviewers were there to record grievances for the government. In addition, the census is conducted by government officials for the government, tending therefore to identify all research activities with the government (Turan, 1975, pp. 12–14).

African experience suggests that villagers' circumspection toward outsiders is well founded. As one village elder in Kenya put it (Kearl, 1976, p. 169):

People in the community have grown accustomed not to trust people who come from outside. No-one comes from outside with good intentions. Everyone comes here to take something away from us and to tell bad stories about us. Some people come here to help us with their research, they say. Then they go back to university to receive degrees, and come back here as government officials giving us instructions and orders.

Suspicion and distrust should not be treated as some kind of irrational backwardness, but as a perfectly rational desire to defend the community against outside intruders. The interview method is an intrusion into rural society, without immediate or visible benefit to the respondent.

More specific sources of non-response error

There are a number of specific ways in which the respondent in a survey in a developing country may be influenced in the responses which he gives. The first of these relate to forms of bias due to behaviour thought to be appropriate to the interview situation. Assuming that the true research purposes of the interview have been recognized, it does not follow that the respondent will give full and frank responses. One form that bias can take is excessive courtesy, discussed by Jones in Chapter 20. Where high social value is placed upon courtesy, avoiding open disagreement and maintaining a pleasant and agreeable atmosphere, the respondent is likely to answer in ways which do not disturb this atmosphere in the interview situation: 'No one will ever go back from this village saying we are not hospitable' (Mamdani, 1972, p. 24).

A more complex form of courtesy bias is ingratiation bias, where the respondent distorts answers in a direction intended to win the approval, attention or favour of the interviewer (Back and Gergen, 1963). Its opposite is 'sucker bias', where respondents make a deliberate effort to mislead or deceive the interviewers, not so much to hide the truth as to trick, outwit or embarrass the interviewer (Keesing and Keesing, 1956). These forms of bias are all examples of cultural response set, where the reception and treatment of the interviewer is conditioned by socially approved values in the society where the research is conducted. For example, according to Robert Mitchell in Chapter 18, people from South-East Asia frequently underestimate themselves and their achievements, while many people in the Middle East overstate their accomplishments and personal merit.

Another major source of bias, particularly common in developing countries, is lack of status congruency between respondent and interviewer. Commonly the interviewer is of higher status, and has other characteristics which marks out his superiority, such as literacy, education, urban residence and wider social experience. Mitchell discusses some of the problems to which this gives rise in Chapter 18, and raises the question whether the equalitarian-oriented interviewing techniques used in the west (see Benney and Hughes, 1956) are appropriate in societies which have sharp status and authority cleavages.

Frey's (1973) experiences on a pilot agricultural survey in Turkey, using regular Turkish census enumerators, illustrates in a rather extreme way the problems which can result. Using census methods for a survey which required a subtle and sensitive approach, data of little value was the outcome of the following procedure which emphasized the status differences between interviewer and respondent as much as possible.

On arriving at a village, the interviewers summoned the village head man (*mulitar*) to them in tones befitting their self-perceived station (that of important government officials) and dress (dark suit, white shirt and tie). The transaction with the head man was appropriately tense and economical. They simply inquired after the nearest ample and shady tree beneath which they could establish themselves. Then they presented the head man with a list of the villagers whom they wanted to interrogate, much like the Grand Jury at the Assizes. The head man thereupon hurried along to inform the selected respondents of The Call, and the alarmed peasants, pausing only long enough to don their own Friday-best, duly appeared, were questioned, prevaricated, and withdrew (one suspects, rear-end first in the ancient Ottoman fashion). Despite an excellently prepared sampling plan, the pilot-study results were largely worthless (Frey, 1973, p. 241).

This experience also highlights the possible errors arising from public or semi-public interviews. In a survey in Nepal, for example, respondents were interviewed, typically, with the entire village watching and listening. This may have had a beneficial effect for certain kinds of factual information, for example, amount of land under various types of cultivation, because the villagers would freely correct and supplement the respondent's replies. It no doubt, however, had a very serious negative effect on sensitive questions relating to number of births, family planning, etc. (Bergsten, 1980, p. 73).

The biasing effect of the presence of other persons at the interview is discussed by Mitchell in Chapter 18 under the heading 'clinical witnesses', (p. 233) but can be generalized as social desirability bias, where respondents distort their answers to conform to the prevailing norms and values in their own community or the wider society. Where the interview takes place in public, or other members of the respondent's family are present in their own residence, this effect may be expected to operate.

Experience varies in the success of research teams in minimizing this problem. In the Fiji Fertility Survey, only 7 per cent of interviews were conducted in the presence of the spouse, and 15 per cent in the presence of other adults (typically mother, mother-in-law, or sisters). 'In a few instances, enumerators, sensing that the persistent presence of a mother-in-law would harm rapport, abandoned the attempt and discreetly discovered a time when the relative would be absent and a successful re-visit could be made' (Sahib *et al.*, 1975, p. 43). In Choldin, Kahn, and Ara's research reported in Chapter 21, interviewers often found it impossible to keep older women and children out of the room in which the interview was conducted.

Discussing Turkish experience, Turan (1975) suggests a further factor operating which may be confounded with social desirability bias, but is in fact distinct from it, though the outcome may be similar. This he calls the community orientation of respondents. The idea that individuals have views and opinions of their own is itself a cultural value. Some research has developed in countries where there is belief in the value of ideas of the individual. The survey method is a means of tapping these ideas. However, in other societies, particularly where localities are isolated from the mainstream (as in many rural villages), identification with the community is much stronger and there is a greater likelihood that people will regard themselves as a part of the community, rather than as individuals. This has consequences for their pattern of response — the stronger the community orientation, the more likely it is that socially desirable answers will be given.

On the basis of Indian experience, Rudolph and Rudolph (1958) suggest that 'where life is lived communally, the unit of opinion is likely to have a communal base', and is more likely to be the extended family, the subcaste or the village rather than the individual. Opinion on many subjects is a product of group deliberation or tradition. The practical problem posed was how to deal with groups who formed themselves around those being interviewed, helpfully answering questions directed at the respondent seated at the centre, sometimes by other individuals, sometimes after discussion among the group (1958, pp. 327–328).

A communal orientation also influences how outsiders are perceived. The stronger the local community orientation, the more likely it is that outsiders such as interviewers will be viewed with suspicion. In urban areas, on the other hand, interviewers are seen as less threatening since urban dwellers are more used to talking to strangers about their answers.

Non-response in survey research is a potential source of bias wherever surveys are conducted, and a major source of concern to survey practitioners throughout the world. There is some indication, however, of types of non-response in surveys in the developing world which may lead to different sorts of bias depending on where the survey is conducted. In village studies, for example, refusals and resistance are frequently encountered both from women and from poorly educated lower-class or caste people, who cannot believe that their opinions are of any importance. 'Why ask me? I am only an ignorant woman. Ask my husband!' (Rudolph and Rudolph, 1958, p. 238). 'Why ask me? I am only a poor farmer.' Western survey research assumes that each person's view is of equal value. A primary aim of the survey is to collect comparable information from each respondent which is then aggregated (Benney and Hughes, 1956). In developing countries, the field force has to be persistent in the face of respondents who believe themselves unworthy to be interviewed. Rudolph and Rudolph cite a case where a poor female respondent and her neighbours believed so strongly that her opinion counted for nothing that they suspected that the interviewers were police interrogators. Another woman believed the interview was a preliminary to criminal proceedings, and wept throughout until the interviewer abandoned the interview.

The problem is discussed further in Chapter 19 by Hershfield *et al.*, but should not be discounted as a significant source of non-sampling error. Turan (1975) suggests that such behaviour is a manifestation of a community orientation, which may sometimes reflect the local power structure. This is plausible in the Indian context, where weight of opinion can be related to caste. (Rudolph and Rudolph (1958, p. 238) report community leaders asking with great consternation why Harijan respondents were to be questioned, saying that they themselves were much better sources of information. In Turkey, a share-cropper may hesitate to take part in an interview unless his *aglia* (landlord) agrees. Fear of the local elite may also reflect the fact that communications with the outside world are channelled through occupants of particular statuses, such as landlords, merchants or agricultural traders.

A further source of non-sampling error can be seen in the examples given at the beginning of this chapter — that respondents are unable to answer certain questions, such as the Nepalese survey lacking adequate age data. This may be the result either of a general inability to answer certain types of question, or failure to answer in respect of specific items. In their Indian survey, the

Rudolphs found that many respondents did not have an 'opinion' on many subjects about which they were questioned. Articulating an opinion requires a degree of self-consciousness and self-awareness, enough to see that custom and tradition are not the only source of ideas and beliefs. Many of their respondents, when questioned about political culture, did not have 'opinions' which could be clearly expressed. This difficulty clearly relates to the existence of a community orientation, and reliance on the collectivity for the formation and expressed of social beliefs and attitudes.

Individual items, too, may fail to yeild meaningful responses. This problem was touched on in Section IV on data collection. It arises whenever a research instrument is translated from one language to another. Will the translated question make sense and be meaningful in another language? (see Deutscher, 1968). Several examples of questions which did not yield meaningful answers are given in Chapter 21 on cultural complications in fertility interviewing.

Remedies for errors and biases

The tenor of discussions of non-sampling error is often one which suggests that the problems are so serious that little can be done to improve matters. This is far from being the case. Some suggestions will be briefly sketched, and the reader is referred to fuller discussions of Third World survey research practice for guidance as to how to proceed in the field (Casley and Lury, 1981, pp. 115–129; Hursh-César and Roy, 1976, pp. 299–320; Warwick and Lininger, 1975, pp. 182–219).

The most essential requirement for dealing with error and bias is self-conscious awareness that it exists and has to be countered. Too often, technical effort in survey research has gone into sample design issues and attempts to reduce (measurable) sampling error, while neglecting non-sampling error. As emphasized in Chapter 7, introducing the section on sampling, in surveys in developing countries, non-sampling error is likely to be greater than sampling error, and therefore requires particular attention. Nothing will be gained by pretending that it does not exist, and a great deal of harm will result.

The quality of data collected in any survey depends in the last resort upon the capabilities and skills of the interviewer. Who does the interviewing is therefore a vital consideration. The Turkish example cited earlier, where census enumerators proved quite unsuitable for the much more sensitive work involved in an attitude survey, is a cautionary tale. The kinds of people employed as interviewers will vary from country to country, cultural group to cultural group, type of area (urban or rural) and subject-matter of the survey (see, for example, Wilson and Armstrong, 1963). Nevertheless, certain characteristics may be identified to which careful consideration should be given in recruiting interview staff, with a view to reducing cultural and status differences and facilitating easy communication with respondents.

In areas with more than one language or ethnic group, ability to speak the language of the respondent is essential, and membership of the same ethnic group desirable:

Most interviewers find it extremely difficult to explain their work as objective data collectors to villagers who have no meaningful frame of reference within which to place survey interviewing. The task is easier when the interviewers and respondents are alike in terms of social origin, religion, language and dialect, geographical area and can understand, appreciate and observe common customs. Sharing these characteristics reduces barriers to communication and is expected to improve acceptance and trust (Hursh-César and Roy, 1976, p. 305).

Matching interviewer and respondent on several attributes is often difficult, or in multilingual or ethnically diverse areas impossible without a two-stage procedure (see Smith (1976) for such an example). Nevertheless, the general point should be borne in mind. Linguistic competence is particularly essential.

The sex of the interviewer poses problems. In many societies, and for some subjects such as fertility, it is only acceptable for interviews to be conducted by a member of the same sex. But in Muslim societies, as Chapter 21 shows, there may be problems in gaining the acceptance of female interviewers, and problems of women interviewers travelling and staying overnight alone in strange places because culturally unacceptable may be insuperable.

Moreover, a degree of toughness is required of interviewers, whether men or women. In rural surveys, they must have the stamina to endure field conditions living rough, working unusual hours and in poor conditions. Interviewing may be fatiguing, psychologically disturbing and on occasions dangerous. Considerable travel is involved, often using rather primitive means of transport. Health conditions are frequently poor.

Personal qualities are also important. The interviewer must like interviewing, present himself or herself well without being uncouth in appearance or manner, and be able to relate to the respondent. These qualities can be developed by training, but also can be judged when selecting individuals on personal and background characteristics. Honesty and diligence are also necessary qualities.

Education, for example, is important, but there is no necessary correlation between more education and better interviewing. Interviewers need to be literate, numerate and able to respond to training, so that they can understand the purposes of the research and record meaningful answers. However, they also have to relate to those whom they are interviewing. In many rural societies, the status gap between highly educated university graduates and rural peasants is so wide as to be unbridgeable. Such interviewers are often far from being the best choice for rural surveys, and people with primary or secondary education may be much more suitable (Hursh, 1971).

Experience previously of social research work is an advantage, but particular care has to be taken in recruiting government officials who have previously worked as census enumerators. A census is compulsory, and is often carried out in a markedly authoritarian manner, as a requirement with which the citizen must comply. Though confidence and firmness are necessary in approaching survey respondents (on how to do so, see Warwick and Lininger, 1975, pp. 203–219), an authoritarian approach is likely to markedly increase the error rate.

The age of interviewers may also be important, particularly in societies where social status is linked to age. Young interviewers may have considerably difficulty in interrogating their elders, and this point should be considered during recruitment.

Some surveys have been carried out in developing countries by recruiting interviewers in the actual village where the study was conducted. Such a use of 'insiders', rather in the manner of anthropological informants, may occasionally be justified but is best avoided, for it is difficult for the local person known to respondents to achieve the necessary detachment. Respondents are more likely to be reticent with those who are already known to them. It is better to recruit interviewers who are indigenous to the *area*, but not to the immediate locality, and to plan work so that interviewers do not work in their own village.

Such an itemization of desirable characteristics has its limitations. Who, then, actually will be employed as interviewers?

Interviewers have been recruited from many groups, with varying degrees of success: government census takers, office clerks, rural school teachers, agricultural field workers, village women, secondary school students, public health nurses, unemployed school-leavers, and so on (Hursh-César and Roy, 1976, p. 309).

Robert Mitchell on p. 237 discusses the practice in different countries as it was in the 1960s. A recent review of rural research in Africa suggested that alternative types of interviewer were university students, extension agents, teachers and locally unemployed people (Kearl, 1976, pp. 115–120). Frey's (1973) experience in Turkey showed that village school teachers were effective and knew the region and its idiom and mores well. Where extension workers, public health or community development officials are used as interviewers, their training must emphasize the difference between research interviews and other types of intervention, stressing the necessary lack of involvement, and the need for detachment, on the part of the interviewer.

If students are to be used, it may be better to use unemployed primary and secondary school gradutates rather than university students. Properly trained and supervised, the former tend to be better and cheaper staff than urbanized, high-class, university students the use of whom is often disastrous. Most students are 'elitist', on the road to becoming members of a privileged class. Serious communication problems can result from their employment. They can frequently have great difficulty in abandoning their high status roles to establish rapport with illiterate, subsistence-level peasant farmers (Hursh-César and Roy, 1976, p. 308).

Another source of bias, referred to earlier and in the chapters by Mitchell and Choldin, is the presence of others at the interview. Privacy for the interview should be sought wherever possible, by avoiding interviewing in public, and making appointments to visit people in their own homes. In the Fiji fertility survey, a successful strategem for keeping husbands and other males out of the way was the suggestion that 'this interview concerns women only and is unsuitable for male ears' (Sahib *et al.*, 1975, p. 43).

In planning the logistics of rural surveys, a topic touched on in Chapter 21 by Choldin, Kahn and Ara, decisions have to be taken about procedure which have major effects on bias and error. In particular, should interviewers in rural surveys be used as a team to cover selected villages intensively in turn, or should single or pairs of interviewers be left in particular villages for several days or weeks to complete the programme more gradually. The former is sometimes called the 'invasion' method, the latter the 'immersion' method. The 'invasion' method is the norm in large-scale surveys, partly for operational reasons, but also in the argument that if interviews are completed within one day by a team, there is less chance for feedback between those interviewed and those still to be interviewed, less opportunity for rumours to build up. Proponents of the immersion method, however, argue that spending time in the village permits interviewers to gain familiarity with local conditions and to develop rapport with respondents. In this respect, the arguments in its favour bear some resemblance to those put forward in favour of more intensive, ethnographic types of research which are considered in Section VI on methodological marriages.

References

Back, K.W. and Gergen, K.J. (1963). Idea orientation and ingratiation in the interview: a dynamic model of response bias, *Proceedings of the Social Statistics Section*, pp. 284–288, American Statistical Association, Washington DC.

Benney, M. and Hughes, E.C. (1956). Of sociology and the interview. *American Journal of Sociology*, **62**, 137–142.

Bergsten, J.W. (1980) Some sample survey design problems in Syria, Nepal and Somalia, American Statistical Association, Washington DC. *Proceedings of the Section on Survey Research Methods*, pp. 72–74.

Bulmer, M. (ed.) (1979). *Censuses, Surveys and Privacy*, Macmillan, London.

Casley, D.J. and Lury, D.A. (1981). *Data Collection in Developing Countries*, Clarendon Press, Oxford.

Deutscher, I. (1968). Asking questions cross-culturally: some problems of linguistic comparability. In H.S. Becker *et al.*, (Eds) *Institutions and the Person*, pp. 318–341, Aldine, Chicago.

Frey, F.W. (1973) Surveying peasant attitudes in Turkey. In D.P. Warwick and S. Osherson (Eds) *Comparative Research Methods*, pp. 227–247, Prentice Hall, Englewood Cliffs, NJ.

Goldman, N. *et al.* (1979). *The Quality of Data in the Nepal Fertility Survey*, International Statistical Institute, World Fertility Survey, Scientific Report No. 6, Voorburg, Netherlands.

Hursh, G. (1971) *Interviewers and Interviewing*, Council for Social Development, Survey Research Training Course, October, New Delhi.

Hursh-César, G. and Roy, P. (1976). *Third World Surveys*, Macmillan of India, Delhi.

Kahn, R.L. and Cannell, C.F. (1957). *The Dynamics of Interviewing: Theory, Technique and Cases*, Wiley, New York.

Kearl, B. (ed.) (1976). *Field Data Collection in the Social Sciences: experiences in Africa and the Middle East*, Agricultural Development Council Inc., New York.

Keesing, F.M. and Keesing, M.M. (1956). *Elite Communications in Samoa: A Study in Leadership*, Stanford, Stanford University Press.

Mamdani, M. (1972). *The Myth of Population Control: Family, Caste and Class in an Indian Village*, Monthly Review Press, New York.

Marsh, C. (1982). *The Survey Method: The Contribution of Surveys to Sociological Explanation*, Allen and Unwin, London.

Neale, W.C. (1958). The limitations of Indian village survey data. *Journal of Asian Studies*, **17**, 383–402.

Pausewang, S. (1973). *Methods and Concepts of Social Research in a Rural Developing Society: A Critical Appraisal Based on Experience in Ethiopia*, Weltforum Verlag, Munich.

Rudolph, L. and Rudolph, S.H. (1958). Surveys in India: field experience in Madras State. *Public Opinion Quarterly*, **33**, 235–244.

Sahib, M.A. *et al.* (1975). *The Fiji Fertility Survey: A Critical Commentary*, International Statistical Institute, World Fertility Survey, Occasional Paper No. 15, Voorburg, Netherlands.

Smith, D. (1976). *The Facts of Racial Disadvantage*, Political and Economic Planning Broadsheet no. 560, London.

Teer, F. and Spence, J.D. (1973). *Political Opinion Polls*, Hutchinson, London.

Turan, I. (1975). *Survey Research in a Developing Country: Field Work in Turkey*, University of Iowa, Comparative Legislative Research Center, Occasional Paper No. 7, Iowa City, Iowa.

Warwick, D.P. and Lininger, C. (1975). *The Sample Survey: Theory and Practice*, McGraw-Hill, New York.

Wilson, E.C. and Armstrong, L. (1963). Interviewers and interviewing in India. *International Social Science Journal*, **15**, 48–58.

Social Research in Developing Countries
Edited by M. Bulmer and D.P. Warwick
© 1983, John Wiley & Sons, Ltd.

CHAPTER 18

SURVEY MATERIALS COLLECTED IN THE DEVELOPING COUNTRIES: SAMPLING, MEASUREMENT, AND INTERVIEWING OBSTACLES TO INTRANATIONAL AND INTERNATIONAL COMPARISONS

ROBERT EDWARD MITCHELL

Scholars, government officials, and commercial interests in the developing countries are increasingly recognizing that survey research methods provide the only means by which systematic information can be collected and analysed for a wide range of purposes of both scholarly research and policy–making. American and European scholars and policy-makers are also becoming increasingly interested in using survey materials collected in developing countries for intranational and international comparisons (Hoffman, 1963; Wuelker, Chapter 12). However, there is ample reason to suspect that many of the materials — perhaps the vast majority — are of such questionable quality that they cannot be used for research on numerous topics. For example, validation checks conducted in the course of fertility studies sometimes reveal major discrepancies in simple factual information (Fortes, 1954); a validation check performed in the course of a study of capital formation in a rural area of a developing country showed a 15 per cent discrepancy in basic economic figures; other studies of household budgets and economic surveys have disclosed extremely sloppy work and serious inaccuracies in the reported figures (Neale, 1958).

Despite the criticisms which can be made of those who conduct survey research in the developing countries, and also those which can be made of their data and the ways they are used, there is no indication that the growth of this

Reprinted from *International Social Science Journal* (1965), **17** (4). 665–685. © 1965, UNESCO.
Reproduced by permission of UNESCO.

research approach will be curtailed by the existence of methodological and technical obstacles. Rather, with governments expressing more and more demands for information, and with scholars expressing an increasing interest in basic social science research, there will very likely be an accelerated rate of reliance on survey research methods.

The present chapter attempts to outline and catalogue some of the major issues involved in the conduct of survey research in the developing countries. A concern with the use of existing materials for purposes of secondary analysis, especially for international comparative purposes, initiated this review. In addition, however, the lessons learned from this examination of the strengths and weaknesses of existing materials are of particular relevance for those wishing to collect original data.

The analysis of available materials is under three headings or types of bias: sampling, measurement, and interviewer bias.

Sampling errors

Poor workmanship

In many countries it is only an analytical fiction which permits one to discuss sampling and non-sampling errors separately, for the same staffs and procedures used in interviewing respondents are also used in preparing the samples. This is the situation in particular with regard to preparing samples of certain specialized populations for which no locator or parameter information is available. In these instances, the interviewing staffs frequently prepare the information which is used in drawing the sample.

Relatively few countries have adequate sampling information even for their major metropolitan centres, and, as a consequence, various incomplete, outdated maps are used, or, in the absence of alternative registers (for example, voting or housing registers), agencies will pre-list their sampling areas. Some studies in non-urban areas employ random-walk procedures (Fink, 1963) without the benefit of pre-listing and, therefore, the interviewer is at the same time a sampler. Interviewers also often select the respondent within the household, although it appears to be an increasingly common practice to have the interviewer first list the members of the household and then use a table of random numbers to select the actual person to be interviewed. Interviewers, of course, play a crucial sampling role in studies based on quota samples.

Unfortunately, there is abundant reason to question both the competence and honesty of interviewing-sampling field staffs in many countries, and, consequently, to question the adequacy of the samples which are drawn. Perhaps samples drawn by government agencies are of less dubious quality than others, but the sampling resources of these agencies are seldom made available to those involved in non-governmental social science research.

An example of shoddy workmanship was discovered in a major Asian city where the leading (and in many ways most competent) research agency prepared house listings which were subsequently used in drawing a number of samples. The listings consisted of house addresses. Approximately 8 months after the listings were prepared, they were loaned to a local university research group for a government-sponsored study, when it was discovered that approximately one out of the four addresses did not exist. The agency which prepared the listings must surely have been aware of their limitations as a sampling frame. However, this did not deter it from using the frame for a number of studies. Such practices, it is suggested, are not uncommon.

Coverage and comparability of sampling frames

Given the lack of sampling resources available in developing countries, and given the sampling obstacles created by poor and often mobile populations, it is probably inevitable that sampling frames often fail to include large segments of the population within a single country and that samples used for international comparative purposes are typically based on non-comparable sampling frames.

These difficulties can be found in the valuable and interesting five-city (Tokyo, Manila, Singapore, Bangkok, and Bombay) general public opinion study called the 'Asia Poll', a regional equivalent to earlier 'World Polls'. The sampling procedures differ considerably in these cities, with quota procedures being used in some and probability samples in others. Even if all five research agencies drew probability samples, the comparative researcher would still encounter difficulties, since the frames in each city would differ in their coverage. For example, a voting registration list might include 70 per cent of one city's population, a housing registration list might include 80 per cent of another city's population, and an area probability sample might be 90 per cent complete in another city. In this situation, the researcher would have problems in deciding whether on some items— for example, occupational mobility— the apparent differences between two cities were significant (if he were to dare ask such a question of his data).

Similar problems of comparability can be found in the recent international comparative study of social stratification and mobility conducted in Rio de Janeiro, Montevideo, Buenos Aires, and Santiago. These are exceedingly interesting and worthwhile studies, although local scholars have raised serious questions about the completeness of the various samples used.

These problems of the comparability of frames between countries are no less serious within single nations. For example, one might question the comparability of Rio de Janeiro samples with samples of Sao Paulo. Since survey studies in most developing countries tend to be conducted within the major city or in the city where the major research agencies are located, the sampling resources are differently distributed throughout the nation. Therefore, a so-called 'national urban sample' based on a number of cities will utilize sampling frames which differ considerably in their completeness. Differences can even be found between two agencies in their samples for a single city, and, furthermore, one agency will differ in samples it prepares at different times for a single location. For example, in evaluating the adequacy of existing materials it acquired, the International Data Library and Reference Service of the University of California's Survey Research Center discovered the following discrepancies in three separate samples drawn by two agencies in the same city: one study found no respondents earning less than 10 (US) dollars per month; another study found approximately 9 per cent; and a third, which seems to be the most accurate, found 70 per cent in this category.

Maintaining adequate sampling frames is an especially difficult problem in rapidly expanding cities such as exist in most developing countries, especially in Africa and Latin America. For example, in some African cities there has been a rapid change in housing from huts to flats, a process which destroys the sampling value of carefully prepared city maps (Barber and Prothero 1961). The expense of keeping these frames up to date is usually prohibitive, and, in fact, it is not uncommon for agencies·to use outdated frames. Since adequate parameter data are seldom available, the researcher is not able to assess the exact nature and extent of the sampling biases in his materials. Too often, as will be noted again later, the only available checks are provided by results produced in earlier studies by the same agency. Misleading information in these instances is used to corroborate deficient data.

Cluster and quota sampling

Unfortunately, descriptive terms such as 'national probability sample' or 'quota sample' based on certain criteria are so general and vague in meaning that the consumer and user of data cannot determine the degree to which his sample is representative of some larger population or the degree to which two samples in the same or different countries are comparable. Only three of many issues relevant to these problems will be mentioned here: the ultimate sampling unit, clustering procedures, and quota sampling procedures — all of which are closely related to problems of sampling frames as discussed earlier.

Critical but ill-informed opponents of sample surveys and quantitative procedures for research in developing societies have argued that sampling necessarily leads to studies based only on individuals considered independently of the social networks in which they are involved (Leach, 1958; Merritt, 1966). Evidently, these critics are unaware of the possibility of interviewing all members of a single household, of a kinship line, or of any other collectivity; nor are they aware of snowball sampling. Furthermore, they fail to recognize the possibilities of various kinds of relational analysis, analytical procedures which have been given a welcome fillip by recent computer developments.

Although these criticisms are not well taken, at least they turn our attention to sampling units and the assumptions underlying their use. There are obvious differences in sampling units based on voting registers and those based on households; the former may consist primarily of men who are highly politicized, whereas the latter may have a surplus of apolitical women. The latter might also include a much higher proportion of all adults in the total universe. However, there may also be problems in the use of the household. Often, the household is defined as a group of people eating around a common kitchen or kettle, whereas in random-walk procedures it might refer to a single hut, regardless of the eating arrangements. Still other samples define a household as all those who share their earnings. After a household has been selected, standard procedures may or may not be used to select the respondent to be interviewed.

Often the average size and complexity of the household differs in different parts of the interviewing area, for example, between rural and urban areas or areas populated by families with different kinship systems. In these sampling units and ratios used to select respondents may overweight certain portions of the population, and alter the selection probabilities of various segments of the universe.

Obviously, the sampling units used in a study must be relevant to the research purposes and to sociological reality. It would be folly for any researcher to proceed blindly to draw his sample without first becoming thoroughly familiar with the major features of the local scene, including kinship structures. However, for the most part, it seems that the use of different sampling units is admittedly only a minor issue in a more complicated problem of sampling.

A key element, as described by Philip Converse (1963), relates to the clustering procedures used in preparing samples. Very often the term 'national probability sample' simply means that the study was conducted in more than one metropolitan area (Converse was referring to European practices, although the same remarks apply to the developing countries). Since research agencies in these countries often face serious transportation problems, as well as cost and supervision difficulties, the rural areas included in the sample are typically adjacent to the major metropolitan sampling points. Even when several sampling points are selected, the clustering procedures which are used add greatly to the error margins for materials, especially for items such as education, sophistication, and political involvement — items which tend not to be homogeneously distributed across regions. Given these considerations, the researcher is limited in his ability to project his findings to larger populations; he is limited in the importance he can attach to rural–urban (or centre–periphery) differences; and he is limited in his ability to subdivide his materials statistically by various criteria, especially those criteria highly associated with the major clusters defining the sample. Since scholars are generally unaware of these problems, they may tend to over-interpret their findings.

A number of difficulties involved in comparing two sets of probability samples have been noted by others (Abrams, 1964). For example, the two major commercial polling agencies in Great Britain disagree as to the proper base for national samples, and, as a result, the two agencies are reported to differ consistently in their electoral predictions. They also differ in the criteria used in determing socioeconomic position, thereby making it hazardous to compare blue-collar workers from one agency's sample with blue-collar workers from the other agency's sample.

When sampling resources are not adequate and funds are scarce research agencies typically resort to quota sampling. Much research needs to be done comparing the relative merits of quota and various kinds of probability samples in the developing countries. As survey research, especially commercial research, expands in the developing countries, it is quite likely that there will be an increasing number of opportunities to do this. One confidential study shown me recently made such a comparison for two samples used in two commercial surveys in a large Latin American metropolitan city, and the comparisons indicated a very close congruence on many relevant items. However, this one example is countered by other experiences. An investigation by the Organization for Economic Co-operation and Development (OECD) concluded that quota sampling procedures used in different European countries were so divergent and uncontrolled that one could not compare results obtained from the various samples (Kapferer, 1964).

Preliminary investigation of quota sampling procedures in the developing countries tends to support the OECD's conclusions. For example, some agencies will select their respondents by house calls made only during the day; others interview outside factories and office buildings, while others use various other techniques. Research agencies naturally defend their samples, but often on entirely erroneous grounds. On the basis of accepted parameter or universe data, the agency selects its various quotas — so many working women between the ages of 35 and 45, so many male blue-collar workers between the ages of 40 and 50, etc. When the interviewing materials are tabulated, the marginal distributions on demographic items typically agree with the distribution of these items in the universe. However, to claim, as some agencies do, that this agreement guarantees the representativeness of the sample is merely to confirm the predetermined consequences which bear no logical relationship to the degree to which the sample is truly representative.

Since research agencies have trained their clients to compare their sample figures with the known universe data, an apparent discrepancy in the sample can prove embarrassing. It is partly for this reason, and partly from a genuine interest in producing quality samples, that research agencies resort to various *post hoc* weighting procedures, or return to the field to pick up the needed extra respondents for particular population segments. Again, a comparison between the universe and sample figures — whether from a quota or a probability sample–need not be relevant at all as far as the representativeness of that sample is concerned.

Social and cultural accessibility (non-completion rates)

Even if a researcher is satisfied with the sampling frames and procedures prepared for his study, he will still have to overcome obstacles created for him by non-respondents, an especially acute problem in comparative studies. Non-respondents are typically not distributed randomly throughout the sample but differ according to variations in the cultural and social accessibility of distinct population segments. On an international scale, Almond and Verba's five-nation study *The Civic Culture* (1963) is an example of this problem. Their non-completion rates range from 17 per cent to 41 per cent. It is not clear whether the non-respondents are the same in all countries. In some countries, they would not be. For example, females account for 64 per cent of the Mexican sample in the Almond and Verba study. According to the contractor, which is surely one of the best agencies found in any developing country, such ratios are not unusual and do not differ significantly from what has been discovered in a number of parallel or interpenetrating replicate subsamples which have been drawn in Mexico.

Unfortunately, the 1960 Mexican census does not support this assumption: only 52 per cent of the Mexican population living in cities of 10 000 (the smallest city sampled in the five-nation survey) or more are women; this figure varies by only a couple of percentage points for different size cities, and different adult age groups. Furthermore, parallel samples can be deceiving here. For example, no matter how many parallel subsamples are drawn in India, men will usually constitute approximately 80 per cent of the interviewed respondents for some agencies. That is, a number of studies and research experiences in Asia indicate that women are culturally and socially inaccessible to interviewers, whereas the experience elsewhere indicates that men are relatively inaccessible, and, as the Almond and Verba study suggests, there are national differences in the availability of different types of respondents even within the western world.

These same problems arise for samples within a single country, since groups may differ in their degree of accessibility to interviewers in different parts of a nation. In Latin America, some of the major intranational differences in response rates seem to occur for members of the upper class, since they are difficult to interview in urban areas.

Intranational as well as international differences in response rates have implications for the way the data can be interpreted. As will be indicated again later, there is good reason to believe that respondents and non-respondents differ in their ability to provide equally good and complete information;

therefore, certain comparisons — such as rural–urban or centre–periphery — will typically introduce biases. For example, the absence of members of the urban upper class may lead to an understatement of rural–urban differences (this understatement may be further complicated if the rural sampling points are closely adjacent to the urban sampling points, as noted previously in the discussion of sampling procedures). If weighting procedures are used to give the correct proportions of upper-class respondents in the sample, some of the bias in single, one-variable marginals may be reduced. However, intensive multivariate analysis based on weighted cards can be highly misleading, especially if the samples are relatively small.

Even these very abbreviated remarks regarding sampling problems should be enough to alert the researcher to the limitations of any one study, let alone several studies which he might wish to use for comparative purposes. Further-more, the issues discussed in this section should suggest some questions which researchers might ask themselves before beginning a study. For example, is it realistic and relevant even to aim for a national sample when the sampling resources are so inadequate and response-rates so flexible? Should some respondents receive only one call-back, thereby releasing resources to permit more call-backs on specified kinds of respondents? The researcher certainly should collect information on the number of call-backs, on replacement pro-cedures used, if any, and the degree to which respondents are self-selected; he should also be thoroughly familiar with the nature of the sampling frame and the procedures used in drawing his samples.

Measurement errors

Sophistication and meaningless evidence

Until recently, social science research in the developing countries was con-ducted almost exclusively by anthropologists, as it is today in a great many areas. Anthropologists have made a number of cogent criticisms of survey research, especially opinion studies. Two criticisms are especially relevant: doubt as to the existence of any such thing as private or public opinion, the mechanisms for decision-making and opinion formation being thought to be absent in lower-class roles, especially in tradition-directed societies. Second, the critics imply that even if the native does harbour personal opinions, it is not possible to measure these opinions by means of standard interviewing tech-niques.

While it might be argued that the proponents of these views tend to gen-eralize experiences gained from observation of primitive societies to the kinds of problems which are likely to be encountered in modernizing areas, and although these critics sometimes ignore the fact that survey research methods are used for gaining factual as well as attitudinal information, there is still considerable general support for their criticisms. For example, almost any study which includes consistency checks within the research instrument will discover a very high proportion of inconsistent responses. Studies being analysed by the International Data Library and Reference Service report very high proportions of 'no answers', 'don't knows', 'no opinion', neutral positions on attitude scales, and undifferentiated responses to manifestly different questions, such as attitudes toward the United States, the USSR, and China. Our preliminary inquiries into the opinion structures of certain groups suggest that the often overtly sophisticated questions framed by many researchers are eliciting meaningless opinion from respondents who have no opinion or only very unstable opinions. Philip Converse (1964) has systematically investigated some of these problems. Using panel data for what might be considered elite American population segments, he raises serious questions regarding the stability of opinion in the 'advanced sections of the most advanced societies'. Even issues considered to be salient to wide segments of the American population were found to have a small public. 'Issue publics' in the developing countries also are liekly to be even more minuscule and limited to a small proportion of the educated. (However, as will be noted again, 'issue publics' as used by Converse should not be confused with 'basic' values.)

The second criticism raised by anthropologists also has apparent support, for there is little doubt that asking questions, as in a personal interview, is alien to many societies. Keesing and Keesing (1956) among others, have argued that to answer a question is to make a decision, which only certain individuals in a society have a right to do. Other studies — for example, Lerner (1958) in the use of the concept 'empathy' — have amplified this issue by noting that lower-class respondents typically are unable to answer questions which require that they take the role of others. These difficulties have encouraged some researchers to sample only known opinion holders (the elite), whereas other researchers, less concerned with general public opinion than with specific behaviour and basic values, have interviewed unsophisticated respondents with considerable success. Family planning studies have probably been most conspicuous in this regard (Freedman, 1961–62).

While recognizing the value of these various criticms, it seems that they are perhaps too general and that, in fact, they suggest a number of dimensions which, once isolated, can help future researchers improve their ability to obtain accurate and meaningful information. Unquestionably, current attempts to measure public opinion and behaviour in the developing countries are imperfect. For example, little or no distinction is made among (a) topics about which the respondent has no opinion or is unable to give an adequate factual answer, (b) topics which are culturally sensitive, and (c) topics which need greater conceptual linguistic, and measuring sophistication in order to draw out information.

Researchers and critics of research seem to be most aware of the 'no opinion' dimension. They claim that research instruments are often so constructed and administered as to elicit meaningless responses. Many studies, of course, are not concerned with general opinions but, rather, with factual information and basic values. One might expect that there would be relatively minor difficulties involved in obtaining factual information on household expenditures and income, media exposure and voting behaviour, and family control techniques and family size. Many of the obstacles to obtaining factual information have been observed by others; for example, demographic surveys have difficulty in obtaining correct information in societies which do not have the western concept of time; and economic surveys in largely non-monetary markets and in rural areas have discovered that employment, income, debt, and consumption vary in size over the farming year, thereby making it impossible to generalize about the economy on the basis of the limited information that respondents are able to recall at only one time period. Even studies which seriously attempt to determine the reliability and validity of their information have discovered fairly serious errors.

Opinion studies which include consistency checks will probably discover even larger 'error rates'. At the present time, no standard method has evolved for handling such instances. One might delete the inconsistencies from the sample, or the whole study might be abandoned if the error rate is high. Some researchers simply treat inconsistency as a finding, and then disregard it in the subsequent analysis (Back and Stycos, 1959). Still others, as will be noted again later, feel that it is best, at least for the key variables in the study, to obtain multiple indicators for a single dimension so that undue reliance is not placed on the answers to any single question.

Of course, some of these suggestions can refer to issues for which respondents have opinions and information just as well as they refer to issues for which this is not the case. For example, it is common practice in media-exposure studies in the United States for the questionnaire to repeat a single question several times and in several variations, a technique designed to help respondents remember whether they were exposed to particular media.

Some non-survey workers have argued that interview studies, especially those which use precoded and leading questions, structure respondents' frames of reference in such a manner as to encourage them to provide answers which under normal circumstances would not be within their capabilities to formulate. However, this is precisely what a well-designed interview schedule is supposed to do, and it presumably has many advantages over traditional research procedures. Rather than collect masses of partially relevant and irrelevant materials, the survey researcher attempts by prior inquiry to isolate major dimensions he wishes to study. And, rather than pore over his notes in an attempt to substantiate (more typically, to illustrate) his major hypotheses, and rather than be in a position where no information is available to test alternative hypotheses, the survey researcher, in the ideal situation, collects data permitting him to perform both of these tasks.

Many of the criticisms against survey research focus specifically on precoded questions, since they obviously provide the answers which respondents might not otherwise be capable of formulating for themselves. To avoid the dangers involved in these questions, as well as similar problems which might arise in open-ended questions, Converse (1964) suggests that the respondent be encouraged to volunteer that he has no opinion on a particular topic. There is no reason why such an invitation or filtering technique could not precede precoded questions, although the general approach could possibly be overtly effective in societies where respondents are eager to give the answer they think you want from them. They would volunteer 'no opinion' when in fact they had one (see the later discussion of 'courtesy bias', p. 253).

The second of the three distinctions made earlier refers to culturally sensitive topics, something quite different from topics for which respondents can be said to have 'no opinion'. Culturally sensitive topics raise special problems for the comparative researcher, since what is sensitive in one country may not be in another. For example, it is said to be extremely difficult to obtain religious information in Moslem Pakistan, but relatively easy to do this in Hindu India. In some African areas, as well as in other parts of the world, there is a reluctance to talk about dead children and the number of people in a household — obstacles to demographic researchers. In the Middle East there is a reluctance to discuss ordinary household events (Prothro, 1961), and Chinese businessmen in any country are reported to be especially secretive about any and all facets of their work and personal lives. In many countries, respondents are reticent about political topics in general and party preference in particular. On the other hand, it is by no means clear that family planning is nearly as sensitive an issue in the developing countries as might be expected.

Questions raised with regard to both meaningless opinions and opinions on culturally sensitive topics suggest the need for new measuring devices, especially devices to measure basic values. To this end, some studies have experimented with projective tests, role-playing, and various sentence-completion techniques, but, unfortunately, the relative merits of these approaches were not reported (Back, 1962). If different measuring devices have varying powers to elicit complete and accurate responses from different population segments, then questions might be raised with regard to the choice of sampling units. For example, for some purposes, husbands seem to be better respondents than are their wives when it comes to family-planning practices (Kiser, 1962).

It will be some time before we can be assured that various segments of a population are offering responses which are comparable in terms of amount and quality. For even though respondents are willing to answer questions asked of them, there remain cultural differences regarding respondents' abilities to express themselves. For example, if one examines marginals from studies conducted in Malaysia, one will notice that the Chinese, when compared with the Indians, have a much higher proportion of 'no answers' to precoded questions and fewer answers to open-ended questions. One of the reasons for this is that the Chinese are quite reticent, whereas the Indians are loquacious. This creates problems in comparing the two groups; and, of course, if the Chinese, Indians, and Malaysians are treated as a single national sample, the Chinese will be underweighted and the Indians overweighted.

Another example of this same kind of problem is suggested by the Almond and Verba (1963) five-nation study. They report that the Italians seem reticent about political topics. And, as was noted before, the Mexican sample has a very high proportion of women respondents least capable of responding to a personal interview. Since this study included a very high proportion of open-ended questions, a much higher proportion than is found in typical American studies, it would seem that the biases arising from cultural differences in sophistication, loquacity and articulateness are especially exaggerated.

Mention might be made of some additional means by which these various obstacles can be overcome, or at least means by which measurement errors of these kinds can be statistically controlled in the analysis of survey materials. For example, if respondents have a short span of attention, then interviewing might be conducted in several sessions, although this might be too expensive a procedure for most project budgets. At least the consequences of a short span of attention could possibly by measured by charting the proportion of 'poorly answered questions' at different phases of the interview session. The proportion should increase towards the end of the session. Another obvious approach is to spend much more time and resources on the pretesting of the research instrument, even if this requires that a smaller sample is interviewed in the final study. Researchers might also establish beforehand the amount of error they will tolerate in their materials, and then, on the basis of a small follow-up survey, decide whether the materials fall within the stated error limits. If not, then the materials and the research project might be abandoned entirely. Another procedure is to include numerous measures of verbosity, sophistication, credulity, conformity, extremism in responses, inability to differentiate, filter questions, information questions, items to measure the strength with which opinions are held, and various reliability or consistency checks. These measures can be used to differentiate population groups whose answers are biased and who need separate consideration. Finally, the researcher might develop various meta-languages which, although they limit the topics which can be studied, help to bypass numerous measurement problems. Charles Osgood has been most intimately associated with attempts to develop such languages (Maclay and Ware, 1961).

The third dimension which was mentioned — that is, the need for greater conceptual and linguistic sophistication — has a number of components. At the core of many of them, as with sampling, is poor workmanship and lack of trained competence among survey practitioners. This lack of expertness can be seen in research instruments which include questions such as 'What was the reason you left your country and came to start work in the plantations; why did you not stay at home?' Even the basic skills of asking the question 'Why?' are rare among overseas researchers. Furthermore, it would seem that much of the criticism against survey research in the developing areas is based on what practitioners in the United States would consider poor representations of the method.

Poorly worded questions are found very frequently in the materials to be used for purposes of secondary analysis. This is especially true for the open-ended questions. Of course, this considerably detracts from the value of these data, for the researcher has no assurance that a question elicits the full range of dimensions implicit in the question, a problem which is further complicated by the typically poor coding schemes developed for categorizing the answers to these questions.

Conceptual and linguistic equivalence

Problems of conceptual equivalence are especially troublesome to the comparative researcher, since he will often find that the concept he is working with is not found in the local culture. Researchers have discovered this difficulty with regard to concepts of time, of the future, of distance or height with regard to visual scaling devices, and of a number of concepts which have clear evaluative overtones, such as 'table manners'. In one recent study, the English word 'aggressive' was used to describe various groups. This created problems in at least one country, since it was later discovered that 'aggressive' had to be expressed either with a negative term or a positive one (one which implied pioneer). The positive one was used, which created some confusion on the part of the client.

Considerable knowledge of the local culture and language is needed in order to gain conceptual equivalence, or, as some call it, 'functional equivalence'. Agencies in the field which are aware of this are becoming increasingly opposed to what some of them refer to as ' "canned questionnaires" sent from the United States'. They feel that a client's attempt to preserve the exact form of his questions, especially precoded ones, can only lead to major errors. One agency now insists that clients attach a paragraph of explanation or a *rationale* to each question submitted. Once the agency discovers the intention behind a question— that is, the kind of answer which is desired and how the question will be used — it formulates its own version.

This approach deserves further exploration, for it attemps to gain functional equivalence with regard to the information which the researcher wants to elicit rather than with regard to the form of the questions used to elicit this information. (For the latter approach see Almond and Verba's (1963) five-nation study.) To attempt to gain functional equivalence in answers may require four questions in one country but only one question in another. While these four questions certainly would add to their value of the information from that single country, obvious difficulties are created for the researcher who wishes to make international comparisons. Not only are different procedures used in gaining the same kind of information, but also, the key terms in the questions are often different. This would occur in studies asking questions about decision-making and authority structures, since the relevant issues and reference groups would be different in different areas (Hollsteiner, 1963).

There is general agreement on how the actual translation of the questions should be made. First, the original instrument is translated into the local language, and then another translator independently translates this translated version back into the original. The original and retranslated versions are compared and the discrepancies are clarified.

A fair amount of linguistic resources are required in order to follow these translation procedures in some countries. For example, a national study in the Philippines will require about nine languages; at least nine are required in India; about 30 are necessary in Indonesia; but only two would be required for a national study in Canada or Belgium.

Unfortunately, relatively few research agencies have these linguistic resources. The implications of this are suggested by a recent study using a number of languages: the client decided to check the language versions which the contractor had prepared and discovered that approximately one-fourth of the translations made for any one language would have led to major biases.

In some areas, no attempt is even made to prepare a translation into the local language. Rather, this is left to bilingual interviewers. This seems to be a fairly common practice in Africa, where many of the languages do not have alphabets. So far as I have been able to discover, some of these African projects do not even decide on common terms for key concepts. Apparently, if the respondent speaks the western language in which the questions are written, this is the language used in the interview. In other multilingual areas, research agencies interview in the language which the respondent speaks in his home.

Needless to say, the language used in an interview may have important implications for the information elicited, for languages may differ considerably in their richness and expressive quality. These problems arise even in a single-language culture, as shown in the class differences in language behaviour in the United States (Labov, 1964). Since those who prepare and translate questionnaires are typically from the middle and upper classes, the instruments they produce are likely to be somewhat inappropriate for large segments of the population.

Interviewer bias

Clinical witnesses

It seems that the personal interview — that is, where an interviewer interviews a person in private — is relatively rare in a great many countries. For example, it has been estimated by some of my informants that at least 50 per cent of the European interviews are conducted in the presence of third parties, whereas in many areas of the developing countries — for example, in non-urban Pakistan — almost all interviews are conducted in the presence of other people. Some researchers have referred to these other people as 'clinical witnesses'.

The implications of these third parties for the data which are obtained seem to depend on a number of factors, including the content of the question, the status characteristics of the third parties, and the general cultural rules defining interpersonal relations. Reports by people working in the field suggest that the 'third-party' effect is considerable in societies characterized by sharp status and authority cleavages. In part, this is because the most important people are often interviewed first. Respondents naturally have difficulty sometimes in understanding why they have been singled out to be interviewed. According to the local status and value scales, the community leaders feel that they 'deserve' to be interviewed, and although the research team may not wish to waste resources in doing this, it is sometimes necessary to interview the local elite purely for public relations purposes. Fieldworkers report that after each answer given by the first interviewed, the assembled crowd nods its approval, saying that the answer also represents the views of others. Not only does this create or help crystalize consensus, it also often produces resistance to being interviewed on the part of others.

As with many other topics previously mentioned, third parties sometimes have a mixed effect. For example, in studies seeking information rather than attitudes, third parties may help keep the respondent honest and also help him to remember the requested information. In other instances, especially with women and younger people, respondents may refuse to be interviewed unless a third person is present. It is common practice in many areas at least to obtain the permission of a third party — the local headman — before commencing fieldwork.

These various examples raise general issues related to sponsorship and privacy in conducting interviews. If consent of local leaders is required, then respondents are likely to feel that the leaders also are sponsoring the study, thereby affecting the respondents' willingness to express certain feelings, especially 'minority' or deviant feelings. A whole range of issues needs to be studied with reference to the other topic, privacy. Certainly, if attempts to secure privacy are associated with witchcraft, as they evidently are in some places, then a public interview is the only means by which information can be obtained. Also, if being asked for one's private opinion gives a respondent prestige in the local community, to deny him the privilege of being questioned in public may seriously reduce the likelihood that he will be willing to be interviewed.

Several procedures have been developed to avoid the assumed consequences of third parties. For example, for some questions the respondent is asked to cast a ballot rather than to give an oral reply. This procedure could possibly reduce biases in politically oriented studies; for example, the presence of third parties in Italy may have played a significant role in the reticence reported by Almond and Verba (1963). A second and administratively popular approach is to use teams of interviewers. The team saturates a village so that the fieldwork is completed in a very short time (Back and Stycos, 1959; Fink, 1963; Frey, 1963). The third approach, which is a more recent development, is to use resident interviewers. These interviewers, like the traditional ethnographer, live in the local community for a fairly long period of time. Some researchers, especially those who have worked in south-east Asia, claim that this is the only technique which can assure complete and unbiased information. The resident interviewer acquires knowledge and contacts to permit him to check on the information he receives; he recognizes errors and inconsistencies which can then be quickly clarified; he may be able to eliminate the recall problem; and by being a member of the community, he is able to overcome the natives' resistance to giving truthful information to outsiders. On the other hand, the use of resident interviewers and fieldwork procedures which assign a very large area to only one or two interviewers limit the number of sampling points which can be used and may, therefore, decrease the representativeness of the sample. Since interviewing assignments cannot be randomized, the entire information for a single sampling point is the product of one man's biases; also, spending long periods of time in one area may involve the field worker in community problems and provide him with so much 'inside' information and so many personal contacts that his respondents refuse to provide him with information because they fear ti will not be kept confidential. For larger studies, the period in the field is lengthened and the costs of the study are increased. Unless the fieldworker is a native of the region he is studying, it may require a prohibitively long time in residence before he is able to reap the benefits presumably associated with being a resident interviewer; and, it is not clear that this is the best procedure for obtaining many kinds of information. One study of American Indian tribes found that it is sometimes easier for an outsider to obtain certain information if the status of the information-seeking person is associated with what outsiders do (Lang and Kunstadter, 1957). Narrolls' (1962) study of the relationship between the length of time anthropologists spend in the field and the information they obtain indicates that length may not be important for some issues and that for other issues a very long period in the field is required. Also, leaving a full-time interviewer relatively unsupervised may not be the best way to control cheating, although to disrupt a man's life by keeping him continually on the move may also create problems.

In any event, the comparative researcher will discover that field staffs and fieldwork procedures are organized very differently, often with very different implications for the quality and completeness of the information which is obtained.

Courtesy bias

The second type of interviewer bias has been referred to as 'courtesy' of 'hospitality bias', a bias which seems to be especially common in Asia, everywhere from Japan to Turkey (Hollsteiner, 1963; Jones, Chapter 20). Courtesy bias means that the respondent provides information which he feels will please the interviewer. He behaves this way because the norms governing interpersonal relations in general and relations with upper-class strangers in specific call for him to do so. However, courtesy bias might also be given a broader meaning, and be taken to refer also to respondents who provide information which they feel a person of their status in their country should give. This would include 'ideological biases', as among refugees who exaggerate their opposition to their home country's regime; or, as in the discussion of culturally sensitive topics, it may inhibit respondents from admitting they voted for certain parties or exposed themselves to certain media channels.

There is some indication that the direction of the courtesy bias is different in different countries. For example, the humility of the Japanese is said to lead them to underevaluate their own achievements, class positions, and the like. On the other hand, some researchers in the Middle East claim that respondents there tend to exaggerate their achievements, class position, knowledge of the world, and extent to which they are modern rather than traditional. In practical terms, this means that the type of question-wording appropriate to western countries would be inappropriate to Japan, and what is appropriate in Japan and the west would be inappropriate in Turkey or Iran.

Some of the effects of the courtesy bias can be reduced by concealing the sponsorship of the study, by more effective training of interviewers, and by more careful wording of questions. With regard to wording, it is advisable to avoid the use of 'moral' words which require either the respondent or the interviewer to pass judgement on the other. Above all, it is important to maximize the ease of giving a socially unacceptable answer, such as might be done through the standard practice of opening the question with 'Lots of people feel this way . . . and lots of people feel the other way. Which direction do you lean toward in . . .' Leading questions also might be appropriate here.

Perhaps courtesy bias is easier to control than its opposite, which might be called the 'sucker bias'. Sucker bias is found in areas where, according to Keesing and Keesing (1956) in a study of elite communications in Samoa, all outsiders are considered fair game for deception.

Interviewer—respondent status congruency

The third type of bias arises from communication obstacles created by the relative status characteristics of interviewers and their respondents. This interaction perspective of social relations has been studied in the United States with respect to age, sex, race, and class, and other characteristics. While these characteristics are important in the United States, they are likely to be critical in other countries. This is because the status of the interviewer is not well known (not institutionalized), which means that other ancillary status factors tend to structure the interviewer–interviewee relationship. These other status factors tend to be more significant than in the United States, since they also tend to maximize the above-mentioned courtesy bias.

In some countries, for example, interviewers are often considered as government employees, and since the local population does not readily differentiate policemen from tax collectors from political party workers, the interviewer has considerable difficulty in socializing the respondent into a new type of questioner–respondent relationship. In these situations, respondents are reported to be very reluctant to provide interviewers with accurate information. This may be one (but only a minor) reason why economic surveys often find that respondents exaggerate expenditures and under-report income, wealth, and savings. To overcome these suspicions, non-commercial research groups often seek an academic affiliation or sponsorship, denying any direct government connection with their activities. Unfortunately, owing to the lack of local personnel, the fieldwork staff are often required to rely on government employees — not only on teachers but, as in some Asian countries, also on 'moonlighting' secret police.

It is often very difficult to hide the political nature of many studies. For example, a poll in Latin America asking numerous questions about De Gaulle's visit, a German poll in Asia or Latin America asking a long list of questions about images of Germany, a poll in Africa regarding British radio programmes and the British government, a poll in south-east Asia regarding views of Japan, or polls in various parts of the world regarding American prestige and foreign policy: all these research projects which never eventuate in scholarly publications may very likely raise questions in the minds of educated respondents regarding the purpose behind the studies in which they are asked to cooperate. A growing number of other countries conduct polls of their citizens, further adding to the suspicions which some groups no doubt have about survey research. (It has been reported that some respondents refuse to talk unless findings are made known to the government. That is, the respondents see the interviewing situation as an opportunity to express an opinion and to influence governmental policy.)

Research agencies in many countries recruit their interviewers from among college students, which means that they come from middle and upper-class backgrounds, and are themselves educated people. This type of interviewer creates a communication problem, since there are certain traditional ways in which members of different classes interact. For example, custom demands that lower-class persons use polite forms of address, be humble, and not express themselves freely to members of the upper classes. Recognizing this, some researchers have questioned whether the egalitarian-oriented interviewing techniques used in the west are appropriate in societies which have sharp status and authority cleavages. Respondents also might be confused if a non-native associated with the former colonial ruling group were not demanding in his questioning.

At the present time there is considerable variation in the composition of field staffs in the developing nations. In Japan, many agencies rely almost entirely on students; in the Philippines, students are used only rarely; one Indian agency has a staff composed primarily of full-time male interviewers, whereas another Indian agency relies primarily on part-time female interviewers; some agencies use only high school graduates, since they show less fear and moral repulsion with regard to interviewing members of the lower class, whereas others rely primarily on college graduates. It is very difficult to assess how well trained these interviewers are and how valid is the information that they collect. However, it is fairly clear that different kinds of interviewers are able to obtain different kinds of information; and, furthermore, it would seem that the different compositions of research agencies is yet another factor reducing the comparability of materials collected for cross-national studies.

Considerable research is needed on a whole range of issues related to biases arising from the interviewer–respondent relationship. Such studies should be of general interest to the social scientist, especially to the sociologist, since they touch on key issues of social relations. Research could be conducted on procedures most appropriate to different phases of the interview: the initiation, structuring, and terminating the interviewer–respondent relationship. Data on the relative effectiveness of different interviewing approaches with different respondent–interviewer combinations are also needed. Perhaps middle-class interviewers should alter their tactics radically, using egalitarian techniques with the upper class and authoritarian techniques with the lower class.

Almost any project can include information which can be used for methodological purposes. For example, future projects could obtain information on the status features of their interviewers, just as they do for their respondents, thereby making it possible to explore the apparent biases arising from different interviewer–respondent status combinations. In short, efforts are needed to define and measure interviewer effectiveness, as well as the relative effectiveness of different interviewing techniques when used in social relations which vary according to the status characteristics of the interviewer and respondent.

References

Abrams, P. (1964). *The production of survey data in Britain*, paper delivered to Second Conference on Data Archives in the Social Sciences, Paris, 28–30 September.

Almond, G.A. and Verba, S. (1963). *The Civic Culture*, Chapter 2, Princeton University Press, Princeton, NJ.

Back, K.W. (1962). *Slums, Projects, and People*, Duke University Press, Durham, NC.

Back, K.W. and Stycos, J.M. (1959). *The Survey under Unusual Conditions: a Jamaica Human Fertility Investigation*. Monograph no. 1, Society for Applied Anthropology.

Barbour, K.M. and Prothero, R.M. (Eds) (1961). *Essays on African Population*, Routledge and Kegan Paul, London.

Converse, P.E. (1963). *The availability and quality of survey data in archives within the United States*, paper delivered to the International Conference on the Use of Quantitative, Political, Social, and Cultural Data in Cross-National Comparisons, held at Yale University, September.

Converse, P.E. (1964). New dimensions of meaning for cross-section sample surveys in politics. *International Social Science Journal*, **16**, 19–34.

Fink, R. (1963). Interviewer training and supervision in a survey of Laos. *International Social Science Journal*, **15**, 21–34.

Fortes, M. (1954). A demographic field study in Ashanti. In F. Lorimer (ed.), *Culture and Human Fertility*, pp. 255–324, Unesco, Paris.

Freedman, R. (1961–62). The sociology of human fertility: a trend report and bibliography. *Current Sociology*, **10–11** (2).

Frey, F.W. (1963). Surveying peasant attitudes in Turkey. *Public Opinion Quarterly*, **27**, 335–355.

Hoffman, M. (1963). Research on opinions and attitudes in West Africa, *International Social Science Journal*, **15**, 59–69.

Hollsteiner, M.R. (1963). *The Dynamics of Power in a Philippine Municipality*, Community Development Research Council, University of the Philippines, Quezon.

Jones, E.L. (1963). The courtesy bias in south-east Asian surveys, *International Social Science Journal*, **15**, 70–6.

Kapferer, C. (1964). The use of sample surveys by OECD, *International Social Science Journal*, **16**, 63–69.

Keesing, F.M. and Keesing, M.M. (1956). *Elite Communications in Samoa, A Study of Leadership*, Stanford University Press, Stanford.

Kiser, C.V. (Ed.). (1962) *Research in Family Planning*, Princeton University Press, Princeton, NJ.

Labov, W. (1964). Phonological correlates of social stratification. *American Anthropologist*, **66**, **December** (2), 164–176.

Lang, G.O. and Kunstadter, P. (1957). Survey research on the Uintah and Ouray Ute reservation. *American Anthropologist*, **59**, **June** 527–531.

Leach, E.R. (1958). An anthropologist's reflections on a social survey. *Ceylon Journal of Historical and Social Studies*, **1**, **January**, 9–20.

Lerner, D. (1958). *Passing of Traditional Society*, Free Press of Glencoe, New York.

Maclay, Howard and Ware, E. (1961) Cross-cultural use of the semantic differential. *Behavioral Science*, **6**, **July**, 186–190.

Merrit, R.L. (1966). *Symbols of American Community*, Yale University Press, New Haven, Conn.

Narroll, R. (1962) *Data Quality Control*, Free Press of Glencoe, New York.

Neale, W.C. (1958). The limitations of Indian village survey data. *Journal of Asian Studies*, **17**, **May**, 383–402.

Prothro, E.C. (1961). *Child Rearing in Lebanon*, Harvard Middle Eastern Monographs, 8, Cambridge University Press, Cambridge.

Russett, B., Alker, H.R., Deutsch, K.W. and Lasswell, H.B. (1964). *World Handbook of Political and Social Indicators*, Yale University Press, New Haven.

Social Research in Developing Countries
Edited by M. Bulmer and D.P. Warwick
© 1983, John Wiley & Sons, Ltd.

CHAPTER 19

FIELDWORK IN RURAL AREAS

ALLAN F. HERSHFIELD,
NIELS G. ROHLING,
GRAHAM B. KERR
AND
GERALD HURSH-CÉSAR

Villagers in many parts of the developing world frequently just do not trust outsiders. Villages are often divided into antagonistic factions and there are frequent conflicts. Land disputes, quarrels over water rights, marital conflicts, commercial fraud, class/caste hostilities, and inheritance challenges — disagreements which probably would involve only the injured parties and their immediate families in the industrial nations — frequently become the concern of entire villages. This is especially true where two or three large extended families may comprise one village, and each dispute tends to divide the village along strong kinship lines.

An interviewer who walks into one of these villages without any previous planning or preparation can quickly offend local leaders or representatives of different factions. Most researchers feel it is absolutely necessary for interviewers and/or supervisory personnel to seek out village leaders and get their permission before beginning work. Moreover, interviewers should know a great deal about village life — forms of social organization, leadership, mores, behavioural patterns — before undertaking data collection.

Village entry

When villages are known to be similar in social structure, it is advantageous to have a carefully planned procedure for entering each village in the same manner. A detailed, written village entry scheme is an important part of every

Reproduced by permission of Macmillan India Limited and the Council for Social Development from the authors' chapter in G. Hursh-César and P. Roy (Eds.) (1976), *Third World Surveys* (Macmillan of India, New Delhi), pp. 320–333. © 1976, Council for Social Development, New Delhi.

241

interviewer's field manual. Such a plan might specify the order in which the interviewer is to contact leaders, as well as the types of leaders to be sought — e.g., chiefs, village headmen, elders, patrons, civic influentials, school teachers, priests, herbalists, shrine keepers, major farmers. It might also contain instructions on how to identify prominent local leaders who occupy no readily identifiable *formal* leadership role. Each knowledgeable informant contacted, such as the village school headmaster, is a qualified source of information on the local power structure and can direct the interviewer to other important influentials in village affairs. Sometimes interviewers can find out a great deal about the power structure from conversations at local markets before entering the village. Often, a letter of introduction will prove useful for establishing rapport with local leaders. Interviewers in eastern Nigeria were given a supply of mimeographed copies of a letter of introduction. Appropriate blanks were left so the interviewer could insert the names and addresses of local leaders as he identified them, thus personalizing the approach.

Interviewers should use a fairly standard introduction in meeting individual leaders. After establishing their identity (identification cards and letters of approval from government officials are useful) and affiliation, they might explain the background and objectives of the study and why it can be useful to the community. They should also describe the procedures to be followed, explain why the village was selected, how respondents will be chosen, and perhaps ask for help in spreading the news about the project to other villagers.

Sometimes it takes more than contacting leaders individually to win their approval of and sanction for the study. It may be necessary to arrange for a village meeting to explain the project to the assembled villagers and their leaders. These points should be stressed: the survey is not itself a development programme; it cannot itself bring new development schemes to the village; no promises can be made, because it would probably be impossible to fulfil them later; the research is undertaken to help gather information about village conditions so better developed plans can be made in the future; to get accurate information, it is necessary to come straight to the village rather than sitting in an office in the capital; the village is selected by a lottery system because it is like so many others. The important objective is to prevent interviewers from making false promises and to remain neutral between competing village groups.

Another functional method of village entry is a two-wave system. Quite often census data are not sufficiently accurate or detailed in developing nations to draw a sample of the ultimate sampling unit — 'eligible family planning couple', 'pregnant or nursing mothers', etc. In the preliminary introductions, the leader, help is sought for doing a complete household listing for the sampling frame. The researcher or the supervisor should be involved in this first wave of entry to discuss the purposes of the project with leaders, determine if there are factions, and attempt to overcome hostility. The interviewers during the house-to-house listing get a general orientation to the village and meet potential respondents for brief interviews. This method tends to reduce the non-response rate and is likely to establish a higher level of rapport when the interviewers return for actual interviewing.

To achieve a probability selection of respondents, the interviewers probably will have to draw detailed maps and enumerate all houses in the village. Local guides or informants can be very helpful with this task, and can save interviewers much time in finding the location of each residence and determining who lives inside. Care must be used in selecting the guides. Members of one faction will not do, for obvious reasons. Persons who are reasonably well-known and trusted are most suitable, presuming such persons can be readily identified.

It is unwise to let interviewers enumerate households from which the sample is to be drawn or select respondents without careful on-the-spot supervision. Whichever method of sampling is used (probability, sociometric, purposive), interviewers should have complete written instructions on the exact procedure to be followed to ensure sample validity and uniformity. It is frequently difficult for interviewers to appreciate the necessity for strict adherence to sampling instructions. The supervisors either should make the selection themselves or carefully observe the interviewers performing the task.

The introduction

A basic problem is how to deal with the suspicion interviewers encounter in rural areas. Rural inhabitants have seldom experienced social surveys or census-taking. If they have been exposed to governmental data gatherers, of one sort or another, it may have been with bad results: taxes raised, land taken for some government scheme, personal possessions or crops confiscated, people arrested, men conscripted for the army.

Researchers have encountered this problem over and over again. When approached, rural villagers or even urban residents may be fear that they have done something wrong and that police or tax collectors are after them (Hanna, 1965). There is an extreme reluctance to reveal the details of their economic life (Martin, 1956). Local people regard anything they think may be connected with 'government' with 'an appreciable degree of reserve and suspicion' (Ward, 1964, p. 56). Many of the difficulties interviewers experience are clearly related to this suspicion, and much time and skill is required to try to eliminate respondents' doubts and fears — not always successfully.

After traditional greetings, the purpose of the fairly standard, non-threatening introduction is to get the respondent to agree to be interviewed. The interviewers' initial approach and manner should be respectful, courteous and pleasant in order to begin to allay suspicions or fears and begin to build a feeling of confidence, encouraging the respondent to cooperate willingly.

In the introduction, interviewers might mention whatever is in their background that is localistic and non-controversial — family, village, clan, school, etc. The best kind of affiliation to have is with an organization or institution with which the respondent is most likely to be familiar and, more important, look upon with favour. This may require that the project establishes a network of local area-to-area affiliations. In eastern Nigeria, association with the University of Nigeria was the only affiliation required. The University was relatively new and viewed as a symbol of progress, and had much favourable publicity. Many villagers knew of some young person from their own area who was attending the institution.

As indicated above, it may be unwise to stress an affiliation with the government. While this is frequently the case, it is not always true. In Jamaica, for example, a fertility study was carefully disassociated from government sponsorship during the pretesting stage, and this seemed to work well. In the time between the pretest and the full-scale study, there was a change in government and many of the lower-class respondents saw new hope in the party in power. Therefore a number of people were disturbed at the stated lack of government sponsorship' (Back and Stycos, 1959, p. 8).

In having interviewers describe the study and its background, objectives, procedures and possible benefits to the village, the researcher is often faced with (a) preparing a brief, simple, honest description that respondents will understand and accept as non-threatening, or (b) developing a somewhat vague and diffuse explanation that is satisfactory to respondents but that does not tell them the exact purpose of the study. The first alternative is normally chosen when the topic of study is not sensitive and the value and importance of the study are readily apparent. In the Diffusion Project in eastern Nigeria, interviewers had comparatively little difficulty explaining they were trying to find out how agricultural information spreads among farmers so as to be able to help improve planning and agricultural production. The second alternative is chosen when the research is concerned with more sensitive subjects such as fertility, family planning practices, methods of abortion. While it may be necessary to be somewhat vague, it is unethical and unwise to distort or lie: 'One cannot announce that a study is about folk songs and ask questions about political corruption' (Hanna, 1965, p. 16).

Privacy or 'confidentiality' of answers is not often stressed. Although essential in much of the western world, emphasis on confidentiality of responses may not be necessary nor even desirable. In eastern Nigeria, respondents frequently requested that their names be associated with their responses. They wanted people to know what they had said. During the pretesting stage of the Jamaica fertility study, 'interviewers nearly lost their lives in a rural area after stressing confidentiality' (Back and Stycos, 1959, p. 7). The people did not value privacy and related the interviewers' concern with it to an interest in witchcraft.

After the introduction, interviewers should ask for questions. In societies in which it is gross misconduct to interrupt a speaker, it is important for interviewers to stop and specifically ask for questions that might reveal doubts and suspicions. Respondents' questions normally cover a variety of topics. While their fears are usually evident in their reactions to the introduction, it is frequently apparent that they fail to grasp the true intentions of the study, the meaning of the interviewer's presence in their village, or the implications of their participation. Much care must be exercised in evaluating the degree to which the would-be respondents accept the validity claims of the interviewer.

Establishing the role of the interviewer

The literature on survey research in developing nations is replete with examples of how respondents often misinterpret the role of the interviewer. In one province in the Philippines, 'interviewers were initially mistaken for traveling salesmen, census agents, and tax collectors' (Feliciano, 1964, p. 11). In very conservative, rural, Moslem Pakistan, the village people did not know whether the enumerator had come to give to them (medicine, relief) or to take from them (raising taxes). They did not know whether the interviewers were godless women heralding the end of the world, or the advance guard of some government programme (Choldin, Kahn, and Ara, Chapter 21).

The point is that interviewers must occupy some role respondents can understand. Who the interviewer is *perceived* to be is much more important than his or her actual role. Role perceptions and misconceptions will determine to a great extent the kinds of answers given. Some respondents will 'underestimate their crops or their income; others (will) overestimate their accomplishments' and there will be instances of evasion (Provinse, 1963, p. 4) — all because of misinterpretations of the interviewer's role.

Frequently interviewers can find an analogy that clarifies their role, one that is looked upon with favour or at least as being harmless. It might be a school teacher, a census enumerator, a medical researcher — whichever provides the most suitable analogy.

Some of the most fantastic and bizarre fears and suspicions can be created by rumours concerning the interviewers' reasons for being in the village. In the Pakistan fertility study, a whole set of disruptive rumours had to be proved false before the interviewers could proceed with their work. Among other things, interviewers were said to have come to give injections to people to stop them from having children; to help the government increase land taxes; to seize the crops of the well-to-do; and as fulfilment of a local religious prophecy that some day women would come out of *purdah*. To dispel these rumours, the female interviewers showed the villagers they carried no equipment for injections; they wore the Burkha (a traditional garment for women); quoted from Moslem scripture to demonstrate they were devout Moslems; referred to neighbouring villages which took part in Academy (the sponsoring institution) programmes;

mentioned male census enumerators who had brought no harm; and showed the interview schedule to any villager who could read (Choldin, Kahn, and Ara, Chapter 21).

In India, going to a village in a white jeep can produce fears that the interviewers are a family planning team coming to perform sterilizations. In a UNICEF-sponsored experimental project south of Hyderabad (Deccan), in spite of several long disclaimers, when female interviewers or male project supervisors arrived in a village, they were confronted by bad vasectomy cases. Ultimately, the jeeps were painted green to partly alleviate this role misconception (Roy, 1973). As another example, rumours destroyed a project in Colombia when the word spread that the children were to be ground up for sausage meat.

Usually it becomes apparent during the initial exploratory work before the field study whether and what types of rumours may be major problems. The researcher may decide to use the invasion method described earlier to collect data quickly. But in research involving successive rounds of surveys, rumours have to be tactfully countered and corrected. The problem simply underscores the absolute necessity of intensive prestudy preparation and acculturation.

In industrial nations, by the time the introduction is over and preliminary questions are answered, interviewers are usually inside the respondent's house administering the questionnaire. In traditional societies, however, interviewers normally are expected to make various gestures of goodwill in order to strengthen and sustain the positive relationship they have just begun to establish. Observing local customs of hospitality may take some time before the interview can begin. In much of West Africa, local practices might involve pouring libations to one's ancestors and breaking and eating the kola nut. In the Meghalaya hills of India it may involve taking betel leaves and the fermented areca nut. Refreshments are often served in the middle of the interview. At its conclusion, a visit of respect to the family elder may be expected. The careless interviewer who is surprised by these practices and refused to partake of the food or regards it with distaste will probably lose both the *rapport* and the data sought.

Initial explanations may be sufficient to start an interview, but the chances are the respondent will still have suspicions and fears to overcome. Interviewers in the Jamaica fertility study identified several techniques they found useful at this stage of the interview. Among them were: (a) catharis — sympathetic listening to the respondent venting her aggressions and fears; (b) identification — seeking some basis of common ground with the respondent and discussing it — for example, religion, similar experiences, similar names, ages; (c) praise and flattery — praise and discussion of some unique characteristic of the house, the garden, the kitchen, children, etc. Some of the interviewers also chose to expand upon the purposes and potential results of the study (Back and Stycos, 1959, pp. 8–9).

In a sense, interviewers must 'teach' respondents *how* to be interviewed. In so doing, they themselves must 'learn' to be guests — tolerant of errors and interruptions and prepared to observe local customs graciously and with ease. Once *rapport* is successfully established and it appears that it can be maintained, the interviewer is ready to begin administering the interview schedule. And this may require a second or third return visit.

Refusals and non-response

Unless gross errors are made in entering the village, there are comparatively low refusal rates in rural areas of developing countries. Curiosity, fear, a desire to be hospitable to strangers, and a sense of flattery for being selected for the interview generally motivate respondents to agree to be interviewed. This does not mean, however, that the answers they give are an accurate description of reality. But a high refusal rate at the point of contact usually can be traced back to a failure to meet all relevant local leaders and win their approval for the study and their aid in stopping rumours.

Researchers, surveying various problems in developing nations, report refusals and resistance especially from women and from poorly educated, lower-class people who cannot believe their opinions are of any importance. 'Why ask me? I am only a poor farmer'; 'I am just an ignorant woman, ask my husband' are typical village reactions. In one study the investigators were able to find a local proverb that provided a suitable explanation: 'If you wish to know whether the rice is done, pick out a grain and taste it'. The simplicity of the explanation was its virtue — many subjects were content to know that they were so homely a thing as a kernel out of the Madras rice pot (Rudolph and Rudolph, 1958, pp. 238–239).

While refusals may for many good or bad reasons be low in most developing nations, the problem of *non-availability* can seriously damage any sampling design or raise interviewing costs and time to make the survey prohibitive. In addition, *inaccessibility* to villages by motorized transport in a time-bound survey can result in large incompletion rates. By using the invasion method to sample school children, Roy and Rath (1972) 'lost' 119 out of 330 randomly selected schools on account of inaccessibility criteria: if a village was more than two miles from a jeepable road it was disqualified, because interviewers could not complete all required interviews in one day. As it was, about 10 per cent of the boys selected in accessible villages were not available for interview on the day of the survey. A call-back for one boy out of ten would have typically involved 16–32 km (10–20 miles) of driving and raised logistical costs in time and money by 30–40 per cent.

Planning interviewing logistics involves several practical decisions:

(1) Should the invasion strategy permit reinterviewing attempts, increase

petrol costs 40 per cent and time costs 20 per cent, and thereby reduce non-response from 10 per cent to 5–6 per cent?
(2) Should interviewers walk 3–6 km (2–4 miles) with their equipment and camp in the 'inaccessible' villages overnight?
(3) Should recognition of logistical realities force a compromise of the sampling design (e.g., matched pair rather than a random sample) as was done in the study cited above?

There are no universal answers to these problems, and the researcher in the field must judge when the boundaries of scientific recitutude are being crossed.

As noted in previous chapters, non-response and refusal also may be due to interviewing attempted at time of the day or day of the week that are *inconvenient* for the respondent. For example, an experimental project found that interviewing times were best starting at 6.00–6.30 in the morning before village women started work; and the best times to hold non-formal education classes were after 9.00 at night, after the women were free from their chores (Roy, 1973). Similarly, surveys throughout the world have encountered problems in trying to conduct interviews during busy harvesting or planting periods, on festival days or weekly days of fasting, during the marriage season, during the times of religious observations or annual pilgrimages, and of course during the monsoons.

Non-response and refusals may also result simply from inadequate study preparation and conceptualization. The Diffusion Project in Nigeria, for example, found that respondents could not easily 'see' their village on a 10-step rating scale drawn on paper for comparing village standings in the past, present and future. When the on-paper abstraction was fashioned into a small hand-made bamboo ladder, response levels increased. Another researcher distinguishes *de facto* and *de jure* respondents in studies of dietary practices (Jesudason, 1974). While the housewife is supposed to be the 'legal' respondent, the respondent 'in fact' may often be the mother-in-law.

Bias and privacy

Personal privacy is neither common nor highly valued in the rural areas of most developing nations. Life tends to be centred around the family, kinship group, clan or village. Most dwellings or compounds include a far greater number of people than would be found in similar-sized areas in the industrial nations. Furthermore, village life sometimes is communal: land belongs to the whole village or to large kinship groups, and the people live, work and play together for most of their lives. Altogether, most aspects of village life are self-contained and highly traditional. The appearance of a stranger or group of strangers is quite rare, and most of the villagers learn about such an unusual event very quickly. It is uncommon to have a private interview under these circumstances.

More often than not the interviewer has to administer the interview schedule in the presence of members of the immediate family, assorted cousins, aunts, uncles and groups of curious bystanders. Sometimes a local official or leader will insist on being present during the interview. The presence of third parties can clearly bias the data, particularly if the third person is an official or a person with some power and status (Feliciano, 1964; Sanders, 1956; Weiner, 1964).

Aside from the obvious bias caused when respondents speak for the benefit of officials or leaders present during the interview, there is another effect of the lack of privacy. This is related to the communal outlook of many villagers. It is not unusual to find an apparent lack of private, individual opinions among the inhabitants of the rural areas of developing nations. Opinions aften are expressed by families, clans and castes, but not individuals (Girard, 1963; Wilson and Armstrong, 1963). Thus, as a deliberate field strategy, group interviewing may be undertaken for village-level data, because individual opinions are likely to be fairly uniform or cross-validating among various members of a single group (Andrade and Roy, 1972). On the other hand, a comparative uniformity of opinion may, as well, result from strong feelings of deference to the most important people who normally must be interviewed first: 'After each answer given by the first interviewed, the assembled crowd nods its approval, saying that the answer also represents the views of others. Not only does this create or help crystallize consensus, it also often produces resistance to being interviewed on the part of others' (Mitchell, Chapter 18).

Although privacy is preferable, a third party present during the interview can be helpful when the objective of the interview is to obtain information about the respondent's date of birth, number of marriages, food consumed daily, and the like. The third person will sometimes assist the respondent by providing information the respondent either does not know, is vague about, or does not want known (Mitchell, Chapter 18; Jesudason, 1974). And sometimes, as in the case of the fertility study in Pakistan (Choldin, Kahn, and Ara, Chapter 21), it is impossible to get an interview without the presence of a third party.

A number of ways of overcoming some of these problems and obtaining individual interviews have been used successfully. One researcher in several studies in eastern Europe got rid of local officials by halting the formal interviews in favour of simply walking around the village exhibting idle curiosity. When the officials were tired of waiting, they left. The respondents then were free to seek out the researcher and correct misinformation provided in the presence of the official (Sanders, 1956). Secret ballots with literate respondents have been used to obtain individual opinions where efforts to get private interviews have been unsuccessful (Mitchell, Chapter 18).

Interviewing is often done in pairs in order to get privacy. For example, a pair of female interviewers might work together with one to interview the housewife and the other to segregate the mother-in-law, engaging her in pseudo-interview (Wyon and Gordon, 1971). A team of interviewers composed of male and female partners might be used to interview a man and his wife simultaneously in different locations or at different times in different locations (Bhogle and Kaur, 1972).

Sometimes interviewers work in pairs both for the purpose of getting privacy as well as for obtaining different types of information. For example, one interviewer may assemble as many villagers as possible in a public place and keep them occupied by administering a 'dummy' questionnaire, while the other seeks out designated persons in the crowd, takes them aside and conducts the real schedule in private. A variation of this technique was used in the Diffusion Project in Nigeria as a means particularly of pleasing important leaders who felt personally slighted by the sample selection. Where village-level data — e.g., the number of shops, the distances to nearby markets, the frequency of medical visitors — is wanted and is acceptable by self-reported 'group consensus' estimates, the first interviewer conducts a real interview while the second is free to seek other special information or designated respondents (Andrade and Roy, 1972).

Sometimes the location of the interview can be changed. Information for a fertility survey was obtained by using the interview as part of the normal admission procedure before seeing the doctor (Hill, 1962). Data might also be obtained in a similar fashion in employment offices, agricultural extension offices, etc.

Interviewing respondents where they work is another way of getting more privacy than might be obtained in the more contrived setting of the household visitors' room. Many a farmer has been interviewed as he toiled in the fields (Wyon and Gordon, 1971) and many a housewife as she cooked in the kitchen (Jesudason, 1974). One advantage in interviewing people where they work is that information is often required on such work-related topics as land size, crop yields, food consumption. Such questions take on a higher degree of reality in the work setting, probably increase rapport, and offer opportunities for verification by, for example, foot measurement of cultivated fields or weight measurement of food preparations. Of course, the interviewer suffers some disadvantage in trying to hold onto the respondent's attention as well as to the questionnaire.

Any number of techniques have been successfully used in the home to try to secure privacy: adults have been sent on errands to the market; children have been bribed with sweets to go outside and play; neighbours have been told to go home and wait for the interviewer who would be coming to their house in a short time; and polite but firm insistence of the interviewer has convinced outsiders to leave. In many traditional cultures it is most difficult to convince husbands to permit their wives to speak for the household, and it is difficult to convince the mother or mother-in-law that the younger woman can authoritatively answer questions about child-rearing. In such situations it is frequently impossible to convince the female respondent to either speak in privacy or to give her opinion in the presence of others.

Various kinds of analogies have been used to convince elders and outsiders not to interfere. A typical and useful device is to liken the interview to the classroom and compare the third person's interference with the school children who get their answers from others who speak out of turn. Another device is to make an analogy between the interview and the doctor's examination, saying that the doctor examines only the patient and in private. Another simple and unexpectedly successful technique was used by Diffusion Project interviewers in Nigeria. They saw the respondents some time prior to the interview, made an appointment for a later date, and explained the need for privacy. The respondent generally saw to it that the interview was private.

The majority of survey illustrations in developing countries indicate that the norm is clearly an interview that is *not private*, despite various stratagems to obtain privacy. Methodologically, the number and type of people present at the interview should be recorded, and after the study a comparison made between the response patterns of private interviews and non-private interviews on a number of key items.

Good training and culturally sensitive interviewing attempt to reduce the bias of onlookers and use them functionally to improve the quality of data. Suppose, for example, we were doing a study of traditional midwives, who in India often come from the poorer segments of the lowest castes. Typically, in such interviews, three or four young nursing women may be present. Besides being poor and of low caste the midwives are often very old and may have just received their payment-in-kind of local liquor. Under such (not unusual) circumstances, it takes a skilful interviewer to sensitively parry bystander intrusions, obtain from the respondent truthful and uninhibited responses, and symbiotically use the group for improving the quality of the interview.

Since the private interview is not the normal condition, interviewers should be better prepared than they are in training to cope with and to use the bystander to improve the quality of data. There is some limited evidence that (a) lack of privacy, and (b) respondents' degree of perceived cooperativeness, two 'situational factors' usually recorded in village surveys, may have *nothing* to do with the realiability of such 'factual-type' demographic items as age, number of pregnancies, number of children, level of education, etc. (Mukherjee, 1974). Indeed, the real problem in surveys in developing nations is the inconsistency of data from one time to the next. Until we improve the test-retest reliability of survey data along with improving the validity of the propositions under study, perhaps we are better served by training interviewers to worry less about privacy and more about the integrity of the information.

References

Andrade, C.P. and Roy, P. (1972). *Report on the Pilot Research Project in Growth Centres*, Ford Foundation, New Delhi.

Back, K.W. and Stycos, J.M. (1959). *The Survey Under Unusual Conditions: Methodological Facets of the Jamaica Human Fertility Investigation*, Society for Applied Anthropology Monograph no. 1, Ithaca, New York.

Bhogle, S. and Kaur, S. (1972). *Adoption of Family Planning in Two Industrial Settings*, council for Social Development, New Delhi.

Feliciano, G. (1964). *Limits of Western Social Research Methods in the Philippines: The Need for Innovation*, International Research Institute, East–West Center Conference, Honolulu.

Girard, A. (1963). Opinion surveys in developing countries. *International Social Science Journal*, **15**, 1–20.

Hanna, W.J. (1965). Image-making in field research. *American Behavioural Scientist*, **3**, 15–20.

Hill, R. (1962). Cross-national family research: attempts and prospects. *International Social Science Journal*, **14**, 425–451.

Jesudason, V. (1974). *Problems in surveys in dietary intake*, Agricultural Development Council, paper presented at Workshop on Problems of Data Collection in Rural Areas, Singapore.

Martin, A. (1956). *The Economy of the Ibibio Oil-Palm Farmer*, Ibadan University Press, Ibadan.

Mukherjee, B.N. (1974). A study of some correlates of response in consistency in selected demographic data. *Journal of Population Research*, **December**.

Provinse, J.H. (1963). *Western Research Techniques and Non-western Values*, Council on Economic and Cultural Affairs Inc. New York.

Roy, P.R. (1973). *Non-Formal Education for Rural Women*, Council for Social Development, New Delhi.

Roy, P.D. and Rath, R.N. (Eds) (1972). *School Lunch Programme in Orissa*, Council for Social Development, New Delhi.

Rudolph, L. and Rudolph, S.H. (1958). Surveys in India: field experiences in Madras State. *Public Opinion Quarterly*, **22**, 235–244.

Sanders, I.T. (1956). Research with peasants in underdeveloped areas. *Social Forces*, **35**, 1–10.

Ward, R.E. (1964). The research environment. In R.E. Ward (Ed), *Studying Politics Abroad: Field Research in Developing Areas*, pp. 49–78, Little, Brown, Boston.

Weiner, M. (1964). Political interviewing'. In R.E. Ward (Ed.) *Studying Politics Abroad: Field Research in Developing Areas*, pp. 103–133, Little, Brown, Boston.

Wilson, E.C. and Armstrong, L. (1963). Interviewers and interviewing in India. *International Social Science Journal*, **15**, 43–58.

Wyon, J.B. and Gordon, J.E. (1971). *The Khanna Study*, Harvard University Press, Cambridge, Mass.

Social Research in Developing Countries
Edited by M. Bulmer and D.P. Warwick
© 1983, John Wiley & Sons, Ltd.

CHAPTER 20

THE COURTESY BIAS IN SOUTH-EAST ASIAN SURVEYS

EMILY L. JONES

That south-east Asians who are being interviewed will express only views which they think the interviewer or investigator wants to hear is one of the most commonly held stereotypes relative to the difficulties of conducting opinion and market surveys in the nine countries of south-east Asia. It need not be true and there is an increasing body of evidence to suggest that it is not true when a survey is carefully planned through every step.

The four following assumptions underlie the writing of this chapter:

(1) *'South-east Asia' is a justifiable concept for the purpose of analysing problems of social science research.* Despite certain evident differences — varying degrees or absence of colonial traditions, associations with different European cultures, extent of economic development, or language — the countries of the area have many characteristics in common which are of significance to the surveyor. Common to all these countries is a hunger to learn the techniques of the most modern countries, an historical attention to status, generosity to the stranger and traveller especially in the rural areas, a highly personalized social organization. Throughout the area the Chinese, whether intermarried with leading families or existing as a barely tolerated minority, heavily influence many of the cultural values discussed in this article.

(2) *The standard survey techniques of the West (with fewer adaptations than might be assumed necessary) are applicable to south-east Asia.* Work has already been done using the cross-section survey, special group studies, panels or small groups, élite interviews, mail questionnaires, projection-type questions and pictures, and community studies.

(3) *Courtesy is an important and pervasive value.*

Reprinted from *International Social Science Journal (1963)*, **15 (1)**, 70–76. © 1963, UNESCO. Reproduced by permission of UNESCO.

(4) *The distorting effects of the 'courtesy bias' can be overcome*. Despite the relative newness of the survey as a tool of social science research, there is already enough negative, critical, and 'uncomplimentary' type of honest response to belie the generalization that the 'enigmatic' Asian can be expected to offer only polite, non-committal answers to dupe or flatter.

For any social scientist — whether economist, sociologist, public opinion surveyor or anthropologist — who seeks to collect data via the questionnaire, an understanding of the nuances of what constitutes courtesy is essential. For the surveyor whose primary tool is the structured interview, the problem is the most acute. Without an interpretation of 'courtesy' as a social value in southeast Asia, it is impossible to describe how the negative effects of this underlying behaviour can be eliminated and the positive ones harnessed — both in the interest of obtaining better interviews.

Courtesy and its elements

At the risk of oversimplifying what is a complex code of behaviour, let me summarize what appear to be some of the main ingredients — all of which are more complicated than the 'manners' and 'mannerisms' associated in many countries with 'courteous' conduct:

(1) The atmosphere between people must be kept pleasant and agreeable, free from anger or contradiction.
(2) No one may disagree openly with a person of higher status.
(3) Nothing should be said which wounds or affronts, or causes hurt to another.
(4) If possible, what is said should please and compliment.
(5) Nothing should be said which another would not like to hear.
(6) Courtesy in conversation demands that the main subject be delayed.
(7) To ask personal questions is well within the bounds of courteous behaviour.
(8) The most basic of courtesies — hospitality — is extended to the stranger in the form of food shared or shelter offered from rain or sun. (Hospitality belongs to the pattern of courtesy in any country, but it becomes particularly poignant in countries where there is often little to share.)
(9) Detailed attention to the needs of others is an integral part of the pattern of social behaviour. In cultures where social life is largely unorganized, relationships of all kinds tend to operate on a person-to-person basis. Behaviour illustrative of this ranges from the host's selecting the choicest morsel from the evening's delicacy to place it personally on his guest's plate to the endless effort which will be taken by a comparative stranger to

satisfy some simple remark of need for a fruit or piece of information. People with a personal problem should be helped.

Among the ingredients of courtesy it is obvious, then, that many can act as a deterrent to obtaining useful and reliable survey data and that others can facilitate the same process. Let us consider first how the effects of those which are possible deterrents (points 1–6 above) can be eliminated.

Eliminating the distorting effects of courtesy

One of the first protections against the courtesy bias or the wish to please lies in questionnaire design. Questions must be limited to those for which there is no obviously pleasing answer. This is simple enough on certain types of surveys. There is nothing about citing one's preferred hour for radio listening or the title of one's favourite newspaper which can be figures out by the most astute of respondents as pleasing or not pleasing. Neither can the person being interviewed know whether the interviewer will be complimented or offended if the respondent has a favourable opinion of a country unrelated to either interviewer or interviewee. How can there be a polite or impolite answer to the question, 'Are you better off, worse off, or about the same as you were a year ago?'

Admittedly, in some inquiries, the question which does not leave scope for this courtesy bias is not so simple to devise. For instance, one can estimate that it would be virtually impossible when working with cross-sections of the population in South-East Asia to elicit in the standard ways dependable answers to questions involving criticisms of parents, teachers, the priesthood and perhaps even national leaders. To all those higher on the authority scale, courtesy must be demonstrated by absence of criticism.

However, two methods of modifying the standard ways and making the respondent more comfortable in the expression of critical, negative, or 'impolite' answers look very promising. Both involve 'tipping' the questions towards a negative response.

(1) Pictures have been used as a substitute for a question-item in a questionnaire. These projective-type drawings employ the usual projection technique of being more suggestive than precise, yet they clearly enough suggest a negative or critical act. The respondent is asked only to explain the 'why' and is not burdened with the necessity to suggest that there is something to be criticized. The picture has assumed this for him. Thus, the picture may show a man leaving a movie or turning off a radio. The respondent is asked only: 'Why is he leaving the movie?' or 'Why doesn't he like the radio programme?' From this 'tipping' of the question flows more interesting and seemingly somewhat deeper material than can be

gained from a standard word-question which asks the respondent to admit to not liking the movie or rejecting the radio programme.

(2) Phrases designed to establish the acceptability of an impolite or critical response are used as introductions to questions. 'Many people around here tell me that . . .' or 'I hear people often say that . . .' seem to suggest to the respondent that he is not alone in what he may say and that others have already expressed a critical view of the subject.

Preventing the undesirable influences of courtesy on survey responses involves strict attention to other aspects of survey work beyond questionnaire design. The standard reassurances of anonymity must be reinforced throughout the interview since it can be assumed that the respondent's willingness to be 'impolite' will be in direct proportion to his belief that this impoliteness will never be reported in relation to him personally. Interviewers are instructed to interrupt respondents who may wish to give their names; in some instances of the use of administered questionnaires to special audience groups, the phrase 'You are not allowed to sign your name' has been inscribed at the top of the questionnaire.

Excellent *rapport*, although desirable for any interview, becomes essential if the interviewee is to be made to feel relaxed in the expression of negativity. The first signs of this willingness to be 'impolite' must be quickly commended and a leisurely pace of interviewing maintained lest any further evidences be cut off.

The interviewer's relationship to the respondent must be clarified in order to minimize the effect which it might have in inducing the courteous, 'safe' response. For example, if the interviewer is a teacher or a government official interviewing a townsman, he must be alert to the possibility that his higher status will preclude reliable answers. He must emphasize his connection with the research organization sponsoring the study or with his university (as many interviewers choose to do) and thus downgrade his relationship to the respondent on the status ladder.

In the ability of the interviewer to establish his own integrity lies part of the answer to obtaining answers untainted by a courtesy bias. In south-east Asia where there is little experience with the research survey, an identification card or brief reference to a scientific study is by no means sufficient. Sometimes as much as 10 minutes must be spent in preparing for a 20-minute interview in order to permit the respondent to see clearly where the interviewer fits into the society he knows. Whom might they know in common? What does the interviewer know about the village or city of the interview? What is he really up to? Only when the image of the interviewer is clearly established can there be hope of answers which will cut across the superficial, courteous response.

It is particularly essential that the interviewer should not be identified with any client or sponsor. The South-East Asian reticence to criticize a company or country with which he thought the interviewer was associated would immediately blur or eliminate entirely any helpful criticism of a product or unfavourable shading of a national image.

In leader or elite interviewing, the use of a 'middleman' offers invaluable assistance in breaking through the courtesy barrier. By utilizing the Asian system of personal introductions for any and all relationships, the respondent can be assured by this middleman friend or acquaintance that his remarks will be held in strict confidence and that the interviewer truly seeks his frank opinions. At the same time, the interviewer is assured that the respondent has views which can be expressed.

In small-group interviewing, the reluctance to contradict a 'senior' person present within the panel raises a difficult research problem. One way to circumnavigate this type of courtesy is to use the small group only to represent different audiences within a population and to minimize, thus, the interpersonal effects. A doctor, a teacher and a businessman will not find themselves in any prescribed relationship and can, therefore, disagree or refute with relatively little difficulty. However, if a panel or small group is required to tap the judgements of those who do have a line relationship to one another — student, professor, dean, for example — the only guarantee against the polite acquiescence of the student and the teacher to whatever the dean has said is to prevent the dean speaking at an early moment in the discussion. This ordering of the discussion by the group leader is neither ideal nor foolproof, but it will at least prevent the blanketing effect of a superior's first statement. This same problem appears in a more natural small group like a meeting of village elders. Depending on the subject for discussion, the headman or teacher may be, almost unconsciously, elected to do the talking. The surveyor here also must attempt to restrain the 'spokesman' until others have had an opportunity to express an opinion.

Sample design may sometimes be part of the solution, and it may be necessary to abandon a more sophisticated sample design in favour of taking the opportunity of working in an area where someone in research, rural health or well-digging has already established himself with the population. Let us assume, to take a purely hypothetical case, that a study was to be undertaken as part of welfare planning to measure attitudes in a rural population towards care for the aged. The investigator may know that there are some people who that there are some people who do not like to live with their parents and others who fret at being tied to the village in order to take care of older members of the family. But without this built-in entrée through someone who has already earned the trust of the sample over a protracted period of time, there is little hope of measuring how widespread the stereotyped politeness and respect for elders may actually be. We know, from completed studies, that it is possible for an interviewing team accompanied and associated with this 'middleman' to obtain interviews on rather sensitive subjects free from courtesy distortion.

Using the positive elements of courtesy

Some of the elements of courtesy assist the interviewing process. Some ingredients (points 7–9 in the list above) can be counted upon to improve the chance of obtaining a rich and meaningful interview.

The fact that one can ask personal questions and not be considered discourteous in Asia eases the way for the interviewer who, in the west, would be fully alert to the potential resistance to such questions as 'How much do you earn?' Not so in Asia. This same question may be asked by an Asian of someone he meets for the first time and he may well follow it up by inquiring. 'How much rent do you pay for this house?', 'How much did your automobile cost you?', or 'Do you use an air-conditioner?' To be asked personal questions raises no problem of *rapport*.

The courteous offer of shelter when sun or rain make standing on the threshold uncomfortable both for interviewer and interviewee encourages a more pleasant interviewing situation than is found in countries where the interviewer is often not invited inside the house. In the Philippine village *barrio*, the interviewer climbs the stairs and is asked to sit on the floor with the respondent inside the house. In a *klong*-side house in Thailand there is nowhere to go but *in*. In the cities of Rangoon or Kuala Lumpur only in a rare case would the interviewer be allowed to remain outside.

Further, in hot climates, liquid refreshment is offered on the slightest occasion. Thus, the interview soon acquires a degree of personalization based on the offer and acceptance of coconut milk, the eternal 'coke', or — in an upper economic houehold — iced lemonade, all brought automatically by a servant or another member of the family.

The wish to help others can operate in favour of obtaining a good interview. Many an interviewer has successfully used the ploy, when confronted with an impatient or reluctant respondent, 'But I have to do this as part of my job, and if you will help me I will be very grateful'. This willingness to help can be tapped regardless of who the respondent may be; professors, village headmen or housewives appear equally eager to 'help someone'.

The interviewer and courtesy

Although most emphasis has been placed in this discussion on the influence of courtesy on the respondent's answers and behaviour, courtesy operates in the interviewing situation in yet another way. The interviewer and his own sense of courtesy is still to be considered. Two basic attitudes related to courtesy must be overcome by interviewer training: (a) the desire to help the respondent, and (b) the tendency to retreat in the face of a possible refusal by a person of higher status.

It has been found difficult but possible in interviewer training to undo the interviewer's almost instinctive desire to 'help'. Repeatedly he must be instructed that he must not interpret the question or simplify the problem for a respondent who seeks his assistance. 'Don't tell him', 'Don't help him', 'Don't put words in his mouth' — these are instructions which must be repeated over and over again.

A defence must also be built against the interviewer's courteous behaviour towards a person of status. It is all too easy for an interviewer to be turned away by a person of superior status whose judgement on anything — including his own reluctance to be interviewed — the interviewer is accustomed to accept. Lengthy and repeated training can provide an answer to this. The interviewer must re-see himself as a social scientist practising a profession rather than as a university student or teacher to be automatically awed by a high government official.

The need for further research

It is hoped that nothing in this chapter will suggest that more than a beginning in research has been made in South-East Asia — both in the conduct of opinion and market research surveys themselves and in controlled experiments directed towards the elimination of the effects of the courtesy bias. Some experimental studies along the following lines should be rewarding:

(1) *The importance of 'matching' interviewer and interviewee.* Controlled experiments to determine the relative importance of variables like sex, superior status, inferior status, language (regional), origin of interviewer in relation to similar and contrasting characteristics of interviewee as they may affect the operation of the courtesy bias.

(2) *The use of the small group in highly structured societies.* To the body of literature already available as the result of many years of experimentation with the small group in the west should now be added systematic approaches to the problem of using the small group for social science research in South-East Asia. As has already been pointed out, the problems of inducing free-flowing commentary are numerous.

(3) *Mail questionnaire versus personal interview.* The mail questionnaire with its obvious advantages of economy and ability to reach the inaccessible portions of the population may offer some opportunities for greater impoliteness than the face-to-face situation. There are no dependable figures, however, to show what percentage of responses can be expected.

(4) *Use of the informal depth interview as a check on quantitative data.* An experiment might well be devised to check on the degree of 'politeness' recorded in the cross-section type of nterview by intensive interviewing later with a sample of the sample. This approach might be amplified by arranging for quantitative interviews in a universe well known to the

investigator who could himself recheck the appropriate answers with people thoroughly familiar to him and from whom he could expect no courtesy bias.

Social Research in Developing Countries
Edited by M. Bulmer and D.P. Warwick
© 1983, John Wiley & Sons, Ltd.

CHAPTER 21

CULTURAL COMPLICATIONS IN FERTILITY INTERVIEWING

HARVEY M. CHOLDIN,
A. MAJEED KAHN,
AND
B. HOSNE ARA

Introduction

The increase in volume of fertility surveys in underdeveloped nations produces a need for the examination and adaptation of current research methods. Increasingly, fertility surveys must be made in rural areas among populations with low literacy levels and no previous exposure to social research of any kind. This paper reports experiences in a fertility survey of women in five villages in what was then East Pakistan (now Bangladesh) in 1963. The paper includes the description of a training programme for 'indigenous fieldworkers' and the kinds of unanticipated responses to the interview situation in the villages and to particular standards items included in the interview. This close examination of the events in the field is presented to aid in the understanding of data collected in this type of setting and in improving research instruments and fieldwork techniques.

The problems inherent in the use of survey techniques in fertility research, especially in underdeveloped nations, have not gone unnoticed. Scattered references to problems of survey interviewing under 'unusual conditions' have been made in reports of field research on fertility and on knowledge, attitudes, and practices concerning family planning (KAP). Detailed reports on survey methods have appeared from Jamaican and Indian studies (Back and Stycos, 1959; United Nations, 1961).

The problems range from the selection and training of the interviewers through question-wording and item translation. They also include reliability problems and considerations involving the interviewing situation. Recently,

Reproduced by permission from *Demography* (1967), **4**, 244–252. © 1967, Population Association of America.

Mauldin (1965) has reviewed the subject of the use of survey methods in fertility research. However, there are relatively few analyses and descriptions of particular fieldwork techniques and problems. Back and Stycos (1959) have provided a detailed presentation of their methods and fieldwork experiences in Jamaica, and the *Myson Population Study* presented similar materials (United Nations, 1961). Yaukey (1961) has described field methods and interviewing problems in Lebanon and more recently in Dacca, East Pakistan (now Bangladesh) (Yaukey, Roberts and Griffin, 1965) Driver (1963) presents some discussion of the field situation in his study in the Nagpur district, India. Other scattered references to fieldwork problems appear in the fertility literature.

Fertility research through survey or other methods in underdeveloped areas provides data-collection difficulties of considerable importance. The data-collection process merits continued and additional scrutiny.

Academy and pilot projects

The fertility and KAP survey discussed in this chapter was undertaken as a part of a family planning pilot project in a rural area in East Pakistan (now Bangladesh). This pilot project is one element in a multipurpose, integrated rural development programme at the Pakistan Academy for Rural Development at Comilla. At the time this fertility survey was begun, the development programme had been under way for approximately 4 years and the family planning pilot project for more than 2 years in selected villages.

The purpose of the survey was to gather baseline information on fertility; knowledge, attitudes, and practices concerning family planning; and religious practices affecting exposure to the risk of pregnancy. After the baseline survey, the family planning programme was to be expanded into the villages studied. The relative success of the academy development projects was widely known among the villages in the area, and this reputation was an asset for the fertility survey.

The Comilla rural development and family planning projects are located in a rural area whose conditions are typical of Bangladesh. The especially relevant characteristics of the area for the purpose of introducing family planning and studying fertility are poverty, purdah, illiteracy, and geography.

The population of the area is predominantly Muslim — over 80 per cent — and the Islamic tradition of purdah rules regarding seclusion of women is quite rigidly enforced in this area. This means that a village woman is generally restricted in her movement. She is prohibited from leaving her husband's or father's homestead, she does not work in the fields, and only a small circle of male relatives are allowed to see or interact with her. The only exceptions to the rules of purdah are found among the extremely poor, where women are beggars or scavengers, and in the small class of college graduates in cities, among whom the purdah restrictions are somewhat modified. The purdah system has some obvious ramifications for a family planning programme and for administering a fertility survey with female respondents.

Of the adults in the country 84 per cent are illiterate, and the rate of illiteracy among females is higher yet. Those who are literate read mainly religious literature. The effects of illiteracy are that knowledge of the subject of fertility is limited and many non-scientific and traditional beliefs and fears prevail. These factors tend to complicate the interview situation.

Geographically, the area consists of rice fields with scattered small villages, connected by dirt paths or roads to the few paved single-lane roads. These dirt roads, of course, become nearly impassible in the monsoon season. Consequently, interviewers usually travelled to the villages by bicycle-rickshaw and by foot.

Village women as survey enumerators

Previous research experience among males in this area had shown village men with some education to be better interviewers for many purposes than college students, since they worked more diligently and established better *rapport*. Over a period of 2 years, a team of male village enumerators had been developed. It was decided that the advantages of good *rapport*, low 'visibility', and knowledge of the village dialect recommended this approach for trial among village women. However, there are so few literate village women and the idea of village women travelling about was so novel in this area that much planning and a long training programme were needed.

In May 1963, the first female enumerators' class was held at the rustic project headquarters of the Academy for Rural Development with 13 literate married women attending. They had been recruited through an announcement given to the organizers of village cooperative societies at their weekly meetings. The notice called for women who had studied up to class 5 and who could read and write. All who joined could at least read and write simple Bengali, and they ranged in educational attainment from the third to the tenth grade. The low level of enumerators' education meant that a type of training was needed that is not required in the usual sample surveys.

The enumerators received 5 months of training and met one day a week for classes. The training included such elementary topics as reading and writing improvement, interviewing and recording technique, and practice with village women. There were a series of quizzes and an examination. Before the beginning of the survey, they studied the interview schedule intensively. During the training, the women received a travel allowance to cover ricksha fare from their homes to the academy. To keep their lessons fresh, they continued to have a weekly class after the final examination.

Eight women comprised the final interviewing team, including two late-comers with a tenth-grade education, virtually the highest in the area. The influence of the local culture had already been felt, for some of the women who completed the course were prohibited from doing actual fieldwork by their husbands. Six of the remaining enumerators were married and had children, one was single and living with her mother, and another was newly married. Two lived in villages near the large town; all the rest lived in villages ranging from 8 to 25 km (5 to 16 miles) from town. There were six Muslim and two Hindu women. Four were from villages with cooperative societies. Educationally, they came from the very small number of literate village women in the area.

The enumerators were supervised by a research assistant, a young woman who had studied to the MA level of social work. They were preceded in the villages studied by a young male fieldworker who made preliminary censuses and maps of the villages.

First entry into the villages

Before the interviewing began, the enumerators thought that it would be very easy; they would just walk in, sit down, and become friends with the village women, who would cooperate with them. The research assistant told them that it would not be so easy, but they did not believe her. She also emphasized the extremely delicate nature of interviewing on the subject of family planning.

They were disappointed when they started fieldwork. When they first went to the village, they explained that they were from the academy and asked if the villagers knew about it; if they did not, the enumerators explained the work of the academy and assured the people that they had not been sent by the government. They explained that they had come to get information only, that the information was necessary for some new programme, but that they did not know exactly what the programme was. The enumerators had been told not to make any kind of promise, because any unfulfilled promise would hurt their work and the projects.

Various rumours arose and spread after the enumerators' first visits to the villages. Some villagers doubted that the enumerators were not from the government. Some said they were using the academy's name but that really they were from the government. There was a rumour that they had come to give injections to people with many children to prevent them from having more. Another rumour was that the government was going to increase land taxes. Another fear was that the crops of those who were doing well would be seized. The most spectacular rumour was that the enumerators were fulfilling a local religious prophecy that someday women will come out of purdah and go about in the open; to the villagers this would be a very bad thing, and when they saw these women coming, they said that the women had come to destroy the faith.

The enumerators tried to reassure the villagers in several ways. They showed them that they had no injections with them and that they were just women like the village women, wearing *burka* — a traditional garment covering the head, face, and much of the body often worn by local women when they are outside their homes. They explained that the interviewers were not out to destroy the faith, and they quoted from the Muslim holy writings to show that they were good Muslims. They also pointed out that the villagers' kinfolk in nearby villages participated in academy programmes. Enumerators reminded the villagers of the recent census made by the male investigator, which had brought no harm, and showed the interview schedule to anyone who could read.

Often a group would form, and some people in the group, knowing about the academy, would support the enumerator by saying, 'These women are our women; they look like us and talk like us. Why shouldn't we trust them?'

Individual interview items

One of the tasks of the interviewers and their supervisors was to instruct the respondents concerning the meanings of the questions and to direct them to relevant responses when possible. When the interviewer herself was unable to accomplish this sufficiently, a supervisor would visit the respondent and carry out the interview. Yaukey (1961, p. 109), also indicates the need for judgement on the part of the researcher with regard to the relative reliability and the validity of responses to various questions in the absence of better measures.)

In this study the complications arose because of lack of importance in the culture of the population studied concerning maintenance of precise personal information (on age, for example), religiosity and fear concerning the disclosure of some opinions or items of information, and definition of the role of the housewife which denied her access to some kinds of information about her husband.

A list of inappropriate responses to individual interview items is illuminating with regard to the general problem of transplanting research instruments into a new culture. The following responses are presented with no measure of the frequency with which they occurred, as none was available, but their occurrence was frequent enough to indicate the point of view of a considerable portion of the respondents.

Age

Some respondents claimed that they had never been asked about or concerned with their ages and did not know their husbands' ages. Some were curious as to why anyone wanted to know their ages; some asked the enumerator to invent an age.

In some cases, age was determined roughly by reference to major historical events such as the Marriage Law (1933), Military Law (1941), famine of 1943, and so forth. When reference to events was unsuccessful, an older member of the family was called in for assistance.

Characteristics of husband

Some women would not even say their husbands' names because they felt that to do so was a sin. Very conservative or newly married women often could not be persuaded to tell the name but asked the enumerator to talk to the husband's mother. Some said that they thought their husbands' lives would be shortened if they told their names. In answer to this question, as well as to others, some other person was called in to participate in the interview.

Women knew their own level of education, but they often knew only whether or not their husbands could read and write. Some said that they had once asked their husbands but were told that that was not a thing for them to know.

Often the wife did not know exactly what her husband's occupation was and said that she had been told it was none of her business. Sometimes the wife seemed indifferent to what her husband did for a living; she indicated that her only concern was that he provide for the family. Here again the enumerator might inquire of some other member of the household.

Number of times husband had been married

Wives seemed proud if their husbands had been married only once. Often the husband would hide the number of his marriages (if more than one) in the village census, but the wife would tell. Sometimes a comparison of the census and the wife's interview showed that the wife did not know how many times her husband had been married.

Household data

It appeared that all respondents attempted to hide their means of support for fear that it would be seized; as a result, the income item became a very difficult question. Even if the family was clearly well off, they would say, 'Oh, we get along somehow'. The enumerator had to work very indirectly here, asking whether the family was able to help its neighbours and if it was free from debts. Then she put the family into one of the broad categories of prosperity. But it seems that there is very great variation in the economic conditions of families put into the same groups.

Another reaction of respondents to this question was to tell all their troubles and ask the academy to help. It was difficult to get a picture of economic conditions because everyone wanted to show his conditions to be as bad as possible, and it was difficult to convince the villagers that the academy had not come to give them something. At this point, the enumerators sometimes explained village cooperatives (a part of the rural development programme) and told them that they could learn more of this at the academy.

A household is defined in this area as the group sharing the food prepared in one kitchen; this definition was used for studying household composition. However, in Hindu villages, difficulty was encountered in enumerating the household members since the survey was made during a time of communal rioting and some individuals were emigrating to India. Respondents wanted to conceal this fact and included members of the household who had left. In Muslim villages, some respondents tried to include as many people as possible in order to show how poor they were. Another reason for including persons who were absent was that some women felt that they should be feeding their husband's mothers, for example, in accordance with traditional rules; they would say that they were doing so even if this were not the case. Finally, some respondents included visiting kinfolk and married daughters who had left the household.

Marital status

Some women did not understand a question concerning number of years of present marriage and gave the total number of years of marriage, including two or three marriages. The question 'Is this your first marriage?' was often taken as insulting, despite the acceptability of remarriage in Islam. This question indicates one kind of unanticipated response in that the general Islamic position permits remarriage of widows but in the villages this is done covertly, perhaps because of local Hindu influence. A study director could not be expected to know this kind of fact unless he knew the local culture well. A question on duration of marriage and number of years of cohabitation also caused difficulties. Many women hesitated to answer because the answer concerned the number of years that they had had sexual relations with their husbands. If the enumerator were younger than the respondent, it was more difficult because the wife would say, 'You are shameless. How can I talk about such things with someone my daughter's age?' Young, newly married women were also shy about this.

The enumerators tried to discover the number of years of cohabitation by finding out what the husband's occupation was and whether he had been at home all the time of his marriage. Or they asked at what age the wife was allowed to live with her husband, or how many years she had lived with her mother-in-law (a young bride often lives with her mother-in-law until she reaches puberty). If men were present, this question had to be skipped until they left.

Knowledge, attitudes and practices concerning family planning

An item concerning knowledge of methods of contraception became embarrassing for the enumerator as well as the respondent, since the enumerators had to explain the question to the many respondents who had no previous knowledge of birth control. When asked if they wanted to learn more about contraception, many respondents asked if it were against their religion. Often the respondent indicated interest but declined to answer the question directly before talking with her husband.

The first reaction to a question concerning knowledge of methods of induced abortion was often one of shock: 'No, no, we don't know about such things'. The enumerator explained that she was not accusing the respondent of this practice but only wanted to know if she knew about it. (Yaukey, 1961, pp. 113–115).

References to supernatural powers were in response to items concerning preferences in the area of fertility. One reaction to the item concerning desire for additional children was, 'This is a funny question. How can you say whether you want more children or not?' Respondents said that it was a sinful question, since its answer lay with Allah. Others said that they wanted more children and asked for help. Some childless women were saddened by these questions.

With regard to child spacing, some objected that this too was in the hands of God. Newly married girls were shy about this question and sometimes referred the enumerator to the mother-in-law, who, if present, sometimes answered for the respondent. In such cases, the enumerator had to record no answer.

Many respondents did not understand a question concerning ideal family size. Sometimes the use of an imaginary woman helped, but very conservative women would not answer. Some replied that they had never thought of it or that it was in the hands of Allah. Some would not give any answer about the number of living children that they already had, for fear they would bring harm to the family.

A question on sexual abstinence on religious days proved to be very embarrassing. Respondents became agitated, fearing that the enumerators would make public their answers. Lack of privacy for the interview became crucial here. Many women said that the question was unnecessary since every married person knows the answers. Respondents sometimes changed their answers to this question if the interview situation became private.

Pregnancy roster

The interview contained a pregnancy roster which also had an item concerning the health of living children. Some high-parity women who had had abortions, or some of whose children had died, had forgotten the exact number of pregnancies. They were likely to ask other relatives to help remember. Others hesitated to tell the number for fear that some of their children might die or become ill. Others, when they thought of the dead children, became very sad and were sidetracked from the interview. The women did not understand why a list of the dead and aborted children was needed. 'Can you bring them back to life?' they asked.

The women often could not remember the recent health problems of their living children. At this point in the interview, some respondents brought out ailing children, expecting the enumerator to treat them and provide medicine. Then the enumerators had to explain that they were not physicians and had no medicine with them.

Fieldwork logistics

Other considerations, such as transportation, privacy, food, suspicion, and timing, posed problems in the fieldwork.

Transportation became a problem as a result of the inaccessibility of some of the villages. It was sometimes difficult to get bicycle-riskshaws at the right time, and some villages could be approached only by foot via dirt roads or paths. Bicycle-rickshaws were used rather than motorized vehicles because of the shortage of jeeps and because the style of the fieldwork was to try to make as few social barriers as possible between the interviewer and respondent. One of the villages could be approached only by a 8 km (5 mile) walk, which required a strong woman. One enumerator became so ill after making several such trips that she had to be hospitalized.

In case of heavy rain or nightfall, the interviewers were stranded, and, since it is unheard of for a woman to spend a night in a strange village, this posed a problem. Interviewers were told to leave by 3.00 or 4.00 pm, but on one occasion a woman was stranded and spent the night at a relative's house. Men in the village considered this highly immoral behaviour.

Although the women were easier to find than the men, since they were always at home, privacy in the interview was seldom achieved. The respondent's mother-in-law or sister-in-law often could not be escaped and posed particular problems in the interview, since she presumably enforces traditional attitudes.

The difficulty of achieving privacy in interviews has been noted in several studies in scattered locations, including India and Jamaica. The experience in the Bangladesh study reported here was that interviewers often found it impossible to keep older women and children out of the room in which the interview was conducted. Poti, Chakraborti, and Malaker (1962, p. 65) in Calcutta and Driver (1963, p. 17) in urban and village settings in central India imply that it was not possible to guarantee the privacy of the interview in these settings. On the other hand, Back and Stycos (1959, p. 12) imply much more success in maintaining private interviews in their description of interview techniques for ejecting 'outsiders' from the interview situation.

In the villages there were no places for the enumerators to rest and eat. The poor respondents rarely offered food, the enumerators could not ask for food, and eating their own food would have been 'improper behaviour'.

A generally negative attitude hindered the fieldwork; some people hesitated to cooperate, saying there was nothing in it for them. They requested payment for their answers, saying that if they gave good answers the enumerator would get more pay and they did not want to help the enumerator with no reward for themselves. Occasionally, the enumerators helped with household work, such as husking rice, and then the people were more willing to talk.

Some women said that the enumerators were shameless and would do anything for money and that their husbands would not allow them to talk to such women. The research assistant visited the village in such cases. The atmosphere was very strained. She dealt with the village people in a sympathetic manner and talked with them. Some of them were willing to answer the questions for her.

During the communal disturbances, the two Hindu enumerators had difficulty in one Muslim village. People were suspicious of them and would not talk, and in one house their lives were threatened. Then Muslim girls were sent along with them. To hide their identity, the Hindu girls washed the red marks that indicated their religion off their foreheads. These problems made the enumerators nervous, and they omitted questions, failed to check, and so forth.

Field supervision

The type of interviewers and the difficulties in the fieldwork necessitated special supervision of the enumerators. The eight women completed 643 interviews in 10 weeks. They met the research assistant and study director weekly for continuous inservice training, in addition to seeing the research assistant in the office or in the field more frequently. In the weekly meetings, they read aloud from their field diaries, discussed cases, and submitted their completed interviews, which were then closely examined. In many cases, repeat visits were made to households to unscramble contradictory information or to complete unanswered items. The research assistant did a great deal of troubleshooting in the field.

Conclusion

The fertility survey can be and has been successfully transplanted, but a close examination of what happens in the confrontation of interviewer and respondent in the context of the respondent's home in the village indicates that new meanings are involved in individual items which can hinder the research project. An appreciation of the fieldwork situation adds to the knowledge gained in the interview.

In the design of the research instrument, the researchers will have to become aware of the meaning of local concepts; for example, the meaning of 'household' in the Pakistani context differs from the researcher's definition, and use of either definition requires careful training of interviewers.

Some accepted ideas about sociological intervening techniques will have to be modified in new settings. For example, the idea of the private interview does not seem feasible in the context described.

The result of the experimental use of indigenous enumerators is mixed. They required a great deal of close supervision, and they were not freely accepted in the village. They did gather a great deal of intimate data, however. Their greatest utility in the future may be in supplying objective data about their own communities. Perhaps total outsiders may find more success in the villages, although they may gather data of less intimacy.

Additional ethnographic data on fertility and family planning in villages are recommended, especially to gather local meanings of concepts in research instruments.

The purpose of this chapter is not to be viewed as destructive. Fertility surveys are producing valuable data throughout the world, but our understanding of the data increases as we understand the research instrument better.

The role of the interviewer or enumerator from outside the village is completely undefined in the village. The village people did not know whether the enumerator had come to give to them (medicine, relief) or to take from them (taxes). They did not know whether the interviewers were the godless women heralding the end of the world or the advance guard for some government programme. Similarly, the purpose of scientific research is also unknown. In the case described, the study became involved with various aspects of community life.

References

Back, K.W. and Stycos, J.M. (1959). *The Survey Under Unusual Conditions: the Jamaica Human Fertility Investigation*, Society for Applied Anthropology Monograph no. 1, Ithaca, NY.

Driver, E. (1963). *Differential Fertility in Central India*, Princeton University Press, Princeton.

Mauldin, W.P. (1965). Application of survey techniques to fertility studies. In M.S. Sheps and J.C. Ridley (Eds) *Public Health and Population Change*, pp. 93–118, University of Pittsburg Press, Pittsburg.

Poti, S.J. Chakraborti, and Malaker (1962). Reliability of data relating to contraceptive practices. In C.V. Kiser (Ed.) *Research in Family Planning*, Princeton University Press, Princeton.

United Nations, Department of Economic and Social Affairs (1961). *The Myson Population Study*, United Nations, New York.

Yaukey, D. (1961). *Fertility Differences in a Modernising Country: A Survey of Lebanese couples*, Princeton University Press, Princeton.

Yaukey, D., Roberts, and Griffith, (1965). Husbands' v. wives' responses to a fertility survey. *Population Studies*, **19**, 25–31.

SECTION VI

METHODOLOGICAL MARRIAGES

Social Research in Developing Countries
Edited by M. Bulmer and D.P. Warwick
© 1983, John Wiley & Sons, Ltd.

CHAPTER 22

ON METHODOLOGICAL INTEGRATION IN SOCIAL RESEARCH

DONALD P. WARWICK

The past two decades have seen a growing recognition of the need for merging two or more research methodologies in the same study. As the social science disciplines have critically examined the epistemological foundations of their data sources, they have come to appreciate the limitations of single methods. Speaking generally about scientific knowledge Donald T. Campbell, a leading social science methodologist, comes to this sober conclusion: 'all scientific knowing is indirect, presumptive, obliquely and indirectly corroborated at best. The language of science is subjective, provincial, approximate, and meta-phoric, never the language of reality itself. The best we can hope for are well-edited approximations' (Mahoney, 1976, p. 126). At the end of a review on survey research and sociocultural anthropology, Bennett and Thaiss (1967, p. 307) reached much the same conclusion: 'The human reality must be apprehended by a variety of viewpoints, not by one alone, because this very reality is always in part a construct, always in part an image, and only by encouraging difference in perspective and approach can one obtain the needed richness of imagery, and consequently, theory'. This section of the book basically accepts that point of view for social research in the developing countries, and offers some examples of how methodological diversity can be brought about.

The briefs in favour of overlapping data sources have taken different forms in different disciplines. In the quantitative branches of psychology and socio-logy two articles set the stage for much of the current discussion on integration. The first, whose impact was mainly in psychology, was a paper by Cronbach and Meehl (1955) on 'construct validity' in psychological tests. While osten-sibly having little to do with methodological integration as such, this article called into question the somewhat mechanical notions of test validity then prevailing and argued for a broader approach. Specifically, Cronbach and

Meehl held that the validity of a construct (some postulated attribute of people assumed to be reflected in test performance) could not be established by simple correlations between a test and some external measure of performance, such as grades in school. Instead, the case for construct validity must be based on the total pattern of relationships between indicators of the construct and other relevant areas suggested by a theory.

Following on that logic, Campbell and Fiske (1959) published a path-breaking article on validation by the 'multitrait—multimethod matrix'. Their key point was that the validity of measurement for a given trait requires evidence of convergence among different measures of that trait. If a questionnaire measure of interpersonal dominance shows a higher correlation with two other indicators of dominance obtained by different methods than it does with a measure of other traits by the same method, a case can be made for convergent validity. But if the correlation of the dominance measure is greater with questionnaire measures of other traits (such as trust and compliance) than it is with measurements of dominance by independent methods, the validity of the dominance measure would be suspect. In other words, the case for validity in measurement must rest on the pattern of associations between the trait in question and (a) measures of different traits obtained by the same method; and (b) measures of the same trait obtained by different methods. Through this article, which was widely used in social science methodology courses, Campbell and Fiske (1959) spurred quantitatively oriented social scientists to broaden their reach in data collection.

In sociocultural anthropology and the qualitative branches of sociology the impetus for methodological fusion came less from shifts in the philosophy of measurement than from the need for a broader range of data. Though anthropology had long been identified with intensive qualitative methods, in fact lists, censuses, and other quantitative approaches were often used in village studies. In *Argonauts of the Western Pacific* and *Coral Gardens and Their Magic* Bronislaw Malinowski (1922; 1929) adopted various statistical techniques to document the quantifiable aspects of village life. As anthropologists took up the study of urban areas and 'complex societies' the demands for representative samples and quantitative data increased. Bennett and Thaiss reported (1967, pp. 279–80): 'A check of the contents of the *American Anthropologist* over the past six years showed that about one-third of the research articles in the field of sociocultural anthropology were based upon data acquired by the use of (survey) instruments. Nearly all of these were segments of larger studies, segments in which specific hypotheses were tested with the use of instruments on a survey basis.'

By the 1970s there was mounting awareness that debates pitting the virtues of one method against the weaknesses of another were not only simplistic but counterproductive. They were counterproductive because, by emphasizing the extremes, they diverted attention from a large middle ground where fruitful combinations could be made. Reflecting this shift in mood was an essay by Reichardt and Cook (1979) called 'Beyond qualitative versus quantitative methods'. The book in which it was published (Cook and Reichardt, 1979) was also novel in advocating both quantitative and qualitative methods in evaluation research, a field that had been dominated by quantitative approaches. More recently Light and Pillemer (1982) applied the logic of integration to research reviews, arguing that the aggregation of findings across many research studies is handled most effectively by combining the traditional strengths of narrative reviews with appropriate quantification. By 1980 the methodological chauvinsim of earlier decades had abated and the benefits of combined approaches were more widely appreciated. At the same time the number of studies in which extensive and intensive approaches were brought together as methodological equals remained small.

Examples of integration

Two examples can be cited of conscious attempts to draw on the advantages of overlapping data sources in the same study. The first is a study by Whyte and Alberti (1976), part of which is included as Chapter 23, on highland Peru. In an effort to understand the sources of conflict, cooperation, and other aspects of community behaviour the authors and their collaborators made use of both anthropological research and sample surveys to gather data on key topics. In addition, they drew on historical materials as well as administrative records to provide a broader perspective on community life.

   The second study, which was still in progress at the time of writing, draws on an even broader range of data sources. This is the Development Program Implementation Study (DPIS) being carried out in Indonesia by the Harvard Institute for International Development and several national counterpart organizations.[1] The main purpose of the study is to identify the factors explaining why some large-scale development programmes are more successfully implemented than others, and why even the same programme varies in its success across different regions of the country. The research covers four nationwide development programmes: (1) family planning; (2) primary education (Inpres Sekolah Daser); (3) rice intensification; and (4) village public works (Inpres Desa). All four of these programmes reach from the central government to the villages, have mass coverage rather than being aimed at special groups, and are concerned with social services or community development rather than with just physical construction. The reason for choosing four different programmes was to permit the study to explore the effects of such influences as the task to be accomplished, organizational structure and management systems, client demand, and the motivation of field implementers.

   The DPIS design called for systematic and overlapping data to be collected in four provinces: East Java, West Java, South Sulawesi and South Sumatra. These provinces were selected to permit analysis of the sources of regional variation in programme success. For the four programmes under study East Java was considered, on average, relatively successful in its implementation record, West Java and South Sulawesi mixed, and South Sumatra relatively unsuccessful. A similar sampling was used for lower levels of government within each province. Thus data were collected from a more successful, average, and less successful regency (*kabupaten*). And within each regency information was obtained from a more successful and a less successful sub-district (*kecamatan*) and, within each subdistrict, from a more successful and a less successful village (*desa*). The design also specified that intensive anthropological research would be carried out in a subdistrict rated as average on programme success and, within that subdistrict, a typical village. Overall the main part of the research called for data collection of some kind in four provinces, 12 regencies, 28 subdistricts, and 52 villages. The staff also conducted a limited number of interviews and gathered existing information about programme performance in five other 'less intensive' provinces.

From the outset the DPIS was designed to incorporate the respective strengths of several disciplines (economics, anthropology, organizational behaviour) and data sources. While it is difficult to discuss data sources without presenting the overall conceptual and analytical framework of the project, for present purposes it is enough to note the main components of the DPIS and the kinds of information collected within each. These were organizational analysis, anthropological studies, and economic studies.

Organizational analysis

A key aim of the study was to understand how the organizational context of a given programme affected its implementation. Toward that end the DPIS included interviews with about 500 public officials and other programme implementers in the four provinces chosen for detailed research. Respondents were asked about the history of the programme in their region; how it was carried out, and by whom; the main successes as well as obstacles in implementation; how obstacles were overcome; who supported, criticized, or opposed the programme, and suggestions for improvement. The theory behind these interviews was that field implementers could provide valid information about those aspects of implementation with which they were most familiar, especially their own immediate work.

Anthropological studies

The most 'intensive' part of the research was a set of anthropological studies conducted in four villages and their corresponding sub-district (*kecamatan*) capitals. Researchers lived in each village from 6 months to a year or more and gathered various kinds of data. In addition to recording their observations on programme implementation and community life more generally, they conducted a complete census of village households and then a sample survey of about 150 households per village. They also prepared life histories on from 20 to 30 villagers, with particular emphasis on their experience with the programme under study, and carried out interviews with implementers working at that level. The observers in the subdistrict capitals likewise interviewed key implementers and watched them in action where possible. The assumption behind this approach was that the anthropological data would be particularly useful in understanding who participates in the four programmes and why; who receives more and less benefits from each; how implementation relates to local patterns of decision-making; and how clients react to the programmes overall and to the specific services delivered.

Economic studies

The third source of data and an additional perspective on implementation came from what were called 'economic studies'. In addition to providing an economic viewpoint that pervaded many aspects of design and analysis, this component involved three specific contributions to the research. The first was the collection and analysis of secondary data, including statistics on programme inputs and outputs. The main objective was to shed light on the cost effectiveness of the programme under investigation. The second source of economic data was interviews with programme implementers and other officials. The focus there was on how financial administration operates for each programme and on its consequences for implementation. The third kind of economic data included information on programme efficiency at the local level.

The research design provided for substantial, though not total, overlap among the three main data sources. All three kinds of analysis were carried out in the same provinces and in certain cases the same regencies, but not necessarily the same villages. Hence the design of the organizational studies involved data collection in the same regency as the anthropological studies, but not in the same villages and subdistricts. The main reason for this separation was to avoid the saturation of the anthropological field sites by too many outsiders. Similarly, the economic studies overlapped with both the organizational and economic studies, but not completely. The DPIS is probably the single most ambitious attempt at methodological integration seen to date in the developing countries. Completion of the analysis should show just what each data source was able to contribute and how well the different components came together in illuminating key aspects of implementation.

Reasons for integration

Although there are many advantages to merging data sources in the same study, not every study will profit from such integration. If a study's objective is to prepare an exact count of the population in Arequipa, Peru, the techniques traditionally used for a population census might be sufficient in themselves. With reasonable cooperation from residents and local officials it might be possible to obtain a precise count of the population by visiting each household at a specifed time and asking about who lives there and is present, who lives there and is away, and so on. Should there be problems of cooperation, however, or other difficulties in the straightforward application of census techniques, additional steps may be necessary both to count the population and to understand likely errors in measurement. If, for instance, residents in a certain neighbourhood refuse to take part in the census or show signs of falsifying their answers, it may be helpful to use one or more qualitative approaches to understanding the situation. At the very least some informal, open-ended interviewing might be done with community leaders and other influentials to explore the nature of local reactions to the census. Depending on the purposes of the research and the importance of accuracy, it might even be worthwhile to have an anthropologist or qualitatively oriented sociologist live in the area for a few months to study relevant aspects of community dynamics. If previous censuses were carried out in Arequipa with no major problems, historical data on changes in that city might be useful in helping to understand the current difficulties. In short, the advantages of adding information from separate data sources depend entirely on the purposes of the research and the feasibility of obtaining the additional information sought.

In general, there are six main reasons for bringing together two or more data sources in the same study. Not all of these are relevant to all kinds of social research, but they are sufficiently salient across the usual range of studies to make them worth citing here. Whether or not a given reason is applicable to a particular study will depend on the purposes and needs of that study and the resources available for the research.

Additional categories of information

The most obvious reason for expanding the number of data sources is to obtain crucial information that is not available from a single method. In the Development Program Implementation Study in Indonesia the research team sought data on the costs per unit of service delivered and similar kinds of financial information. Although the study design included two major and overlapping data sources — anthropological research and a survey of field implementers — neither supplied the required financial data. Hence the specifications also called for a third component, called 'economic analysis', to gather information on costs and expenditure patterns for the programmes covered. In Chapter 23

Whyte and Alberti likewise show the value of official records as a supplement to both survey research and anthropological observation. On such questions as who attends community meetings, who turns out for cooperative work projects, and who pays fines for non-compliance with community obligations such official records have a validity that would be hard to duplicate by the most careful of sample surveys. In line with the next point, the confidence that could be placed in this information was enhanced by the fact that official data corresponded very well with on-the-spot observations by anthropologists.

Improved accuracy in measuring a single phenomenon

A second reason for combining data sources is to increase confidence in the accuracy of measurements or observations made on a given phenomenon. Where the first reason was basically concerned with gathering information by one method that is not available from others, this reason has to do with overlapping data supplied by two or more methods. As used here accuracy can be defined as the generalizability of the measurements or observations made of one phenomenon to all the measurements or observations that might have been made of the same phenomenon at the same time (Cronbach, Rajaratram, and Gleser, 1963). This notion of accuracy is an abstract construct, for there is virtually no situation in which all possible measurements or observations of a single phenomenon can be taken at more or less the same time. While there may be a dozen or more conceivable measures of social class, the case for the accuracy of any given set of measures increases when the same results are obtained by independent or at least somewhat independent methods. The logic of the previous definition suggests that consistent findings from two or three methods are more likely to represent all the possible findings that might be obtained than are findings from a single method.

In a study of social stratification in a small town in the United States, Vidich and Shapiro (1955) used both participant observation and survey research to obtain prestige ratings in a community. The participant observers assigned ratings to a sample of residents on the basis of observations on social status during field work. The survey items used to measure prestige included sociometric questions such as the following: 'If some person were to be selected to represent this particular part of town at a special meeting of the town board, who would *you personally* want to go?' The observational and survey data were generally consistent and, in the view of the authors, complementary: '. . . the techniques of participant observation and the sample survey are not competitive, but, in the well-conducted community study, will be complementary. The survey provides representative information which will be given meaning by the anthropological observer' (Vidich and Shapiro, 1955, p. 33). The possibilities of complementarity were enhanced in this study by the choice of a common focus and explicit coordination in data collection.

An even more ambitious attempt to integrate data from survey and anthropological methods is seen in Schwab's (1954) study of an urban Yoruba community in south-west Nigeria:

The basis of the methodological procedures employed was an attempted integration of survey techniques and intensive anthropological methods. Customary procedures — such as interviewing selected informants, collecting case histories and genealogies, observing group and individual activities — were augmented by the use of questionnaires, field guides, and sampling devices. Field assistants were trained to observe and record the individual and group activities of selected families over a period of one year. Moreover, available documentary data, such as political and economic reports, price indices, court records, and other miscellaneous material, were examined in detail.

Because Schwab's account focuses mainly on the methodology of this project it provides little detail on the ways in which the two data sources overlapped on specific topics. There are hints, however, that on such questions as kinship the two methods provided generally consistent information while on others, including the traditional social structure, they differed. But overall 'they were, in fact, complementary, and the division between them somewhat artificial. Each was a stimulus to the other, for it was data collected by the asssistants that provided, as it were, the substantiating facts for a continuing sequence of ethnographic hypotheses' (Schwab, 1954, p. 19).

At times the greatest value of overlapping methods is to show that data from one source are either totally false or seriously flawed. The usual butt of such research is, with some justification, the quick sample survey, but there are enough instances of invalidity with other methods to make this a generic concern. One of the more dramatic cases of cross-method inconsistency comes from the dissertation research conducted by John Marshall (1972) in India. As part of this study Marshall and his wife lived in a village with the fictitious name of Bunkipur. During the course of their stay the village was visited by the local family planning programme. Fieldworkers carried out a motivational campaign and then, to test their success, conducted a version of the Knowledge–Attitude–Practice (KAP) survey. In this survey respondents are asked in different ways whether they are familiar with birth control methods (Knowledge), how they feel about the idea of limiting births (Attitude), and what, if anything, they are currently doing on that front (Practice). Because the Marshalls were interested in fertility control and had collected information on many of the same questions through observation and informal discussion, they could compare the results of the KAP study with their own findings. The discrepancies were striking, especially on knowledge and practice. The survey data showed, for instance, that modern contraceptive techniques had been adopted by twelve villagers, the same number indicated by their village research. According to the survey these twelve included ten Thakurs, one Brahman, and one Jyogi. The observational data, by contrast, revealed that it was five Thakurs, five Chamars, one Bhangi, and a Jyogi, half of whom were more than 60 years of age. As Marshall put it (1972, p. 264), 'the correspondence between the actual contraceptive users and those reported in the survey was accidental'. Lest one conclude that sample surveys have a monopoly on falsification, Whyte and Alberti (Chapter 23) report instances in which anthropological observation resulted in serious errors. In one case an observer reported an unusual type of committee within the local government of a community. A restudy provided no information whatsoever on this committee which, in fact, did not and never had existed. The points to be underscored here are that *all* methods are susceptible to errors of this kind, and that the best defence against falsified or otherwise mistaken information is cross-checking by independent but comparable data sources.

Qualitative depth

A common lament about quantitative data is that in themselves they lack depth and meaning. Findings may attain high levels of precision and statistical significance, but still be very difficult to interpret outside a qualitative framework. Schwab (1954, pp. 18–19) cites an example from his study of the urban Yoruba:

A social fact is significant in itself and acquires full meaning only when understood in its historical perspective and in its functional and structural relationships to the society . . . . Let us consider the problem of the religious composition of the Oshogbo: the field assistants collected data in a questionnaire that indicated that the religious composition of the community was 80 per cent Muslim, 13 per cent Christian, and seven per cent Native. These data showed that there had been a shift from a predominantly Native community to one that was predominantly Muslim. However, these data gave no indication, for example, of the complicated and various reasons that caused this shift, and could not reach such problems as complex changes in morals and sanctions, and codes and values, that were crucial to the understanding of religious changes.

Although Schwab understates the extent to which a well-designed survey might shed light on the dynamics or religious change (for example, through the adroit use of brief life histories), his point is well-taken.

A related limitation of survey methods used alone is that they are ill-suited to the study of complex social relationships and intricate patterns of interaction, such as kinship obligations or gift exchange. Their contribution is also limited when the aim of the research is to obtain first-hand *behavioural* information on such processes as leadership and influence in small groups or to construct a qualitative picture of a certain situation or flow of events. Under those circumstances the methods associated with participant observation would often be more suitable as the primary source of data. The skilled observer can develop an intimate understanding of the context of relationships and events, and has the distinct advantage of being able to match norms against behaviour, word against deed. Rather than just ask villagers about who holds power in the community, observers can actually watch and record who wields power of different sorts, and on what occasions. These advantages are partially offset by the limited coverage of most observational studies, the inherent difficulties in replication, and the inescapable need for subjectivity in interpreting the results of the study. Perhaps the main point of the contribution by Whyte and Alberti (Chapter 23) is to show that qualitative depth can profitably be combined with quantitative measurement in the same study.

Generalizability of findings across units

Another reason for combining research methods in a single study is to augment the possibilities of generalizing the results to a broader population. With the exception of a census, which by definition covers the population about which conclusions are to be drawn, most studies hope to generalize beyond the confines of the units actually covered. A sample survey is usually defined as a study in which information is gathered from a fraction of the population chosen to represent the whole (Warwick and Lininger, 1975, Chapter 1). By using a representative sample of individuals, households, or other units, survey research aims to collect data that can be used for drawing conclusions about the population in question. But even the anthropological study confined to a single village hopes to be able to generalize to a broader geographical region or human population. It is a rare anthropologist who is happy to analyse what happens in a small part of the society and stop there. Typically students of village life aspire to generalizations about regional culture, social structure, the dynamics of change, socialization, or other phenomena of broad import. Village studies leading to policy recommendations also make implicit generalizations when they suggest that the results from a few units of observation can serve as the basis for policy guidance in regions not studied.

In principle the greatest single advantage of the well-designed sample survey is that its results can be generalized to a larger population within known limits of error. The greatest single drawback of small-scale observational studies is that the limits of generality are unknown and usually unknowable. A community study may provide a masterful portrayal of society, culture, and personality and deep insights into the human condition, but still be of indeterminate generalizability. A sample survey may be qualitatively superficial and flawed in other ways and yet provide a solid basis for generalizing about key areas of information (household composition, housing characteristics, age structure, and so on). The overriding argument of this section is that, where feasible, extensive and intensive methods should be combined to enhance both generalizability and qualitative depth.

But how can that be done? Is it really possible to bring together small-scale, intensive studies with the more extensive coverage of the sample survey? The obstacles to such marriages are indeed formidable, as much for psychological as for administrative reasons, but the studies done to date suggest some promising possibilities. In material not reprinted here Whyte and Alberti (1976, p. 282) argue that the most effective strategy for combining survey and anthropological methods is to begin with the surveys, which can be completed fairly quickly, and use the results to choose the best sites for intensive field research.

If we were now utilizing our experience for national planning, we would begin by selecting a sample of 6 to 10 villages in each of the major regions of the country. Then in region X, we would survey villages A and B, repeating the process in the other regions. We would not undertake any anthropological studies until we had completed the first-year surveys and scanned the patterns of responses. We would then pick out a few villages whose response patterns appeared to be particularly interesting for theoretical and/or policy purposes: for example, villages very high or very low in confidence in their ability to solve village problems . . . . We would design our anthropological field work in these villages in order to probe for the social processes underlying the survey findings. . . . In the second year, in region X, we would survey villages C and D, repeating the procedures outlined above. For the third year, we would survey E and F, and so on.

In the Development Program Implementation Study, the research team applied the logic, if not the exact procedures, of probability sampling to the selection of villages for intensive study. As noted, the research called for anthropological studies to be conducted in four different provinces. Within each province there was to be intensive research in one village and its corresponding subdistrict capital. To select those units the researchers used various kinds of available information, including government classifications of villages and statistics on programme performance, to choose a 'typical' village for each province. While the samplers had no illusions that any village would be truly typical of a region, the procedures used went as far as possible to ensure that the areas selected were not obviously *atypical*. In reaching their judgements the research team used quantitative data such as population size and the number of villagers per district, as well as the qualitative judgement of informed observers. Although this procedure was far from perfect, it did work to ensure at least rough comparability among the four pairs of units chosen across provinces. Both this study and that discussed by Whyte and Alberti in Chapter 23 argue strongly for systematic attention to the selection of villages or other sites for intensive work. Given the high costs and heavy time demands of such intensive research, with field studies often running a year or more, the investment made in a careful sampling strategy seems exceptionally worthwhile.

Historical interpretation

In certain kinds of research it is crucial to explain events or situations in the present by reconstructing the past. In such cases historical data can profitably be combined with whatever methods are being used to understand the present.

This historical information may be qualitative, as is the usual case, or quantitative, as when census records, administrative statistics, or even public opinion polls are analysed over time. Lipset (1968) rightly points out that voting statistics and other quantitative data may have great utility in testing hypotheses about social change.

Several examples can be cited of attempts to blend historical analysis with research primarily oriented to the present. One is the Project on Cultural Values and Population Policies conducted by the Hastings Center in collaboration with scholars in eight developing countries (for an overview of this study see Warwick, 1982). The project's primary objective was to understand the formulation and implementation of contemporary population policies in Egypt, Kenya, Mexico, the Philippines, the Dominican Republic, Haiti, India, and Lebanon. The principal methods of data-collection were a combination of indepth interviews with key officials, less intensive interviews with field implementers, documentary analysis, and sometimes other sources. It quickly became clear, however, that in several countries contemporary population policy could not be adequately understood without reference to the past. In Lebanon the key fact to be explained was why the government could not have even a population census, much less an overt public policy on fertility control. As Khalaf (1978) makes clear, any discussion of population policy in Lebanon is virtually inseparable from historically rooted conflicts over ethnic and religious balances. An analysis of population policy that failed to take account of this historical dimension would be seriously incomplete, if not totally misguided.

Similarly, in Mexico a critical fact was that in 1972, after fifty years of public pronouncements in favour of a larger population, the government announced a new policy favouring birth limitation. From the standpoint of the research project it was important to know what effect, if any, this abrupt shift would have on the possibilities of implementing the new policy. Leñero (1979) and his associates concluded that to deal with this question it would be necessary to trace attitudes as well as policies on population at least to the 16th century. By drawing on historical information, including newspaper articles on population size over the previous three decades, the Mexican team was able to portray the historical momentum of Mexico's pronatalism, including its carryover to the present. At the same time their interviews and other research on the present showed how these inertial forces pressured Mexican leaders to design a population strategy that would minimize political and social dislocations brought on by the sudden reversal of policy.

In Chapter 23 Whyte and Alberti document some of the ways in which historical data can help to explain differences in the contemporary conditions of Peruvian villages. By integrating historical materials with both survey research and anthropological observation they were able to shed light on such questions as the difference in dynamism across villages in the same region.

They comment (Whyte and Alberti, 1976, p. 280): '. . . we can exploit the diachronic focus of history to bring to life the social processes that are vital to our understanding of community life'. Other fruitful possibilities are suggested by the work of Vansina (1965). By merging historical with ethnographic techniques he was able to reconstruct the history of non-literate peoples from their oral traditions. Whatever the particular form of integration, there are many kinds of social research in which an historical dimension will be useful, if not essential, for interpreting the phenomena at hand.

Testing associations

In most forms of social research it is important to test associations within the data collected. Creating the possibility for the systematic exploration of associations is usually the foremost reason for conducting a sample survey, but the same need likewise arises in research billed as qualitative. Whatever one's data sources, it is often critical to answer questions such as these: Who participates? Who benefits and who is harmed by a given situation or intervention? What is the relationship between caste or class and behaviours in the society? Who conforms most and least closely to social norms and expectations? And how do attitudes, values, and beliefs differ across religious and occupational groups? Research stereotypes to the contrary, such questions arise as often in anthropological or qualitative sociological studies as in conventional survey research. The difference between these research traditions is often less the questions asked than the strategies adopted for answering them. And it is precisely in developing a more effective approach to testing associations that creative combinations of research methods come into play.

In his research on caste and world views in India Joseph Elder (1969) combined survey research with field observation, partly to have the data necessary to test key associations. At the beginning his research techniques were mainly those associated with anthropology: participant observation, interviews with village informants, census-taking, tracing lineages, and taking copious field notes. But near the end of his stay he added a sample survey of 200 respondents drawn from five different groups considered important for the research topic. The survey data, as usual, permitted comparisons of replies by caste, age, income, religious belief, and other categories. Elder notes that for some questions, such as what happened to Muslims in the village at the time of partition, three or four good informants were sufficient. But for other questions, such as 'On the whole, would you say that the mill has brought more benefit or more harm to the village?' the responses differed across social categories. Moreover, careful attention to the tabulated results forced Elder (1969, p. 174) to change some of the conclusions he drew from his anthropological data sources.

For example, my general impression was that the poorer villagers looked back with nostalgia on the days of the British; whereas the richer villagers were glad that India was independent. When I had totalled my interview returns, however, I saw that the rich–poor distinction was not as important as the caste distinction, with the highest and lowest castes feeling things had become better since independence while the middle classes felt things had been better under the British. Unless I had systematically interviewed a sizeable sample of the population, I would not have been able to correct my initial error.

Along with most survey researchers, Elder (1969) also found that 200 cases were too few for pursuing all the critical questions that arose in his study. With substantial overlap between education and caste, it was difficult to find lower-caste respondents who were highly educated. Hence, 'when the two groups differed in outlook, as they frequently did, there was no way in which I could attribute difference to caste, education, or urbanization'. In a later study with a sample of more than 2500 respondents Elder collected the data necessary to test associations on a more solid basis. There he was able to introduce the controls necessary to determine whether apparent associations, such as that seen between caste and fatalism, were real or spurious.

The case for multiple data sources is especially strong in the developing countries for the simple reason that the data collected by any one method are often subject to substantial error. Survey research, in particular, is likely to suffer from such drawbacks as sampling bias; respondent incomprehension of the method itself; fears about the uses to which the survey data will be put (military conscription, taxation, political repression); difficulties in reaching certain remote areas; errors arising from interviewers, who may be inexperienced, poorly trained, and inadequately paid; and other sources of error. Such problems are endemic to the sample survey anywhere, but are often accentuated in countries or regions with a weak tradition or professional survey research and social conditions, such as illiteracy, that are not conducive to either initial cooperation or valid response. Anthropological field research may likewise suffer from the lack of experienced professionals in that field, governmental suspicion or regulation of village studies, and local scepticism about the purposes and uses of such research. A combination of methods, while no panacea for the ills of social research, at least holds the promise of counteracting as well as comprehending the biases of single data sources.

Finally, experience to date with integrated methods should serve to dispel the notion that qualitative intensive research should always precede quantitative or extensive methods. For many years researchers of a quantitative bent have acknowledged the contribution of qualitative work, but mostly as a source of ideas that can be tested with "hard" data. As Whyte notes (1976, p. 215):

. . . research is a two-step process: the researcher begins with 'soft' methods to develop ideas, and then moves on to the 'hard' science methods of testing those ideas. After that, he/she starts over, with another project, and goes through the same old one-two. . . . That is the conventional wisdom in sociology — and it is dead wrong. It distorts reality and understates the value of *both* research methods.

Whyte points out that, while the original idea for his research on Peruvian communities came from reading an anthropological report, 'it was only when I checked the marginals for the surveys on the three Mantaro Valley communities that I realized I might have an idea worth developing as well as testing' (Whyte, 1976, pp. 215–216; for a related discussion, see Sieber, 1973).

Whyte recommends a strategy of weaving back and forth among methods through the various stages of research. This approach has much to commend it, and not only when the combination at stake involves anthropological and survey methods. Sometimes, for example, data collected through survey research may suggest an association that is worth checking by other quantitative methods, such as administrative statistics. While analysing survey data from the Development Program Implementation Study, I found an apparent association between levels of programme input (staff, salaries, supplies, and supporting services) and the success of the country's national family planning programme. This tentative finding prompted a closer examination of the relationship between inputs and programme effectiveness as seen in aggregate programme statistics compiled by the government. The significant point is not the order in which one or the other method is used, but the extent to which one data source can suggest hypotheses that can be pursued by different and ideally overlapping methods.

Types of overlap

The most obvious advantage of multiple data sources is that one approach can provide information on topics that are not covered at all or are covered very lightly by others. In the Development Program Implementation Study, for example, the anthropological research proved to be the only solid source of information on village level decision-making in the local public works programme (*Inpres Desa*). Interviews with field implementers and other officials touched on the question of decision-making, but for various reasons did not yield quality data on that subject. Similarly, the organizational interviews were the main source of statistical information about implementation problems and their differential frequency across provinces. Wtih 500 interviews it is possible to establish the frequency of implementation problems with some confidence. And by design the economic studies were the major source of data on cost effectiveness and related questions of expenditure in each of the programmes. Overall, the greatest single advantage of multiple data sources is that they permit the collection of critical data on one topic that are not available from other sources used in the same study.

But more creative possibilities of integration arise when the same topic is covered in the same study by two or more data sources. It is here that the limitations of single methodologies become potential strengths, even when the data from separate sources appear inconsistent. If both an extensive survey and a set of intensive village studies show that the implementation of a family planning programme follows a certain pattern, the findings will have a stronger empirical foundation than if the same pattern emerged from just one data source. But even if separate methods produce different results on the same topic, something important has been learned. The researchers may later find that the inconsistency is only superficial and that there is a deeper congruence in the data, or they may conclude that the difference is real and requires further study, perhaps by a third data source. Whatever the outcome, viewing the same topic through different methodological lenses will usually be worth the effort.

Experience to date with methodological integration suggests four main ways in which the data generated by different methodologies will cluster around a given topic: separate information with little overlap; convergent overlap; divergent overlap; and inconclusive overlap. Some examples will illustrate these various possibilities.

Separate information with little overlap

Sometimes the different data sources will yield independent data on the same topic, but with little or no overlap on the subareas covered. A significant question in the DPIS, for example, is the ease or difficulty farmers have in selling their rice to the local government sponsored cooperatives. It could happen that both the organizational and anthropological studies would find that farmers faced problems in selling their rice. However, given their specific data source — the field implementers — the organizational studies might come up with information highlighting difficulties within the cooperative (shortage of capital, storage space). With a view from the village the anthropological research might well come up with a different set of reasons, such as the greater profit to be made from growing local varieties of rice that are not purchased by the cooperatives. At a general level the findings would converge in showing the existence of problems in the sale of rice. But when it came to the precise nature of those problems, the results would neither converge nor diverge; they would simply be different. In that case one might want to conduct further research by those or other methods to obtain more specific information on the questions at hand.

Convergent overlap

Perhaps the happiest outcomes of methodological marriages arise when different methods produce information on the same topic that is overlapping, fundamentaly consistent, and yet different enough to enrich the analysis. If data from the different sources are almost identical the researchers might feel gratified at the congruity but dismayed that nothing new has been learned. But when the overlapping data are both congruent in their basic thrust and disparate in their details one can feel that the investment was demonstrably worthwhile.

A clear example of convergent overlap comes from the Project on Cultural Values and Population Policies. (The general study on population policy in the Philippines can be found in Lopez *et al.*, 1978. The anthropological study was issued as Garcia-Yangas and Prill-Brett, 1978). In the Philippines the project was able to conduct both intensive and extensive research on the implementation of the government's family planning programme. The extensive study itself used various data sources, but drew heavily on interviews with several hundred programme implementers, including top officials. The intensive study was an anthropological analysis of implementation in two sites, one near Manila and one in a somewhat isolated rural area. While the studies were independent in their execution, they were part of the same overall project and addressed many of the same questions about implementation. One of these was the reaction of field workers to promotion of sterilization. With independent data sources both studies found that local implementers were reluctant to motivate for sterilization, especially when the intended clients were men and when the couple had fewer than four children. While the anthropological study had the edge on observational detail, the implementer survey provided much more extensive coverage than was possible with intensive research. But the point to be underscored here is that both methodologies produced essentially the same picture of implementer reactions to motivation for sterilization. This convergence increased the confidence that could be placed in the findings of the study as a whole on that point.

Divergent overlap

Data from different sources will sometimes overlap on the same topic but yield apparently inconsistent findings. The inconsistency itself is no cause for panic, for it will typically prompt a more thorough analysis of the data than would otherwise be the case and sometimes lead to the collection of more information. Typically there will be two outcomes of the initial analysis: results that can be reconciled by data from within the study, and inconsistencies that cannot be reconciled without further research.

The following is a hypothetical but plausible example of an apparent discrepancy that could be resolved by data from within the study. In the implementer interviews an agricultural extension worker claims that he visits village *A* once a week and while there convenes farmers for a discussion of problems in applying new techniques of growing rice. However, the anthropologist living in village *A* reports that the extension worker comes there only once a month and during his stay almost never convenes the farmers. The report from another anthropological observer stationed in the subdistrict capital, the extension worker's home base, confirms that the latter goes to village *A* no more than once a month. In this case, barring any disconfirming evidence, it is reasonable to assume that the fieldworker was overstating both the frequency of his visits to village *A* and the number of times he convened meetings of the farmers. In such circumstances one would expect the extension worker to overreport contact with farmers, especially if there were official guidelines suggesting a frequency close to what he stated. Assuming that they are independent, the convergence of the reports from the village and sub-district anthropological observers provides more convincing evidence than reports from the extension agent. The picture would change, however, if there were evidence of conflicts between this individual and one or the other of the anthropologists. In all such cases judgements must be made about the reliability and validity of data from different sources, but often the evidence to support one or another interpretation is clear enough to resolve the inconsistency.

The analytical outcome is less satisfying when findings from different sources are divergent and not reconcilable with the data at hand. Suppose, for example, that in the DPIS family planning workers in Sumatra stated that a major difficulty in their work was in bringing villagers together for meetings to discuss the programme. The main reasons they reported for this difficulty were that settlements are widely scattered and, especially in the swampy areas, transportation is difficult. Problems of interpretation would arise if the anthropological studies in that area concluded that the main reason for the implementers' failure to convene the villagers was not the physical environment but their own apathy. Even if the conclusion of the anthropological team were well-founded there would be an immediate problem of interpretation. Where the interviews with implementers were held with respondents in twelve villages and six subdistrict capitals, the anthropological observations were based mainly on one village and one subdistrict capital. And these last two sites did not overlap at all with the sites of the other interviews. In this situation one would want to be very careful in interpreting that part of either study and, if possible, do some further checking in the data and outside to see if the inconsistency can be settled. But even if the discrepancy remained the analysis as a whole would be helped by being alterted to a key area of ambiguity in the data.

Inconclusive overlap

The findings generated by different research methodologies may also overlap in ways that are neither divergent nor convergent but simply inconclusive. A study of rural communities might be interested, for example, in the question of who is most and least likely to contribute money and labour to local self-help projects. Interviews with officials responsible for these programmes might lead to the conclusion that those contributing the least are the poor farmers. According to those officials poor farmers have little or no money to contribute and they are so busy earning a living that they have no time to offer labour. By contrast, anthropological research in other communities shows that, whatever the demands on their time, many poor farmers are rounded up to provide labour on community projects.

There are several plausible explanations for this apparent inconsistency. First, because the two sets of studies were dealing with different villages they were tapping different realities. Perhaps in the villages studied by the anthropologists farmers are rounded up to provide labour, while in the villages covered by the other interviews they are not. Second, it is possible that the officials commenting on self-help contributions were simply ill-informed about what was really happening in the villages. Third, the picture may have been mixed: some poor farmers may have been rounded up in some of the villages, while others were so busy earning a living that they could not be found. In this last case both the extensive and intensive data could be partially correct. But without further information to resolve the seeming inconsistency the over-lapping data would have to be rated as inconclusive.

Several of the examples point up a major benefit of results from multiple and overlapping methods: uncovering the need for additional analysis or data. Particularly when overlapping findings are divergent or inconclusive the researcher will be under pressure to resolve discrepancies by digging deeper into the problem at hand. Such pressure may arise, of course, from data generated by a single method. In the DPIS, preliminary analysis of data from the organizational studies suggested that a prime source of differences across regions in the success of the family planning programme was the level of programme inputs (staff, honoraria, supplies, visits by medical teams, and so on). That hypothesis, in turn, indicated the need for additional and ideally quantitative data on programme inputs for each area under study. But such pressure for further analysis rises when there are two or more apparently inconsistent data sources for each major topic under consideration.

Some barriers to integration

Let this chapter convey a misplaced euphoria about the prospects for methodo-logical integration, I should note some of the reasons why the systematic merging of data sources in a single study has been rare. There is no shortage of cases in which a second method has been used as a supplement to a primary source of data, as when anthropologists use surveys as an adjunct to field observation or survey researchers use observation as a prelude to question-naire construction. But the number of studies in which different methods have entered the research design more or less as equals has been small, and those in which the intersections of these methods have been discussed in detail are even fewer. The following seem to be the main obstacles to methodological integra-tion in social research.

Limited competence

Probably the greatest single barrier to methodological integration is the sheer lack of capacity to draw on methods other than the one in which one was originally trained. It is both a strength and a weakness of professional training in the social sciences that aspirants to the various disciplines typically learn but one major approach to data collection. It is a strength because competence in one method provides the foundation for high-quality research and works against the shallowness of multidisciplinary omniscience. Donald Campbell has warned about the dangers of creating social scientists who are competent in everything but proficient at nothing. But the narrowness of methodological training becomes intellectually counterproductive when the skills acquired blind social scientists to the complementary potential of other approaches. For the future the best route towards greater integration may not be training in two or three different approaches, for that strategy runs the risk of superficiality, but rather teaching these professionals to understand and appreciate the contribution of other data sources. Interestingly, in his research on Peruvian communities Whyte, whose methodological forte was participant observation, did not try to become an instant expert on survey research. Instead he entered into collaboration with a colleague whose own strong suit was survey research, and through joint work over a period of years came to understand and use that methodology.

Disciplinary ethnocentrism

A second and closely related barrier to integration is the tendency of the various social science disciplines or subdisciplines to exalt the virtues of their dominant methods and disparage those of other fields. Thus many quantitative social scientists fancy themselves as 'hard-heads' — true scientists whose propensity for numbers betokens a deep and undying commitment to truth. Those who do not share this faith are 'soft heads' who do not deserve the name of science. For their part social scientists of a qualitative persuasion often portray their approach as humane, sensitive, intuitive, and comprehensive. In this world view the participant observer is a caring, pulsating human being who identifies with the people being studied and learns as much by being as by doing. Quantitative researchers, by contrast, are methodologically gross, insensitive to contexts, and more often than not wrong in their assessment of community dynamics. Happily these stereotypical images of social research are less common than in earlier decades, but they are by no means dead. Their practical consequence is that they make self-respecting social scientists from one tradition at least initially wary of associating too closely with those of a different persuasion.

Costs

Even for those who would like to take up some form of integration the costs, financial and otherwise, are often high. Projects drawing together two or three different data sources are not only more expensive than those relying on one method, but much more complicated to carry out. What economists call 'transactions costs' are exceptionally high in interdisciplinary projects. At the beginning specialists from the different disciplines, whatever their commitment to the overarching objectives of the project, may have difficulty communicating with each other about methodology. The survey specialist may wonder why anthropological research takes so long, and the anthropologist may question how survey research can ever hope to gather valid data through such brief contacts with respondents. If the aim of the project is to bring about an integration of data sources from the outset, lengthy discussion may be needed to work out a suitable fit among the approaches used. If, on the other hand, each specialist goes his or her way at the beginning, the problem of integration will simply be postponed until later. In short, anyone who thinks that methodological integration is an easy task — financially, psychologically, intellectually, or administratively — has obviously never tried it. But the benefits outlined earlier, particularly the possibility of checking key areas of information by earlier independent sources, make these costs worth bearing.

Opportunities

Finally, a major barrier to methodological integration is the lack of suitable projects for combining methods. Partly this is a matter of financing, for funding agencies often resist studies that appear complex and cost more than those with simpler methodologies. But also at work in many countries is a second-order effect of professional training. Planners with a background in economics may see no need for studies drawing on anthropological methods, particularly when the village research involved requires 1 or 2 years of work in just a few areas. Even if the researchers were to explain the enormous advantages of that fieldwork for policy purposes, the administrators will often ask why the same task cannot be accomplished with more rapid and preferably quantitative methods. Similarly, the problems of integration faced by the researchers themselves, such as how qualitative and quantitative research on villages can best be brought together, will also be problems for sponsors and administrators who have to approve such efforts. Given the paucity of successful cases of methodological integration, there is hardly a book that proponents can bring forth as an illustration of what is to come. There is a vicious circle here in which the absence of live examples of integration makes it difficult to convince funders and other key decision-makers about the feasibility and benefits of multiple data sources.

But this chapter can end on a positive note. Both the following chapter by

Whyte and Alberti and the Development Program Implementation Study provide concrete evidence that methodological integration is not only possible but productive. With more flexible training in graduate schools and greater openness by research sponsors we may hope for more cases of this type in coming years.

Note

1. The Development Program Implementation Study (DPIS) is a joint effort between the Harvard Institute for International Development and several institutions in Indonesia, with funding from the Government of Indonesia. It began in 1979. The principal participants from Harvard University are Donald Snodgrass, Marguerite Robinson, and myself. The major counterpart institution in Indonesia is the Economic and Human Resources Research Center at Padjadjaran University in Bandung. Other participating institutions include Satya Wacana University, Airlangga University, Hasanuddin University and Sriwijaya University.

References

Bennett, J.W. and Thaiss, G. (1967). Survey research and socio-cultural anthropology. In C.Y. Glock (Ed) *Survey Research in the Social Sciences*, Russell Sage Foundation, New York.

Campbell, D.T. and Fiske, D.W. (1959). Convergent and discriminant validation by the multi trait-multi method matrix, *Psychological Bulletin*, **56**, 82–105.

Cook, T.D. and Reichardt, C.S. (Eds) (1979). *Qualitative and Quantitative Methods in Evaluation Research*, Sage, Beverly Hills.

Cronbach, L.J. and Meehl, P.E. (1955). Construct validity in psychological tests. *Psychological Bulletin*, **52**, 281–302.

Cronbach, L.J. Rajaratnam, N. and Gleser, G.C. (1963). Theory of generalizability: a liberalization of reliability theory. *British Journal of Statistical Psychology*, **16(2)**, 137–163.

Elder, J.W. (1969). Caste and world view: the application of survey research methods. In M. Singer and B.S. Cohn (Eds) *Sturcture and Change in Indian Society*, pp. 173–186. Aldine, Chicago.

Garcia-Yangas, R. and Prill-Brett, J. (1978). *Cultural Values and Population Policy in the Phillipines: The Anthropological Study*, Institute of Philippine Culture, Ateneo de Manila University, Manila.

Khalaf, S. (1978). *Cultural Values and Population Policy in Lebanon*, paper prepared for the project on Cultural Values and Population Policies, Hastings Center, Hastings-on-Hudson, New York.

Leñero, O.L. (1979). *Valores Ideologicos y Politicas de Poblacion en Mexico*, Editorial Edicol, Mexico City.

Light, R.J. and Pillemer, D.B. (1982). Numbers and narrative: combining their strengths in research reviews. *Harvard Educational Review*, **52(1)**, 1–26.

Lipset, S.M. (1968). History and sociology: some methodological considerations. In S.M. Lipset, *Revolution and Counter-revolution*, pp. 3–28. Basic Books, New York.

Lopez, M.E., Nemenzo, A.M., Quisumbing-Baybay, L., and Lopez-Fitzpatrick, N. (1978). *Cultural Values and Population Policy in the Philippines: The Sociological Study*, Institute of Philippine Culture, Ateneo de Manila University, Manila.

Mahoney, M.J. (1976). *The Scientist as Subject*, Ballinger, Cambridge, Mass.

Malinowski, B. (1922). *Argonauts of the Western Pacific*, Routledge and Kegan Paul, London.

Malinowski, B. (1929). *Coral Gardens and their Magic*, Liveright, New York.

Marshall, J.F. (1972). *Culture and contraception: response determinants to a family planning program in a North Indian village*, unpublished doctoral dissertation, University of Hawaii.

Reichardt, C.S. and Cook, T.D. (1979). Beyond qualitative *versus* quantitative methods, In C.S. Cook and T.D. Reichardt (Eds), *Qualitative and Quantitative Methods in Evaluative Research*, pp. 7–32, Sage, Beverly Hills.

Schwab, W.B. (1954). An experiment in methodology in a West African urban community. *Human Organisation*, **13(1)**, 13–19.

Sieber, S. (1973). The integration of fieldwork and survey methods. *American Journal of Sociology*, **78**, 1335–1359.

Vansina, J. (1965). *Oral Tradition: A Study in Historical Methodology*, Routledge and Kegan Paul, London.

Vidich, A.J. and Shapiro, G. (1955). A comparison of participant observation and survey data. *American Sociological Review*, **20(1)**, 28–33.

Warwick, D.P. (1982). *Bitter Pills: Population Policies and Their Implementation in Eight Developing Countries*, Cambridge University Press, New York.

Warwick, D.P. and Lininger, C. (1975). *The Sample Survey: Theory and Practice*, McGraw-Hill, New York.

Whyte, W.F. (1976). Research methods for the study of conflict and cooperation. *American Sociologist*, **11**, 208–216.

Whyte, W.F. and Alberti, G. (1976). *Power, Politics and Progress*, Elsevier, New York.

Social Research in Developing Countries
Edited by M. Bulmer and D.P. Warwick
© 1983, John Wiley & Sons, Ltd.

CHAPTER 23

ON THE INTEGRATION OF RESEARCH METHODS

WILLIAM F. WHYTE
AND
GIORGIO ALBERTI

Introduction

This chapter reflects on a research programme which involved the use of several research methods. The programme was carried out in collaboration between the Institute de Estudios Peruanos (IEP) and Cornell University. José Matos Mar was the Peruvian co-director for IEP and William F. Whyte and Lawrence K. Williams the American co-director for Cornell. The co-ordinators for Cornell in Peru were Oscar Alers, for 1965–67 (see Chapter 15), Lawrence Williams for 1967–68 and Giorgio Alberti for 1968–75. The project involved joint and equal Peruvian–American cooperation at all stages. Fieldwork was carried out by Peruvian teachers and students of sociology, with support from Alers and Alberti.

The aim of the project was to study social change in rural Peru and is reported fully in Whyte and Alberti (1976). The study began within the framework of 'modernization theory', which views the rural peasant as naturally tradition-bound, fatalistic and inclined to resist change. In the course of research, this theory was abandoned in favour of a focus on structural change. Peasants were seen as men and women in motion in response to forces generated among themselves, as well as in response to external forces. The focus of analysis shifted from the purely local level to look at the impact of and response to external forces, and to link together the microlevel of community with the larger geographical, political and economic units of area, region and nation. As well as using survey and ethnographical data, historical materials became an important element in the evolving analysis.

Reprinted by permission of the publisher and the authors from W.F. Whyte and G. Alberti (1976). *Power, Politics and Progress: Social Change in Rural Peru* pp. 266–280, Elsevier, New York. © 1976, Elsevier North-Holland Inc.

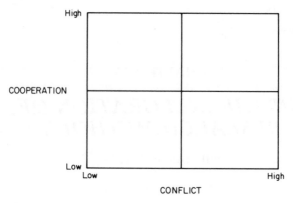

Figure 23.1: The Four Box Conflict-Cooperation Framework

Reference is made in the early part of the chapter to the author's four-box conflict–cooperation framework. This is shown diagramatically in Figure 23.1, which divides the conceptual space into four boxes, representing the crossing of two dimensions, cooperation (from high to low) and conflict (from high to low). The four boxes represent:

(1) high cooperation — low conflict
(2) low cooperation — high conflict
(3) high cooperation — high conflict
(4) low cooperation — low conflict.

The two concepts were measured empirically by survey instruments asking questions about peasants' perceptions of conflict and cooperation in their own villages (Whyte and Alberti, 1976, pp. 223–41). To map the twelve communities studied, the dividing line between high and low on each of the two dimensions was drawn at the mean values for conflict and for cooperation for the total of all the communities, as measured in the survey.

This brief introduction sets in context the discussion which follows, mainly concerned with the integration of methods of research in the project.

Our research programme was launched on the basis of a combination of methods: the survey, characteristicaly used by sociologists and social psychologists, and the interviewing/observational methods commonly used by social anthropologists. As we went along, we found ourselves also gathering extensive historical, economic, and political-bahaviour data.

This chapter presents what we have learned through the use of this array of methods. We seek to show not only the benefits of the use of such a combination of methods but also some of the shortcomings of our efforts, so that other behavioural scientists can learn from both our successes and our failures.

Combining surveys and anthropological field methods

Surveys and anthropoligical methods are customarily looked upon as rival research strategies (Whyte, 1964). (For convenience, we will call interviewing/ observational techniques 'anthropological methods', recognizing, of course, that they are used also by some sociologists and by some other behavioural scientists.) We believe that these two methods should be seen as complementary: the weaknesses of one are the strengths of the other.

The great value of the questionnaire is that it provides us with a large quantity of data at a relatively low cost (in comparison with other methods) and in a readily quantifiable form. But it is not an all purpose instrument. Generally if offers us data of two types: (1) demographic: sex, age, marital status, occupation, years of residence in the community, etc., for each respondent; and (2) the subjective state of the respondent: his attitudes, beliefs, and values regarding himself, his community, and the world around him.

The questionnaire generally gives us very little information regarding the particular events which make up the social processes of community life. The questionnaire can tell us how much confidence the respondents have in their municipal council. It cannot tell us how the councillors have acted to produce this degree of confidence.

Anthropological methods have two great values. They enable a good field worker to develop a relationship with his informants that permits him to penetrate their thoughts and to discover the sentiments that may not be expressed in response to standardized questions. They make possible a description of human activities and interactions and are thus essential for the examination of social processes and the social structure. . . .

With anthropological methods, quantification and standardization are not impossible, but we constantly face this dilemma: when we quantify and standardize, are we not in some way sacrificing the 'richness' of the flow of human events, which led us in the first place to use anthropological methods? However, this dilemma is serious only if we are committed to the exclusive use of anthropological field techniques.

If we use anthropological techniques for examining the culture, social processes, and the social structure and rely upon questionnaires to measure attitudes, values, and beliefs of our respondents, we will be using each method for the special contribution it can make.

The two methods offer different types of data, so that the validity of one type often cannot be fully tested by the other type, but in many cases the data from the two methods fit well together. We then have more confidence in our conclusions than we would have if we had depended solely on a single method. Apparent contradictions should not lead us to try to determine which method is telling us 'the real story'.

We use contradicitions as exercises in research methods, trying to understand the discrepancies, and seeking new data which may permit us to resolve problems of interpretation (Matos Mar and Whyte, 1966).

This combination of methods has proven useful in four stages of research: (1) developing the research design and instruments, (2) interpreting preliminary results, (3) determining future data-gathering needs, and (4) developing a theoretical framework.

Many of the survey items were designed to tap aspects of peasant life as they had been described in anthropological studies. The logic of the survey also led us toward comparative studies of a number of communities — although that logic, of course, did not determine how many communities would provide the necessary variety.

Two examples will illustrate the use of the two methods in the interpretation of preliminary results.

As one example, let us consider the responses in Pacaraos to the item, 'How much power does the *junta comunal* have to solve the problems of this village?' In Pacaraos, 23 per cent respond, 'all the power necessary' and 40 per cent respond, 'the power to do certain things but not others'. Do these figures suggest that the people of Pacaraos have much or little confidence in the power of their *junta comunal*? It might be argued that when 63 per cent of the villagers feel that the *junta* has either all the power necessary or the power to do some things but not others, this is a substantial vote of confidence in this local government institution. But when we look at the figures for Huayopampa and find that 90 per cent say that their *junta* has 'all the power necessary', we get a more valuable perspective on our figures. We still cannot say whether the Pacareños are expressing much or little confidence in the power of their junta, but we can say that the Huayopampinos have much greater confidence in the power of theirs. In other words, the responses to a survey item are not very useful until we compare one village with another, and such comparison requires some degree of standardization, which a survey provides.

As another example, past surveys had indicated that dynamic communities could be expected to show less respect for age and old people than stagnant ones. The finding that age was more respected in Huayopampa than in Pacaraos led us to speculate that the dynamism of Huayopampa was not a recent phenomenon and that people now old had played leading roles in moving that village ahead.

But note that in neither of these two cases did the survey data tell us the whole story. The item on the *junta comunal* did not tell us *why* respondents in the two communities perceived such great differences in the power of their local government. To answer that question, we had to observe the *junta* in action, examine community records, and interview *comuneros* about their local government. Similarly, regarding respect for age, we had to use anthropological methods to confirm our interpretation of survey measures and to trace the economic and social development of Huayopampa.

Our concern with the decline of cooperation and the rise of conflict in Huayopampa illustrates the value of our strategy both for determining future data-gathering needs and for developing a theoretical framework. A key problem for research design in any field is the determination of priorities. Especially in a broad-ranging research programme such as ours, there is no problem in finding 'interesting things' to study. The problem is to make rational decisions regarding the relative importance of these many interesting things.

This is a problem both of data and of theory. If we had not had the 1964–69 data on perceptions of conflict and cooperation in Huayopampa, we would not have recognized the magnitude of the changes that had taken place in that community. But these survey data by themselves did not influence our research priorities. When we reviewed the comparative marginals for all communities in the autumn of 1969, we did indeed note these conflict–cooperation changes, but our response to that finding was simply, 'Isn't that interesting'. At the time, we did not find the changes interesting enough to make further research in Huayopampa a matter of high priority.

It was only in 1973, after we had placed Huayopampa in our four-box conflict–cooperation framework, that we came to recognize the exceptional nature and the importance of the changes that had taken place in that community. And the four-box framework itself depended upon a combination of research methods. Although several of our anthropological field reports might have suggested the possibility of communities that were low in both conflict and cooperation or high in both characteristics, given the past unreliability of anthropological descriptions of peasant communities, we would hardly have rejected the single-continuum model solely on the basis of anthropological reports by student fieldworkers. Only as we turned to survey measures of conflict and cooperation did we see the possibility of developing the four-box model that has provided the framework for our interpretation of peasant communities.

On hard and soft data

In expositions on methods, it is customary to encounter the distinction between quantitative and qualitative, or between *hard* and *soft*, data. We are likely then to find that quantitative, or hard, data are those derived from a questionnaire or survey, whereas qualitative, or soft, data are those derived from the fieldwork of the anthropologist. People who make such distinctions are ready to credit the anthropologist with 'insights' that might point the real scientist toward new types of hard data, but they are inclined to consider the anthropologist more an artist than a scientist.

Applying this logic, we find than an individual's attitudes and opinions expressed in response to survey questions, when they have been coded and punched into cards, become hard data, whereas the fieldworker's observations of the actual behaviour of the same individual are considered soft data. Of course this is ridiculous.

What is involved here is not the question of hard versus soft data but rather the ease with which data can be quantified. Except for open-ended items, a questionnaire is so structured that responses automatically fit into quantitative form. The behaviour the fieldworker observes does not fall so readily into standard categories. The observer must establish his own categories or use categories established by others and then persuade critics that the observational guide permits a reasonable degree of objectivity and that another observer with the same observational guide (if conscientious and well trained) would categorize the same behaviour in a similar way.

Although establishing categories and coding behaviour within these categories is more difficult than placing survey responses into predetermined alternatives, various investigators have worked out methods that meet the test of reliability — producing similar results when the same method is applied by different observers (see, among others, Chappel et al., 1955; and Bales, 1950). The quantitative data gathered by anthropology students in our programme have depended less upon the direct observation of behaviour by fieldworkers than upon official records of behaviour of importance to the community: who did (and who did not) turn out for a given *faena*, who did (and who did not) attend the monthly community meeting, who did (and who did not) pay the fines levied for non-compliance with community obligations, and so on. Since these items of behaviour were of considerable importance to community members and leaders, we assume that the records kept would be accurate, and, indeed, on-the-spot observation by our fieldworkers confirmed this assumption. The most 'hard-nosed' survey expert can hardly deny that these are hard data. And they cannot be dismissed as trivial, for they provide us with essential information regarding community solidarity and the capacity of local government to implement its decisions.

The fieldworkers in Huayopampa and Pacaraos also developed a body of quantitative economic information: amount of land owned by each family, number of cows and sheep per family, occupation of family members, and income from farming and other sources. These data enabled us not only to measure the average difference in income between Huayopampa and Pacaraos but also to note the different shapes of the incomes pyramids for both communities.

Problems in the integration of methods

When reviewing the first reports submitted by the team of anthropology students after their intensive study of Huayopampa, Whyte was impressed by two aspects of their work: (1) the anthropological data confirmed the survey findings in all important respects, and yet (2) the students make no references to the survey data.

When Whyte raised these points in discussion with the team, one of the fieldworkers replied: 'Yes, we did know about the survey, and we looked at it before we started our field work. But we couldn't believe that answers to a questionnaire in a peasant village would have any real meaning, so we just decided to forget about the questionnaire when we did our anthropological study.'

Whyte pointed out that it was not too late to re-examine the survey so that their final report could draw upon both types of data. They agreed; yet, aside from token efforts, they did nothing to provide for such an integration.

Only a few of the students developed interest and competence in the analysis of both types of data. Many more students demonstrated their ability to produce first-rate anthropological field reports, but what integration of the two types of data we have been able to provide is based almost exclusively upon the work of senior staff members.

This problem is by no means limited to Peru. In the United States, students of sociology tend to have little interest in the soft data provided by anthropologists, and students of anthropology have distrusted the numbers coming out of surveys.

Nor were our shortcomings in methodological integration found solely on the side of anthropology. We now recognize that it was possible to make far more use of our anthropological field studies in order to link survey responses to social structure.

Although we did not have enough money or enough able students in all of our communities to make the intensive studies of family income and economic activities carried out in Huayopampa and Pacaraos, we could have built out of these studies short-cut methods to apply in other communities. For example, after a preliminary field study, with the help of key informants, the researcher could have identified the socioeconomic levels generally perceived in the community and representative families that fit into each level. If there were thought to be five levels, he could have undertaken to make intensive studies of the family economies of one family at each level. He could then have had key informants in the village place each respondent in the proposed survey in terms of the five levels and five representative families. When the respondent was surveyed, this socioeconomic placement could have been recorded on the questionnaire and punched into the data cards, along with information given by the respondent himself. The allocation of respondents in terms of these socio-economic levels could then have led to estimates of average income at each level. These estimates would have been much cruder than those derived from studies of each family, but they would have been better than information obtained directly from respondents by surveys, since questions from relative strangers about income, land and cattle ownership, etc., in a peasant community are likely to stir suspicion and give rise to inaccurate answers.

The approach outlined above would need to be field-tested. It is not presented here as a full answer to the methodological problems posed but rather as an illustration of the way we can learn from our field experience to devise short-cut methods that may produce more effective interdisciplinary research.

On the potentialities of anthropological field methods

Our emphasis upon the integration of methods may lead the reader to assume much more uniformity within anthropological methods than in fact exists. Social anthropologists generally gather their data through interviewing and observation, but there are, of course, enormous variations among them in what they are trying to find out and in the ways they work.

Let us make explicit the characteristics of our own use of anthropological methods. Many anthropologists are concerned with the study of culture, but we were primarily interested in the study of behaviour.

Culture

Culture is a concept subject to a board range of interpretations, so we shall have to specify the contrast we have in mind. One important line of anthropological work on culture focuses attention upon the beliefs and practices of a people as they explain them to each other and to outsiders. This leads to a normative emphasis — but the judgements are supplied by the informants and not super-imposed by the anthropologists. The fieldworker seeks to elicit from infor-mants a picture of how their society *ought* to operate; of the values they hold dear; of the obligations they recognize to kinsmen, to clan members, to the community, and so on.

An anthropologist with such interests observes that people's values and beliefs are acted out and reinforced in characteristic social and ceremonial activities. He observes and describes these activities. If several communities in the same general area share many beliefs and values and participate in similar social and ceremonial activities, he concludes that they share in a common culture and continues his efforts to describe the main features of that culture.

Such a focus on culture masks the differences among communities that are to be found at the behavioural level. In the Chancay highlands, there were 27 officially recognized indigenous communities. The similarities among them were important enough to justify considering all of them to be of one type. Spanish was the language spoken, there being few individuals who knew more than a few words of Quechua. They were all predominantly agricultural com-munities. They all had the same basic political structure: *personero, junta comunal*, monthly community meetings, etc. Each community had at least one patron saint and a fiesta system combining Catholic and folk religious elements. Each community had a system of communal labour known as the *faena*. In each community there existed a similar set of beliefs on how people ought to behave.

Such similarities are certainly important. An outsider who deals with any of these communities will need to have some knowledge regarding the ways in which they resemble each other. But if he fails to recognize significant differences among these communities, he makes a serious error. Huayopampa and Pacaraos differed from each other in such important ways as to present the prospective change agent with markedly different sets of problems, possibilities, and limitations. Lampiān had differed from both of these in the severity of its generational conflict.

The same statement can be made regarding the Mantaro valley. That the villages have much in common has long been recognized, yet we found striking differences between Mito, on the one hand, and Pucará and Cajas, on the other. Even between these latter two, differences in occupational structure and in the types of tenancy of church-owned lands, among other factors, contributed to differences in effectiveness in carrying out community projects. In our fourfold conflict–cooperation diagram, each of the three communities falls in a different box.

We must also deal with variability within a given village. The anthropologist dare not assume that interviews with any single individual will represent 'the true picture'. Nor is it sufficient to recognize differences in attitudes and behaviour that accompany age and sex differences. Some of the peasant communities we have studied are highly differentiated in terms of occupation, size of land holdings, and other factors. These lines of differentiation tend to be associated with differences in perceptions and beliefs as to what is good for the community and, therefore, with factional alignments.

We are not denying the existence of uniformities. We are saying that if the investigator begins with the assumption of homogeneity within communities and among communities in a given area, subsequent studies will reveal so much variability as to force him to start all over again. If that is the case, then it is better to start with the assumption of variability and then seek to discover the uniformities that lie beneath the variability.

The uniformities of concern to us are to be found on the level of behaviour. Many of the elements generally considered in cultural studies will enter our analysis in so far as they tend to specify the conditions of behaviour and to categorize the individuals who are behaving. It is unprofitable to seek to generalize about these cultural elements as such.

This focus on behaviour requires a sharp distinction between *what is* and *what ought to be* — whether the moral judgment is applied by the investigator or by members of the community under study. It is not enough to know what members of the community are supposed to do when the *junta comunal* decides upon a project for a *faena*. Conformity is not automatic. Whenever men's actions involve costs in time, effort, and/or resources, they cannot be elicited and maintained without a system of rewards for compliance and penalties for failure to comply.

Approval or disapproval by one's fellows can be a powerful sanction, but compliance will also depend upon material or physical sanctions for use on those who are not sufficiently motivated by the thoughts and feelings of others.

We are not suggesting the man acts solely in order to gain an immediate reward or to escape an immediate penalty. Social psychologists speak on the *internalization* of values. Through prior experience, the individual learns to do what he feels is right even when he perceives no offer of reward or threat of penalty. At the same time, the individual is aware of the extent to which those around him are meeting or failing to meet their obligtions. an occasional and isolated failure of others will have little effect upon the individual's own conception of his obligatons. But when increasing numbers of people are failing to comply, a person asks himself 'Why should I carry the load?' and soon we find him among the non-compliers. Evasion of duties becomes contagious, and social control breaks down.

It is of little scientific value to know how people think they and others should behave. In some communities (Huayopampa, for example), we found a high degree of correspondence between expressed norms and observed behaviour. In others (Pacaraos, for example), we found striking discrepancies between expressed norms and behaviour.

Nor is it enough to note such differences from community to community, if we are interested in the prediction and/or control of behaviour. We must ask: What sanctions are available to support normative behaviour? When someone deviates from the norms, who brings sanctions to bear, how, and with what results?

We are not dealing simply with a schedule of rewards and penalties. We must determine also in what ways and how effectively these sanctions are *applied*, as we have noted in comparing the effectiveness of Huayopampa and Pacaraos in collecting fines for the same types of offenses.

This emphasis upon the study of behaviour and its variability has been well stated by Frank Cancian in the following words (1955, pp. 2–3):

The use of extensive samples of individual behavior may be contrasted with two other approaches to the study of social structure: (1) the approach that generalizes about social structure on the basis of intensive analysis of a few 'crucial' cases, and therefore carries little information about the actual proportion of the population that follows any particular pattern; and (2) the approach that generalizes about social structure on the basis of information about norms, and therefore carries virtually no information about what people actually do. Many anthropologists are able to argue convincingly that the proper goal of a field study is the production of a report showing how the native system makes coherent sense as a way of looking at the world and a way of living. I cannot object to this goal, but I think that the usual way of attaining it leaves too much to the imagination of the anthropologist. The more powerful his intellect and imagination, the more likely the anthropologist is to use this power to create coherence, whatever the actual situation. Careful attention to extensive samples of behavior may help avoid these dangers.

On restudies and team research

In most cases, a study of a given community has been carried out by a single student, but in the Chancay valley project, with Huayopampa and Pacaraos, we had teams of four to five people in the community at the same time. The results have been sufficiently encouraging as to suggest the value of team efforts. A team can provide for a division of labour, with one individual examining the records of the communal government, observing *junta* meetings, and interviewing about local government activities while another student concentrates on the organization of the economic activities and upon the measurement of income. A team effort also provides for protection against the biases of a single individual. The members learn from each other as they spend hours, in the course of the field period, discussing and comparing their findings and arguing about their interpretations. For example, in the course of what was our *third* fieldwork period in this village, five able students spent 6 months in Huayopampa. We suspect that this team approach produced better results than would have come from the investment of the equivalent of $2\frac{1}{2}$ man-years on the part of an equally able single investigator.

We had originally hoped that during 1964 we would complete not only the surveys but also the anthropological studies in each of our villages. We did get several first-rate anthropological reports, but even the best of the reports had serious deficiencies. We recognized then that our original plan had been unrealistic. Although we had planned each year after 1964 for additional fieldwork in these villages, these new efforts were to be only brief expeditions for the purpose of checking anything that might have changed from the previous study during the year. However, instead of simply bringing each village up to date, we carried out full-scale restudies, designed to check the original findings, to fill in gaps, and to re-examine interpretations made on the basis of the orignal study.

In some cases, restudies revealed serious errors of the original studies. Our first study of one community described an unusual type of committee functioning under the local government. The restudy provided no information on this committee. When we checked with the research team of the restudy, we found that the committee in question did not exist and in fact had never existed. How could such a mistake be made? The student who did the first study described the committee on the basis of information given him by a single informant. This informant had a record for urging changes that frequently were not carried out. The minutes of the meetings of local government do record the establishment of the committee, but the idea was never implemented.

In another community, after making a much more careful and systematic examination of the economic aspects of community life, our restudy team developed figures to indicate that the first study's family income estimate was twice as large as it should have been.

It might be argued that such errors can be avoided by a single good anthropologist if he uses good methods. We agree that a well-trained and experienced anthropologist will bring in more adequate field data than beginning students, but this history of social anthropology should raise doubts about the wisdom of relying entirely upon the field reports of a single anthropologist, no matter how well trained or how large his professional reputation.

The checking and rechecking process also stimulated our students to raise their standards as to quality of their data. They explained to us, 'The information you had was simply wrong because the man who made the study got it from a single informant and did not check it with anybody else.' Or: 'Those original income estimates were just based on sloppy methods. We have talked with Fulano, and he himself has admitted that this part of his study was no good.' As students recheck the work of their predecessors, they have the incentive to raise their own standards of performance. As they prepare their reports, they must be inclined to look over their shoulders not only at the professors who will read their reports but also at future students who will follow them and check up on their work.

The quality of our studies has been improved by the writing of comparative descriptions and analyses about pairs or sets of communities. When a research director reads over reports on communities A and B, deficiencies may escape his attention until he is required to write a chapter comparing the two communities. He then finds that he has excellent information on one aspect of life in community A, but the information from community B on this aspect does not refer to some points considered important by the writers of the A report. For example, impressed by the Pacaraos report on the low frequency of collection of fines, we looked for comparable data in the Huayopampa monograph — and did not find any. Since Huayopampinos paid 100 per cent of their fines, collection did not seem a problem there and thus was not reported. When we compared the two villages, Huayopampa's success in collecting fines was clearly as important as Pacaraos's failure. Thus, the task of comparison enriched our understanding of the data needed for analysing the dynamics of community life.

On the uses of historical data

In the original outline for the field studies in anthropology, Whyte proposed that history be used simply to provide general background and that we should not trace the historical record beyond the last 50 years. Our students had too much interest in history to abide by this limitation. We now have data on land ownership and changes in tenure in the delta of the Chancay valley going back to the conquest of Peru. Similarly, the fieldworkers traced the history of Huayopampa and Pacaraos back to the conquest and developed an historical record of increasing detail for each subsequent century. This work has produced information of value in a neglected field, the development of rural Peru, but has it contributed anything beyond 'general background' to our present studies? We can point to several important contributions of history to our current understanding of these villages — and all of these go back beyond our original 50-year limit.

In the literature of sociology, anthropology, and community development, we generally find the rural community presented as a passive entity in relation to dynamic urban centres. Particularly if it is far removed from an urban centre, the village is seen as a tradition-bound unit, conserving its own culture and being inclined to resist interventions from the city. We doubt this picture even for more remote parts of rural Peru. The village records show that as much as 100 years ago, the people of Huayopampa and Pacaraos were making strenuous efforts to develop an educational system that would put them in touch with the modern world. The records provide frequent statements to the effect that the village should make such and such a change in order to put itself in harmony with modern (city) methods. History does indeed provide examples of men from the cities intervening in the local community, but in these cases it is clear that for at least 100 years, Huayopampinos and Pacareños have sought to integrate themselves more closely with the nation.

A striking example of the uses of history is provided by study of land distribution in Huayopampa and Pacaraos. By coincidence, final distribution of communal lands was begun in both villages in the year 1902. Whereas Pacaraos distributed this land to permanent ownership, Huayopampa retained title to the land and rented it out. We see, therefore, that the difference in the strength of community organization in the two villages can be traced back at least to the fateful decisions of 1902.

A researcher who looked only at the material resources available for development today would find no clues to the decadence and stagnation of Mito and the dynamism of Pucará and Cajas. It was only as Alberti traced the political decline and dismemberment of Mito and the gain in political position of Pucará and Cajas that the differences in present conditions and future prospects became understandable.

We find history an important corrective for a form of myopia common among behavioural scientists. The most popular research techniques focus upon present-time data and provide the researcher with a static picture of the scene under study. Since the researcher knows that human beings act through time, he seeks to infer from his data what may have happened in the past, but he is on shaky ground when he tried to draw dynamic conclusions from static data. History is a discipline organized in terms of time sequences. Few historians try to establish the generalizations of interest to the behavioural scientist, but we can exploit the diachronic focus of history to bring to life the social processes that are vital to our understanding of community life.

References

Bales, R.F. (1950). *Interaction Process Analysis*, Addison-Wesley, Cambridge, Mass.

Cancian, F. (1955). *Economics and Prestige in a Maya Community*, Stanford University Press, Palo Alto.

Chappel, E.D. *et al*. (1955). Behavioral definitions of personality and temperament characteristics. *Human Organisation*, **13** (4).

Matos Mar, J. and Whyte, W.F. (1966). *Projecto de Estudios de Cambios en Pueblos Peruanos*, Instituto de Estudios Peruanos, Lima.

Whyte, W.F. (1964). High level manpower for Peru. In C. Myers and F.H. Harbison (Eds) *Manpower and Education*, McGraw-Hill, New York.

Whyte, W.F. and Alberti, G. (1976). *Power, Politics and Progress: Social Change in Rural Peru*, Elsevier, New York. (available from the Center for International Studies, Cornell University, Ithaca, New York 14853).

SECTION VII

ETHICAL AND POLITICAL ISSUES IN SOCIAL RESEARCH

Social Research in Developing Countries
Edited by M. Bulmer and D.P. Warwick
© 1983, John Wiley & Sons, Ltd.

CHAPTER 24

THE POLITICS AND ETHICS OF FIELD RESEARCH

DONALD P. WARWICK

Whatever its disciplinary and institutional origins, field research in the social sciences inevitably raises questions of politics and ethics. Politics in one form or another impinges on a study from the initial choice of a topic to the final interpretations made of the results. And no field research, whether a sample survey, an observational study, or even the secondary analysis of existing data, is immune to such ethical questions as informed consent, harm resulting from research findings, and policy recommendations based on flimsy evidence. Studies crossing national borders or cultural boundaries within the same country raise all the ethical and political issues seen with single-culture research and others as well. Whereas a field project carried out in one nation may arouse controversy because of its perceived links to contending domestic interests, a cross-national study can readily play into and aggravate disputes tied to international politics. Project Camelot remains the paradigm for international conflicts touched off by social science research, but it is not the only case that could be cited.[1] And the special circumstances of cross-cultural research, whether across or within countries, raise ethical questions that are different in degree, and sometimes in kind, from those seen in unicultural projects.

The present discussion and the chapters that it introduces focus on ethical and political issues that are more or less distinctive of field research in the developing countries. (For more detailed essay on these topics see Warwick (1980). The following discussion draws on that source.) The main emphasis is on studies in a developing country that involve funding, personnel, conceptual frameworks, or methodologies from outside that country. As the chapter by Zuñiga (Chapter 25) makes eminently clear, one need not have foreign staff physically present to incur the wrath of political critics for ideologically biased research. His experience during the Allende period in Chile showed that the political slanting of entire disciplines — in that case psychology — can provoke sharp clashes over approaches to research. This chapter will also consider

315

political and ethical issues arising when researchers from one part of society, particularly the dominant group, attempt to study other groups, particularly minority groups, in the same society. The two foci of this section come together when foreign funding and/or personnel are used in a study involving data gathered by one social group on others.

A basic premise in this chapter is that the politics and ethics of cross-national and cross-cultural field research are analytically distinguishable but closely connected in practice. *Politics* refers to interactions revolving around power, influence, and authority. Research is political to the extent that it affects the ability of individuals or groups to impose their will, to pursue their interests, or to be seen as legitimate authorities. *Ethics* deals with questions of moral goodness or evil and with the proper standards for human action. The politics of research raises problems of ethics particularly when the use of power, influence, and authority causes harm to persons or groups or serves the interests of some at the expense of others. Ethical issues can become political when, for example, infringements on the rights of individuals, groups, or even countries become a source of controversy or demands for regulation.

Research Politics

The politics of field research in a given developing country depends on the specific political context of that country, the state of international politics, and the links between the two. The greater the polarization in domestic politics and the greater the association between the research project and the principal points of contention, the more likely is there to be controversy about the project. Consider the probable reception of a survey on attitudes toward birth control in countries *A* and *B*. Country *A* is a relatively small, ethnically homogeneous nation which has been ruled for many years by the same government. Domestic disputes do arise, but they are readily accommodated within the political system and are not closely connected to the issue of birth control. Country *B*, by contrast, is one of the largest in its region, is badly divided along ethnic lines, and has had a record of political instability. While often quelled by military governments, domestic political debate is turbulent and closely tied to ethnic group interests. One of the charges often made by critics of the government is that the largest ethnic group is plotting to impose a national scheme of birth control to hold down the numbers of the smaller groups. Other things being equal, we would expect that in country *A* it would be politically more feasible to conduct a survey on attitudes toward birth control than in country *B*, where that question is linked to the divisive issue of ethnic dominance.

A similar point can be made about the interplay of field research, domestic politics, and international relations. Assume that in country *A* the survey on birth control is sponsored by a Scandinavian country which is relatively inconspicuous on the international scene and with which the country has enjoyed two decades of amicable relations. In country *B* a similar survey is being promoted, financed, and organized by the western nation which, until two decades earlier, had been the colonial power in that region. In addition to its links to ethnic group politics, a survey on birth control could evoke images of colonialism ('they are trying to keep us from being a major power by keeping our numbers down'), racism ('they don't want too many non-white people in the world') or even genocide ('what they once did with slavery they are now doing with birth control').[2] It is again very likely that the survey in question would meet with much less resistance in country *A* than in country *B*. To the extent that the opposition in country *B* could credibly link the study of birth control to support by the western nation for the dominant ethnic group, the obstacles to acceptance would be even greater.

The point here is that the political reactions to a given field study are often situation-specific. An American-sponsored project in Indonesia will typically raise a different set of issues than an identical project in Latin America, and even there political contexts vary considerably. The fact of American sponsorship will typically be more of a political liability in Latin America than in Indonesia and, within Latin America, usually more controversial in Mexico than in Paraguay. Those about to fund or conduct studies in countries other than their own would do well, on both political and ethical grounds, to pay close attention to the unique configuration of interests and issues in each setting.

Despite substantial variations across countries and regions, there are generic issues of research politics that come up in most cross-national and cross-cultural field studies. And even when they do not surface overtly during the course of a project they may lurk in the background as constraints or as unstated but implicitly recognized sources of support. For example, the fact that a project is sponsored by the US Agency for International Development, the foreign aid unit of the US government, may not be raised as an explicit political issue during negotiations over the design and implementation of a sample survey. Still, both the American participants and their counterparts in the developing country may recognize that such sponsorship is a political drawback to the research and one that could, in a worst-case scenario, bring the study to a halt. Therefore, without ever mentioning the matter of sponsorship those involved in the negotiations may design the study in such a way that it does not lend ammunition to potential enemies. A review of the politics of research in the developing countries over the past three decades suggests the following as the major points of contention or areas of political influence.

Sponsorship

The sponsorship and auspices of research will often be issues in themselves and influence other aspects of the research process. In the wake of Project Camelot almost any piece of social science research sponsored by the US Department of

Defense, regardless of its intent and content, will be controversial in most developing countries. Opponents will say that no matter what its design and how 'pure' it is as science, any work financed by the Defense Department must have an overt or covert military purpose. And the vehemence of the reactions to this funding source will be directly proportional to the salience of the US military intervention as an issue in the country or region. In the Latin American area, which has experienced US military incursions first-hand, the matter will be more sensitive than in West Africa, which has had no such interventions. In other cases the sponsor's image can be a distinct asset for research, even facilitating studies that would be politically difficult or impossible without such support. The most obvious case is the United Nations and its specialized agencies which typically, though not always, carry the image of political neutrality and professional legitimacy. In the field of population studies the United Nations has sponsored field research, such as the World Fertility Survey, which in some countries would be politically risky for governments to undertake on their own initiative.

In their relations with the implementers of field research, sponsors cover the gamut from the zealous promotion of a single mission to utter timidity in the face of potential controversy. Some donors make it known, directly or indirectly, that they want not only results, but results of a certain kind. For over a decade the Office of Population of the US Agency for International Development was known as a sponsor with a decided preference for results showing the feasibility and efficacy of family planning programmes in the developing countries. Fairly or not, many recipients of its funds felt that their chances of additional funding would be much better if they came up with the desired pattern of results rather than data that were ambiguous about the value of family planning. At the opposite extreme were several United Nations agencies that seemed afraid of even the slightest controversy about population matters, and thus gave their implicit blessing to blandness. (For a specific example of UN resistance to controversy see the Preface to Warwick, 1982a.) These preferences and proclivities of research sponsors can, and often do, affect the conceptualization, design, methodology, interpretation, and uses of field research.

Research topic

Some topics will almost inevitably stir controversy in developing countries, and doubly so if brought in under the aegis of certain sponsors. Much depends on the local and international political context, but there are few developing countries in which field research on abortion, political corruption, and tax evasion would not be sensitive. As Beals (1969) points out,

It appears that potentially any study of politicalization, political attitudes or behavior, political parties or factions, or governmental policies may be sensitive, especially if social tensions are high . . . . Whether a study is judged to be sensitive often depends on the political relations of the investigator and, in the case of foreign investigators, the home and host countries.

The single most explosive study ever undertaken in the developing countries was the ill-fated Project Camelot. There the conjunction of an inflammatory topic (domestic insurgency) and a disputed sponsor (the US Army) touched off a political outburst whose repercussions can still be felt. The project itself was to be a multimillion-dollar study whose aim was to develop sophisticated social science models for predicting and explaining social conflict and social change in the developing countries. While still in the design stage Camelot created a furore in 1965 when a Chilean-born social scientist tried to explore the interest of Chilean colleagues in this undertaking. The press in Chile and elsewhere quickly lambasted the project and its design as a thinly veiled manifestation of American militarism. Faced with an outpouring of hostilities to the study and its sponsors, the Army cancelled the project and the US State Department was given responsibility for reviewing all federally financed overseas research projects. To this day the phrase 'Project Camelot' conjures up images of political ineptitude in the conduct of cross-national research and is used as a shibboleth by those opposed to foreign sponsorship of social science initiatives in the developing countries.

In Chapter 27, Kleymeyer and Bertrand show how the combination of an explosive topic, a hasty entry and local politics can produce devastating effects for a community study (see pages 365–77). The site was a Latin American city, the topic the attitudes of female slum dwellers toward birth control, and the researchers three visiting North Americans. With little groundwork and apparently not much attention to the political climate of the slum, the research team set out on their study of birth control. Before long they found themselves in the midst of accusations that they were not really researchers but rather agents for sterilizing children during a government-sponsored antimeasles vaccination campaign. As concrete evidence to support their charges community leaders came forth with a bottle of measles vaccine bearing the English word 'Sterile'. The authors candidly show how these misunderstandings arose from the confluence of local politics, errors by the researchers on such matters as where they lived, the brevity of their visit, and various unfortunate coincidences. Their analysis suggests that the concrete meaning of a research topic in a given area depends as much on the connotations it takes on from local interpretations as from the denotations laid out by well-intentioned researchers.

Staffing and collaboration

Political considerations may also enter into the selection of research staff and subsequent collaboration among those chosen (see, for example, Portes,

1975). International donors as well as national sponsors may press hard to have certain researchers be responsible for the study. Their reasons could include a sincere belief that the persons in question are the most qualified; a conviction that these individuals will come up with the 'right' answers or otherwise cause no trouble; a desire to reward political favorites for past services rendered; and the desire to spread research assignments across different institutions or parts of the country. United Nations agencies will be under strong pressure to employ local personnel to the extent possible, even when some of these individuals are not especially well-qualified for the work at hand. In one study sponsored by the United Nations Fund for Population Activities (UNFPA) a government agency in Canada insisted that, to the extent possible, funding for the project go directly to participating institutions in the developing countries rather than to an American coordinating organization (this sequence of events is discussed further in the Preface to Warwick, 1982a). When the UNFPA followed that advice, the cost was a complex process of research clearances that set the project back by more than a year.

Particularly delicate political issues arise in research projects involving collaboration between scholars from North America or Europe and the developing countries. More often than not the basic concept, if not the specific design, of the research has been established before the local collaborators are brought on board. Such arrangements are difficult to avoid, if only because one needs a project to obtain the funding necessary to seek the local collaborators. But the structure of such projects has built-in difficulties, especially when the collaborators are well-qualified social scientists who could contribute significantly to the project's design and who may resent being left out. Still other problems emerge when local social scientists agree to do the research and accept funds for that purpose, but then deliver little or nothing. In that situation the foreign coordinator is in the difficult position of trying to exert pressure for results without destroying the collaborative relationships that may be necessary for the project's continued legitimacy in the country. Form (1973) discusses problems of this kind experienced in his cross-national study of automobile workers. Other studies leave a more positive impression of the dynamics of collaboration (see, for example, Holtzman, Diaz-Guerrero, and Schwartz, 1975; Triandis et al., 1972).

Access

Some of the most thorny political problems in cross-cultural research arise around the question of access to the field. With cross-national studies the first challenge is in getting into the countries involved, and sometimes this is far from easy. In the Project on Cultural Values and Population Policy, the United Nations Fund for Population Activities decided that formal approval from the respective governments would have to be obtained for the countries serving as major studies and informal approval for those serving as secondary sites (for additional details see the Preface to Warwick, 1982a). Among the first set, approval was gained immediately for one country and delayed for a year or more in the other three. In these three cases the principal reason for the delay was some form of bureaucratic politics. In one there were apparently tensions between the proposed research director and one of the government agencies involved in the clearance process. In another disputes arose over who was to receive the research funds and in the third the research subcommittee of the clearing body insisted on a detailed rationale for the study and further details on research design. Among the countries originally proposed for smaller studies one was vetoed by the local representative of the United Nations on the grounds that the topic was too controversial. Despite their appearance of bureaucratic neutrality, such clearance processes frequently open the door to personal and institutional jealousies and other forms of domestic politics.

Even when approval has been granted for the project as a whole clearance may have to be obtained from local authorities before fieldwork can be undertaken. The government of Indonesia, is, on the whole, quite open to social research, but sensitive about studies conducted in rural areas. Thus a project calling for interviewing, anthropological observation, or other field work in villages will usually need the specific approval of officials in the regional government. And even when permission is granted it may be suspended for certain periods, such as the weeks immediately preceding the national elections. Before the congressional elections in May 1982, an instruction from the Minister of Home Affairs specifically called for the cessation of field research for the two preceding months.

The politics of access can become highly complex when field research is to be conducted on minority or ethnic groups. Access will be most difficult when the study deals with groups that have been oppressed or exploited by the larger society, when the research topics are sensitive within the group, when the political leadership of the group is ambiguous or divided, and when the group's experience with the type of research in question has been negative. As Joan Moore notes in connection with her research on Mexican-Americans (1967, p. 225):

In a general way, the minority sits inside a delicate and complicated structure of political and moral postures. Imbedded in this structure are the group's deepest aspirations and frustrations. To enter this fabric, no matter how gently, means that this structure of frustration and aspiration is somehow altered.

Moore goes on to note that even very careful arrangements are no guarantee of trouble-free access. Though she and her colleagues went to great lengths in consulting the Mexican-American community and in establishing an all-Mexican Community Advisory Board, political problems still arose.

In recent years minorities as widely separated in distance as the Hesquiat band of Indians in Canada and the Aborigines of Australia have made very similar demands concerning access by researchers to their groups. In brief, these and other groups are demanding more control over what is studied and by whom, and are insisting on tangible benefits from the research for the communities involved (Effrat and Mitchell, 1974, pp. 405–407). Such pressures affect not only the possibilities of field research but the topics open to study, the methodologies used, and ultimately the nature of the findings. Zuñiga (Chapter 25) likewise notes the drastic implications for psychological research of a regime strongly committed to popular participation. The politics of access can thus affect not only the entry of a research group to conduct a given study, but also the content, method, and style of that study.

Conceptualization and research design

The politics of research can further affect the conceptualization of the problem to be studied, the choice of methodology, the specific design used for data collection, the wording of questions, the extent of quality control in the field, and other aspects of the research process. The degree and kind of political influence varies from study or study, but it is always present to some extent. Field research in the developing countries is particularly susceptible to influences arising from donor agencies, which may have a particular programmatic mission to advance through the research, from domestic politics, and from rivalries among social scientists working in the same general area, such as population or agriculture. In Chapter 26 Warwick documents some of these influences in the case of the Knowledge–Attitude–Practice (KAP) survey.

Chapter 25 by Ricardo Zuñiga provides one of the most vivid discussions now available on the political antecedents and consequences of conceptualization. One of his central points is that the discipline of psychology as taught in the United States is so deeply 'American' in concept and method that it is difficult to apply in a Latin American setting, particularly one undergoing revolutionary change.

A problem that was specific to psychologists and that made their integration among the social sciences very difficult was the cultural homogeneity of their training or, to put it more bluntly, the unanalyzed 'Americanness' of their science. Much of the professional arsenal of Chilean psychologists was not only culturally relative but culturally dependent. . . . The ethnocentrism in the training of American psychologists which is ever-present but irrelevant for all practical purposes suffers a radical qualitative transformation when it is mechanically transported to a different cultural context. What was only a localized deficiency becomes a universalistic ideology and an unconscious (or guilt-ridden) advocacy of a cultural intrusion that is often extremely naive (see below, page 338).

Zuñiga specifically notes the political implications of a person-centred or even person-blaming defintion of social problems:

> ... the redefinition of a social problem in terms of the attribution of centrality to psychological variables usually implies a radical shift in the object of inquiry. Since the definition of the problem determines the research strategy, the selection of a social action delivery system, and the criteria for evaluation, a tendency to assign causal significance to person-centered variables produces a significant shift in understanding (see below, page 341).

The practical implication in Chile during the Allende period was that research growing out of this conceptual tradition clashed head-on with an entirely different notion of social change, one that put much heavier emphasis on structures and contexts than on the characteristics of individuals.

Political concerns, including those emanating from funding agencies, may also bear on the choice of methodology for a given study and every other aspect of data collection. Donors interested in rapid results that can be easily summarized may press for a research design involving a sample survey, a prestructured questionaire that calls for a little probing, brief interviews, and only cursory quality control. As Warwick notes in Chapter 26 such donor pressures, often combined with the personal commitments of researchers to family planning, may have contributed to the 'quick and dirty' quality of many KAP surveys. At the opposite extreme from such mission-oriented research are studies in which the interests of sponsors are served by results showing a highly mixed pattern of outcomes. The need for muddy data is particularly strong in evaluation studies in which administrators may be blamed for poor performance if the results on that front are very clearly negative. The expedient answer may be a research design allowing the collection of a variety of data, including qualitative observations. When the results from such research are finally in it may be very difficult for critics *or* supporters to say anything very definitive about what was produced by the programme under scrutiny.

Interpretation and dissemination

Political influence is often particularly heavy at the point where the findings of field research undergo interpretation and some form of dissemination. Pressures to produce a particular pattern of results or a specific policy recommendation are especially strong when the research is linked to a highly visible or controversial question of public policy; when the funding agency or other sponsor is identified with a particular policy line, such as cooperatives, birth control, or non-formal education; and when the researchers themselves are part of an interest group or even lobby urging a certain kind of policy. Even a cursory review of the history of KAP surveys will show that in several countries those responsible for conducting and interpreting the research were among the most visible academic proponents of governmental action on family planning. While advocacy is not incompatible with objectivity in research, the temptation to accentuate findings favouring one's preferred views and to play down other results will be great. In Chapter 26, Warwick argues that the results of KAP surveys were regularly and systematically overinterpreted to show the existence of client demand for family planning.

Some of the most vehement battles over social research in the developing countries take place around the question of disseminating controversial findings. In highly repressive countries the question may never come to a head for the simple reason that the researchers decide unilaterally not to publish potentially critical data. Elsewhere government agencies may refuse to grant permission for publication or dissemination of research results or even put pressure on the investigators to change the findings. These manifestations of research politics are seen to some extent in every country, but when, as in some developing countries, there is no tradition of academic freedom and governments maintain tight control over most kinds of publication, the costs for research objectivity can be very high. The situation is so extreme in some cases, such as in Iran under the Shah, that one would be unwise even to commission a potentially controversial study in an area of concern to the government.[3] Unfortunately, for the very reasons leading to censorship by self or others, there are few cases available to document the effects of such repression on social science research. Scholars remaining in the countries are typically fearful of discussing such matters, while those outside may be embarrassed to admit that they capitulated to political pressures on their research.

The ethics of cross-cultural research

The foregoing discussion of research politics leads directly to the question of ethical standards for cross-national and cross-cultural research projects. To what extent should sponsors be allowed to influence the design and interpretation of social research? Should some research topics be avoided, particularly when they are likely to touch off domestic or international controversy? What standards should govern the researcher's access to the group being studied? What are the responsibilities of a foreign social scientist to national colleagues working on the same project? Does the social scientist have any moral obligations concerning the conceptualization, design, and execution of a field study? What standards should apply to the analysis, interpretation, and dissemination of research findings, particularly in areas of controversy or sensitive matters of public policy? Recent articles by Tapp *et al*. (1974), Warwick (1980), and by Kleymeyer and Bertrand (1980) have addressed these and other questions of ethics in the specific context of cross-cultural research, and all have proposed concrete standards of ethics. An essay by Warwick and Pettigrew (1982) likewise analyses the distinctive problems arising in the application of social science research to public policy and offers some provisional ethical guidelines for that area. Here I can do little more than note the main areas of concern expressed in discussions of research ethics and show the general directions of the ethical standards suggested to date.

Commentators on the ethics of cross-cultural research have focused on four main topics: (1) the professional relations between the researchers and others involved in organizing and conducting the research; (2) the obligations of the researchers to the populations studied: (3) the professional standards that should govern study design and data-collection; and (4) the standards that should apply to the analysis, interpretation, and diffusion of social science data. The first two topics have received the greatest attention in the literature, but all four are relevant to the present discussion.

Professional relations

The single most frequent topic in discussions of cross-cultural research ethics has been the relationships between foreign scholars and local collaborators in the developing countries (Adams, 1969; Portes, 1975; Whyte, 1969). Much of the concern behind these discussions arose from allegations that well-financed outsiders had employed local social scientists as 'hired hands' or otherwise treated them in a demeaning manner. To prevent such abuses and to promote effective working relations among scholars from different countries, Tapp *et al.* (1974), Warwick (1980) and Kleymeyer and Bertrand (1980), recommend genuine collaboration in the conceptualization and design of a cross-cultural project. Drawing on his extensive experience in Peru, Whyte (1969, p. 28) further argues that foreign scholars working in developing countries '. . . give as much thought to developing more effective models of international research collaboration as we do to our own research design and data analysis'. Warwick (1980, pp. 359–360) also suggests that cross-cultural studies incorporate mechanisms for surfacing ethnocentrism and political biases; that all collaborators be informed of the sponsorship, funding sources, purposes, and intended uses of the research; that social scientists should not agree to take part in a study unless they are in a position to honour the time commitments and standards of quality required; and that publication agreements should be discussed early in the study, be the subject of mutual agreement among all collaborators, and take account of varying national and local circumstances. In some cases it might be agreed that publication within the country will be delayed or even suspended if it is likely to bring serious harm to the researcher or others connected with the research. Given the hostility with which certain kinds of social science research are viewed in highly repressive countries, such cautions are well-advised.

Future discussions of ethics might also take up the question of relations between sponsors or funders and the researchers. The development of suitable ethical guidelines would require a more careful analysis of the issues at stake than has been seen thus far. Most observers would concede that funders have the right to support those kinds of research that they consider important, even if the range covered is limited. The more difficult questions come up when, within a given conceptual or methodological tradition, donors put pressure on the researchers to move in certain directions. Most would consider it improper for funding agencies to insist on research strategies obviously violating professional norms of data-gathering, such as using loaded questions or deliberately leaving out critical areas of information. But short of that extreme there are areas of negotiation whose outcome bears directly on the research process and whose morality is by no means obvious.

Obligations to the population studied

The most general obligations of researchers to the population studied are to be truthful, to avoid physical or mental harm, and to show respect. While those obligations apply to any kind of social science research, their application to a cross-national or cross-cultural project often requires special care and sensitivity to contexts. For example, certain kinds of interviewing practices followed in the United States, such as having a male interviewer speak privately to a female respondent for an hour or more, might be considered offensive or worse in traditional Islamic societies. In such circumstances showing respect to the respondents and the society might mean radically altering the procedures for data collection developed in the United States or Europe. The following are some specific suggestions that have been made for ethically acceptable cross-cultural studies (The section is a paraphrase of Warwick, 1980, pp. 361–364.)

(1) Researchers should avoid actions violating the ethical standards or cultural understandings of the group being studied. The case cited above would be one example.

(2) In their conceptualization, design, and execution projects should show sensitivity to each political and cultural situation. Studies should avoid questions or techniques that are likely to be offensive, poorly understood or perceived locally as nonsensical. Research should not be carried out if the chances are high that it will set off internal conflicts, polarize the population studied, or be widely misunderstood. The kinds of conflict brought on by the Latin American birth control survey mentioned earlier serve as a negative illustration of sensitivity and respect (see Chapter 27 below).

(3) Research participants should be informed of the general purposes, funding source, and, if relevant, other sponsorship of the project. Such disclosure is especially important when the sponsor or funding source is, or could easily become, highly controversial in ways that may harm the participants. In

some cases it may not be possible to provide meaningful explanations about sponsorship and the like to all participants, particularly those who are illiterate or simply unfamiliar with such matters as field research. In those circumstances the study should at least be explained clearly to community leaders or others who can pass the information along in appropriate ways to the participants. Respect for culture implies a willingness to adapt all research procedures, including the explanation of the study, to local situations.

(4) The study should take culturally appropriate steps to ensure informed consent and to avoid invasions of privacy. Where potential participants have little understanding of social research — a common situation in the rural areas of the developing countries — it may be necessary to use 'cultural interpreters' to explain the study in terms that are locally intelligible. Given the wide cross-cultural differences in the value and meaning of privacy, great care must be taken on that front as well.

(5) The research experience should not cause physical, mental, social, or political harm to participants, including embarrassment, demeaning treatment, damage to one's reputation, anxiety, or reprisals from the government. Researchers must be especially sensitive to the political dangers that may befall participants in extremely repressive systems. Experiences in Argentina and Chile over the past decade suggest that it is no longer far-fetched to be concerned about the lives of informants in certain kinds of politically sensitive research.[4]

Professional standards in research

Recent discussions of research ethics, especially in public policy, have paid increasing attention to the standards of the 'craft' that should prevail in field studies. The issue of quality is most acute in studies with high aspirations for policy impact, for there the question of relevance is not academic. If the future of an entire area of agricultural, educational, or population policy hinges to a large extent on the results of a social science evaluation of existing programmes, the stakes are high and the issue of data quality central. With such situations in mind Warwick and Pettigrew (1982) have proposed guidelines such as the following for social science research related to public policy:

(1) Within the limits of available resources the most powerful methods appropriate to the problems should be chosen. In complex areas of policy or where public debate about the research findings is likely to occur, multiple rather than single methods should be used.

(2) The samples drawn, whether of individuals, households, communities, events, or other populations, should be representative of the populations about which generalizations will be made. In reporting the findings

researchers should also provide detailed information about the sample and make clear its limitations for the interpretations made about policy.

(3) The items used in questionnaires or interview guides should not be leading, loaded, or otherwise contribute to response bias. The questioning process should also have the depth necessary to address the policy-related concerns of the study.

(4) Researchers should avoid known sources of bias in causal attribution (for example, regression artifacts). Where such sources of bias cannot be avoided in the research design, investigators should make every effort to limit the bias in their analysis, discuss the problem openly, and restrict their interpretations accordingly.

In one sense these standards do not have any special bearing on the cross-national and cross-cultural studies discussed here, for they apply across-the-board to all policy-related research. But in another sense they deserve to be taken particularly seriously in cross-cultural studies, for there the danger of slips in quality is especially high. When, as is the case in many of the poorest countries, the materials available for random sampling are limited and the options for remedying the situation are few, extra care must be taken to analyse the biases flowing from the samples used. The same point applies to the quality of interviewing and field supervision, coding, and other operational aspects of field research. And when political, administrative, or other constraints make key respondents hesitant to disclose critical problems in the politcs under study, the norms proposed for the validity of interview data take on particular force.

Analysis, interpretation, and dissemination of findings

A final area of ethical concern has to do with the way in which social science data are analysed, interpreted, and presented to the public. On the issue of analysis the main obligation of researchers is to be faithful to their data. Whatever the pressures from self or others, researchers should not draw conclusions that are not supported by their data nor fail to carry out analyses that are directly germane to the questions at hand. Further, unqualified statements about the population should not be made on the basis of data from samples, and significant variations or nuances in the findings should not be compressed into oversimplified summaries.

The main ethical abuses seen with the interpretation of social science data are overinterpretation, including the simplification of complex research findings, and drawing policy recommendations whose normative and empirical foundations are not clearly separated. With the KAP survey ambiguous data derived from flawed questionnaire items and dubious interviewing procedures were often portrayed as showing a strong 'latent demand' for family planning.

An accurate interpretation would have paid more attention to the limits of the questions used and the difficulties posed by rapid interviews with women who in many cases had little understanding of any social science research. And the logical extension of overinterpreted data is a 'policy recommendation' firmly supported by the research at hand. In the case of the KAP survey the most common recommendation was that governments establish voluntary family planning programmes to meet the demand indicated by the KAP surveys. But there and in many other studies the researchers failed to distinguish between the facts established by the research and the values adduced to support a recommendation for governmental action. For obvious political reasons, researchers often try to create the impression that policy implications are based entirely on science rather than personal, social, or political values. Even the assumption that the government should act to meet the stated demand of women for family planning services implies a value judgment about governmental actions that many would not accept *a priori*. In their paper on social science research and public policy Warwick and Pettigrew (1982) specifically suggest that the values lying behind policy recommendations be stated honestly and openly rather than hidden in language connoting a purely scientific basis for the proposed actions.

The chapters in this section explore various aspects of the politics and ethics of social research in the developing countries. The essay by Zuñiga offers a powerful commentary on the cross-cultural limitations of social science, particularly psychology. By contrasting the assumptions and practices of the social science in which he was trained with the revolutionary situation in Allende's Chile, he vividly illustrates how latent ideologies can create manifest political difficulties for the social scientist. In Chapter 26 Warwick follows with an analysis of the politics and ethics of perhaps the single most frequent form of cross-national survey research: the KAP survey. He argues that the politics of promoting family planning in the developing countries led to an actual decline in the quality of survey research on matters related to fertility. Both this decline and the uses made of KAP data raise significant questions of professional ethics.

Notes

1. The best source on Project Camelot remains I.L. Horowitz (1967); see also Deitchman (1976). Another controversial study involving social research was the Himalayan Borders Country Project carried out by the University of California and funded in part by the Department of Defense. This is discussed in Berreman (1969).
2. Field research conducted through the Project on Cultural Values and Population Policy showed that, in fact, such issues did arise when a national family planning programme was launched in Kenya; see Warwick (1982a), especially Chapter 6.
3. As Project Manager for the Hasting Center's eight-nation Project on Cultural Values and Population Policies I had occasion to explore the feasibility of objective field research in Iran. At that time (1974) my conclusion, based on observation as well as conversations with Iranians,

was that any study critical of national policy would be difficult to carry out and even more difficult for Iranians to publish.
4. For a more detailed discussion of the types of harm arising from social research see Warwick (1982b).

References

Adams, R.N. (Ed.) (1969). *Responsibilities of the Foreign Scholar to the Local Scholarly Community*, Education and World Affairs Publications, New York.

Beals, R.L. (1969). *The Politics of Social Research*, Aldine, Chicago.

Berreman, G.D. (1969). Not so innocent aborad. *The Nation*, **10, November** 505–508.

Deitchman, S.J. (1976). *The Best Laid Schemes*, MIT Press, Cambridge, Mass.

Effrat, B. and Mitchell, M. (1974). The Indian and the social scientist: contemporary contractual arrangements on the Pacific Northwest coast. *Human Organization*, **33**, 405–407.

Form, W.L. (1973). Field problems in comparative research: the politics of distrust. In M. Armer and A. Grimshaw (Eds) *Comparative Social Research: Methodological Problems and Strategies*, pp. 83–116, Wiley, New York.

Holtzman, W., Diaz-Guerrero, R., and Schwartz, J. (1975). *Personality Development in Two Cultures*. University of Texas Press, Austin, Texas.

Horowitz, I.L. (Ed) (1967). *The Rise and Fall of Project Camelot*. MIT Press, Cambridge, Mass.

Kleymeyer, C.D. and Bertrand, W.E. (1980). Towards more ethical and effective carrying out of applied research across class or cultural lines. *Ethics in Science and Medicine*, **7**, 11–25.

Moore, J.W. (1967). Political and ethical problems in a large-scale study of a minority population. In G. Sjoberg, (Ed.) *Ethics, Politics and Social Research*, pp. 225–244. Schenkman, Cambridge, Mass.

Portes, A. (1975). Trends in international research cooperation: the Latin American case. *American Sociologist*, **10**(3), 131–140.

Tapp, J.L., Kelman, H.C., Triandis, H.C., Wrightsman, L.S., and Coelho, G.V. (1974). Continuing concerns in cross-cultural ethics: a report. *International Journal of Psychology*, **9**, 231–249.

Triandis, H.C., Vassiliou, V., Vassiliou, G., Tanaka, Y., and Shamagun, A.V. (1972). *The Analysis of Subjective Culture*. Wiley, New York.

Warwick, D.P. (1980). The politics and ethics of cross-cultural research. In H.C. Triandis and W.W. Lambert, (Eds) *Handbook of Cross-Cultural Psychology*, *Vol. 1*, pp. 319–371. Allyn and Bacon, Boston.

Warwick, D.P. (1982a). *Bitter Pills: Population Policies and their Implementation in Eight Developing Countries*, Cambridge University Press, New York.

Warwick, D.P. (1982b). Types of harm in social research. In T.L. Beauchamp, R.R. Faden, R.J. Wallace Jr., and L. Walters, (Ed) *Ethical Issues in Social Science Research*, pp. 101–124. Johns Hopkins University Press, Baltimore, Md.

Warwick, D.P. and Pettigrew, T. (1982). Toward ethical guidelines for social science research in public policy. In D. Callahan and B. Jennings (Eds) *Ethics, The Social Sciences and Public Policy*, Plenum, New York.

Whyte, W.F. (1969). The role of the US professor in developing countries, *American Sociologist*, **4**(1), 19–28.

Social Research in Developing Countries
Edited by M. Bulmer and D.P. Warwick
© 1983, John Wiley & Sons, Ltd.

CHAPTER 25

THE EXPERIMENTING SOCIETY AND RADICAL SOCIAL REFORM: THE ROLE OF THE SOCIAL SCIENTIST IN CHILE'S UNIDAD POPULAR EXPERIENCE

RICARDO B. ZUÑIGA

Forms of social consciousness in radical reform: Chile 1970–73

The existence of alternative political projects

One of the characteristic traits of the recent Chilean political history has been the fluidity of a multiple party structure, which has changed and reshaped itself in great numbers of fusions, divisions, and coalitions. At the time of the 1970 elections, the political scene was structured in three main blocks loosely organized around the National Party, the Christian Democracy, and the *Unidad Popular* coalition.

The National Party, and related groups and sectors, was the representative of conservative thought and vested interests. Espousing capitalism as the only social project fully compatible with democracy, its strategy was centred in depoliticization. Its programme emphasized the threat of international communism as the end of individual liberties and private property; an interpretation of most social changes as subtle advances in communist influence and control; and a positive emphasis on a 'natural' order of social reality, with stability and social order as the natural rewards of hard work. The political platform was clearly oriented toward the business, industrial, and farming interests and their spheres of influence. Its platform was amplified by the social movements and groups that stemmed from it, and which, free from the constraints of electoral strategies, carried the programme to its logical conclusions.

Reprinted in abridged form by permission of the publisher and the author from *American Psychologist* (1975), **30 (2)**, 99–115. Copyright 1975 by the American Psychological Association.

First among these was 'Family, Tradition, and Poperty', a spiritualistic, traditional-Catholic revitalization movement, with abundant references to the threat of communism as an atheistic force destructive of the three values the movement centred around. It was superseded by 'Fatherland and Liberty', a frankly political paramilitary organization with a clearcut programme of replacing the democratic forms it saw eroded through demagoguery and weakness by an authoritarian government backed by direct military intervention.

The Christian Democracy, a reform party stemming from the political right, went to the polls in 1970 as a progressive party. Explicitly anticapitalistic in its platform, it had the aim of continuing Frei's (the Christian Democratic president from 1964 to 1970) programme of a 'communitarian society' by working toward social transformations that would produce a distribution of social power without disrupting the Chilean democratic tradition. Its programme proclaimed itself as a 'Revolution in Liberty'.

The third political project was the *Unidad Popular*, a coalition of six political groups centred around the communist and socialist parties, both of which were explicitly marxist, and the Radical party, which was a social-democratic traditional one. The electoral platform was that of a leftist coalition. It called for a gradual transformation of the socioeconomic structure toward socialism. How gradual or how radical this transformation was to be became a source of internal discrepancies and a target for opposition attacks. The left outside the spectrum of political legitimacy included groups like the Revolutionary Leftist Movement, which insisted on the need to leave open the possibility of an armed confrontation, and of smaller groups like the National Liberation Army, which was exclusively oriented to an armed struggle. These groups, like those mentioned to the right of the legitimized conservative forces, grew in importance during the 3 years of the *Unidad Popular* government, as the possibilities of political exchange first dwindled and then disappeared. Both left and right 'extremist' groups were always important as unrestricted expressions of the basic appeal of the parties with which they were associated.

The importance of the political alternatives stemmed from their equal claims to political legitimacy, their radical incompatibility, and the degree to which political life subsumed all aspects of social life. A long history of political awareness had given the citizenship a degree of consciousness of the social roots of political programmes that made the 1970 elections a choice among ways of life. The left spoke of land reform, nationalizations, and the extended role of the state in social welfare, industrial planning, and channels of product distribution. It spoke to the dispossessed in the language of radical vindication. The right spoke to the fears of massive confiscations and incarcerations, of a police state, of the beginning of social chaos, and of the reign of terror that would be imposed by the communist party with the support of the mobs. The Christian Democracy spoke against the left and against the right, condemning both Marxism and capitalism. It favoured both social justice and the social stability of existing institutions. It warned both against the threats to democracy and the ruthlessness of capitalists (Debuyst and Garcés, 1971).

The elections brought a relative majority to Allende and the *Unidad Popular*. The Christian Democracy, the majority party in Congress, had to choose to support him in the Congressional runoff elections or to add its strength to that of the candidate of the right, the second majority. It had to choose between the safety of the existing social order and the risk of social transformations. It decided on the latter and joined the *Unidad Popular* in Congress, voting the parliamentary majority that gave the power of the executive branch to the left. The alliance was brief. The 3 years of the *Unidad Popular* government show a rapid identification of the Christian Democracy with the opposition. The social order versus social transformation polarization was soon replaced by a social integration versus social confrontation polarization in which the left accepted the costs of radical social transformations, while the opposition insisted that those costs would destroy the nation. In one camp were the defenders of the fatherland, democracy, nationalism, and social harmony; in the other were the defenders of the people, of justice, of national independence from American economic control and from the exploitation of multinational corporations. The fusion of the right and the Christian Democratic blocks into a unified opposition against the governing left created the conditions for total social polarization.

Commitment demands of the generalized alternatives

The gradual redefinition of everyday life in terms of its reference to mutually exclusive and totally incompatible political projects did not remain at the level of cognitive organizations. It was both the product and the cause of profound transformations of the conceptions of social life. This emphasis on commitment, participation, organization, and militancy extended throughout the social structure. These aspects are especially relevant to the understanding of the Chilean scientific community.

First, the 3 years of the *Unidad Popular* government saw an impressive growth of social organization. The increased political clout of the Central Workers Union, dealing for the first time with a government it could call its own, facilitated a renewed campaign toward unionization. This growth helped to integrate and politicize previously marginal sectors such as rural labourers. The counter-effect was an active process of organization by the opposition of sectors that had been unstructured, such as small business owners, farmers, and service sector employees, both public and private. The activation and politicization of professional organizations also became intense and added to the opposition the powerful and influential voices of groups such as the professional colleges of medicine, engineering, and law. They had the legal right to control the licensing process of their respective professions and to impose and collect membership fees. Their powers, when politicized, could transform a political disagreement into a charge of professional impropriety, punishable with penalties ranging from suspension to loss of right to practise the profession. The occupational organizations were complemented by residentially based associations in the form of neighbourhood government structures, communication networks of both protective and aggressive character, and regional organization of work associations. These developments represented new forms of political education and organization. Where prior organizations had included only males from the organized sectors of the work force, these new organizations integrated people whose activities had lacked collective forms of consciousness and expression.

The second aspect of social activation was the political activation of groups that previously had remained marginal. Rural labourers, Indian communities, women, high school students, and the well-to-do discovered their community of interests in major social, economic, and political questions. Though their initial awareness was often triggered by the sense of a threat to individual interests, their new-found sense of community is evidence of the degree to which a latent national community became aware of its own existence. That recognition clarified the intentional nature of the decision processes which mould that existence and the underlying visions of ideal states and ideal means of achieving them.

The third aspect of social organization processes was that of the increased social pressures toward explicit allegiances and commitments. Given the degree to which political options determined interpretive viewpoints, sympathies, and allegiances (whether direct or remote, conscious or unconscious), the identification of those options became the most useful information about a given individual, group, or institution. The predictive power they offered made them a prized target of investigation. Social rituals of making conversation to strangers included comments about the scarcity of products, the incidents of violence, or generalizations about the state of the economy, placed as bait to bring the guarded opinions of the other into the open. Many households put up signs testifying to their political allegiances. The pressures toward visible alignment were more and more evident as the numbers of mass demonstrations increased (marches and rallies of hundreds of thousands were by no means rare). The pressures toward political self-revelation coexisted with sophisticated techniques of political intrusion, such as the empty-pot symbol. A generalized informal agreement among the women of opposition parties was to express their anger at scarcities for which they blamed the government. They chose to step out of the house every night at exactly 10.00 pm and bang empty pots with spoons for a while, producing a deafening political testimony, exhilarating for the opposition and vaguely disquieting and highly frustrating for government supporters. These marches, demonstrations, and political symbolic expressions reinforced the commitment of participants and gave them the pride of belonging and the self-congratulation of their courage. They gave adversaries food for thought about the size and resolution of their opposition and strengthened in both groups their allegiances, their compromise with a political option, and their disposition to confront the sectors of the national community that were increasingly perceived as alien to their commitments and their life.

The impact of alternative social projects on the social sciences

The preceding description is impressionistic, overly general, and simplified, and it could be construed as relevant to the scientist but not to science. The charges are justified. The description of the social consciousness of groups and individuals faced with difficult choices, divided allegiances, and the feelings of uncertainty of generalized changes deserves a systematic treatment that it has not yet received. This is not the occasion for it. The illustration of its relevance beyond the subjective dilemmas of its actors is the main task of this point.

Miller (1969, p. 1063) describes quite accurately the dilemma most social scientists felt and tried to cope with. As citizens, they could not disregard the social forces that moulded their lives and their work and that competed persistently and strenuously for their allegiance. As scientists, the vast majority struggled in a long and intense fight against personal tensions and external pressures in order to save the scientific character of their action.

This struggle can be viewed at different levels of analysis. The definition of the role of the social scientists was first of all a problem of self-definition, involving commitments to conceptions of science around which their professional lives were organized, their work defined, and even their modes of interaction determined. The absence of an adequate rationale for action was also an intellectual embarrassment. Many social scientists found themselves avoiding the controversies that would demand from them clarifications about their social commitments and the concrete characteristics of the social interactions triggered by their work that they were not ready to discuss. It also involved a political option: the application of scientific procedures involved concrete choices that were inseparable from political considerations. This point is further developed in three successive steps.

Social concreteness of scientific research

No formulation of the role of the social sciences in Chile can ignore the analysis of the social determinants of the production of knowledge and the heightened awareness of the scientific community of this area of analysis. A first factor derived from sociological conceptualizations of the national patterns of growth, modernizatin, and development. The double reality of a national autonomy in formal political terms and the limitations of that autonomy by processes of economic subordination and external political influences moulded the social analysis of both the Christian Democracy and the left. The analysis of scientific strategies of development and the planning of human resources in the academic community were necessarily referred to this broader framework of analysis. In this context, it was obvious that the short history of the social sciences in Chile and the absence of advanced graduate studies and doctoral programmes made the social sciences derivative in their initial stages, dependent in their growth, and marked by a time lag in their evolution. Developments in leading countries made belated impact in the Chilean scientific community and arrived with a magnified discontinuity. The arrival of recently trained scholars marked distinctive stages of growth. The physical presence of such individuals in a country with grave economic limitations on access to foreign publications and library resources meant the forceful irruption of hitherto unknown perspectives. The phenomenon triggered both an increased personalization of paradigms and persistent reinforcements of cultural dependency.

A second factor in the development of the social sciences in Chile was the obvious limitation of the available resources. It made brutally clear the need for limiting alternatives and emphasized the necessity of rationalizing those choices in terms of coordinated planning and research programmes with explicit aims, priorization of alternatives, clearly defined expected payoffs, and corresponding evaluation procedures. Research funds came from very few sources — the government, universities, and American research foundations with offices in Chile — and all of them were pressured toward developing explicit criteria for resource allocation. The criteria developed went far beyond tradition. The scientific background of the researcher and subjective judgements of peers on project feasibility remained but had to be complemented. The complements included the more controversial problems of degree of institutional support, the place of specific projects in lines of continued research, and the relations of individual researchers to the institutions they were supposed to represent. Preference was given to team projects over individual ones, and judgements were made on their social relevance and the presence or absence of secondary benefits of providing training to younger scientists. Taken as a whole, these criteria challenged the equation of scientific freedom with absolute choice of research topics by the researcher and limited the autonomy of both projects and researchers.

A third factor was the increased awareness of social scientists of the internal functioning of the resource-allocation institutions. Appointments and elections of officers were crucial for determining which projects would be funded and therefore became legitimate concerns of the scientist, dealt with openly, and handled like any other social situation of power allocation. Institutional approach–approach conflicts tested severely the traditional beliefs in understanding the scientific process as the activity of a specific community, with scientific knowledge as the concrete manifestation or product of that community.

Political correspondence of scientific paradigms

The issues that were permanently in discussion were of a theoretical nature, but their importance was fused to the political implications of the alternatives. In their usual formulations, they referred to the nature of scientific rigour, the growth of scientific knowledge, and the social determination of scentific orientations.

That science is a reflective endeavour, in which the process of knowledge production is in itself part of the object of study, was a truth abstract enough to produce general agreement. The problem appeared when different scientists evaluated the rigour of others. Those of a positivistic bent stressed verification, especially in terms of internal consistency, communicational univocity, and validation. These concepts, on which there were both nuances of discrepancy and agreement, were not attacked by marxists as irrelevant but were criticized by them for the implicit restriction of the analysis of scientific growth to the conditions within the control of the scientist. Scientific voluntarism was interpreted as an ideological smokescreen that hid the relationships of dependency of the scientific community. Marxist analysis stressed scientific rigour primarily in terms of the fullest possible understanding of the grounding of social research in a scientific analysis of the conditions of its production and utilization. Scientific rigour is only possible when there is full awareness and explicit, systematic analysis of the factors that guide the definition of the problem and the decisions on where to study them, how to interpret results, and how to utilize these results. The emphasis on socioeconomic determinants brought on the marxists' accusations of reductionism and of making knowledge epiphenomenal to power relations. Their counter-attack pointed at the systematic refusal of the positivists to understand science in its historical reality and the resultant disembodiment, making it an idealistic progression of ideas related only to each other. This approach denied the need for social causation analysis of the generation and the selective facilitation or obstruction of these ideas. If science is understood as primarily a verification process, efforts concentrate on the internal logic of inquiry and the procedural rigour of the verification. If it is focused primarily on the understanding of the generation of modes of understanding and of the historical interaction of these modes, then the task can be conceived as a history of ideas. A third possibility is that of an empirical sociology of knowledge, analysing the concrete determinants of social thought. That these three were not integrated into a comprehensive strategy of empirical analysis of social knowledge was a permanent and bitter source of misunderstandings, reciprocal stereotyping, and political attributions of intention. They broke down scientific concerns in terms of allegiance to a single approach, often undercutting the importance of the others. Examples of these unfortunate limitations were the refusal of student sectors to take basic statistics courses on the grounds that they were incompatible with their political standpoint, the suppression of courses of theory of personality and Freudian analysis on the grounds that they were not scientific, and the rejection of empirical sociology of knowledge as a marxist infiltration plot. These instances sadly illustrate one consequence of political confrontrations among social scientists: it pushes them to hide their private lopsidedness and makes them politicize their ignorance.

A problem that was specific to psychologists and that made their integration among the social sciences very difficult was the cultural homogeneity of their training or, to put it more bluntly, the unanalyzed 'Americanness' of their science. Much of the theoretical background and the totality of the professional arsenal of Chilean psychologists was not only culturally derivative but also culturally dependent. The relative underdevelopment of the consciousness of American psychology of its own cultural rootedness (Allport, 1961; Brandt, 1970) and the marginal character of the study of its history in graduate programmes have an intensified impact on the formation of psychologists from other countries who get their training in the United States or through textbooks and professional tools that are usually translations of American products. The ethnocentrism in the training of American psychologists which is ever-present but irrelevant for all practical purposes suffers a radical qualitative transformation when it is mechanically transported to a different cultural context. What was only a localized deficiency becomes a universalistic ideology and an unconscious (or guilt-ridden) advocacy of a cultural intrusion that is often extremely naive. It often isolates the psychologists from other social scientists with disciplines in which competing centres of production make comparative and critical modes of thought necessary. The production of psychologists is significantly more alientaed from their national reality, and their dependency on culturally extrinsic thought patterns is often a source of friction with other disciplines. Neither economists nor sociologists had to introduce electric shock punishment as a necessary tool for the production of knowledge. Neither social workers nor political scientists thought of human beings as 'subjects' or spoke of 'running subjects'. That a psychologist might or might not think and be influenced in his behaviour by the terminology he uses is of course a matter subject to experimental verification and the mould/cloak controversy. The rejection he can provoke in people outside the profession because of his unanalysed assumptions of human universality and his cross-cultural insensitivity to his own culture was unfortunately tested often enough. The impact on the psychologist was often traumatic and made him bitter about 'the politicization of science'. It made him retreat to areas in which he would not be challenged on a host of issues that he himself had never challenged. As psychology is the least political of the social sciences and psychologists are the least politicized of the social scientists, both had great difficulty in coping with a social reality that intruded in unexpected forms and that interpreted their existence in terms totally unfamiliar. I shall return later to the problem of the political implications of the unquestioned assumption of scientific universality in the social sciences.

The experimenting society and radical social reform

Campbell's (1972) description of an experimenting society, one ready to try an experimental approach to social reform, has a multiple and direct relevance to the experience of the Chilean social scientific community, especially in the case of psychologists. It represents the only action blueprint for the integration of psychologists to planned social action projects. It represents the methods-oriented definition of the scientist as a maximizer of external selectors of truth incrementations and as a minimizer of the biasing effects of internal selectors derived from its characteristics as a concrete social system (Campbell, 1972). Its impressive record in developing techniques for the assessment of the impact of planned social change coincides with the growth of concern with social evaluation in Chile during the last decade. It represents an attempt to deal with social changes within a continuity, however minimal, with preceding social states. This minimum of continuity was a characteristic of the total Chilean situation, which stressed both transformation and continuity. If Allende's government had in mind a socialist historic project, the chosen road was that of a non-violent, democratic transition to socialism. It is in this interpretive perspective that the political context has been described as a radical social reform. The aims of the process were the replacement of a socioeconomic mode of production; the means were those of a change in continuity, utilizing the available instruments to advance the social formation to a different social mode.

The extrinsic definition of the role of the social scientist

The job of the methodologist for the experimenting society is not to say *what is to be done*, but rather to say *what has been done*. The aspect of social science that is being applied is primarily its research methodology rather than its descriptive theory, with the goal of learning more than we do now from the innovations decided upon by the political process. As will be elaborated later, even the conclusion-drawing and the relative weighting of conflicting indicators must be left up to the political process (Campbell, 1971).

When pressures toward social utility make psychologists more aware of both the expectations on their contribution and their own desire to fulfil them, several strategies for their integration become apparent.

The first and easiest is the jump on the social-change bandwagon. It seems both easy and conflict free to fuse a social evolution perspective, one that stresses the historical necessity of a modernization process that is indistinguishable from increased democratization, social harmony, and rationality, with a sense that genuinely scientific contributions can only be opposed by the devil and politicians. From the uncritical confusion of definitions of the levels of analysis in social change (Andreeva and Leontiev, 1974), it is relatively easy to derive a view of a world that is imputed with a need for enlightenment and a capacity to recognize it in the contributions of the social scientist. The social sciences are thought to be able to provide a set of beliefs grounded on empirically acquired knowledge to replace the contents of traditional commonsense. Statements such as 'All men are created equal', 'One truth underlies all controversy', and 'Conflict is generally inevitable' are seen as belonging to an early understanding of the social nature of man, one which has been modified gradually by the contributions of the social sciences. Now, the social scientist can proudly replace them: 'All men are created equal' is replaced by 'There are great individual differences between humans'. 'Conflict is generally inevitable' can be replaced by 'Human conflict is no more inevitable than disease and can be solved or, even better, prevented'. The belief that 'One truth underlies all controversy', which in the presocial science list appeared with 'Most behaviour is economically motivated', can now be replaced with another great conflict-solving discovery: 'Perceptions are more relevant to social problems than "true facts" ' (Varela, as quoted by Rodrigues, 1972, pp. 291–292).

The dangers of such an approach are obvious and coextensive with those of idealistic optimism and superficiality of social analysis, to say nothing of the political option they represent. In the Chilean experience, few psychologists espoused it, perhaps because the critical development of social theory had made such forms of thought too primitive to receive attention. But the pressing character of the challenges continued to push relentlessly toward the commitment of scientific knowledge to the clarification and solution of social problems. This pressure pushed for a second strategy of participation: the redefinition of problems in psychological terms.

The problem of the 'psychological' study of 'social' issues was a painful one. Psychology has yet to find an adequate niche in the array of scientific activities, and its internal spread is broad enough to make it a reluctant member of classificatory interests. While most academic committees accepted the presence of psychology among the social sciences, it was usually on the understanding that some individual psychologists perceived themselves in these terms, even though their basic training had made a scant contribution to their professional definition as social scientists. The psychologist, for his part, realized that his training did not prepare him directly to deal with social problems and that therefore his contribution had to be strictly psychological in order to be rigorous. The personal starting point from which the commitment to social action stemmed was a sense of the moral imperatives of relevance, a concept as slippery and extrinsic to the discipline as necessary for the defence of judgements of relative importance in problem definition:

> The concept of relevance lacks the power of pointing to the frame of reference with respect to which the sought relevance is to be relevant. The removal of the objective or contextual aspect from relevance is due to the supposition that it is self-evident that relevance entails concern for human beings as they exist and conceive of themselves in the present. Yet there is, as is very often the case, a kind of warning in the slogan of relevance that is raised against the overmethodological character of academic disciplines and their overhasty identification of substance with method (Rotensreich, 1972, p. 253)

The personal starting point pushed toward an apparently consistent integration of an extradisciplinary problem definition with an intradisciplinary definition of research objectives. The strategy, almost as old as the professional respectability of social concerns, was insufficient to cope with the novelty of the social situation. Its methodological underpinnings and political implications have been analyzed effectively by Caplan and Nelson (1973) as the 'person–blame' causal attribution bias in psychological research on social problems.

First, the redefinition of a social problem in terms of the attribution of centrality to psychological variables usually implies a radical shift in the object of inquiry. Since the definition of the problem determines the research strategy, the selection of a social action delivery system, and the criteria for evaluation, a tendency to assign causal significance to person-centred variables produces a significant shift in understanding. If industrial productivity is studied as worker productivity, if political education is analysed as attitude change, if ideology is understood in terms of motives, if alienation is defined in psychological terms, then in all these cases the analysis of the social situation has been effectively displaced to a marginally explanatory role. Such an organization of research will not necessarily show the arbitrariness of the problem transformation. Verification methods do not have the power to alter the definition of the problem under study.

Second, person-centred analysis has subtle yet significant decontextualizing and atemporalizing effects that mask the interplay of social forces in a specific historic moment. The Chilean situation was overwhelming in its specificity and the difficulties it imposed on any attempt to understand it in comparative terms. A leftist coalition aimed at the transformtion of a society toward a socialist mode of production through a gradual process within a democratic and unaltered framework of social institutions. Supporters had to work toward that transformation burdened with a demand for perfect institutional continuity. The opposition had to deal with a process that was gradual in the transformations it utilized but radical in its explicit aim of total substitution of socioeconomic structures. In this setting, the available methodological arsenal of psychologists was woefully inadequate for recognizing qualitative transformations of social processes.

Third, and perhaps most important, the tradition of person-centred social analysis is deeply steeped in a 'person–blame' causal attribution bias which is consistent in its built-in political bias. As Caplan and Nelson (1973, p. 207) observed, 'the criteria by which social scientists select "problem" groups for study are not unlike the criteria by which the broader culture selects certain groups as scapegoats'. Not only the definition of the problem and the causal interpretations, but the recommendations for policy-making that derive from the analysis become person-centred. The strategy for social action becomes psychologically oriented, and the psychologist finds herself in the bewildering situation of being accused of being a Weberian, a label that is baffling because it is beyond his habitual realm of intellectual competence (Seve, 1972; Veron, 1972, Chapter 4).

An experience that was decisive for many social scientists, especially those working with *Unidad Popular* programmes, was that of the patterns of interaction forced on them by many popular organizations. The intial contact usually took the form of a request for a descriptive analysis or an evaluation. The challenging novelty in both cases was the more or less explicit understanding of those groups— trade unions, neighbourhood organizations, and political education and worker training programmes — that what they demanded was not a 'study', but a skill. They wanted to learn how to study a production process flowchart, an organizational structure, task programming, or educational evaluation. The scientist was supposed to have the 'how', and he was asked to teach it. The study that put him in contact with their organization was understood to be a means, not an end. Implicit in the definition of the request was an insight into the nature of the scientific inquiry. If the major contribution of science is a growth in planning, adaptive, and coping rationality, should not the scientific mode of thought be a skill of all self-determining collective actors and possibly of all individual actors? In this perspective, the role of the scientist was understood as a vicarious input, being a necessary extrinsic help to social units still lacking sufficient reflective rationality, charged with the remedial task of elevating self-governing bodies to the level of full selfconscious and self-evaluative capacities. The analogy with the psychotherapeutic process flowed naturally. A process of working in close contact with a patient, sharing his experience but adding a degree of liberty through the relationship, a relationship that is resolved when the patient has acquired sufficient rationality so as to cope with the extrinsic determinants, the emotional pressures that made it difficult for him to analyse his situation or act according to his own planning— this was an easily understood model for psychologists and for those who sought their cooperation. Psychotherapy does not define itself as a permanent input but rather as a temporarily limited help in actualizing an existential project. It does not aim to make a psychiatrist out of every patient and is not threatened by this possibility. The role of the social scientist could profit from this revision, this alternative formulation. It was perhaps one of the most important contributions and certainly one of the most rewarding experiences for Chilean social scientists. It could serve to test for a possible history of ideological displacement of the scientific process outside of the social actor. The next point to be discussed is complementary, in the degree that it can be conceived of as an 'upward' displacement of the scientific process.

The insertion of scientific inputs in higher levels of control

The understanding of the scientific process of abstraction in terms of control of variables as a precondition for knowledge can perhaps be analysed with the help of an analogy that is admittedly a bit of a caricature from the realm of photography. A persistent characteristic of Brownie-camera photography that is a source of wonder for the uninitiated, of pride for the author, and of envious frustration for the owner of more expensive equipment, is the fact that most of these photos are good. A closer analysis of the homogenous quality can nevertheless tell something about the costs of the results achieved. Brownie photography follows three basic rules. First, keep the subjects far away, if possible at the same distance to the camera in all takes, regardless of topic. This solves the problems of focusing, angle, and perspective. Second, put your subjects always in the sun, and facing it, and photograph at high noon. This will take care of the problems of lighting and unwanted shades. Third, tell them not to move. This will facilitate composition and will control for blur. The result of strict adhesion to the three rules will give high 'reliability'. The subjects will become rigid, square-shouldered, far-away, squinting statues, but the proud camera owner will have the satisfaction of 'never losing a picture' . . . .

The Chilean experience was rude, even brutal to social scientists. The degree of real displacement of power put the areas of crucial decisions in the hands of those involved in the generation of social innovations, and undercut radically the possibilities of manipulation available to social scientsists. Lacking a tradition of academic coercion of students into experiments, lacking the resources to pay subjects, and having little luck in the recruitment of subjects for the undefined (from the point of view of the subject) aims of traditional research, the only way in which social research was conceivable was as the joint activity of a community of interests, in which all participants defined an agreement on social aims, in procedures to study them, and in the utilization of the knowledge to be generated. As the social power of the scientist was reduced to a minimum and by the same people he was to study, his role escaped his own total control, and he had to learn to see it redefined according to the issues under consideration, the intentions of participants, their time availabilities, the time spread of the research, and the introduction of a permanent feedback system between researcher and other actors. The knowledge generated was simultaneously fed back into the situation, altering the scientific research model into a fluid one, in which the scientific products were diffused as they were produced and were immediately utilized to alter the situation that had originated them. The manipulative techniques, so common in otherwise bene-volent scientific intentions (Argyris, 1974; Argyris and Schon, 1974) were made impossible by the requirement of full disclosure of information to subjects and full agreement on research objectives by all actors. In a politicized situation, one in which the aim of almost any conceivable research project was in one way or another the evaluation of the impact of a political decision, the social philosophy of the scientist became relevant and necessary information, and those who thought they could defend a disconnection of their procedural science from their metaprocedural ideology found their research opportunities greatly curtailed. For many others, the social demands of a socialist project still to be defined led them to think in audaciously positive terms. If the social sciences have an abstract intention of fostering rationality and reality testing, do not they have in the social realm the moral obligation of fostering the types of social relations that are implicit in the aims of increased rationality of social actors?

An evaluation model of social research

The demands for social rationality that stemmed from the awareness of the scarcity of resources available for research and from the awareness of the political decisions that the allocation of those resources required created a strong pressure toward increasing the rationality of the process of production of scientific knowledge. A definition of scientific freedom in terms of 'studying whatever the scientist feels like studying' does not stand the scrutiny triggered by social confrontations. Nor does a belief in the economic strategy of random research allocation regardless of topic. The discussions inevitably centred on making explicit a model of decision-making for scientific growth, and such a need made the underpinnings of an idealistic postulate of 'natural' order and directionality of the growth of knowledge as untenable and obvious as the absence of a coherent alternative model.

The problem was posed in terms of the need and possibility of a relatively autonomous analysis of the social production of knowledge. The element of autonomy was the differentiation from an epistemological level of analysis, both necessary and conceptually distinct from an empirical analysis of the social relations of production that defined, triggered, supported, diffused, and utilized knowledge. It did not question the validity of the study of the collective flow of thought and of the intrinsic phenomena of the mechanisms for introduc-ing variation, consistent selection processes, and mechanisms for preserving and reproducing the selected variations (Campbell, 1969; Campbell, 1974; Kuhn, 1970). The autonomy was limited and made relative precisely in the preservation of the epistemological level and in the awareness of the dangers of transforming the sociology of knowledge into a mechanistic attempt to derive total understanding of scientific knowledge from the socioeconomic analysis of its production, the type of vulgar marxism that Marx decried (Engels, 1968a, 1968b; Goldmann, 1970; Veron, 1972, Chapter 5; Zuñiga, 1973).

Given that human behavior is a relative totality, only an element of the men-nature totality, but a total fact nevertheless, all attempts to separate its 'material' and 'spiritual' aspects can only be, in the best of cases, provisional abstractions, always implying grave dangers to knowledge. The researcher must therefore exert himself in finding reality in its totality and concreteness, even though he knows he will only be able to reach it in a limited manner. To achieve this aim, he must integrate in the study of social facts both the history of the theories about these facts and the relation of the study of these facts of conscience to their historic rootedness and to their economic and social underpinnings. (Goldmann, 1970, pp. 20–21).

The task was a difficult one. Subjectivism was deeply entrenched and ingeniously camouflaged in research proposal evaluation. The opinion of experts in the field was undercut in its reliability by the difficulty of finding several truly independent informants for each project, and was undercut in its validity by the inevitable interpersonal and institutional ties characteristic of specialized areas in a small research community of authors, sponsoring institutions, and evaluators. The attacks on the establishmentarian or political biases of entrenched evaluators were influenced by the same factors plus the additional burden of the rigid hierarchies of seniority, chronological accumulation of scientific respectability, prestige, and control, which produced a persistent correlation of radical innovation and drastic reformulations with junior status, youth, and institutional powerlessness. Lengthy and acid discussions centred on the integration of habitually incompatible sources of criteria for judgement: those derived from the professional prestige of the researcher, seen as a guarantee of project success, and those derived from the social relevance of the topic, as defined by those who shared the political perspective of the researcher. No provisions existed to assign teams of research evaluators to a completed project in order to obtain a measure of its final value. No pressures on the researcher demanded from him a personal report on the impact of the research in terms of a loss–gain analysis for the agent and the target of the research, the sponsoring institution, and society at large, of the type of the one Zimbardo (1974) has outlined around the ethical aspects of his Stanford prison experiment.

Redefining the scientific community

The persistent pressures on the scientific community during the *Undiad Popular* period were basically demands of democratization and openness, and they produced the gradual broadening of the collective consciousness inherent in the scientific endeavour. The transformation of an understanding of science from that of a collectively generated set of propositions to that of a community of knowledge production led to the insight into its character as a community of concern, which included all those who were involved in producing a better understanding of an experienced social reality, all those who were involved in producing social knowledge, and all those were affected by it. Utopian as most of the early manifestations were, the realization of the equality of dignity and equality of rights of all participants began to unveil new understanding of the role of the social scientist. At its humblest levels of attainment, it multiplied the headaches of the psychologists who accepted the relative loss of control of their own activity implied in their integration in massive education projects, and who struggled in the search of non-manipulative and egalitarian relations of social research. The process involved displacement of research efforts to permanent feedback strategies, and the redefinition of the social scientist as a participant, with responsibilities to his community of belonging that derived not from his parallel commitments as citizen but from the very essence of his scientific endeavour.

Conclusion

The experience of a community of social scientists in the context of a radical social reform like that experienced in Chile during the 3 years of the *Unidad Popular* government was a disorienting one, especially for psychologists. We had to learn too much in too short a time. Our rather frantic practical efforts and theoretical elaborations after abandoning the accepted paradigms that were proving inoperative attained a sense of internal conviction of the legitimacy and scientific honesty of the search. They did not attain an explicit reformulation of a changed understanding of social reality and social verification. The psychological arsenal we had available was not universal and culture free. Nor was it politically neutral, sufficiently democratic in its implications, nor sufficiently aware of itself to be fully rational.

The experience of a community of social scientists in times of radical reform can be a sad one. The effort to prolong an exchange of critical rationality over discrepant commitments requires an act of faith in the basic possibility of scientific research to contribute a specificity of reflective negation of appearances of conventional life (Schroyer, 1973) and of creating the conditions for the falsification of beliefs (Lakatos, 1970). The realization of the subordinate character of scientific paradigms to broader frames of reference, philosophical and political, shows the limits of the possibility. An experimenting society needs the contribution of the social sciences, but that contribution must go beyond the elements of understanding it can provide. An experimenting society also needs the example of the social relations through which the social scientist points at the concrete requirements of a democratic society, committed to an equality of respect and an equality of control. It also needs the example of a community of social endeavour in which the passion for understanding and the desire to help are coupled with an acceptance of the concrete,

societal, and historical determinants of the limits of ideal, abstract bene-
volence.

References

Allport, G.W. (1961). European and American theories of personality. In H.P. David
   and H. von Bracken. (Eds), *Perspectives in Personality Theory*. Basic Books, New
   York.
Andreeva. G.M. and Leontiev, A.N. (1974). *Methodological problems of studying the
   psychological aspects of social change*, paper presented at the European Conference
   on Social Psychology, Budapest, Hungary, May 1974.
Argyris, C. (1974). *Some dangers in applying results from experimental social psycho-
   logy*, unpublished manuscript, Harvard University, Graduate School of Education.
Argyris, C., and Schon, D. (1974). *Theory in Practice*, Jossey-Bass, San Francisco.
Brandt, L.W. (1970). American psychology. *American Psychologist*, **25**, 1091–1093.
Campbell, D.T. (1969). *Objectivity and the locus of scientific knowledge*, paper pre-
   sented at the meeting of the American Psychological Association, Washington, DC.
Campbell, D.T. (1971). *Methods for the experimenting society*, unpublished manuscript.
Campbell, D.T. (1972). *Critical problems in the evaluation of social problems*, paper
   presented at the meeting of the Division of Behavioral Sciences, National Academy of
   Sciences, Washington, DC.
Campbell, D.T. (1974). Evolutionary epistemology. In P.A. Schilpp (Ed.). *The Philo-
   sophy of K.R. Popper*, LaSalle, Ill., Open Court.
Caplan, N. and Nelson, S.D. (1973). On being useful: The nature and consequences of
   psychological research on social problems. *American Psychologist*, **28**, 199–211.
Debuyst, F. and Garcés, J.E. (1971). La opcion chilena de 1970. Analyisis de los tres
   programas electorales. *Revista Latinoamericana de Ciencia Politica* (Santiago, Chile).
   2, 279–369.
Engels, F. (1968a) Carta a Heinz Starkenburg, 1894. In *Marx, Engels: Sobre Arte y
   Literatura*. Ciencia Neuva, Madrid.
Engels, F. (1968b) Carta a Joseph Bloch, 1890. In *Marx, Engels: Sobre Arte y Literatura*.
   Ciencia Nueva, Madrid.
Goldmann, L. (1970). *Las Ciencias Humanas y la Filosofia*, Neuva Vision, 1970,
   Buenos Aires.
Kuhn, T.S. (1970). *The Structure of Scientific Revolutions*, University of Chicago Press,
   Chicago.
Lakatos, I. (1970). Falsification and the methodology of scientific reserch programmes.
   In I. Lakatos and A. Musgrave (Eds), *Criticism and the Growth of Knowledge*,
   Cambridge University Press, Cambridge, England.
Miller, G. (1969). Psychology as a means of promoting human welfare. *American
   Psychologist*, **12**, 1063–75.
Rodrigues, A. (1972). The integration of pure and applied research and its application to
   the design of national development programmes. *Inter-American Journal of Psycho-
   logy*, **6**, 287–295.
Rotensreich, N. (1972). Relevance examined. *Ethics*, **82**, 239–53.
Schroyer, T. (1973). *The Critique of Domination*. George Braziller, New York.
Seve, L. (1972). *Marxisme et Theorie de la Personnalité*. Editions Sociales, Paris.
Veron, E. (1972). *Conducta, Estructura y Comunicacion*. Tiempo Contemporaneo,
   Buenos Aires.
Zimbardo, P.G. (1974). On the ethics of intervention in human psychological research:

with special reference to the Stanford prison experiment. *Cognition*, **2**, 243–256.

Zuñiga, R. (1973) *La determinacion de la practica scientifica*. Documentos de trabajo, Universidad Catolica, Instituto de Sociologia, Santiago, Chile.

Social Research in Developing Countries
Edited by M. Bulmer and D.P. Warwick
© 1983, John Wiley & Sons, Ltd.

CHAPTER 26

THE KAP SURVEY: DICTATES OF MISSION VERSUS DEMANDS OF SCIENCE

DONALD P. WARWICK

For over two decades one of the most common types of sample surveys in the developing countries was the Knowledge–Attitude–Practice (KAP) study. In essence, this was a household survey in which respondents, usually women, were asked about their knowledge, attitudes, and practices on matters related to fertility and birth control. Beginning with a Puerto Rican survey in 1948 and continuing into the 1970s, several hundred KAP studies were carried out in several dozen countries (For the Puerto Rican study see Hatt, 1952; another early study using the approach, but not the name, of the KAP survey was Freedman, Whelpton, and Campbell, 1959). A manual on the KAP survey (Population Council, 1970) listed 135 separate studies as of that time, but there were many others not reported in that source. In the wake of strong criticism about its methodology, a drop in funding, and a gradual decline in its political utility, the KAP survey in its classical form was slowly abandoned, though some stalwarts may still be carrying on.

Aside from its sheer frequency, which is of historical interest, the KAP survey raises profound questions about the politics and ethics of social research. This was one of the few areas of social science research in which there was an average decline in the quality of work done over a 20-year period. Moreover, it was the *only* area known to this writer in which eminent social scientists stoutly defended what more critical colleagues considered careless work. It was also a line of work whose political uses were discussed openly by defenders and practitioners, and one in which political influences were fairly apparent in the design, execution, and especially interpretation of research.

The basic argument of this essay is that the decline in quality, the defence of carelessness, and the susceptibility of research to political influence can all be explained by the mission-orientation of the KAP survey. While it may have begun as an instrument of scientific understanding, it gradually became an

349

effective tool of political persuasion. Throughout its history there was a running tension between the scientific and the political objectives of this research, with a few practitioners holding fairly closely to the former and many more allowing themselves to be heavily influenced by the latter. The willingness of social researchers to lower their scientific standards in the interests of gathering politically useful data further raises basic questions of professional ethics. To what extent, if at all, is it ethically acceptable for researchers to sacrifice generally recognized standards of quality in the interests of gathering data to serve a given social or political mission, such as population control? This question emerges sharply with the KAP study.

The politics of the KAP survey

To support my argument about political influence, I must first demonstrate the existence of political motivation in the KAP survey. This is not difficult to do with only the published literature on the subject. J. Mayone Stycos, a leading expert on population research, was quite frank about the political uses of KAP studies in Latin America. After noting their value in showing that social science research on a delicate subject can be carried out in that region, he cited two specifically political advantages (Stycos, 1964, p. 368):

2. The most important function of such surveys is similar to any market research project: to demonstrate the existence of a demand for goods and services, in this case for birth control . . . the elite in most societies believe that their people have many children because they want many children . . . They believe that to run counter to such a profound array of beliefs, drives, behavior patterns, and norms would either be political suicide or a waste of time. And, indeed, they would be correct if such assumptions were true. But, repeatedly, surveys demonstrate that couples want a moderate number of children, that they are convinced of the economic disadvantages of a large family, and that they are eager for information on what to do about it. Such information, if believed, can show that a program of population control could win votes rather than lose them.
3. A third function of such studies relates to the fact that research is a relatively uncontroversial way of initiating activity in population control, in countries where direct efforts are not possible. The research itself, in addition to providing valuable information for possible future programs, stimulates the interest of those directly and indirectly involved, and may serve to accelerate the whole process of policy formation.

In other words, the KAP survey can help to legitimize population programs by showing that they are the people's choice, and they can also be an entering wedge for action in countries where the subject of population control is still taboo.[1]

Similar arguments were put forth by Bernard Berelson of the Population Council, one of the most vocal and respected commentators on population policy (1964, p. 11):

Such a survey should probably be done at the outset of any national program — partly for its evaluational use, but also for its political use, in demonstrating to the elite that the people themselves strongly support the program and in demonstrating to the society at large that family planning is generally approved. Within not too large limits, the major results of such surveys can now be pretty well predicted, but they are still highly useful for their persuasive and informational impact.

Related comments were made by other leading figures in the population field, including John D. Rockefeller III (1969, p. 493–498). More to the point, many of the same individuals later argued that the KAP survey not only *could* but *did* have a political impact in legitimizing population programs. 'As an example,' Bernard Berelson writes, 'the 'KAP survey done in Turkey in 1963 was given wide attention and contributed to bringing about the recent change in national population policy' (1966, p. 665). Research on the development of population policy in the Philippines shows a similar role for KAP studies in that country (Lopez et al., 1978).

The assumption and then demonstration of political utility was followed by a dramatic increase in the amount of money made available for KAP surveys. In the 1960s the Population Council, the Ford Foundation, and later the Agency for International Development let it be known that funds would be found for those who wanted to launch this kind of study. In some cases the lure of easy funding was accompanied by direct efforts at persuading reluctant nationals in the developing countries to become involved. As the mission-orientation of the KAP survey increased, the professional qualifications of its practitioners often declined. The net result in many cases was surveys that were not only far below the quality of studies conducted earlier but of poor quality in an absolute sense.

From the perspective of the sociology of knowledge it is certainly significant that two of the best surveys ever carried out on human fertility were completed in the 1950s and that most of those conducted later were simply not in the same league of technical competence. These surveys were the study on Puerto Rico by Hill, Stycos, and Back (1959) and the Jamaica Human Fertility Investigation carried out by Back and Stycos (1959). In an exemplary monograph dealing specifically with methodological issues in survey research on human fertility, Back and Stycos (1959) probed further than anyone before or since into such questions as response bias and inconsistency in fertility surveys. In the 1960s and 1970s there were also some KAP surveys meeting high standards of quality, but these were few considering the total number of such studies. (The fertility studies conducted by Ronald Freedman and his colleagues were notable among those maintaining high standards of survey research; see, for example, Freedman and Takashita, 1969). To judge from published reports, the garden variety KAP survey was biased or flawed in almost every respect, from its initial conceptualization to the final interpretation of the data.

In most areas of social science research such a notable decline in methodological rigour would have met strong criticism, if not professional outrage. But with the KAP survey the dominant response was silence. Over the years the

Population Council did make various efforts to improve the quality of this research, and in 1970 published a manual aimed in that direction. But in that organization and elsewhere there was always an ambivalence about being too critical of KAP studies. A review of the publications of the Population Council, including its series *Studies in Family Planning*, shows a pattern of sporadic but muted criticism coupled with enthusiastic advocacy of KAP research. One has the sense that professionals in the field were well aware of the limitations of KAP surveys, but hesitated to speak out too vigorously on the subject for fear of reducing their political utility.

An even more clear sign of political influence is seen in statements defending the existing quality of KAP surveys and questioning the need for either scientific skepticism or greater rigor. In 1966 Bernard Berelson wrote (p. 657):

It is easy to make technical criticisms of such studies, but it is not easy to do better . . . in my opinion, the sampling has been fairly good, the formulation of questions acceptable or better, the interviewing at least adequate, and the analysis, if anything, overdone (again, from the standpoint of administrative requirements).

Contrast Berelson's complacency about KAP methodology with the following comments about KAP and similar surveys in Africa (Caldwell and Gaisie, 1971). The senior author of the article from which the comments are taken, John Caldwell, is an experienced researcher and one thoroughly familiar with KAP studies in Africa.

The weakest point of many African surveys is the sample frame. Even where censuses have been held, the enumeration areas are often inadequately mapped or described (a major weakness also in the censuses themselves) a fact that is not always appreciated until the attempt is made to use the official maps or descriptions in the field . . . (p. 54). KAP surveys in Africa, and doubtless elsewhere, are beset by problems of communication, definition, and clear thinking. The subject is delicate; probing often does not go far enough, especially in such areas as the limitation of sexual relations between spouses. There is often a reluctance to describe the matters being investigated — a reluctance which can exist between organizer and interviewers as well as between interviewers and respondents — and there are often local terms for condoms and *coitus interruptus* and sometimes no term at all for the latter even when widely practiced. The investigators have often not defined to the interviewers or themselves whether some practices, such as postnatal continence, are contraceptive in either effect or intent (pp. 57–58).

The authors mention other problems with KAP surveys, including memory lapse, problems in obtaining accurate statements about age, the validity of responses to questions that may not be understood by respondents, and unexplained differences in fertility, mortality, and contraceptive practice between adjoining survey areas. Their concern for quality contrasts sharply with Berelson's complacency about standards.

Other statements by eminent figures in the field suggest a suspension of the usual scepticism of science when interpreting KAP data. In discussing whether verbal statements of interest in family planning will be followed by actual practice, Ronald Freedman (1966, p. 815) noted that there could be a gap between stated assent and subsequent adoption.

Does this mean that the responses are not based on conviction or are only intended to please the investigator? Although this may be true to some extent and in some places, the fact that a population perceives that family planning ideas are held by such respected 'others' as the investigators is in itself a significant basis and reinforcement for social change. The small family idea, at least, must be there.

By the usual norms of survey research Freedman's interpretation would be considered a *non sequitur*. It is stretching the data to argue that statements made to please an interviewer have movitating power simply by virtue of the fact they are made for that purpose. Freedman goes on to argue specifically against excessive doubt about the validity of KAP responses (1966, p. 815):

In any case, I would accept the responses on such surveys as valid initially until they are tested by a really effective, persistent, all-out service and information effort. Devious psychological explanations of why the respondents did not mean what they said may be too easy a rationalization for a feeble or insufficiently thorough effort.

This is a clear example of the effects of mixing commitment to programme success with the evaluation of KAP data. Under the usual norms of scientific scepticism one would do the opposite of what Freedman suggests: treat the data as of unknown validity until there is evidence of their relationship to behaviour. But in the passage quoted Freedman suggests that such caution may work against programmatic success by giving administrators an excuse for weakened effort. From the standpoint of survey quality Freedman's advice could have the additional effect of rationalizing 'a feeble or insufficiently thorough effort' to test the validity of responses to the KAP survey.

In short, the history of the KAP survey shows a continuing tension between the demands of science and the dictates of mission. The aims of science are served when the design and conduct of research are guided above all by a commitment to accuracy. The mission is advanced when the research produces findings that are of rapid and direct use in promoting certain practical aims, in this case population control. When these two imperatives come into conflict, as they often did in KAP surveys, researchers are forced to choose between professional quality and programmatic utility. The record of KAP surveys suggests that in many studies quality was sacrificed in the interests of utility.

The scientific costs of mission politics

The main effect of the politics just described was a set of surveys that, on the whole, fell below the technical standards of comparable work in the 1950s and that often violated accepted norms of survey research at the time they were conducted. It is unlikely that anyone ever sat down and consciously decided to do careless work that would serve the ends of family planning. Rather a climate developed in which 'quick and dirty' KAP studies were not only tolerated by tacitly encouraged by sponsors seeking immediately usable results. Funds for KAP surveys were made available without too many questions being asked about methodology, and the general mood of the times was 'let's get on with it'.[2] With leading figures proclaiming that the results of KAP surveys were fairly well knowable in advance and that one need not worry too much about sampling, questionnaire construction, and other technical matters, it is not surprising that less eminent researchers pushed forward without great concern for technical quality. While this is not the place for a thorough review of the conceptual and methodological limitations of KAP surveys, some of the more common weaknesses can be noted.[3] (One of the most detailed critiques of the KAP survey ever published is Marino, 1971, pp. 36–75. This would be a good place to begin for those who wish to pursue this line of discussion in greater detail.)

Conceptualization

Many of the difficulties with KAP studies began with the way in which the research problem was conceived. The typical KAP survey assumed that reproductive decisions are an individual matter and one largely controlled by women. Husband–wife interactions, kinship structures, and the surrounding culture may be important in the abstract, but to find out the real market for birth control one must go directly to the ultimate consumer — the woman of reproductive age. This assumption of individual choice is consistent with the western ideology of free choice and also critical to a research design relying heavily on interviews with individual respondents. (This point is emphasized in Godwin, 1973, pp. 131–143). Within this paradigm results showing a positive interest in family planning could then also be interpreted as indisputable evidence of 'the people's choice'. After all, what stronger evidence could one find for an interest in birth control than direct statements by eligible respondents of their own interest?

This individualistic conceptualization of the research problem was not the only option available. Even within the framework of sample surveys, population researchers could have interviewed both husbands and wives and compared the pattern of their responses. Do they think alike on these matters, and is there consistent evidence that they even talk about birth control? While still fraught with methodological problems, this approach, which was rarely used, would have increased the base of coverage. A broader approach to survey research might also have paid explicit attention to the question of whether respondents really had an opinion on such questions, and whether they felt that they had personal control over their own fertility. A still more sophisticated methodology would have tried to explore decisions on fertility in the context of the immediate household and the larger social structure. The Nigerian sociologist F. Olu Okediji argues, for example, that in Africa,

the opinion of an elder carries more weight than that of a young mother and also the opinion of a husband carries more weight than that of his wife or wives. It will be recalled that most KAP surveys in tropical Africa usually solicit information from wives and not from husbands; and this precedure is not in consonance with patterns of authority in traditional African societies (1974, p. 43).

Other circumstances bearing on actual, as distinct from idealized, family size preferences include the value of children for farming and other economic activities, for old-age security, for religious ceremonies, and for such traditions as naming. (For an enlightening discussion of the potential influence of naming customs on fertility preferences see Herzog, 1971, pp. 89–94.)

A study that wanted to predict not only individual interest in birth control but probable use of family planning services might also have considered the impact of such opinion leaders as midwives and local religious figures. The idea that individuals will execute their individual preferences without regard to community pressures carries individualistic rationalism to an ethnocentric extreme. However, it was a rare KAP study that looked beyond the potential consumer of family planning to the larger social and political environment. Yet it was precisely such blunders in conceptualization that returned to haunt the KAP survey when it often proved to be a poor predictor of individual behaviour *vis-à-vis* family planning programmes.

Questionnaire design

While conceptualization was the root of many evils, their most obvious surface manifestation was a low-quality questionnaire. Many of the difficulties apparently arising from questionnaires actually went back to deeper problems in concept and method. One of the most basic was that some respondents, and perhaps a substantial percentage in certain surveys, had little real understanding of the household survey. Because few KAP studies tried to determine the extent to which the survey itself was understood by respondents, it is difficult to be specific on this point. Yet experience with other surveys in the developing countries strongly suggests that the methodology is foreign to many, especially poorly educated individuals living in rural areas. In the typical KAP study, the interviewer arrived unannounced, located the respondent (typically a woman), gave a quick explanation of the research, made hasty arrangements for some semblance of privacy (itself a concept that is not universally understood or accepted), asked structured questions about some of the most sensitive aspects of the person's life, and left after an hour or so. For individuals who had no idea of what a sample survey was supposed to be, who were not accustomed to sharing their most intimate thoughts and behaviour with total strangers, and who had no experience in compressing their opinions into the rigid response categories of a KAP questionnaire, this fleeting encounter was unlikely to create the conditions for high quality data. As a result the responses obtained might be valid for some items, invalid for others, and mixed for still others. Without careful study, which was absent in most KAP surveys, one can never know which answers have what degree of validity. Yet researchers went ahead on the assumption that most respondents understood the survey itself and that most, if not all, of their responses were valid on their face.

Another background difficulty with KAP questionnaires was the assumption that respondents had thought enough about fertility to have crystallized opinions in that area. Although the literature on opinion research had long warned about the dangers of measuring opinions when there were none, and one respected writer had raised this issue specifically with regard to KAP surveys, investigators typically collected data as if the problem did not exist (Stephan, 1962, pp. 423–431). Instead of designing interview schedules in which the presence or absence of an opinion and its salience to the respondent could be assessed by the research itself, KAP researchers used structured items assuming the presence of a salient opinion. The following item, for example, was part of the model KAP questionnaire recommended by the Committee on Comparative Studies of Fertility and Family Planning of the International Union for the Scientific Study of Population (Population Council, 1970, pp. 2a–19):

Many couples do something to delay or prevent a pregnancy, so that they can have just the number of children that they want, and have them when they want them. How do you feel about this? Would you say that you approve, disapprove, or feel uncertain about this?

While this phrasing is more acceptable than the loaded language of some earlier studies, it makes no attempt to determine whether the respondent actually thought about the matter of fertility control before the interview. Moreover, the response categories for that item include only three options: approve, disapprove, and uncertain. Even within the structured format, the question might have allowed for an answer of 'don't know' or 'never thought about it'. In areas such as birth control, both of those responses are perfectly reasonable, and yet they were effectively excluded by the question format. In studies that did allow for such answers, more than a few respondents opted for them. A Turkish survey showed that about half of the women interviewed had never thought about the number of children they wanted to have (Berelson, 1964, pp. 155–158). Another study in Lima, Peru, found that a majority of lower-class and a third of upper-class women had not thought about the number of children they wanted (Stycos, 1968). An early KAP study in

Indonesia found that almost half of all respondents simply did not understand a question about birth spacing (Gille and Pardoko, 1966, pp. 518–519). The authors commented: 'It is questionable whether the villagers understood what the question really was about, since their knowledge of family planning was almost totally absent . . . and no detailed explanations were made during the interview' (Gille and Pardoko, 1966, pp. 518–519). It was experiences of this kind that led Philip Hauser to a pessimistic conclusion about the validity of KAP data: 'It is quite possible that many of the responses in KAP surveys are efforts at politeness to meaningless queries or forced responses to questions which the respondent really has no answer either before or after the question is put' (Hauser, 1967, p. 404).

Apart from the difficulties just noted, several of the critical items in KAP questionnaires were leading or loaded. In a study of rural Thailand two investigators included the following items (Hawley and Prachuabmoh, 1966, pp. 537–538):

1. If you knew of a simple, harmless method of keeping from getting pregnant too often and of having too many children (more than you want), would you approve or disapprove of its use?
2. Would you like to do something to keep from getting pregnant in the future?
3. Are you interested in learning more about how to keep from getting pregnant too often or having too many children (more than you want)?

By the usual standards of survey research, questions containing words such as 'too often' and 'too many' would be regarded as leading the respondent toward an answer, in this case, approval. At the same time, a question beginning 'Are you interested in learning' would be regarded by most specialists on questionnaire design as biased toward a positive response. In most countries it is considered good to be interested in learning and backward not to be so interested. Commenting on the general pattern of questionnaire wording in KAP surveys, Marino (1971, p. 47) notes:

Given the use of phrases like 'too often', 'too many', or 'more than they want' as explicit cues to the respondent, we may well marvel not at the fact that a majority approve of 'this kind of thing', but that anyone could possibly disapprove. Moreover, since the specific action of 'something' is never defined for the respondent, each person may define it as he wishes.

It is hard to escape the conclusion that in most KAP surveys the data derived from questions about attitudes toward family planning are, at best, suspect and in many cases totally devoid of scientific validity. But in most cases we shall never know, for the studies were not designed so that response validity could actually be checked.

Had KAP researchers and their sponsors been of a mind to do so, they could have included several proxy indicators of validity even in the questionnaire.

One of the most useful, and one that was used in a large survey carried out in the early 1960s, is the 'random probe' technique developed by Howard Schuman (1966, pp. 218–222). In brief, this technique has the interviewer use follow-up probes for a set of items randomly chosen from the interview schedule for each respondent. By asking the person to 'explain a little' of what he or she had in mind in answering a closed question, the random proble elicits information on whether the question was understood at all and whether the meaning perceived by the respondent was the same as that intended by the study designers. Schuman made apt use of this technique in a study of 1000 factory workers and cultivators in what was then East Pakistan (now Bangladesh). He found that the results obtained shed qualitative light on the quantitative data, but that they were no panacea for the usual difficulties of closed responses. Other methods of checking validity include a combination of open-end and closed questions and intensive probing on key items. Most of these techniques were known in the 1950s and 1960s, but were rarely adopted by researchers conducting KAP surveys.

Interviewing and quality control

It is well known that the validity of survey data depends to a large extent on the quality of the interviewing in the field and on the care taken with administrative control. Even with a soundly designed questionnaire, bias can easily be introduced by interviewers who are poorly trained, insensitive to the needs and concerns of respondents, or bent on obtaining the 'right' answers. The chances of bias from interviewers increase when those assigned to gather data also have operational responsibilities, such as administering family planning clinics, and when the study directors indicate that they hope for some answers more than others. Reports on KAP surveys only rarely provided any detail on the procedures used in training and supervising interviewers, and still more rarely discussed the extent of error from that source. One exception was a study by John Laing in the Philippines: (1970, p. 283):

In the Dumaguete study, there is all the more reason to expect interviewer effects to be important . . . . During the training period, an attempt was made to mitigate them by stressing the problems of population growth and the economic problems of raising too many children. This instruction seems to have had the latent dysfunction of instilling in them a sort of missionary zeal and a feeling that they were expected to promote family planning. They were also aware that the clinic staff was planning to hire field-workers for the motivational campaign and that they would be likely candidates. It became evident that at least two of the interviewers were reporting excessively high motivation for family planning among their respondents, despite pleas to the contrary from the research director.

Laing also reported large variations across interviewers in the distribution of responses to attitude items, a further indication of bias.

Critical to the quality of interviewing as well as field operations more generally is capable supervision. In their textbook on sample surveys, Warwick and Lininger observe (1975, p. 220):

Successful field work requires not only a theoretical understanding of the interview and a command of practical techniques, but also a carefully organized system of field administration. In most surveys the quality of the data is no better than the quality of the field organization. Interviewers may perform well as individual *virtuosi* during the training sessions, but fail to satisfy the needs of the study because of inadequate supervision or low productivity. Similarly, a study which begins well may lose momentum after a few weeks as a result of poor morale among the interviewers, high attrition because of other demands on the staff's time, improper scheduling, or a lack of coordination between the field sites and the central research office.

With the KAP survey it is difficult to estimate the quality of field organization and supervision, for there are few explicit reports on that topic. However, both the usual silence on the matter and some published comment suggest that the standards of quality control were often low. Writing about KAP surveys in Africa, Caldwell and Gaisie (1971) note that 'shortage of adequate supervisors and low levels of supervision are a more common feature of African surveys than a shortage of trainable interviewers'. In many other studies the entire question of field supervision appears to have been given little attention.

Analysis and interpretation

The weaknesses in KAP research did not prevent the authors of study reports and others in the field from drawing clearcut conclusions about the extent of demand for family planning 'demonstrated' by the data. Beyond consistency checks and data cleaning, the first level of survey analysis deals with what the data actually *say*. Even at this level there was often substantial overinterpretation of findings. For example, responses indicating a willingness to 'do something' about birth limitation were typically reported as a readiness to engage in family planning. In the study of Thailand mentioned earlier, the authors decided that respondents giving positive answers to all three of their questions about family planning could be described as highly motivated, while those who gave a qualified approval to contraception in general and positive answers on the other two items would be rated as moderately motivated. Thus even at this first stage of analysis, an inference was made about respondent motivation. The authors decided that a statement of approval for a method of 'keeping from getting pregnant too often and having too many children' was tantamount to motivation to practise contraception. But that is not necessarily the case. Even leaving aside the loaded wording of the question, someone could approve 'doing something' in general and still not be motivated. The obvious example would be the woman whose first child is a daughter and who desperately wants a son. This person might well say that she approves 'doing something' in general, but she herself would not be motivated to practise contraception, at least for the time being. Many other examples of this kind could be cited to illustrate the massive overinterpretation of ambiguous KAP data even at the level of 'findings'.

The level of inflation was much greater in comments on what KAP data *mean*. Here even experienced social scientists threw caution to the winds as they read into the data all of their hopes, aspirations, and preconceptions about family planning. One of the most blatant cases of overinterpretation was this statement from a report by the Population Council to the Government of Kenya (Population Council, 1965, p. 41):

(a) *A Study of Knowledge, Attitudes and Practice* — This study should be done on a sampling basis to determine the people's knowledge, attitudes, and practices regarding family planning. Studies in other developing countries have almost invariably shown that although family planning is very little practised by most of the people, the majority would welcome information, would like to limit the size of their families, and would favour a Government-sponsored programme.

This statement goes far beyond the KAP data in stating that the 'majority of the population' in any country has made such statements. In every case samples were used, and often samples of unknown representativeness but with a distinct urban bias. The statement that the majority would welcome information, etc., is also an inaccurate summary of the results. All that the data really 'say' is that a certain proportion of respondents state that they would like an ideal family size of x children, that they would like to 'do something' to avoid having too many children, and that they approve of learning more about means of limiting births.

The excerpt quoted is modest, however, in comparison with sweeping claims, based mainly on interpretations of KAP data, that couples are almost universally interested in family planning and family planning programs. In its 1966 Annual Report, the Population Council made one such claim: 'It is often argued that in the traditional societies people are not ready for or interested in family planning. The experience of the Council is that people are amazingly ready and that the difficulty lies in the failure of governmental personnel to realize the fact' (p. 16). The main empirical basis for this optimism was none other than a series of KAP surveys.

The point to be emphasized is that promoters of family planning often permitted their enthusiasm for that mission to transport them well beyond the data in interpreting KAP results. In making such expansive interpretations these advocates failed to draw a clear distinction between their personal or institutional values and the empirical evidence at hand. While the interpretation of data in any survey is almost always a complex matter and one in which inferences are inescapable, in many KAP surveys the empirical inferences drawn were not supported by the data collected and the policy recommendations based on those inferences showed a heavy dose of personal preference and mission values.

The ethics of policy research

Let me conclude with a few comments on the ethical problems posed by KAP surveys. The core problem has to do with the relationship between personal or institutional mission and the craft of research. What standards should apply to research conducted in sensitive areas of public policy, especially when the researchers themselves and their sponsors would like to see a certain pattern of results emerge? Warwick and Pettigrew (1982) suggest a number of ethical guidelines that apply to this and similar situations. They suggest, above all, that social scientists adhere strictly to the standards of their craft, whatever their own and their sponsor's value convictions. In areas where they are likely to be tempted to distort the research process or cut corners to come up with the desired results they should build in checks against their own bias. As one specific source of prevention they should agree from the outset that the data collected will be open to secondary analysis by others, and take steps to make such analysis possible. And in making policy recommendations based on their research, investigators should consciously try to distinguish between the empirical and normative bases of their suggestions.

When the full history of the KAP survey is written it is likely to emerge as a classical case in which the failure to separate personal, professional, and political agendas created serious threats to the integrity of social science. Perhaps its main lesson is that no one can serve two masters in social research, especially when their demands are incompatible.

Notes

1. While living in Peru from 1964–66 I participated in a discussion in which representatives from the Ford Foundation tried to convince my Peruvian counterparts about the need for population surveys in that country. As we left the meeting, one of the Peruvians said that he did not want to get involved with this kind of research because it would just be the beginning of birth control, which he opposed.

2. This attitude of moving ahead without much concern for technical quality was especially strong in the mid-1960s. As the volume of funds for this type of research began to swell, the concern for technical standards diminished. Some donor representatives were almost frantic in their search for takers and transmitted a clear message that what was wanted was results.

References

Back, K.W. and Stycos, J.M. (1959). The survey under unusual conditions: methodological facets of the Jamaica human fertility investigation. *Human Organization*, **23(1)**, supplement.

Berelson, B. (1964a). National family planning programs: a guide. *Studies in Family Planning*, **5 (December)**, 11, supplement.

Berelson, B. (1964b). Turkey: national survey on population. *Studies in Family Planning*, **1**(5), 1–5.

Berelson, B. (1966). KAP studies on fertility. In Berelson, B. (Ed.), *Family Planning and Population Programs*, p. 665, University of Chicago Press, Chicago.

Caldwell, J.C. and Gaisie, S.K. (1971). Methods of population and family planning research: problems in their application in Africa. *Rural Africana*, **14**, **Spring**, 54.

Freedman, R. (1966). Family planning programs today: major themes of the conference. In B. Berelson (Ed.), *Family Planning and Population Programs*, p. 815, University of Chicago Press, Chicago.

Freedman, R. and Takeshita, J. (1969). *Family Planning in Taiwan*, Princeton University Press, Princeton, NJ.

Freedman, R. Whelpton, P.K. and Campbell, A.A. (1959). *Family Planning, Sterility and Population Growth*, McGraw-Hill, New York.

Gille, H. and Pardoko, H. (1966). A family life in East Java: preliminary findings. In B. Berelson (Ed.), *Family Planning and Population Programs*, pp. 518–519, University of Chicago Press, Chicago.

Godwin, K. (1973). Methodology and policy. In R. Clinton (Ed.), *Population and Politics: New Directions in Political Science Research*, pp. 131–143, Lexington Books, Lexington, Mass.

Hatt, P.K. (1952). *Backgrounds of Human Fertility in Puerto Rico*, Princeton University Press, Princeton, NJ.

Hauser, P.M. (1967). Family planning and population programs: a book review article. *Demography*, **4**(1), 404.

Hawley, A.H. and Prachuabmoh, V. (1966). In B. Berelson (Ed.). *Family Planning and Population Programs*, pp. 537–538, University of Chicago Press, Chicago.

Herzog, J.D. (1971). Fertility and cultural values: Kikuyu naming customs and the preference for four or more children. *Rural Africana*, **14**, **Spring**, 89–94.

Hill, R.J., Stycos, J.M. and Back, K.W. (1959). *The Family and Population Control*. University of North Carolina Press, Chapel Hill.

Laing, J.E. (1970). The relationship between attitudes and behavior: the case for family planning. In D.J. Bogue (Ed.), *Further Sociological Contributions to Family Planning Research*, p. 283, Community and Family Study Center, University of Chicago, Chicago.

Lopez, M.E., Nemenzo, A.M., Quisumbing-Baybay, and Lopez-Fitzpatrick, N. (1978). *Cultural Values and Population Policy in the Philippines: The Sociological Study*, Institute of Philippine Culture, Ateneo de Manila University, Manila.

Marino, A. (1971). KAP surveys and the politics of family planning. *Concerned Demography*, **3**(1), 36–75.

Okediji, F.O. (1974). *Changes in individual reproductive behaviour and cultural values*. Lecture delivered at the World Population Tribune, Bucharest, Romania. Paper published by the International Union for the Scientific Study of Population, Bucharest, p. 43.

Population Council (1965). *Family Planning in Kenya*. A report submitted to the Government of Kenya by an Advisory Mission of the Population Council of the United States of America, p. 41, Ministry of Economic Planning and Development, Nairobi.

Population Council (1966). *Annual Report*.

Population Council (1970). *A Manual for Surveys of Fertility and Family Planning: Knowledge, Attitudes and Practice*, Population Council, New York.

Rockefeller, John D. III (1969). The citizen's view of public programs for family planning. In S.J. Behrman *et al.* (Eds). *Fertility and Family Planning: A World View*, pp. 493–498, University of Michigan Press, Ann Arbor.

Schuman, H. (1966), The random probe: a technique for evaluating the validity of closed questions. *American Sociological Review*, **31**, 218–222.

Stephan, F.F. (1962). Possibilities and pitfalls in the measurement of attitudes and opinions on family planning. In C.V. Kiser (Ed.), *Research in Family Planning*, pp. 423–431, Princeton University Press, Princeton, NJ.

Stycos, J.M. (1964). Survey research and population control in Latin America, *Public Opinion Quarterly*, **28(3)**, 368.

Stycos, J.M. (1968). *Human Fertility in Latin America*, Cornell University Press, Ithaca, NY.

Warwick, D. and Lininger, C. (1975). *The Sample Survey: Theory and Practice*, McGraw-Hill, New York.

Warwick, D. and Pettigrew, T. (1982). Towards ethical guidelines for ethical research in public policy. In D. Callahan and B. Jennings (Eds), *Ethics, the Social Sciences and Policy Analysis*, Plenum Press, New York.

Social Research in Developing Countries
Edited by M. Bulmer and D.P. Warwick
© 1983, John Wiley & Sons, Ltd.

CHAPTER 27

MISAPPLIED CROSS-CULTURAL RESEARCH: A CASE STUDY OF AN ILL-FATED FAMILY PLANNING RESEARCH PROJECT

CHARLES D. KLEYMEYER
AND
WILLIAM E. BERTRAND

Introduction

Nearly two decades after Project Camelot and its aftermath, social scientists from developed countries have not succeeded in adequately mending their established ways of carrying out applied social science in developing nations (or, for that matter, in less developed or culturally different strata of developed societies). Subjects are becoming less compliant, and problem-oriented studies are still on occasion producing problems rather than solving them (see, for example, American Sociological Association (1974), Form (1970); Gouldner (1970); Josephson (1970); D. Lewis (1973); Portes (1975); Salmen (1974); Vargus, 1971). Nevertheless, there is a continuing proliferation of international research efforts falling under the rubric of 'applied social science'. We want to emphasize from the outset that it is not our intention in this chapter to place blame on individual actors. The presence or absence of given social conditions and processes make up the critical causal factors associated with the incident.

Our objective in this presentation, is to use the case study to make explicit certain problems inherent in applied research and to examine some of their methodological implications and ethical consequences. Others have encountered and dealt with similar difficulties — Adams (1955); O. Lewis (1955); Selser (1966); Silvert (1965); Tax (1958); Rainwater and Pittman (1967) — and

Reprinted by permission in abridged form from the authors' chapter in Margaret Stacey *et al.* (Eds) (1977), *Health and the Division of Labour*, pp. 217–236. Croom Helm, London. © 1977 Croom Helm Limited.

concern has been expressed in many areas of the social sciences regarding these problems — Form (1973); Horowitz (1967); Miller (1965); Portes (1972, 1975); Rodman and Kolodny (1965); Roy and Fliegel (1970). We will attempt to add to this growing literature by presenting a description and analysis of a relevant case.

The case

The core incident centred around an accusation (which was false, though believed by many and considered seriously by many others) that North American social scientists were involved in a plan to sterilize local children within a government sponsored antimeasles vaccination campaign. This campaign was under the local auspices of an established maternal-childcare programme, developed and administered jointly by a prominent local university and by the City Health Department.

Context and setting

'Esperanzas' is a slum or poor *barrio* not significantly different from other such settlements which ring major cities throughout Latin America. It had its origin nearly two decades ago as an illegal squatter settlement which was nipped in the bud by pragmatic landowners and the government who quickly 'urbanized' the threatened area, laying out streets and tiny lots. Esperanzas grew rapidly as the rural poor streamed hopefully into the departmental capital of 'Bolivar'. Bolivar's population itself increased from 638 000 in 1964 to slightly under one million today. The population of Esperanzas rose accordingly — today numbering about 70 000 individuals.

Politically, Esperanzas has a history of being in opposition to the government and to various other outside influences. It is considered by many to be leftist, and there is no mistaking the strength and considerable popularity of the left among the people. The *barrio's* historical distrust of outsiders includes not only foreigners but outsiders of higher class, status and power (and usually, therefore, of lighter skin). As we shall see, such is particularly true of outsiders who move in and become fixtures in terms of their daily occupations or, at an even higher level, in terms of their place of residence. The occasional visitor is nearly always treated with an abundance of graciousness and hosptiality. As is to be expected, it is the more permanent intruder who tends to provoke suspicions.

The most conspicuous outsiders in the *barrio* at the time the incident was brewing were the three North American social scientists whom we shall discuss shortly. However, a less obvious but in some ways equally problematical group of outsiders was the team of middle-class health professionals from the University and the City Health Department (hereafter called 'the health team'). Even though they were testing a 'progressive' model of health care delivery which differs rather significantly from the norm in terms of its organization and form of delivery, this team (with one or two important exceptions) consistently relied on traditional forms of social interaction and organization characteristic of the class, culture and nation in which the team is imbedded. Suffice it to say that the resulting social relations between the health team agents and *barrio* clients are of a nature generally classified as 'patron–client' by anthropologists and 'vertical' or 'powerful–dependent' by sociologists.

To complete this description of context and setting it is necessary briefly to mention two additional aspects of the general ideological/phenomenological backdrop which impinges upon the behaviour of the people of Esperanzas *vis-à-vis* outsiders, especially those of North American heritage. It almost goes without saying that anti-Americanism and anti-imperialism are strong factors, especially when individuals allow themselves to be identified with the goals and politics of the United States. Another factor is the sensitive nature (locally, nationally and internationally) of the topic of population control as well as its close relation, human sexual behaviour, both being topics which played important roles in the incident.

The prelude

Some 4 months before the incident itself (the false accusation linking the researchers to an alleged campaign to sterilize *barrio* children), the future project leader passed through Bolivar on a talent and site search covering several countries and under the auspices of a well-known international organization. Meanwhile, the university-based institute for which the project leader was working received word from its funding agency that budgets would be cut and that productivity would be looked upon favourably. This news produced a set of predictable tensions and pressures, and the project leader was encouraged to try out some previous ideas concerning applied methodology and family planning (including the cultural acceptability of specific birth control methods). Additional incentives derived from the prospect of publications, further research experience and a month in Latin America. This time span was determined partly by pressures from the funding agency and by competing professional and personal activities.

A few weeks before the study began, the project leader again visited Bolivar, this time to lay the groundwork for the forthcoming month-long investigation. After spending several days making contacts with the University-affiliated members of the health team and with a University-based population research centre, the project leader was successful in getting the tentative approval of these two groups for the study (though with some reservations, such as those regarding the small sample size for the home interviews). The City Health Department was approached informally, but the health centre personnel and *barrio* leaders were not contacted at all.[1] *En route* to another country, the project leader stopped in the national capital and contacted the national planning commission and the local representatives of the US government funding agency. Thus, the top of the pyramid was well covered, including some persons in the upper echelons of the Bolivar academic structure.

To understand why individuals and institutions in Bolivar gave their approval to the project, we must consider the complex and varied pressures, perceptions and social processes which were at work at the time. First, there were some persons who were genuinely interested in the objectives of the project (though at odds with certain aspects of its approach). Of these persons, some were merely curious, while others saw prospects for direct application of the results. A second general factor in the gaining of approval was that of direct face-to-face persuasion. Skilfully applied and culturally sound social pressures coming from a prestigious professional (as are the majority of visiting North Americans and Europeans, phenomenologically speaking) often prove to be quite effective in the Latin American sociocultural setting in gaining support for, or compliance with a project, regardless of its practical or scientific merits.

A third factor in gaining approval of the project falls under the general rubric of 'reciprocity and professional politics'. In addition to standard local hospitality, there exists a strong desire to build and maintain relationships with outside sources of funding and other research-related benefits. The resulting 'politics of research' is well understood by some visiting professionals, while others become convinced that it is their personal worth as researchers or problem solvers that elicits such solicitude, hospitality and willing compliance. To expand somewhat on this point, university and government persons and groups frequently perceive visiting professionals — especially those that represent renowned organisations and foundations — as potential sources of goods and services. These range from trips, grants, scholarships, jobs and consulting fees (for themselves, their friends, or their relatives) to free books and publications, invitations to conferences, valuable future contacts, embellishment of personal and/or group reputations and other benefits, both real and imagined. Thus, those numerous local individuals and groups who perceive a broad existing network of institutionalized payoffs and other valued outcomes, are often hesitant to alienate any sector or representative of that network. In fact, they frequently go out of their way — expending large (sometimes exorbitant) quantities of time and energy— to maintain their inter-institutional and personal contacts and relationships, generally by taking good care of official and unofficial visiting institutional representatives.

A final factor at work in the project's approval was the common one of compliance with or indifference to projects perceived as representing little or no cost or risk. Several local persons involved took a more or less 'who cares?' attitude towards the project due to their interest and involvement in other activities and due to their general assessment that there was nothing to lose by letting the project take place.

The research project

A month after the project leader's second short visit, the research team — two anthropologists and a social psychologist — arrived in Bolivar. The next day, a Saturday, they made arrangements to live in an empty house owned and used by the Catholic church in the *barrio* and immediately left town for the weekend. Monday morning they were back in Bolivar, meeting first with professionals at the university and later in the week with authorities of the City Health Department. At once, obstacles began to arise — ranging from a lack of official communiction between the University and the Health Department, to internal conflicts in the target health centre. The Health Department had never been officially informed of the project and thus held off permission to study the health centre for what seemed to them to be an appropriately extended delay — one-third of the study period. Finally, the project was approved in its totality. In the meantime, the month had been quickly slipping by, so the two anthropologists had long since moved to the *barrio* and had promptly begun doing standardized home interviews. When permission came later for the health centre study, the social psychologist joined them.[2]

With the exception of subsequent weekends of rest and travel and short periods of predictable illnesses, the remainder of the month was spent in the *barrio* collecting data. Interviews and observations were done in the clinic, focusing on the inner workings of that institution. Simultaneously, women were interviewed in their homes concerning their family planning practices, values and attitudes, as well as other topics related to health, health services and procreation. The women were also questioned about their knowledge of the reproductive parts of their bodies (entailing the use of a body chart which rather closely resembles charts used in local family planning courses).

Due to various prior obligations, the three social scientists staggered their departures from the research site. Of an average span of 30 days in Bolivar (counted from the day of arrival until the day of final departure), the mean number of days that each researcher spent in the barrio came to 11. Though the shortness of this timespan may seem extreme and may do damage in the minds of some readers as to the applicability of our chosen case to other situations, we have observed many similarities between this study and others of longer duration.[3]

Furthermore, there were other problematical aspects of the project, in addition to the short amount of time *in situ*, which add to the representativeness of the case. Let us briefly cover several of these problem areas. One aspect — closely related to the extreme limits on time — was the precipitous nature of the researchers' entry into the *barrio* and of their initiation of data collection. This is to suggest that 11 days of intensive interviewing after 2 or 3 months of on-site preparation might have been a suitable time period — at the very least, it would have lessened the chances of misunderstandings and accusations. In contrast,

11 days of intensive data-gathering beginning immediately after arrival proved to be risky and counterproductive.[4] Also, the fact that the three unattached researchers lived in a house owned by the local Catholic church led to both ambiguous attributions and later problems because the drug dispensary was in the same house. In addition, one always takes chances when one steps outside the local cultural norms, especially in terms of lifestyle. An unattached person, for example, renting a room with a family in Esperanzas would be much less likely to arouse suspicion and questioning than three unrelated persons living alone in a temporarily abandoned church house.

Other sources of suspicion and misunderstanding were the researchers' gift-giving and their failure adequately to explain the purpose of their interviews, plus the sensitive content of those interviews. At least one of the researchers innocently and altruistically showered gifts on the *barrio* children, reportedly even making lists of requests for clothing, school supplies, etc. As a rule in such sociocultural settings as Esperanzas, children receive presents only from a relative or godparent, so this particular case of gift-giving fell outside any understandable cultural context and was interpreted by many as an attempt to buy off the children. As regards the interviews themselves— especially those in the home — the *barrio* women reportedly were not adequately briefed either publicly or parivately on the nature and purposes of the interviews and thus were left to fill in the blanks, so to speak, with their own interpretations. Finally, the actual content of the interviews was controversial, anxiety-producing and politically volatile. At this moment in Latin America few topics are hotter than the issue of birth control methods and policies.

Two additional and closely related problematic aspects of the research project proved to be serious ones. One was the common practice among US researchers (due to earlier training and dominant contemporary trends in the various professions) of ignoring the possible significance to their research of local, national and international political factors and processes. Some US professionals even argue that such phenomena are 'unscientific' or irrelevant and deliberately do not take political factors into account. Whether this omission be due to innocence or ignorance, it leaves much applied research badly flawed and/or in shambles.

The second, and related, problematic aspect was the previously mentioned failure of the researchers to contact and to gain the approval of the local *barrio* leadership for the realization of the project. Perhaps from the distant perspective of the US, those involved felt that by contacting various University people and one sector of the health team they had indeed contacted local authorities. Certainly, in making these contacts they were improving on the practices of many foreign-based research projects of the past. However, they overlooked at least one group — which later turned out to be the key group — the political leaders who make up the *barrio's* official governing *junta*.

The incident itself

Two days after the final researcher left the barrio for good, a group of *barrio* leaders came looking for the three North Americans. These leaders had been informed that the City Health Department was going to carry out an anti-measles vaccination campaign in conjunction with the University health team. They had also heard that a team of North American health workers had recently been thrown out of an eastern state of the country for allegedly using a vaccination campaign to sterilize children.[5] This ejection had taken place approximately a week before the researchers arrived in Bolivar, and at least one of the persons involved reportedly had the same first name as one of the researchers. The sterilization story had received national and international coverage — front page in the national papers — the accusations being formally retracted several days later (on inner pages). Nevertheless, key persons in the *barrio* made their own interpretations — in the context described above of problematical relations with the researchers as well as with the health team — and the accusation stuck that the researchers were the same persons who had previously been thrown out of the eastern state.

After four visits in four consecutive days, the group of leaders gave up hope of finding the researchers and went to a prominent *barrio* priest (a fairly radical and very activist European who is highly trusted and well-liked by the people). Acquainted with the researchers, the priest's reaction to the leaders' accusation was that he thought they were completely wrong, but that if they felt they were right, they should bring him proof. At that, the leaders went to the church house where the three researchers had stayed and returned with a phial marked in English 'STERILE'. The priest explained to them what the word meant in this context, but to no avail. At his request, a highly respected nurse who lives in the *barrio* (and is also a leftist) explained the different meanings of the word sterile — also to no avail. Finally, the priest took aside the treasurer of the *barrio's junta* (a man who also happens to be a Sunday school teacher in the parish church) and told him that the people would panic and even more rumours would spread. The treasurer shrugged his shoulders and went on his way.

Soon, young radicals got hold of a portable loudspeaker and paraded through the *barrio* in an automobile shouting, 'Yankee imperialists go home!', 'Our children will be sterilized!', etc. Handbills carrying the same basic messages were distributed, and a local radical paper printed a scathing anti-American editorial likening this 'sterilization campaign' to US atrocities in Vietnam. Thus, in a loose coalition, the older politicos and the young radicals were consciously or unconsciously, sincerely or opportunistically, playing a catalytic and at times incendiary role. The scandal quickly obtained explosive force. *Barrio* members began saying they would refuse to have their children vaccinated during the measles campaign, and other clear signs of trouble appeared on the horizon.[6] At that, the health team decided to confront the accusers, before the news media got wind of the incident and things became even worse.

Several intense conversations and meetings were held over a 2-day period, culminating in a large meeting which was attended by the *barrio* leaders, the priest and nurse, the head of the health centre and a doctor and two social workers from the University sector of the health team. At this meeting, the community leaders made three major demands: (1) to receive a sample of the vaccine which would be injected into their children; (2) to receive an official confirmation from the local health authorities that this was a legitimate campaign and that no foreigners were or would be involved; and (3) to be informed in the future of all studies which were planned for the *barrio*, studies which would be well screened by the health team.

The demands were so reasonable and the health team was so alarmed that all points were accepted forthright. The next day a conservative Bolivar newspaper printed the story of the meeting under the headline, 'Measles Vaccine Does Not Produce Sterility'. Several days later the National Health Ministry felt obliged to put out a nationwide news release assuring the country that the various ongoing vaccination campaigns were most definitely *not* sterilizing anyone. By then, things were calmed down in the *barrio*: apparently people had got what they wanted. The *barrio* members had their fears of sterilization assuaged, and the leaders had shown off their concern, responsibility and significance. Perhaps most important of all, they had gone to the mat, so to speak, with the higher-class, higher-power professionals from the health team and had won hands down. Even had they lost in terms of one or all of their demands, they would still have felt victorious because they had forced the powers that be to take them and their constituents into account — at least on this occasion, and perhaps in the future.

The aftermath

The immediate consequences and future ramifications of the incident were numerous, due in part to the many and changing targets of both the accusations and the *barrio's* wrath (in other words, the researchers, the health team, outsiders in general, paternalism and imperialism). Fortunately for many of those involved, the incident was well contained and the accusations refuted. These two outcomes were achieved by a combination of the political skills of the health team, the efforts of some respected *barrio* members and what was either the responsible nature or the ineffectiveness of local press and radio coverage (which was minimal and subdued). Consequently, the progressive health programme survived, the vaccination campaign went off not only on schedule but with no major resistance from the people, and two other North American based research projects in the same *barrio* were not adversely affected.[7]

An analytical summary

The incident that we have chosen to describe and analyse is only one of many comparable ones that have occurred in the past few decades. As we have documented, many social scientists have confronted issues of ethical and methodological problems in other cultures. Yet both the particular nature of this case study and its representativeness of that which is presently occurring in various parts of the world has encouraged us to attempt more than an illustrative description of a set of events. Thus, it seems necessary and useful to separate out several primary causal categories which we feel are worth further emphasis and explication.

(1) To begin with, the uncontrollable matter of coincidence clearly aggravated the described situation. The fact that the local press carried news of North Americans being accused of sterilizing children and that at least one of the names mentioned was the same as that of one of the researchers, helped set the stage for the events which followed.

(2) Second, the matter of relevant structural factors of a sociopolitical nature was of no small importance. The researchers were unavoidably associated with the United States, a country whose political and corporate representatives are often in a dominant role *vis-à-vis* nationals of the country where the incident took place. The United States is also viewed by some groups of nationals as having imperialistic intentions in its dealings with the country and as being the major source of the country's ills. Furthermore, the paternalistic design, if not the intent, of local health care programmes is characterized by a vertical structure as regards the delivery of services and tends to condition the ways in which an associated group of visiting professionals will be viewed and dealt with. As a result of these structural factors the fieldworkers were perceived by many as outsiders with ulterior motives — as intruders who would have to prove thoroughly the integrity and innocuousness of their motives. Those *barrio* dwellers who were not so suspicious, were at least open to suggestion and, ultimately, to the accusations. In many social science research endeavours the above factors are present, but even more so in a study which is characterized by high visibility of researchers perceived as belonging to dominant groups, by short exposure to the community under examination and by a delicate, politically volatile subject matter.

(3) Social psychological factors, related both to individual behaviour and to cross-cultural misinterpretations of that behaviour, provide the third major explanatory category. Among upper middle-class North Americans, it is considered appropriate to give gifts, relate directly to children and indulge in gratuitous, unexplained (and difficult to understand) altruistic acts. In a social system where these North Americans are outsiders and power figures (as discussed above) any strange actions can

create confusion or can be interpreted as suspicious. Thus, whether due to cross-cultural indifference or ignorance or to simple naîvety, individual actions taken out of their native cultural context can be most problematical within another cultural context. Often, of course, they produce only discomfort or laughter. In other circumstances, the reaction is serious indeed.

Equally difficult for lower-class Latin Americans to interpret is the fact that North American (or any middle- or upper-class) professionals would be willing to reside in the slums. Knowing little of the value (admirable and necessary as it may be) that some branches of the social sciences place on complete immersion in the field setting and on first-hand contact with the social world, the local population applies its own value sets in attempting to explain such strange behaviour. This in turn leads to stories that such persons are secret agents, are reaping huge personal benefits from such sacrifices, and so on. The same phenomenon of cross-cultural misinterpretations led in this case to the researchers' weekend travels being explained by *barrio* dwellers as trips to the United States to make reports and pick up sterilisation serum.

Filling out this third explanatory category are several factors falling within the broad realm of social processes, such as the institutional pressures felt by the researchers, the bilateral desires for professional favour-trading on the part of the health team, and the researchers and the *barrio* members' needs to be taken into account and to assert themselves in the face of familiar irritants. As regards the latter group of persons, we must take into account the broad existing social climate among Third World lower classes which entails not only distrust of outsiders, but also a general alienation from society's institutions and a resentment of past and present exploitation — both economic and academic (especially at the hands of North Americans and other foreigners, and middle- and upper-class nationals).

(4) Another general matter which no investigator can afford to overlook is the importance to field research of political factors (see Beals, 1969; Berreman, 1969; Dos Santos, 1970; Galtung, 1966; Horowitz, 1967). These factors change from moment to moment and range from the actions of national governments, to the struggles and bargaining of local politicians, radicals and small-time opportunists. In the present case, the publicized position of the United States regarding birth control and the resultant availability of millions of dollars for international work in the area of family planning represented one of those political factors. Local leftist are religious opposition to that stand was another political factor. Widespread anti-American and anti-imperialist sentiment was yet another. The involvement of any social scientist in matters related to population control in developing countries carries with it the risk of political reprisal. It would seem that to ignore this, or to deny it, is to court danger.

(5) The final causal category deals with certain factors of an operational nature. Among these were the brief duration of the fieldwork and the precipitous entry into social territories, especially *barrio* homes, by highly visible outsiders. Also important was the failure to contact the *barrio* leaders at any stage of the research and the sometimes problematic relations between the health team and the *barrio* people. Finally there was the tendency on the part of both the researchers and the health team to rely on an *ad hoc*, crisis-intervention approach to dealing with problems, and the practice of the latter group of giving mere lip-service to the goal of 'community participation'.

The above five categories and their components entail the more salient and important of the causal factors at play in the incident. For the sake of brevity we have left others out which seem obvious from the analytical parts of our previous description of the case.

Conclusions

Elsewhere we have presented a broad set of measures (operational, methodological, conceptual, goal-related and ethical) in a discussion of the necessity of fieldwork reform in cross-cultural settings (Kleymer and Bertrand, 1980). Numerous researchers have already touched or concentrated upon one or several such measures in previous works (for example, Adams, 1969; Barnes, 1970; Becker, 1970; Blair, 1969; Clinard and Elder, 1965; Cochrane, 1971; Denzin, 1970; Fals Borda, 1970; Foster, 1969; Gjessing, 1968; Goodenough, 1963; Graciarena 1965; Horowitz, 1967; Maruyama, 1974; Peterson, 1974; Portes, 1972; Roy and Fliegel, 1970; Salmen, 1974; Sathyamurthy, 1973; Spiegel and Alicea, 1970; Vargus, 1971; Webb, 1966; Whyte, 1969; Willner, 1973).

It goes without saying, that problems such as those we have discussed in this paper are at one time or another inevitable. Intervention into social problems generates problems: partly because such intervention is usually, in the final analysis, a political action. The fact that applied social science entails problems and politics should not, however, produce an ostrich effect in us, but should force us to make that fact a continual object of study and a component of our methodology (Gouldner, 1970). Furthermore, it just might be that current bureaucratic and funding constraints are incompatible with scientific research (see Blumer, 1967; Bogdan, 1975; Clinton, 1975; Galliher and McCartnery, 1973; Sjoberg, 1967), and still other problems arise from the conflicting interests of researchers, study population and local and national institutions and pressure groups (Clinton, 1975; Rodman and Kolodny, 1965).

It should be reiterated that this case study has relevance not only for North Americans in Third World countries (as was the case here), but also for *any* social scientists who cross cultural or class boundaries to carry out applied (or 'pure') research. These could be Latin American researchers in the Amazon Basin, Europeans in their own or other countries, or North Americans on Indian reservations or in the inner city. At stake is our effectiveness in the face of monumental world problems, as well as the accuracy of the first and last words of the term 'applied social science'.

Notes

1. According to the project leader, a University official did agree to make all necessary contacts. However, before the research team arrived this official had to leave the country for several months on extended business.
2. Meanwhile, a local psychologist was hired, in a research assistant role, to help interview in the health centre. The project leader insists that this person was a fully fledged team member (thus balancing out somewhat the heavily foreign and anthropological make-up of the research team). However, this local professional played no role in the research process either before or after data collection, during which time she functioned as an employee of the project. Significantly, she was not perceived locally — either during or after the study or the resulting incident — as a member of the research team.
3. One finds evidence that such haste is well-known among Latin American researchers and other professionals — they often call such quick-entry–quick-exit research teams *paracaidistas* (parachuters). A high official in the Bolivar City Health Department had an alternative epithet for such research projects — he classified this particular study as *Plan Turista* (Tourist Plan). Indicative of the changing climate in Latin America regarding such research is the fact that he said this not in private after the researchers had left the country, but to their faces in a meeting— with a polite smile of course. Yet another observer classified this and similar research projects as examples of *'veraneo academico'* (roughly, 'academic summering').
4. Incidentally, the brevity of the study — and the resulting limits on data collection concerning local background and current events — led not only to repercussions during and just after the study period, but to later ones as well. For example, an elementary and sensitive error was made in the introductory comments in the final report — a mistake so glaring in nature as to all but destroy the credibility of the document.
5. Apparently, the local bishop had taken advantage of the North Americans' presence to strike a blow at a prominent family planning programme.
6. What is notable here, of course, is not that the charges were *made*, but that they were — in varying degrees — listened to, believed *and acted upon* by considerable numbers of people.
7. It is interesting to note that both of these latter two projects employ local fieldworkers, have local professionals as co-workers, are focused on relatively non-controversial but relevant topics (immunology and the relation between nutrition and learning), offer highly valued services to participating families (such as medical care, education, food and clothing), and have been in the *barrio* for several years (not without opposition, but surviving).

References

American Sociological Association (1974). Survey research problems getting worse, study shows. *ASA Footnotes* (newsletter of the American Sociological Association), **2(5)**, 2.

Adams, R.N. (1955). A nutritional research program in Guatemala. In Benjamin D. Paul (Ed.), *Health, Culture, and Community: Case Studies of Public Reactions to Health Programs*, pp. 435–58, Russell Sage Foundation, New York.

Adams, R.N. (Ed.). (1969). *Responsibilities of the Foreign Scholar to the Local Scholarly Community*, Education and World Affairs Publication, New York.

Barnes, J.A. (1970). Some ethical problems in modern fieldwork. In William J. Filstead

(Ed.), *Qualitative Methodology: Firsthand Involvement with the Social World*, pp. 235–251, Markham Publishing Co., Chicago.

Beals, R.L. (1969). *Politics of Social Research: An Inquiry Into the Ethics and Responsibilities of Social Science*. Aldine, Chicago.

Becker, H.S. (1970). Whose side are we on? In William J. Filstead (Ed.), *Qualitative Methodology: Firsthand Involvement with the Social World*, pp. 15–26. Markham Publishing Co., Chicago.

Blair, C.P. (1969). The nature of US interest and involvement in Guatemala: an American view, In Richard Adams (Ed.), *Responsibilities of the Foreign Scholar to the Local Scholarly Community*, Education and World Affairs Publication, New York.

Blumer, H. (1967). Threats from agency-determined research; In I.L. Horowtiz, (Ed.), *The Rise and Fall of Project Camelot*; pp. 153–174. MIT Press, Cambridge.

Bogdan, R. (1975). *Conducting evaluation research — integrity intact*, Center on Human Policy, Syracuse University, mimeograph.

Clinard, M.B. and Elder, J.W. (1965). Sociology in India. *American Sociological Review*, **30**, 581–751.

Clinton, Charles A. (1975). The anthropologist as hired hand, *Human Organization*, **34** (2), 197–204.

Cochrane, G. (1971). *Development Anthropology*, Oxford University Press, New York.

Denzin, N.R. (1970). Who leads: sociology or society?' *American Sociologist*, **5**, 125–127.

Dos Santos, T. (1970). The structure of dependence. *American Economic Review*, **60**, 231–6.

Etzkowitz, H. (1970). Institution formation sociology, *American Sociologist*, **5**, 120–124.

Fals Borda, O. (1970). *Ciencia Propia y Colonialismo Intelectual*, Siglo Veintiuno, Mexico.

Form, W.H. (1973). Field problems in comparative research: the politics of distrust. In Michael Armer and Allen D. Grimshaw (Eds), *Comparative Social Research: Methodological Problems and Strategies*, pp. 83–117, Wiley, New York.

Foster, G.M. (1969). *Applied Anthropology*, Little, Brown and Co., Boston.

Galliher, J.F. and McCartney, J.L. (1973). The influence of funding agencies on juvenile delinquency research. *Social Problems*, **21** (1).

Galtung, J. (1966). Letter to the Ministry of Interior of Chile, In Gregorio Selser (Ed.) *Espionaje en America Latina: El Pentagono y las Tecnicas Sociologas*, pp. 134–145. Ediciones Iguazu, Buenos Aires.

Gjessing, G. (1968). The social responsibility of the social scientist, *Current Anthropology*, **9**, 397–402.

Goodenough, W. (1963). *Cooperation in Change*, Russell Sage Foundation, New York.

Gouldner, A.W. (1970). *The Coming Crisis of Western Sociology*, Basic Books.

Graciarena, H. (1965). Algunas consideraciones sobre la cooperacion internacional y el desarrollo reciente de la investigacion sociologica, *Revista Latinoamericana de Sociologia*, **2**, 231–242.

Horowtiz, I.L. (1967). *The Rise and Fall of Project Camelot*, MIT Press, Cambridge, Mass.

Josephson, E. (1970). Resistance to community surveys. *Social Problems*, **18**, 117–129.

Kleymeyer, Charles D. and Bertrand, W.E. (1980). Towards more ethical and effective carrying out of applied research across cultural or class lines. *Ethics in Science and Medicine*, **7** (1), 11–25.

Lewis, D. (1973). Anthropology and colonialism. *Current Anthropology*, **14**(5), 581–602.

Lewis, O. (1955). Medicine and politics in a Mexican village. In Benjamin D. Paul (Ed.), *Health, Culture, and Community: Case Studies of Public Reactions to Health Programs*, *Russell Sage Foundation*, New York, pp. 403–434.

Maruyama, M. (1974). Endogenous research vs. delusions of relevance and expertise among exogenous academics. *Human Organization*, **33**(3), 318–322.

Miller, S.M. (1965). Prospects: the applied sociology of the center-city, In A.W. Gouldner and S.M. Miller (Eds), *Applied Sociology: Opportunities and Problems*, The Free Press, New York, pp. 441–456.

Peterson, J.H. Jr. (1974). The anthropologist as advocate. *Human Organization*, **33** (3), 311–318.

Portes, A. (1972). Society's perception of the sociologist and its impact on cross-national research. *Rural Sociology*, **37**(1), 27–42; also published as Perception of the US sociologist and its impact on cross-national research. In Michael Armer and Allen D. Grimshaw (Eds). (1973). *Comparative Social Research: Methodological Problems and Strategies*, pp. 149–169, Wiley, New York.

Portes, A. (1975). Trends in international research cooperation: the Latin American case. *American Sociologist*, **10**, 131–140.

Rainwater, L. and Pittman, D.J. (1967). Ethical problems in studying a politically sensitive and deviant community, *Social Problems*, 14, 357–66; also in McCall, G. and Simmons, J. (1969). *Issues in Participant Observation: A Text and Reader*, Addison Wesley Publishing Co., Reading, Mass., pp. 276–288.

Rodman, H. and R.L. Kolodny. 'Organizational Strains in the Researcher-Practitioner Relationship', in Alvin W. Gouldner and I.M. Miller (eds.). (1965). *Applied Sociology: Opportunites and Problems*. New York: The Free Press, pp. 93–113.

Roy, Prodipto and Frederick C. Fliegel. (1970). 'The Conduct of Collaborative Research in Developing Nations: The Insiders and the Outsiders', *International Social Science Journal*, vol. 22, no. 3, pp. 505–523.

Salmen, Lawrence, F. (1974). 'Perspectives for Long-Term Co-Sponsored (U.S.-Latin American) Research in Urbanization', Presented at the Seminar on New Directions of Urban Research, Institute of Latin American Studies, University of Texas at Austin, May 1974.

Sathyamurthy, T.V. (1973). 'Social Anthropology in the Political Study of New Nation-States', *Current Anthropology*, vol. 14, no. 5, December, pp. 557–565.

Silvert, Kalman H. (1965). 'American Academic Ethics and Social Research Abroad: The Lesson of Project Camelot', American Universities Field Staff. West Coast South America Series, vol. XII, no. 3, July 1965.

Sjoberg, Gideon. (1967). *Ethics, Politics and Social Research*. Cambridge, Massachusetts, Schenkman.

Tax, S. (1958). The Fox Project. *Human Organization*, **17**, 17–19.

Spiegel, H.B.C. and Alicea, V.G. (1970) The trade-off strategy in community research. In Louis A. Zurcher, Jr. and Charles M. Bonjean (Eds), *Planned Social Intervention: An Interdisciplinary Anthology*, pp. 481–92, Chandler, Scranton, Penn.

Vargus, B.S. (1971). On sociological exploitation: why the guinea pig sometimes bites. *Social Problems*, **19**(2), 238–248.

Webb, E.J., *et al.* (1966). *Unobtrusive Measures: Nonreactive Research in the Social Sciences*. Rand McNally, Chicago.

Whyte, W.F. (1969). The role of the US professor in developing countries. *American Sociologist*, **4**, 19–28.

Willner, D. (1973). Anthropology: vocation or commodity? *Current Anthropology*, **14**(5), 547–554.

Selser, G. (1966). *Espionaje en America Latina: El Pentagono y las Tecinas Sociologicas*, Ediciones Iguazu, Buenos Aires.

AUTHOR INDEX

379

SUBJECT INDEX